Policing Cities

WITHDRAWN

Policing Cities brings together international scholars from numerous disciplines to examine urban policing, securitization, and regulation in nine countries and the conceptual issues that these practices raise. Chapters cover many of the world's major cities, including New York, Beijing, Paris, London, Berlin, Mexico City, Johannesburg, Rio de Janeiro, Boston, Melbourne, and Toronto, as well as other urban areas in Britain, the United States, South Africa, Germany, Australia and Georgia.

The collection examines the activities and reforms of the traditional public police, but also those of emerging public and private policing agents and spaces that fall outside of the public police's purview and which previously have received little attention. It explores dramatic changes in public policing arrangements and strategies, the exclusion of urban homeless people, new forms of urban surveillance and legal regulation, and securitization and militarization of urban spaces. The core argument in the volume is that cities are more than mere background for policing, securitization, and regulation. Policing and the city are intimately intertwined. This collection also reveals commonalities in the empirical interests, methodological preferences, and theoretical concerns of scholars working in these various disciplines and breaks down barriers among them. This is the first collection on urban policing, regulation, and securitization with such a multi-disciplinary and international character.

This collection will have a wide readership among upper-level undergraduate and graduate-level students in several disciplines and countries and can be used in geography, urban studies, legal and socio-legal studies, sociology, anthropology, political science, and criminology courses.

Randy K. Lippert is Professor of Criminology at the University of Windsor, Canada, specializing in security, governance, and policing. He is co-editor of two other Routledge publications, *Eyes Everywhere: The Global Growth of Camera Surveillance* (2012) and *Sanctuary Practices in International Perspective* (2013) as well as author of *Sanctuary, Sovereignty, Sacrifice: Canadian Incidents, Power and Law* (2006).

Kevin Walby is Assistant Professor of Sociology at the University of Victoria, Canada, specializing in surveillance and policing. He has authored or co-authored articles in *Policing and Society, British Journal of Criminology, Criminology and Criminal Justice, Punishment and Society, Social and Legal Studies, International Sociology*, and *Current Sociology*. He is the Prisoners' Struggles editor for the *Journal of Prisoners on Prisons* and co-editor of *Bro____ ____ ____ ____ Freedom of Information Process in Canada*, with N

Routledge Frontiers of Criminal Justice

Policing Cities

Urban securitization and regulation
in a twenty-first century world

Edited by
Randy K. Lippert and Kevin Walby

Routledge
Taylor & Francis Group

LONDON AND NEW YORK

First published 2013
by Routledge
2 Park Square, Milton Park, Abingdon, Oxon OX14 4RN

Simultaneously published in the USA and Canada
by Routledge
711 Third Avenue, New York, NY 10017

*Routledge is an imprint of the Taylor & Francis Group, an informa
business*

British Library Cataloguing in Publication Data
A catalogue record for this book is available from the British Library

Library of Congress Cataloging-in-Publication Data
Policing cities: urban securitization and regulation in a 21st century
world / [edited by] Randy K. Lippert, Kevin Walby.
pages cm.—(Routledge frontiers of criminal justice)
1. Law enforcement. 2. Police. 3. Community policing. 4. Criminal
justice, Administration of. I. Lippert, Randy K., 1966– II. Walby,
Kevin, 1981–
HV7921.P584 2013
363.2'3—dc23
2012049758

ISBN13: 978-0-415-54033-9 (hbk)
ISBN13: 978-0-203-10736-2 (ebk)

Typeset in Times New Roman
by Book Now Ltd, London

Contents

Illustrations

Figures

Tables

Contributors

Kafui Attoh is a PhD Candidate in Geography at Syracuse University. He has published several articles on urban political struggle including "What *Kind* of Right Is the Right to the City?" *Progress in Human Geography* (2011); "The Bus Hub: Poem and Song" *ACME: An International E-Journal for Critical Geographies* (2011); and "The Transportation Disadvantaged and the Right to the City in Syracuse, NY" *The Geographical Bulletin* (2012).

Anna Barker is Lecturer in Sociology (crime and deviance) in the School of Social and International Studies at the University of Bradford. She completed her Economic Social Research Council-funded PhD "Local Perceptions of Insecurity and Reassurance: A Socio-Spatial Perspective" at the University of Leeds in partnership with the Leeds Community Safety Partnership and Leeds City Council. Her previous publications include an article in *Déviance et Société, the leading French criminology journal.* Her broader interests lie in development of socio-spatial criminology through interdisciplinary methodological approaches.

Julie Berg is a Senior Lecturer in the Centre of Criminology, Public Law Department at the University of Cape Town, South Africa. She is currently undertaking research on the functioning, regulation, and accountability of non-state security governance, particularly the private security industry and urban improvement districts.

Nicholas Blomley is Professor of Geography at Simon Fraser University. He has a long-standing interest in the geographies of property, which he has pursued in areas such as gentrification, urban gardening, public space and indigenous treaties. He is the author, most recently, of *Rights of Passage: Sidewalks and the Regulation of Public Flow* (Routledge, 2012).

Nelson Arteaga Botello is a Researcher in Latin American Faculty of Social Sciences, Mexico, specializing in issues of violence, security and surveillance in Latin America. Publications include "Privacy and Surveillance in Mexico and Brazil: A Cross-National Analysis," in *Surveillance, Privacy and the Globalization of Personal Data* (McGill-Queen's University Press, 2010) and "Security Metamorphosis in Latin America" in *Security and Everyday Life* (Routledge, 2011).

Irus Braverman is Associate Professor of Law and Adjunct Professor of Geography at the University at Buffalo, The State University of New York. Her main interests lie in the interdisciplinary study of law, geography, and anthropology. She has researched illegal houses, trees, checkpoints, public toilets, and zoos. Her publications include *House Demolitions in East Jerusalem: 'Illegality' and Resistance* (2006) (Hebrew), *Planted Flags: Trees, Land, and Law in Israel/ Palestine* (Cambridge University Press, 2009), and *Zooland: The Institution of Captivity* (Stanford University Press, 2012).

Adam Crawford is Professor of Criminology and Criminal Justice and Director of the Security and Justice Research Group of the Building Sustainable Societies Transformation Fund project at the University of Leeds. He is also the Pro-Dean for Research and Innovation in the Faculty of Education, Social Sciences and Law. His recent publications include: *Legitimacy and Compliance in Criminal Justice* (co-edited with A. Hucklesby (Routledge, 2013); *International and Comparative Criminal Justice and Urban Governance* (Cambridge University Press, 2011); and *Crime Prevention Policies in Comparative Perspective* (Willan, 2009). He is Editor-in-Chief of the journal *Criminology and Criminal Justice*.

Diane E. Davis is Professor of Urbanism and Development at Harvard's Graduate School of Design. Her primary research interests are conflict cities, violence, and the role of police in urban regulation. She has been a Carnegie Scholar and John D. and Catherine T. MacArthur Fellow (Program on Global Security). Her publications include: *Cities and Sovereignty: Identity Conflicts in the Urban Realm* (co-edited with N. Libertun de Duren); *Discipline and Development: Violence, Coercion, and Rights in Contemporary Latin America* (co-edited with A. Pereira); *Irregular Armed Forces and Their Role in Politics and State Formation* (co-edited with A. Pereira); and *Urban Leviathan: Mexico City in the Twentieth Century*.

Volker Eick is a Political Scientist at the Faculty of Law, Center of European Law and Politics, Universität Bremen, Germany. His research endeavors include the commercialization of security, labor market policy (workfare), urban security regimes, security in sports, and security technologies. He has authored numerous articles and chapters on private policing.

John Flint is Professor of Town and Regional Planning in the Department of Town and Regional Planning at the University of Sheffield. He has researched and written widely on urban governance, policing and security, including articles in *Sociological Research Online, Housing Studies, Urban Studies, British Journal of Criminal Justice, Criminology and Criminal Justice* and *Economy and Society*. He edited *Housing, Urban Governance and Anti-social Behaviour* (Policy Press, 2006).

Matthew A. Light is Assistant Professor of Criminology at the Centre of Criminology and Legal Studies, University of Toronto, Toronto, Canada. He holds a PhD in Political Science from Yale University. He is also a Doctor of Jurisprudence. Professor Light's doctoral and post-doctoral research has focused on issues of migration control, individual rights, police reform, policing and security in post-Soviet Russia.

Randy K. Lippert is Professor of Criminology at the University of Windsor, Canada specializing in governance, law, and security. He is co-editor with S. Rehaag of *Sanctuary Practices in International Perspectives* (Routledge, 2012) and with A. Doyle and D. Lyon of *Eyes Everywhere: the Global Growth of Camera Surveillance* (Routledge, 2011). He is also author of *Sanctuary, Sovereignty, Sacrifice: Canadian Incidents, Power, and Law* (University of British Columbia Press, 2006).

Setha Low is a former president of the American Anthropological Association and director of the Public Space Research Group at the City University of New York. Her recent research includes an ethnography of residents in gated communities in Texas and on Long Island as well as a study of urban parks. Low's research includes work on the anthropology of space and place, urban anthropology, landscapes of fear, security/insecurity, and gating in Latin America, the United States, and cities of Western Europe. Her publications include *Behind the Gates: The New American Dream* (Routledge, 2003); *On the Plaza: The Politics of Public Space and Culture* (University of Texas Press, 2000); and *Theorizing the City: The New Urban Anthropology Reader* (Rutgers University Press, 1999).

Virginie Milliot is Associate Professor of Urban Anthropology at the University of Paris 10 Nanterre La Défense. Since 2006, she has been conducting research on conflicts in public space in Paris. She first completed a study of public life in the Goutte d'Or neighborhood, and since 2009 has been conducting ethnographic research on poverty markets. These research projects allow her to examine the impact of weak ties on urban socialization, the dynamics of the construction of the public, and mobilizations on the street.

Don Mitchell is Distinguished Professor of Geography at Syracuse University. He is author of numerous articles and book chapters on social justice and public space. His books include *Justice, Power and the Political Landscape* (Routledge, 2009) (co-edited with Kenneth Olwig); *The People's Property? Power, Politics, and the Public* (Routledge, 2008) (authored with L. Staeheli); *The Right to the City: Social Justice and the Fight for Public Space* (2003); *Cultural Geography: A Critical Introduction* (Blackwell, 2000); and *The Lie of the Land: Migrant Workers and the California Landscape* (University of Minnesota Press, 1996).

Darren Palmer is convener of the Criminology program at Deakin University, Geelong, the Victorian Executive member of the Australian and New Zealand Society of Criminology, and Chair of the Australian Surveillance Studies research group. He is a regular commentator on crime and socio-legal issues in the Australian media and has conducted extensive research on the problematic nature of several contemporary policing, crime control and regulatory problems. He has authored and edited numerous Australian and international works examining the evolution of modern public and private policing and has won several awards for his ongoing community-based research.

Guillermo Ruiz de Teresa is an architect and researcher in Mexico City.

Gary Sigley is Professor of Asian Studies at the University of Western Australia. He has conducted several major research projects in China and has published widely in refereed journals such as *Economy and Society* and *Asian Studies Review*. He is former director of the University of Western Australia's Confucius Institute.

Susan Silberberg is Lecturer in Urban Design and Planning in the Department of Urban Studies and Planning at MIT where her teaching focuses on arts and cultural development in communities and also on the nexus between urban design and economic development. Susan's research includes the design and perception of public space post 9/11, and she received a Boston Society of Architects Research in Architecture Grant for this work. She consults with municipalities and non-profits in a wide range of areas including public space design and planning, urban commercial district revitalization, and arts and culture in communities. She has served as Associate Director of the MetLife Innovative Space Awards, which recognized innovative affordable artist space and artists' engagement with community across the United States.

Lynn A. Staeheli is Associate Professor of Geography. Her interests are in political and urban geography. Her research examines how local political processes shape the development of urban areas. She has investigated the consequences of the electoral process, the provision of public services, and the role of women in urban politics. She is author of numerous articles and book chapters and co-author of *The People's Property? Power, Politics, and the Public* (Routledge 2008, with D. Mitchell) and co-editor with J. Kodras and C. Flint of *State Devolution in America: Implications for a Diverse Society* (Sage, 1997).

Stéphane Tonnelat is an associate of the research faculty of the CNRS, at the LAVUE research center in Paris, France. He is the author of articles and book chapters in French and English on ethnography and urban public spaces, such as streets, gardens, and subways. His main research terrains are Paris, New York City and New Orleans.

Jürgen von Mahs is Assistant Professor in Urban Studies at The New School in New York and holds a joint appointment in the Urban Studies Program at Eugene Lang College and the Department of Social Sciences at the New School for Public Engagement. He has published numerous articles on the regulation of homeless people.

Kevin Walby is Assistant Professor in the Department of Sociology at the University of Victoria, Canada, specializing in surveillance, security, and policing. He has authored and co-authored articles in *Policing and Society*, *British Journal of Criminology*, *Punishment and Society*, *Crime, Law and Social Change*, *Criminology and Criminal Justice*, *Antipode*, *Social and Legal Studies*, *Sociology*, *International Sociology*, and *Current Sociology*. He is the Prisoners'

Struggles editor for the *Journal of Prisoners on Prisons*. He is co-editor of *Brokering Access: Power, Politics, and Freedom of Information Process in Canada* with M. Larsen (UBC Press). He teaches policing, law, deviance, and qualitative research methods.

Ian Warren is a Senior Lecturer in Criminology at Deakin University, Geelong, Australia. He has researched and published in several areas relating to comparative and international crime control policy. His research examines comparative and global policing and justice approaches to illicit drug control, violence and disorder in the night-time economy, and the role of information privacy in surveillance, justice policy and crime prevention.

Foreword

As I walk the streets of Vancouver, I often encounter a rather disheveled man who plays tunelessly on a mouth accordion in order to solicit small change from passersby. Subservient and ingratiating, he seems fairly harmless (unless one had to work close by). Yet, judging by extant law and policy, he is a recalcitrant and inveterate offender, potentially contravening the City's panhandling bylaw, as well as a bylaw governing street use. I also very much doubt that he holds, as is required, a "street entertainment permit." Even if he did, he would be governed by a matrix of rules (only 60 minutes in one location; no blockage of circulation; no use of sharp or dangerous objects, such as chainsaws or flaming objects; no voice amplification, except if he were rapping, in which case, an exception may be made). As is made clear by the City, he would be expected to self-regulate by respecting the wishes and needs of neighbors; accommodating other performers; not aggravating a "captive audience"; and keeping volume to "reasonable" limits, etc. If this fails, and there is a complaint, the City will act, by mobilizing either the police, or a "Street Use Inspector" who are empowered to move on the performer. Repeated infractions will lead to the denial of a permit (City of Vancouver 2012).

The lowly busker, it seems, is a legal object, subject to a mixture of complex and overlapping forms of regulation. But what sort of object is he? In common with other forms of street activity, particularly that involving the socially marginalized, he is also a potential object of interest for the following: private security forces, employed by local business organizations, who may regard him as a nuisance; urban policy pundits, who may treat him as a manifestation of urban diversity, or as a "broken window," depending on ideological leanings; civil libertarians, for whom he is a citizen, engaged in valued forms of expressive activity; urban engineers, who view him through a lens of circulation and traffic flow; public space scholars, who treat him as engaged in the production of a space of encounter and difference, and so on.

He is also an *urban* legal object. This is important, given that the city is a distinctive legal space. Not only do we find, as noted, a complex and poorly understood agglomeration of rules, policies and codes, driven by diverse projects of policing, security and regulation, conducted by state and non-state officials, but the city also has a distinctive logic that may depart quite significantly from "state" law. It is in the city, for example, that anxieties concerning public disorder (or optimism concerning political change) can be at their most acute. Behind the regulatory impulses that govern the lowly busker are a set of subterranean concerns relating to the well ordered society. "Policing" cities, in that sense, entails the operation of a "police" mindset, predicated on the regulation of the internal life of a community so as to promote salubrity, safety and wellbeing. Policing, in this ancient and deeply entrenched sense, works through the city, in particular, in defense of the community as a whole, seeing to suppress threats to wellbeing. The sidewalk upon which the busker performs is not, from this perspective, part of a Habermasian public sphere, but is understood as municipal property, to be governed according to a rationality of circulation and safety, and subject to a dense array of provisional permissions, licenses, and prohibitions.

Understanding urban law is thus no easy task. It is too easy to treat the regulation of the city through a narrow or singular focus. This collection promises something different, allowing us to make sense of the intersections and collisions of these diverse forms of urban legal practice and knowledge. It is also tempting to generalize from the experience of certain parts of the world. The chapters in this collection, however, provide a welcome window on a geographically diverse and fast-changing phenomenon, and draw from a rich and varied range of disciplinary perspectives.

Nicholas Blomley
June 2012

Reference

City of Vancouver (2012) http://vancouver.ca/engsvcs/streets/retailuse/busking.htm.

Acknowledgments

Randy K. Lippert acknowledges loving support and patience of Francine Lippert while co-editing this volume. He also acknowledges the influence of the late Richard V. Ericson. Richard's famous, ground-breaking policing scholarship, and his lesser known unwavering devotion to the graduate students whose lives he touched, one can only try to emulate.

Kevin Walby thanks Seantel Anaïs for all her encouragement and creativity.

Special thanks are due to each contributor for embracing this project from the beginning and following through with insightful and fascinating chapters about policing in the world's cities. We feel fortunate to have had an opportunity to exchange ideas with so many leading scholars researching and writing in their disciplines today. In some cases contributors were facing serious challenges in their professional lives due to institutional budget cuts and related pressures that are fast becoming the norm in academia. We truly appreciate their remarkable effort in following through. All the contributors' profound dedication to scholarship about policing and about cities continues to inspire us.

Special thanks also to Nicola Walker for her comments.

Finally, this collection would not have been possible without the excellent, efficient and amiable people at Routledge, especially Thomas Sutton and Nicola Hartley.

Introduction

How the world's cities are policed, regulated, and securitized

Randy K. Lippert and Kevin Walby

Policing is integral to cities. The need to understand policing has reached a critical juncture, as the world's population has become an urban population for the first time (Davis 2007). Social scientists long ago noted this trend toward urbanism as a way of life (Wirth 1938), and the connection between cities and security is an age-old theme (Weber 1958). Yet these perennial issues have taken on new importance and are worth reflecting on at the beginning of this millennium. Our collection is about policing this twenty-first century urban world. It comprises sixteen original chapters written by prominent international scholars. These contributing authors are experts in criminology, geography, sociology, political science, anthropology, urban planning, socio-legal studies, or Asian studies. They explore developments in cities across the USA, the UK, Australia, Canada, China, France, Georgia, Germany, Mexico, and South Africa and thus focus on cities of the Global North, on metropolises of the South, and cities continuing to transition from communist rule in the East.

Policing Cities is a double entendre that initially implies that this collection is about the public police, the urban spaces they traditionally patrol, and forms of conduct falling under their purview. But policing refers to wide-ranging efforts that seek to influence conduct or maintain order in urban spaces. By policing, we mean practices of public police as well as private and hybrid authorities and agencies that are neither obviously public nor private. Policing is a varied set of practices enlisting an array of technologies, practices, spaces, and persons to accomplish numerous order maintenance objectives, with complex consequences and implications. Scholarship on urban policing can no longer focus only on public police, as they are becoming less directly involved in policing cities and are being outnumbered by other agents. Some chapters that follow explore the ties among public police and other authorities in cities. This "pluralization" is significant given that public police now openly acknowledge what has been perhaps evident to many observers since their modern Peelian beginnings in nineteenth century London: public police cannot be everywhere and must share the heavy load of security provision (Shearing and Marks 2011). In urban Australia, for example, as the chapter by Ian Warren and Darren Palmer shows, securitization of major sporting events has resulted in public police becoming merely a "back up" when required. In Mexico City, Diane Davis and

Guillermo Ruiz de Teresa similarly demonstrate how security is changing from a political project, in which public police play a starring role, to a spatial project, in which they become less relevant. And the chapters by Volker Eick and Irus Braverman on Berlin and Buffalo respectively point to the array of agencies involved in policing cities today.

Yet any account of policing cities that ignores the public police does so at its peril. Public police, despite comparatively fewer in number, remain firmly entrenched and at times anchor other agencies' and authorities' policing. This is certainly the case where public police act as representatives of current or post-authoritarian regimes, as Gary Sigley and Matthew Light indicate in their respective chapters on cities in China and Georgia. But it applies in places where private security has made a mark too. For instance, Anna Barker and Adam Crawford examine the relationship between public police and community policing in this age of austerity budgets, with a focus on how community policing intersects with the private sector. Similarly, in their chapter on UK cities, Don Mitchell, Kafui Attoh and Lynn Staeheli note that "community cohesion is a policing-*centered* project." They argue that public police remain integral to policing cities even if their role is changing. It is especially important to explore the reasons behind and the means through which the public police role is changing.

The title's second, less obvious meaning is that the space and materiality of the urban (Ford 1994) and policing are deeply intertwined. As Michel Foucault remarked in his famous "security, population, territory" lectures, "to police and to urbanize are the same thing" (Foucault 2007: 337) and, more intriguingly, said "police . . . [is] a condition of existence for the urban" (Foucault 2007: 336). These assertions lend understanding to this second meaning of *Policing Cities*. In much previous work on urban policing, the city is typically an inert background rather than the main stage or the protagonist influencing the outcome of the story. However, the second meaning highlighted by our title refers to the integral relationship between policing and the urban form. This is evident where walls and segregation are stark, as in gated communities (Low 2003; Caldeira 1996) but also where spatial and material divides are subtle and gradual. The space and materiality of the urban should interest all scholars concerned with policing, not only urban planners or architectural theorists. As Julie Berg notes in her chapter on security provisions in South African cities, "urban space itself plays an important role." Nelson Botello makes a similar point about built space and surveillance in Mexico City. These and other chapters about policing in the world's cities underscore that such processes and the urban are entangled; the policing/urban nexus is not incidental. For Foucault "police" connotes not public police but regulation more generally, especially its spatial elements (Elden 2001). In his lectures, Foucault quotes Catherine II on developing a code of police: "The things of police are things of each moment . . . .. Police is concerned with little things" (Foucault 2007: 340). It is these little things and spaces in the fleeting moments of urban life, remarked upon in the chapters below, which become subject to "indefinite regulation" (Foucault 2007: 340). Our quoting of Foucault is not to suggest the following chapters are primarily Foucauldian but instead to imply there is more to policing than might first appear, and that the space and materiality of the city need exploration too. Issues of built space and architecture are integral to policing, and policing in turn shapes the city.

This collection's aim is to move beyond case studies of policing cities – in both senses of the phrase – from one perspective or country by bringing together international scholars from multiple disciplines to interrogate urban policing, securitization, and regulation; to reveal these practices as more intricate and mutable than previously thought; and to consider the thorny and intriguing theoretical and conceptual issues these explorations raise. Some concepts used to make sense of recent developments in the world's cities, like *regulation*, are old, yet remain vital even where urban populations and conduct are not *directly* targeted; others, like *securitization*, are newer, and offer additional ways to think about policing cities. Typically securitization means the regulation and fortification of buildings, spaces, and things (Aradau 2010). In New York City co-op housing arrangements, as Setha Low's chapter reveals, securitization can also mean the "financialization" of life, a process that can detrimentally affect those seeking affordable urban housing. John Flint notes a similar trend across the UK in his chapter on urban public housing. But if policing entails strategies "intended to offer guarantees of security to subjects" (Johnston 1999: 10), then there is overlap among policing, regulation, and securitization practices. Our position is that these practices are inseparable. Certainly policing as the broadest of the three concepts often encompasses regulation and securitization (Walby and Lippert 2012). The overlap of these practices within cities remains underplayed and little recognized in scholarly work. Disciplinary distinctions made about these practices may stunt rather than nurture conceptual cross-fertilization and refinement among criminologists, geographers, sociologists, political scientists, anthropologists, socio-legal scholars and others seeking understanding of policing cities.

Much previous research and theoretical reflection on urban policing, securitization, and regulation have involved perspectives and research literatures that talk past one another. Consider how different disciplines have traced the influence of the "broken windows" thesis, rarely acknowledging similar analyses in adjacent fields. More generally, urban geographers have focused on public urban space but discuss exclusion of homeless people in a manner similar to socio-legal scholars and criminologists. Other geographers explore the militarization of cities in ways more consistent with security studies; socio-legal scholars interrogate forms of legal regulation in the city and invoke space more akin to urban planners; cultural and critical criminologists investigate public and private security networks in city centers using anthropological research methods, and so on. As adroit as these various accounts may be, our position is that there is more to be gained through greater conversation among them since there is often overlap among their empirical foci, methodological preferences, and theoretical puzzles. Many of the following chapters topple barriers among these disciplines by offering cross-disciplinary theorizations and empirical analyses of urban policing.

Most of the chapters that follow demonstrate how their perspective advances knowledge in the field of urban securitization, policing and/or regulation and the theoretical and/or methodological strategies stemming from it. The chapters seek to advance understandings in a particular discipline but also bridge disciplinary divides to show what one discipline can learn from another. The volume underscores the value of dialogue among these disciplines since they often confront similar conceptual issues and themes as it concerns urban policing, securitization and/or regulation while working from within seemingly detached domains.

This inevitably means new questions will be asked. To be sure, older normative questions like "who has the *right* to the city?" despite much scholarly attention since Lefebvre (2000) first posed it in 1967, retains critical currency (Harvey 2008). Indeed, to see this, one need only read the chapters by Jürgen von Mahs on Berlin and by Susan Silberberg on Boston. This question speaks to growing numbers of homeless people, deepening spatial insecurities, rising class and racial/ethnic inequality, and destruction of public space in the world's cities. But in the wake of relentless urban neo-liberalization, decade-long post-9–11 maelstroms, and arrival of the Great Recession, the sum of the facts of accelerating urban securitization and novel uses of regulation have provided a stark answer to Lefebvre's inquiry. As the chapters below show, the answer is this: urban dwellers who are deemed risky or threatening to unfettered commercial activity on retail strips and at major sporting events, to free passage on sidewalks and streets, to near sanitized residential living, or to a preferred urban aesthetic, are presumed to have relinquished any right to the city. This policing produces categories of moralized and criminalized urban people that include "weak social elements" migrating to the cities from rural areas of China, street peddlers and crowds in the Barbès neighborhood of Paris, homeless people sleeping or panhandling in Berlin's railway station, street vendors in illicit markets selling "knock-offs" in Mexico City, tipsy sports fans over-celebrating in Melbourne's docklands, families raising rural (farm) animals as urban pets in Buffalo, and distrusted co-op housing applicants in New York City. These urbanites are to be excluded, watched, arrested, fined, jailed, banned, and any signs of a fleeting presence (e.g., cups, mattresses, beer cans, barnyard smells, and "denied" applications) forcibly removed, cleansed or disposed of as so much garbage (also see Walby and Lippert 2011). These persons and their artifacts are determined to be too risky, a nuisance to consumption, an affront to the ideals of private property, a barrier to elitist projects of urban civility, and a moral stain on a carefully crafted urban aesthetic (also see Smith 2002; Walby and Lippert 2012). These all preclude recognition of any rights to the city. Moreover, there is far less public urban space to which to claim a right, or collectively use, than in 1967, due to relentless privatization and the failure to include public space in urbanization projects. Embedded within urban geography, the question of "the right to the city" provides a crucial starting point from which to inquire about urban policing practices. Yet as Blomley (2011: 11) notes, an exclusive focus upon this question can obscure elements equally integral to the urban that call out for consideration.

The continued value of Lefebvre's question and others with which the chapters in this volume engage also butt up against far less critical questions currently asked of cities. One recent exemplar is the title of a best-selling book by urban scholar Richard Florida: *Who's Your City?* Florida (2008) tells us the city in which you choose to reside will profoundly influence your life chances. His treatise speaks to would-be urban gentry, a "creative class," which can prosper in a "spiky" rather than flattened globalized urban world. It matters in which city you live, says Florida, so ask which cities are spiked, and then relocate there. But Florida's question is neglectful of the realities of those immobilized in and displaced from urban spaces, those unable to *choose* their city, their neighborhood, or their residence, and those who remain trapped in places only to be policed as urban authorities deem fit, or are forced from traditional neighborhoods no longer affordable due to gentrification's less celebrated effects. These processes are exacerbated by the (latest) Great Recession, but were present in cities long before its onset. Ignored are towering urban spikes and yawning blighted valleys, and the physical walls, roadways, and other policing strategies demarcating them *within* cities. Florida, for example, mentions Toronto (exquisitely spiky) and Detroit (not so much), both cities in which he has lived. But he is quiescent about how Toronto's Jane-Finch corridor differs from the downtown's new "condoland" and about Detroit's infamous Eight Mile Road separating a primarily poor urban African American population from more affluent White Flight suburban sanctuaries as well as the different policing that defines and divides these spaces and inhabitants. Florida does not say much either about the experiences of urban exclusion and police violence like those that Virginie Milliot and Stéphane Tonnelat describe in their chapter on the Barbès neighborhood of Paris. In many major cities of the world, housing is now mostly private and financially out of reach (choosing your city in fact means purchasing property there). What dwindling public or subsidized housing stocks remain in the world's cities (see, for example, Lippert 2012) are inadequate to shelter vulnerable populations. And as John Flint shows regarding cities in the UK, housing is also about urban policing. Policing therefore directly influences life chances of urban populations. Asking "Who's Your City?" tends to obscure startling mutations in how the world's cities, along with their segregated populations and spatial inequalities, are being policed, securitized, and/or regulated.

Rather than relying only on Lefebvre's, or embracing those like Florida's, other questions are raised in the chapters that follow, illuminating ever more securitized, hyper-regulated realities of the twenty-first century urban world. If many cities are following the securitizing trajectory of what Davis (1992) called decades ago 'Fortress LA' to describe Los Angeles, what are the new keys to the world's cities and who keeps them? The ascendency of transnational governance through globalization rhetoric has not resulted in a declining regulatory role for the world's cities in the twenty-first century (Valverde 2011: 307), so how has a rescaling of policing and security to the urban level transpired and with what effects? How are police seeking to remain legitimate through reforms amidst dramatic fiscal cutbacks in the UK or in cities where they have all but lost legitimacy due to past ties with authoritarian government, as in Mexico, Georgia, and China? And what new forms and uses of urban governance are being deployed that foster this shift or which permit populations to be regulated by non-state policing agents? In some countries and regions community policing is the key signifier, though the type and content of community and the role of public police within this rhetoric remain in question and vary across cities. What are the roles of the new or hitherto ignored policing agents that range from police community support officers (UK), to citizen volunteer patrols, to non-profit security agents, to for-profit private security agents, to animal abuse officers, to military personnel? From where do these policing agents receive their power and authority? What do recent changes in policing cities mean for those residing in and frequenting urban spaces? How and from where are logics like "zero tolerance" and "broken windows" transferred to new locales in Mexico, Germany, and South Africa, such as by former New York mayor Rudy Giuliani's security consulting firm? What are the broader backdrops of policing cities that range from falling levels of social welfare, to reduced access to affordable urban housing, to neo-liberal privatization, to authoritarian intervention by higher levels of government, to drastic police budget cutbacks, to declared wars on drug lords, to spatial responses to the events of September 11, 2001? These are only some of the questions addressed in this collection.

Organization of chapters

There is a continuity of purpose among the volume's four parts, each of four chapters, bound together as they are by a focus on policing cities.

Part I, "Public police reform and community policing in twenty-first century cities," focuses on more traditional topics of policing cities, namely developments in public police reform (Barker and Crawford; Light) and community policing (Sigley; Mitchell *et al.*).

Part II, "New modes of urban policing and governance," comprises empirical case studies of new organizational forms and developments in policing cities, including unique kinds of legal exclusion and surveillance (Palmer and Warren), networks of private policing, non-profit and public police (Eick), rescaling of security to the urban level (Davis and Ruiz de Teresa), and neglected types of urban policing (Braverman).

Part III, "Policing city spaces and regulating conduct," offers chapters describing empirical research on policing urban residential space (Flint), securing privatized urban spaces in a network (Berg), effects of policing on urban homeless people (von Mahs), and on regulating urban public spaces (Milliot and Tonnelat).

Finally, Part IV, "Securitization of twenty-first century cities" covers new forms and effects of militarization (Walby and Lippert) and securitization (Low; Botello; Silberberg) of cities.

References

Aradau, C. (2010) "Security that Matters: Critical Infrastructure and Objects of Protection." *Security Dialogue,* 41(5): 491–514.

Blomley, N. (2011) *Rights of Passage: Sidewalks and the Regulation of Public Flow,* London: Routledge.

Caldeira, T. (1996) "Building up Walls: the New Pattern of Spatial Segregation in São Paulo." *International Social Science Journal,* 48(1): 55–66.

Davis, M. (1992) *City of Quartz: Excavating the Future in Los Angeles,* New York: Vintage.

Davis, M. (2007) *Planet of Slums,* New York: Verso.

Elden, S. (2001) *Mapping the Present: Heidegger, Foucault and the Project of a Spatial History,* London: Continuum.

Florida, R. (2008) *Who's Your City? How the Creative Economy Is Making Where to Live the Most Important Decision of Your Life,* New York: Basic Books.

Ford, L. (1994) *Cities and Buildings: Skyscrapers. Skid Rows, and Suburbs,* Baltimore: Johns Hopkins University Press.

Foucault, M. (2007) *Security, Territory, Population: Lectures at the Collège De France,* M. Senellart and A. Davidson (eds). New York: Palgrave Macmillan.

Harvey, D. (2008) "The Right to the City." *New Left Review,* 53: 23–40.

Johnston, L. (1999) "Private Policing in Context." *European Journal on Criminal Policy and Research,* 7: 175–96.

Lefebvre, H. (2000) *Le Droit à la ville* (2nd edn), Paris: Anthropos.

Lippert, R. (2012) "Governing Condominiums and Renters with Legal Knowledge Flows and External Institutions." *Law and Policy,* 34(3): 263–90.

Low, S.M. (2003) *Behind the Gates: Life, Security, and the Pursuit of Happiness in Fortress America,* New York: Routledge.

Shearing, C. and Marks, M. (2011) "Being a New Police in the Liquid 21st Century." *Policing,* 5(3): 210–18.

Smith, N. (2002) "New Globalism, New Urbanism: Gentrification as Global Strategy." *Antipode,* 34(3): 427–50.

Valverde, M. (2011) "Seeing Like a City: the Dialectic of Modern and Pre-modern Ways of Seeing in Urban Governance." *Law and Society Review,* 45(2): 277–312.

Walby, K. and Lippert, R. (2011) "Spatial Regulation, Dispersal, and the Aesthetics of the City: Conservation Officer Policing of Homeless People in Ottawa, Canada." *Antipode,* 44(3): 1015–33.

Walby, K. and Lippert, R. (2012) "The New Keys to the City: Uploading Corporate Security and Threat Discourse into Canadian Municipal Governments." *Crime, Law and Social Change,* 58(4): 437–55.

Weber, M. (1958) *The City,* D. Martindale and G. Neuwirth (trans). New York: Collier Books.

Wirth, L. (1938) "Urbanism as a Way of Life." *American Journal of Sociology,* 44(1): 1–24.

Part I

Public police reform and community policing in twenty-first century cities

1 Policing urban insecurities through visible patrols

Managing public expectations in times of fiscal restraint

Anna Barker and Adam Crawford

Introduction

On 10 May 2012, some 30,000 police officers took to London's streets to protest against the government's 20 per cent reductions in police funding, changes to the service and cuts to police pay.[1] This extraordinary reaction to contemporary events indicates that public policing is undergoing rapid and fundamental change. This is especially so in the British cities that gave birth to modern professional policing, a quintessential dimension of which always has been visible patrol officers. They represent what Thomas (1945) sardonically described as the '"scarecrow" function of the police'. The evolution of professional policing has long been tied to shifts in the nature of insecurities fuelled by the changing face of risks and the manner in which these are perceived by powerful elites (Reiner 2010). Contemporary insecurities, moreover, coalesce and take on acute meaning within the city as both host to, and generator of, diverse forms of crime and anti-social behaviour. Consequently, concerns about disorder and urban safety directly inform debates about the urban condition and the nature of city governance.

This chapter reflects upon public policing through visible patrols in a changing climate of fiscal restraint,[2] a flurry of government reforms, and volatile public expectations. We chart policy and economic shifts and consider their implications for policing insecurities in cities across England and Wales.[3] In particular, we assess the rise of the 'reassurance policing' agenda under the New Labour Government (Povey 2001); unfolding relations between public and private provision of security; and, for the first time, the election of a Police and Crime Commissioner (PCC) for each force area outside of London introduced by the Police Reform and Social Responsibility Act 2011. We question the extent to which these changes signal the eclipse of reassurance policing and foreshadow a recasting of public police ambitions. We conclude with speculation on future trends in light of projected police budgetary cuts, opportunities for further private sector involvement in policing, and plans for democratic oversight.

The future shape and ambitions of public policing are uncertain. Nevertheless, policing is now on a radically altered course, largely defined by several interconnected influences. These include abandonment by the Coalition Government of the previous political shibboleth of increasing police officer numbers, described by Ian Blair (2012a) as constituting a 'straightjacket' on police budgets; political and ideological commitment to greater private sector involvement in the delivery of public services as *the only rational response* to conditions of austerity, thus increasing the pluralized provision of 'policing beyond the police' (Crawford 2008); and a radical reform to police governance through publicly elected PCCs, deepening efforts to make policing 'citizen-focused' and enmeshing its operational delivery more significantly in public expectations and popular demands. In an interesting example of policy transfer, this unique model of police governance borrows from, but modifies, US models of police 'democratic' accountability. In the reconfiguration, 41 new PCCs will become primary fund holders and be responsible for planning and accounting for policing strategy and services to be delivered by the Chief Constable or other providers in their police area.[4] PCCs will preside over the central government police grant, local council tax precept and various other funding streams, including current Community Safety Partnership funding and Home Office special grants, as well as new forms of income generation such as the levy on night-time economy service users. These will be streamlined into a single PCC funding pot by 2014/15 (Home Office 2012). Significant here is the level of discretion elected figures will have over these resources.

This chapter's first objective is to consider the implications of these developments for policing urban insecurities. The dark shadow cast by spending cuts and the *volte face* on police numbers loom large over the earlier policy preoccupations with reassurance policing and allied goals of managing subjective insecurities and impressions of order. Nonetheless, in explicitly tying the fortunes of PCCs to the policing of public demands, including the insatiable desire for a visible police presence, their arrival heralds potentially contradictory implications for continuation of the reassurance agenda. This is a timely juncture at which to reflect upon the recent fortunes and future prospects of reassurance policing and the extent to which government reforms signal its eclipse or its reinvigoration. Our second objective is to consider the unfolding relations between public policing and private security, notably in relation to visible patrols in cities.

This chapter analyses contemporary public policy shifts from a criminological perspective. It highlights the key dynamics of governmental intentions and speculates on future implications. Evidently, it has less to say about the manner in which these logics and ambitions are played out, interpreted and contested on the streets of cities across England and Wales. These are empirical questions for another day.

The rise of 'reassurance policing'

The past two decades have seen several significant twists and turns in the direction and priorities of policing in British cities. Whereas the 1990s saw a narrowing of the police mission to a preoccupation with 'crime-fighting' and 'priority crimes', the 2000s witnessed a more expansive vision of policing tied to efforts to manage public insecurities. Managerialist concerns about the efficient targeting of police resources to crime-related performance indicators (often concerned with detection) emerged as the dominant logic in the late 1980s – exemplified in the 1993 White Paper's mantra that 'the main job of the police is to catch criminals' (Home Office 1993: para. 2.2). This relegated to the margins less measurable dimensions of policing, including public engagement through locally tied community patrols (FitzGerald *et al*. 2002). Crime reduction displaced order maintenance and visible street patrols due in part to the acknowledgement that the latter had little direct impact on crime rates (Clarke and Hough 1984).

Things changed dramatically soon after 2000, against a background of declining crime rates. There was a growing recognition of a 'reassurance gap' (ACPO 2001) between public perceptions of crime and the declining risk of victimization and deteriorating public confidence in the police, particularly marked in urban areas. This was combined with fears that the private sector may encroach onto, and stimulate, a market for policing services, including patrols. The then deputy Commissioner of the Metropolitan Police, Ian Blair (2002) somewhat apocalyptically warned of the possible 'Balkanization of policing', whereby 'we may see hundreds of different law-enforcement agencies springing up across Britain', returning policing to the dark ages before the rise of the professional police.

Subsequently, the police mission was recast, in the words of the 2004 White Paper, to include 'both preventing and detecting crime *and* reassuring the public' (Home Office 2004: 18, emphasis in original). This vision of policing signalled both a more capacious ambition of governmental intervention and, simultaneously, a narrower focus on the regulation of individual behaviour and local social order as the crucibles in which the fortunes of governments are to be forged. As the capacity of political institutions to control large-scale economic and social problems has become increasingly circumscribed under pressures of globalization, so we have witnessed a tapering of governmental capabilities. Uncertain of their values and purposes, governments have re-sighted their energies on managing public displays of behaviour. Under New Labour, this expressed itself in a zeal to deliver local public sector reform and tangible changes to quality of life, in ways that would be visible and recognizable to the electorate. A key philosophy behind the shift was that 'numbers are important but not enough: citizens have to see and feel the difference' (Barber 2007: 370). Hence, delivering irreversible change that citizens might notice became a major policy driver. The then Prime Minister Tony Blair (2006) reflected on the importance of public perceptions:

> you can argue about statistics until the cows come home and there is usually a very great credibility gap between whatever statistics are put out and whatever people actually think is happening, but the real point is not about statistics, *it is about how people feel*, and if they feel safer and more confident, because the fear of crime is as important in some respects as crime itself. (Emphasis added.)

Given the close association between the 'crime–disorder–fear' nexus and the city, as well as the importance of urban electorates for political fortunes, the salience of these issues was magnified across British cities. Moreover, the very notion of delivering reassurance through visible policing was tied to a certain image of urban social order. Implicit in this and paralleled in the concurrent 'anti-social behaviour' agenda was a prevailing attempt to re-imagine and re-designate cities as safe places to visit, live and invest in. This was linked directly to entrepreneurial 'urban boosterism' and 'local growth coalitions' (Logan and Molotch 1987), combining municipal authorities and business interests, that have played a crucial role in promoting safety as an essential dimension of regeneration agendas (Crawford and Flint 2009).

In the ensuing period, citizens of cities across England and Wales have become accustomed to policing reforms, backed by sustained funding increases, designed to manage public perceptions of local safety. Key to the delivery of this reassurance agenda have been expanded numbers of police officers and strategies to augment their 'visibility, familiarity and accessibility' (Povey 2001). Hence, the Police Reform Act 2002 introduced a second tier of police patrol officers, Police Community Support Officers (PCSOs), without the full powers or training of sworn constables. The separation of the patrol function from reactive demands means that PCSOs are not subject to the 'tyranny of the radio' or other reactive burdens on police constables. Hence, they dedicate more time to public interactions on the streets. Their introduction and expansion became a linchpin in convincing the public they could 'feel safer and more confident'.

Allied to this was the establishment of a 'National Reassurance Policing Programme' (NRPP) in eight police forces across England from 2003 to 2005. The programme was informed by the signal crimes perspective (Innes *et al.* 2004), suggesting that public reassurance can be engineered by visible policing interventions, such as foot patrols, attuned to key drivers of insecurity identified by communities. Visible policing is argued to influence public impressions about the degree of 'guardianship' and social controls present in an area (Innes and Fielding 2002: 14). The main evaluation of the NRPP found that, compared with their control sites, it 'had a positive impact on crime, perceptions of crime and antisocial behaviour, feelings of safety and public confidence in the police' (Tuffin *et al.* 2006: ix). The NRPP's success informed the introduction of neighbourhood policing teams across England. These locally tied teams aim to provide a response to community concerns. This has seen greater value and resources accorded to visible foot patrols, resulting in a substantial increase in the number of police officers and support staff dedicated to maximize front-line visibility. In contrast to the recent budget cuts, public spending on policing after the turn of the century rose by over 20 per cent (Home Office 2001: 14). By 2010, the size of the police workforce in England and Wales reached an all-time high, at just under 245,000. So too, the number of PCSOs peaked at approximately 17,000.

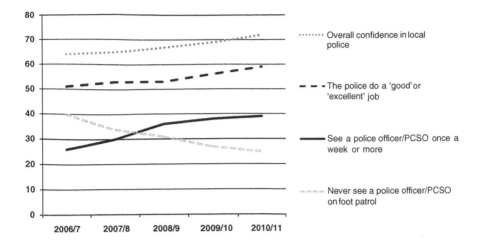

Figure 1.1 Public perception of the police 2006–11 (%).

Source: Crime Survey for England and Wales.

Consequently, the reassurance agenda has been a *public* policing project, associated with the direct activities of state-funded constables, PCSOs and other public sector policing auxiliaries (including neighbourhood wardens).

The broadening of the police mandate combined with additional resources has coincided with significant improvements in traditional measures of police performance. The crime rate continued to decline to its lowest level since 1981. There has been a steady upward trend in perceptions of police visibility with a greater percentage of people reporting sight of a police patrol officer on a weekly basis or more and a marked decline in those who have never seen an officer on foot patrol (see Figure 1.1). We have also witnessed a turnaround in public perceptions of local crime and confidence in the police, apparently delivering on New Labour's reform pledge. The percentage of respondents perceiving a rising local crime rate declined from 54 per cent in 2002/3 to 28 per cent in 2010/11.[5] Both the indicators for public ratings of the local police, measured by whether they do a 'good' or 'excellent' job, and for overall confidence in the police, showed an 8 per cent increase between 2006/07 and 2010/11.

Policing in times of fiscal restraint

The scale of fiscal restraint on policing budgets is unprecedented. The economic challenges go beyond the short-term spending period. HM Treasury (2012) has already indicated departmental expenditure limits until 2017. Moreover, the Winsor Review (2011) forecasts severe restraint in public service finances for decades to come. However, the police austerity programme was due to ideological imperatives as well as economic conditions. As Prime Minister David Cameron (2009) declared:

> Achieving more for less in this age of austerity is not just a technical question of managerial efficiency. It is a philosophical question too. It's about your approach to the big social problems that government must help address. And we have a fundamentally different approach to Labour.

The difficulty for Cameron is that citizens have become accustomed to seeing, and associating urban safety with the provision of, visible police patrols. Public expectations of, and demands for, policing may be at considerable odds with Cameron's philosophical commitments.

Leaner policing: the decline of the reassurance agenda?

The language of 'leaner' and 'smarter' policing has penetrated official police discourse and post-budget mission statements. This new discourse contrasts starkly with the positive messages conveyed to the public in healthier economic times; for example, West Yorkshire Police Authority's (2004) maxim: 'bigger budget = more staff = better policing'. The political 'numbers game' (Morgan 2012: 472) has been suspended and the police workforce is being allowed to enter a period of significant contraction.

As Figure 1.2 shows, total police employees are estimated to decline by 32,300 up to 2015; a 13 per cent fall from its 2010 peak. This includes reductions of 15,600 police staff, 15,000 police constables and 1,700 PCSOs (HMIC 2012: 20).

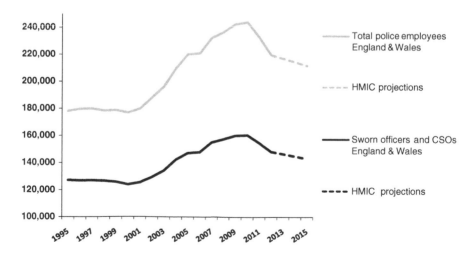

Figure 1.2 Number of police employees with HMIC projections 1995–2015 for England and Wales.

Source: Home Office and HMIC (2012) projections.

Consequentially, police numbers will reach 2004 levels, a time when reassurance policing was emerging and there was a clarion call by politicians for greater numbers of police on the streets. The first year of the financial cuts witnessed the largest annual fall in police numbers in forty years and the first annual decline in PCSOs since their introduction in 2002.

The reassurance agenda always raised implications for its long-term sustainability given its 'ambient' conception of policing (Loader 2006). A prominent critique has highlighted the associated failure to recognize policing as a finite resource, requiring the negotiation and management of a range of competing demands (Crawford 2007). The policing of citizen insecurities has stimulated debate about where to concentrate limited public resources across urban areas, particularly given the awkward relationship between actual crime risks and subjective insecurities, which is particularly acute within and between cities. This resourcing question has even greater resonance in a context where doing 'more with less' is a governmental expectation. These debates exist partly because reassurance policing has been promoted as an additional police strategy, requiring extensive resourcing, to sit alongside crime control and other policing strategies (Innes 2005), rather than as a 'golden thread' integral to all police work (Millie 2010: 230). Moreover, achieving greater efficiency is limited, given that 80 per cent of police budgets goes toward personnel (Winsor 2011).

To what extent do substantial reductions in police numbers signal a move away from an expansionist, proactive model towards minimalist, reactive style of public policing? Given 16,700 fewer police officers and PCSOs, observers suggest there is little prospect that the front-line and neighbourhood policing teams will be unaffected (HMIC 2012). This is where the greatest impact may be felt (Myhill and Quinton 2010) or at least where it may be most visible to the public. The resulting impact might be that the police will attend less to the disorder and anti-social behaviour problems that 'adversely shape public confidence' (Myhill and Quinton 2010: 279). The *Policing for London* study reminds us that a shrinking workforce capacity can contribute to the decline of public confidence in the police (FitzGerald *et al.* 2002). The contraction of the police workforce risks being interpreted by the public as a powerful signal of a 'control deficit' (Innes 2003). Survey research has established a relatively strong association between *seeing* officers on foot patrol and public confidence in the police (Innes and Innes 2012). Declines in this softer policing function could damage public confidence for 'reassurance, like trust, may take considerable time and effort to construct and maintain but may be brittle and easily fractured' (Crawford *et al.* 2005: 89). The provision of increased police visibility over the past decade has inadvertently fuelled an inflated normative standard for visible displays of security. Zedner (2003: 166) notes: 'The more security provision there is, the more people regard it as normal or necessary, and the greater their anxiety when it is not available'. An early evaluation of the impact of PCSOs in two cities in England appears to support this conclusion. For, while the introduction of PCSOs resulted in 25 per cent of respondents to a survey stating they felt safer, 59 per cent of respondents agreed that they would feel less secure if PCSOs were removed (Crawford *et al.* 2004: ix). The unintended consequence may be that public perceptions of crime and insecurity will grow.

Nevertheless, as Neyroud (2010) points out, 'protecting the frontline' has become a political mantra. Against the backdrop of the financial cuts, police forces have been restructuring so that a greater proportion of the workforce is positioned at the front-line. Police forces will need to innovate and strategically realign operational capacity to budgets if they are to continue visible policing. This may include the redeployment of back-office staff to beat duties and making single patrolling routine (Muir and Loader 2011). Additionally, aided by geographical mapping, there may be tactical attempts to align the deployment of foot patrols more 'precisely' with crime and fear 'hotspots'. This may have positive effects, potentially giving patrol officers a clearer sense of purpose and direction, rather than simply seeking to reassure the public as 'mobile scarecrows' (Crawford *et al.* 2005: 57). It is possible that the public may become critical of PCSOs if they are interpreted as *only* providing a visible presence; a criticism directed at the NRPP. Moreover, findings of research in England have identified that the relative reassurance value of police patrols may be reduced in areas with large numbers of semi-formal and organic 'capable guardians' (Crawford *et al.* 2005). Perceptions of safety can coexist with high levels of crime in particular spaces, such as busy thoroughfares, perceived as distinctly safe due to high levels of natural surveillance (Barker 2012). Furthermore, some police forces are seeking to increase the strength of (less costly) Special Constables and volunteers to boost visible policing.

Ambiguously, government appears, once more, to be re-sighting the principal objectives of policing on the prevention of crime and disorder. The 2010 White Paper, harking back to the narrower policing remit of the 1993 White Paper, identified that the 'key priority for the police is to cut crime' (para. 1.22). Interestingly, 'reassurance' does not feature at all, although there are scattered references to 'making people feel safe' (para. 1.21) as a policing goal. The balance between these priorities is left ill-defined.

The introduction of PCCs

This ambiguity is likely to be heightened by the introduction of PCCs, who will be tied via the electoral process to public concerns and have powers to set local policing priorities. In their desire to respond to what matters most to their electorate and embed a 'public voice' into policing strategies, they might place reassurance and the 'politics of fear' centre-stage. Commissioners are to be identifiable, public-facing individuals occupying a central position in the new governance of policing. Described by the Prime Minister as 'a big local figure', PCCs are intended to mark a radical break with the 'shadowy bodies' (Morgan 2012: 473) – as police authorities have been described – which have remained largely unknown to local people. Importantly, PCCs' remit extends beyond the police to encompass responsibilities for crime and community safety. PCCs will have a legal responsibility for appointing (where necessary suspending or removing) the Chief Constable; holding the Chief Constable to account for the 'totality' of policing; setting a five-year plan; deciding the local council tax precept and annual force budget; and commissioning services from *anyone* within their force area, including the voluntary and private sectors.

One uncertainty about incoming PCCs is what policing priorities they will set, given their public mandate. On the one hand, this reform signals an increasing democratization that could strengthen police legitimacy by subjecting their priorities, particularly in light of fewer resources, to an open public debate (Home Affairs Committee 2010) and rendering police services more accountable. This arrangement might enhance public confidence and trust in policing and politics (Muir and Loader 2011). On the other hand, the election of PCCs leads to questions about how and whether concerns over security, voiced by diverse publics, will be listened to and represented by a single elected person.

There are risks that policing agendas influenced by majoritarian sensibilities may be captured by those with the loudest voices, the largest political influence and the deepest pockets; i.e. the 'worried well' and the 'fearful safe' (Home Affairs Committee 2010: 9). We know that public demands for policing tend to be locally based, focused on visible incidents that are not necessarily serious and may evoke punitive sentiments. PCCs may proactively target policing resources towards crimes and disorders identified by the public as triggers of their insecurity but it is unclear the extent to which this may be at the expense of more serious threats with lower 'signal values'. If abstract methods of consultation are used by PCCs to inform priorities, they may distort public views and encourage emotive responses. Politicians sounding 'tough on crime' to appeal to a 'populist punitiveness', or capitalizing on public insecurities for electoral success are by no means unfamiliar. Given that political figures do not tend to rate high on public trust (de Grazia 2011: 4), elected Commissioners may erode the legitimacy of the police, if they seek to fuel uncontained public expectations on which the police are unable to deliver. As with the prior governance arrangements, PCCs are limited to making policy decisions. The operational independence of the Chief Constable continues to be protected by a Policing Protocol Order. Ironically, as Sampson (2012: 11) makes clear, it is these legal differences between the US Sherriff model and English reforms that may lead to a disjuncture between a PCC's campaign and the capacity of police to deliver it. PCCs do not have the 'correlative ability' to deliver operational policing, as in the US model.

PCCs will have greater freedom than police authorities ever had to determine priorities for policing resources. The only significant constraints are laid down in the collective cross-force priorities in the annual 'strategic requirement'. If majoritarian expressions of public opinion come to inform policing priorities via PCCs' electoral commitments, we may see policing drawn into responding to parochial demands and/or intolerant sensibilities. The most consistent response to crime and disorder favoured by the public is more police officers to provide a visible presence (Casey 2008). Some candidates promising this are likely to lower public confidence if the Chief Constable is not able to deliver them (de Grazia 2011).

There are concerns about how possible it is for a single elected figure to represent impartially the geographical breadth and cultural and demographic diversity of urban communities. A key question arising from the reassurance policing agenda is *whose* concerns are accorded prominence in normative discussions about how the police should define social order. The police interact with many different publics in diverse contexts and on the basis of differing relationships. The contemporary discourse of citizen-focused policing tends to reduce all citizens to the same status of recipients of a service, with little acknowledgement that some people – often defined as 'police property' – are the objects of policing and are more likely to find themselves in an adversarial relationship with the police, notably young people. Democratic public policing should not be concerned merely with giving the public what it wants (Crawford 2007: 159), but also ensure equitable and fair treatment and protection for human rights.

Policing cities?

It is within neighbourhoods and cities that policing becomes meaningful for crime and insecurity. It is at the city level that normative governmental agendas to promote civility and tackle anti-social behaviour collide with commercially driven imperatives to promote cities as safe places to consume but also where consumption itself is crimogenic, as in the night-time economy. It is here that policing and crime control become embroiled in political alliances and local economic forces, as well as enmeshed in images of civic identity. More specifically, it is at the neighbourhood level that experiences of local social order serve as a lens through which wider national and global anxieties are refracted. However, the PCC model of representation and accountability is force-wide, rather than at the level of the city or neighbourhood. While PCCs are an attempt to respond to local crime and policing needs, there is a concern that with a large geographical and demographic area to cover, combined with a strategic requirement for national issues, the PCC will not be able to grasp the neighbourhood or city perspective and/or may disregard local variation: 'there is even a substantial question mark over the extent to which the PCC will be able meaningfully and directly to address any citizens' local policing concerns' (Sampson 2012: 12). The city-level dimension is to be found in the creation of Police and Crime Panels, which will be established with representatives from each local authority area.

Yet, there are concerns that Commissioners might appeal to electorates solely on prominent issues within the force area with little regard for national and regional threats and cross-border organized crime. The new National Crime Agency will disseminate the impacts of organized crime on communities to PCCs and foster a 'laminated' (ACPO cited in Neyroud 2010: 3) policing approach, which recognizes the connections between neighbourhood problems and organized crime. In this way, the strategic requirement is an 'important lever' for safeguarding and developing interoperability and collaboration across police forces (Home Office 2011: 9), because there may be little electoral benefit for PCCs. Failure to attend to cross-border collaboration may prompt future Home Secretaries to become more prescriptive over the content of national strategic requirements.

The advent of PCCs is likely to usher in an era in which geographic police areas diverge over the nature and role of contemporary policing. Cities may increasingly vary in their approach to visible reassurance and public safety. The political dimension to PCC elections is likely to result in many Commissioners being affiliated to, or directly espousing, party political values and beliefs. It is not unlikely that police services in large (high crime) metropolitan cities – such as Manchester, Liverpool, Leeds and Birmingham – will see the election of Labour-endorsed PCCs, whilst Conservative PCCs will be more likely to succeed in predominantly rural (low-crime) areas. This may offer an experimental bed in which diverse strategies are tested. However, it may also result in a policing patch-work quilt, whereby cross-border differences are accentuated and cities diverge along fault-lines concerning the purpose and role of the public police. One issue on which we can expect PCCs to have considerable sway (infused by ideological or party political positions) is in relation to the involvement of the private sector in the delivery of policing services.

The privatization of policing?

The recent 'rebirth of private policing' (Johnston 1992) in Britain has been incremental. Nevertheless, the steady marketization of policing has seen the police involved more extensively both in buying and selling services. Whilst the Police Act 1964 allowed police forces to charge for 'special services', such as the policing of football matches, it was the Police and Magistrates Court Act 1994 that opened a wider space for the police to enter the marketplace, including the contracting out of police officer time. The Police Reform Act 2002 not only gave the police a new commodity to 'sell' through public–private partnerships, namely the PCSO, but also enabled chief officers to establish accreditation schemes that grant limited powers (fixed penalty notices) to non-police organizations to contribute towards community safety. The Act marked a watershed in fostering greater engagement with the private security sector.

However, the Private Security Industry Act 2001 did more to lay the groundwork for the current conditions. It established the Security Industry Authority, launched in 2003, to license and regulate all 'contract' private security providers. Regulation was a policy goal that powerful proponents within the industry had long championed as the key to greater legitimacy and hence to open the gateway to wider policing markets. Nevertheless, it has taken a number of 'false dawns' (White 2010) to reach the brink of expansion on which we now stand. A decade ago relations between the public police and private security were marked by hostility and a lack of trust. Research concluded:

> There persists a view within some police units that the police alone should provide patrols and that others merely get in their way rather than seeing others' policing efforts as a resource to be harnessed in the furtherance of public safety.
>
> (Crawford and Lister 2004: x)

In the 2000s, police managers anticipated that they could expand and even capture markets from the private sector, given their brand advantage and their more competitively priced workforce, notably PCSOs, compared with their constabulary colleagues (Crawford et al. 2005). In sum, the assumed relationship was one of professional police hegemony, in which non-state policing served as the 'junior partner' (Cunningham and Taylor 1985).

However, community safety accreditation schemes failed to take off to the extent initially envisaged, despite offering the police opportunities to influence the policing efforts of others and affording private security benefits from enhanced credibility. The business advantages to security providers were offset by the costs and the scheme foundered on the reluctance of many police forces to entertain the idea of granting additional powers to private operators. By the end of 2010, the number of accredited persons stood at only 2,219 across the 26 participating forces (ACPO 2011). The vast majority were local-authority employed wardens or anti-social behaviour enforcement officers rather than staff employed by commercial security companies.

Nevertheless, by the time of the 2010 Comprehensive Spending Review, Britain had a more mature and self-confident private security industry. The implementation of the new, albeit relatively tame (within a European context) regulatory framework for the security industry coupled with innovative experiments in public–private partnerships has provided more fertile soil. In this, the ideological commitment to private sector involvement in the delivery of public services as the accepted response to conditions of austerity has quickly germinated. As the political taboo of decreasing police officer numbers was abandoned by the Coalition Government, the transfer to the private sector of large aspects of policing has been placed firmly on the agenda.

Acknowledging this, the private sector has been adroit at responding to their changed fortunes. In November 2011, a roundtable meeting was held in Parliament, hosted by the British Security Industry Association (BSIA) to encourage greater private sector involvement in policing. Soon thereafter, Oliver Letwin the government Minister responsible for co-ordinating government policy articulated the now prevailing ideological position. He declared that private companies working in hospitals, police and schools will 'no longer be a matter of political debate but straightforward and obvious as a way of conducting business in this country' (Mason 2012). Austerity has thus become the justification for the head-long rush to private sector involvement as a means of making cost efficiencies in the face of considerable reductions in police budgets.

The subsequent pace of events has been remarkable. A landmark was set by Lincolnshire Police when they signed a £200m contract with G4S in February 2012 to build and staff (for 10 years) a police station. The contract accounts for 18 per cent of the force budget, with estimated savings of £28 million. It will incorporate a wide range of functions such as: custody services ('street to suite'); town enquiry officers; force control room; and a crime management bureau. Under the initiative, half the civilian staff (some 575 employees) joined the private company.

West Midlands and Surrey Police forces followed this initiative by issuing a £1.5 billion procurement tender. Activities outlined included: investigating crimes, detaining suspects, developing cases, responding to and investigating incidents, supporting victims and witnesses, managing high-risk individuals, managing intelligence, managing engagement with the public and patrolling neighbourhoods. A West Midlands police authority spokesman explained: 'Combining with the business sector is aimed at totally transforming the way the force currently does business – improving the service provided to the public' (cited in Travis and Williams 2012).

In July 2012, the London Mayor, Boris Johnson revealed that huge parts of the Metropolitan Police could be privatized to cut costs and cover a projected £233 million gap in its finances (after the Olympics). Johnson said that an 'irreducible core' of duties would be protected but claimed private firms could run some Scotland Yard services 'without making the thin blue line any thinner' (Crerar 2012). Many of the policing activities identified in the Surrey/West Midlands tender, including patrolling by PCSOs, and others could be up for grabs.[6] The contract notice was something of a scoping exercise both in its breadth and the fact that it was undertaken for the benefit of all police forces in England and Wales, to avoid subsequent costly procurement exercises. The police management wanted to test the possibilities for new areas of policing to be provided by private companies. This signalled a transition in the attitude of police managers towards private security in which the market came to be seen less as a threat to the public good and more as providing opportunities for efficiency savings. However, publication by *The Guardian* newspaper in March 2012 of the Surrey/West Midlands plans prompted a public furore. The scale and breadth of the contract left few in doubt that this represented a fundamental departure in the organization, delivery and governance of British policing. In light of the ensuing public debate, both police authorities agreed to a short pause in the contracting process to build public confidence in the contracting programme and to seek to dispel the idea it was about privatizing core police services. By contrast, the BSIA (2012) responded by welcoming the opportunity to take over certain police functions.

Attempts to differentiate between 'back-office' staff and 'front-line' personnel have been central to proponents' arguments that contracting out the former will allow police forces to dedicate more resources to the latter, enhancing public-facing police interactions. Yet, such distinctions are complex and frequently constitute something of a semantic fig leaf. Many of the tasks identified for private contracting in recent tenders involve contact with the public in some form or other. The patrol function has already largely been civilianized and devolved from the constabulary to PCSOs, who themselves have been the subject of public–private financing initiatives. Just as the work of traffic wardens (previously police employees) was passed to local authorities and private contractors, so too the work of other police staff following the Lincolnshire experiment has been handed over to private companies like G4S. In the near future, PCSOs may be in line for similar private management. In June 2012, David Taylor-Smith, the head of G4S for the UK and Africa, predicted that private companies would be running large parts of the British police service within five years driven by a combination of 'budgetary pressure and political will' (Taylor and Travis 2012).

However, the brakes to the privatization juggernaut were spectacularly applied when, later the same month on the eve of the Olympics, G4S announced its inability to meet the terms of its £284 million contract with the government to provide 10,400 security staff for the Olympic Games in London, requiring some 3,500 members of the armed forces to stand in. The 'G4S fiasco' underlined that the public sector will be required to bail out private companies when they default on their contracts (Crawford 2006). That is where, and if, sufficient capacity to do so remains. Inevitably, the more that privatization through outsourcing bites into the provision of public safety, the more it will erode the public sector's capability to fill the vacuum created when the market fails. The G4S saga has caused some government ministers, notably the Defence Secretary Philip Hammond, to reconsider the appropriateness of the involvement of the private sector in the delivery of certain services (Wright 2012). In the light of the G4S Olympic failure, Surrey police announced their intention to withdraw from their contract negotiations in the face of active campaigns against the move by some of the declared candidates for the Surrey PCC job (Travis 2012a). The West Midlands police authority reacted to the Surrey announcement by postponing its decision on who should get the contract until after the election of their PCC. This sudden change of events underscores both the contingent nature of developments and the volatile condition of public debate with regard to policing, given the deeply held attachment of the British public to the emblematic 'Bobby' as the symbol of collective identity and public order (Loader and Mulcahy 2003).

It is deeply ironic that at the very moment in history when government is preparing for democratic oversight of the police in the form of PCCs, we are likely to see large parts of policing shielded from public scrutiny under the veil of commercial confidentiality that accrues to such contracts. Contracts with private security providers will also tie the hands of incoming PCCs, as these may be signed for terms of 10 years or more, considerably longer than the term for which a PCC is elected. Given the pivotal role of the PCC as budget holder and the lack of other significant issues of division that separate the established political parties with regard to policing matters, we are likely to find that the 'spectre of privatization' becomes a significant political issue in the election of PCCs, at least in some force areas. Some PCC candidates – like the former Deputy Prime Minister John Prescott, standing in Humberside as a Labour candidate – have made their 'anti-privatization' stance clear. In light of the publication of the Surrey/West Midlands plans, he declared: 'This is extremely alarming, fundamental change to our police system. It needs to be nipped in the bud now. This is about replacing bobbies on the beat with security people' (cited in Travis 2012b). Prescott (2012) later set out a campaign 'to keep the police public'.

Outsourcing, if applied to elements of policing like patrol, may result in priority given to quantitative (rather than qualitative) and more easily measurable indicators of performance as set down in contracts. This would take us back to the kinds of managerial problems that stymied community policing in the 1990s. Furthermore, outsourcing may undermine 'total' or holistic policing, notably where different elements of policing are hived off to diverse providers (potentially subject to differing contractual demands and priorities). Crucially, there are concerns that outsourced private contractors will not be subject to the same regulation, oversight and accountability mechanisms that exist for public police employees. For example, the work of private contractors will not be overseen by the Independent Police Complaints Commission. In all, a deeper constitutional form of democratic oversight of policing is likely to be the long-term loser.

Conclusions

Fiscal restraint and police reforms are set to bring about far-reaching changes to the policing of crime and insecurities in British cities. Many of the governmental responses to urban insecurities over recent years have been framed in terms of police solutions. After a decade of record levels of increased economic investment in the police, it is now accepted that policing will have to be delivered with fewer resources. It is in this evolving economic and policy context that policing urban insecurities will come to look quite different from what the public have come to expect. There are mixed signals in the government's programme of spending cuts and police reform for the continuation of a public reassurance agenda. It seems likely that the new PCCs will add to the dynamic and volatile relationship between the delivery of policing as a demand-led service and public expectations over what that service should constitute. To deal with the range of challenges that policing faces, PCCs will need to be able to debate openly difficult questions with the public about priorities. This depends on the skills of elected Commissioners to engage with public demands, especially around their insecurities, fears and desires for visible reassurance, and their willingness to acknowledge the limitations of policing. It will also entail their engagement with vexed issues regarding who within the 'extended policing family' (Crawford and Lister 2004) should provide different services and what the limits for a market in public reassurance might be. Fundamentally, these issues will engage PCCs and local citizens in essential questions about the function and purpose of police (and policing) in a modern society.

Notes

1　The reduction in funding detailed in the Spending Review 2010 equates to £1.2 billion, taking the main central government policing grant to £8.5 billion in 2014–15 (HM Treasury 2010).
2　The term fiscal restraint captures the conscious political decision-making processes of governments in a post-economic crisis hidden in the notion of an 'age of austerity'.
3　Scotland has followed a different path of police reforms, notably since devolution in 1999, which are not covered in this chapter. Likewise developments in Northern Ireland are excluded from this review.
4　There are a total of 43 police force areas in England and Wales. In London, the elected Mayor (largely via the Deputy) will act as the PCC for the Metropolitan Police area and the City of London Police will continue to be scrutinized by the Common Council.
5　However, the belief that the national crime rate has increased remains stubbornly unaffected according to the Crime Survey for England and Wales.
6　At much the same time, other forces announced outsourcing plans and tendering processes (Taylor and Travis 2012).

References

Association of Chief Police Officers (2001) *Reassurance – Civility First: A Proposal for Police Reform,* London: ACPO.
Association of Chief Police Officers (2011) *A Survey of Employers Involved in the Community Safety Accreditation Scheme,* London: ACPO.
Barber, M. (2007) *Instruction to Deliver,* London: Politico's.
Barker, A. (2012) "Communicating Security? Policing Urban Spaces and Control Signals." Unpublished paper.
Blair, I. (2002) "The Policing Revolution: Back to the Beat." *New Statesman,* 23 September: 21–3.
Blair, I. (2012) "The Police: a Chance to Modernise." *The Guardian,* 4 March.
Blair, T. (2006) *"Community Safety Everyone's Responsibility."* Speech to Safer Croydon Partnership, 10 February. Online. Available at: http://webarchive.nationalarchives.gov. uk/20070701143242/http://www.pm.gov.uk/output/Page9040.asp [accessed 24 August 2012].
British Security Industry Association (2012) "MPs' Talk of Increased Public/Private Sector Partnerships Is Welcomed by Private Security Firms." Online. Available at: http://www.bsia.co.uk/home/bsia-police-public-private-sector-government-secur [accessed 24 August 2012].
Cameron, D. (2009) "The Age of Austerity." Keynote Speech to the Spring Conservative Party Forum, Cheltenham, 26 April. Online. Available at: http://www.conservatives. com/News/Speeches/2009/04/The_age_of_austerity_speech_to_the_2009_Spring_ Forum.aspx [accessed 3 April 2009].
Casey, L. (2008) *Engaging Communities in Fighting Crime,* London: Cabinet Office.
Clarke, R.V. and Hough, M. (1984) *Crime and Police Effectiveness,* Home Office Research Study No.79, London: HMSO.
Crawford, A. (2006) "Networked Governance and the Post-Regulatory State?" *Theoretical Criminology,* 10(2): 449–79.
Crawford, A. (2007) "Reassurance Policing: Feeling is Believing." In A. Henry and D.J. Smith (eds) *Transformations of Policing,* Aldershot: Ashgate.
Crawford, A. (2008) "Plural Policing in the UK." In T. Newburn (ed.) *Handbook of Policing,* Cullompton: Willan.

Crawford, A. and Lister, S. (2004) *The Extended Policing Family*, York: Joseph Rowntree Foundation.

Crawford, A. and Flint, J. (2009) "Urban Safety, Anti-Social Behaviour and the Night-Time Economy," *Criminology and Criminal Justice*, 9(4): 403–14.

Crawford, A., Blackburn, S.J., Lister, S.C. and Shepherd, P. (2004) *Patrolling with a Purpose: An Evaluation of Police Community Support Officers in Leeds and Bradford City Centres*, Leeds: Centre for Criminal Justice Studies Press.

Crawford, A., Lister, S.C., Blackburn, S.J. and Burnett, J. (2005) *Plural Policing*, Bristol: Policy Press.

Crerar, P. (2012) "Thinner Blue Line? Boris Reveals Bid to Privatise Parts of Met." *London Evening Standard*, 11 July.

Cunningham, W.C. and Taylor, T. (1985) *Private Security and Police in America*, Boston: Heinemann.

de Grazia, J. (2011) *The Impact of Elected Police and Crime Commissioners on Operational Independence and Confidence in the Police*, London: de Grazia Associates.

FitzGerald, M., Hough, M., Joseph, I. and Qureshi, T. (2002) *Policing for London*, Cullompton: Willan.

Her Majesty's Inspectorate of Constabulary (2012) *Policing in Austerity: One Year On*, London: HMIC.

HM Treasury (2010) *Spending Review 2010*, London: TSO.

HM Treasury (2012) *Budget 2012*, London: TSO.

Home Affairs Committee (2010) *Policing: Police and Crime Commissioners*, Second Report of Session 2010–11, London: TSO.

Home Office (1993) *Police Reform: A Police Service for the Twenty-First Century*, London: HMSO.

Home Office (2001) *Policing a New Century: a Blueprint for Reform*, London: HMSO.

Home Office (2004) *Building Communities, Beating Crime: A Better Police Service for the 21st Century*, London: TSO.

Home Office (2011) *The National Crime Agency: A Plan for the Creation of a National Crime-fighting Capability*, London: TSO.

Home Office (2012) *Working in Partnership with Police and Crime Commissioners*. Online. Available at: http://www.homeoffice.gov.uk/publications/police/police-commissioner-events/ [accessed 15 July 2012].

Innes, M. (2003) *Understanding Social Control: Deviance, Crime and Social Order*, Maidenhead: Open University Press.

Innes, M. (2005) "Why 'Soft' Policing is Hard." *Journal of Community and Applied Social Psychology*, 15(3): 156–69.

Innes, M. and Fielding, N. (2002) "From Community to Communicative Policing: 'Signal Crimes' and the Problem of Public Reassurance." *Sociological Research Online*, 7(2). Online. Available at: http://www.socresonline.org.uk/7/2/innes.html [accessed 21 November 2007].

Innes, H. and Innes, M. (2011) *Police Presence and Public Confidence in Local Policing: an Analysis of the British Crime Survey*, Cardiff: Universities Police Science Institute.

Innes, H., Hayden, S., Lowe, T., MacKenzie, H., Roberts, C. and Twyman, L. (2004) *Signal Crimes and Reassurance Policing Volume 1: Concepts and Analysis*, Guildford: University of Surrey.

Johnston, L. (1992) *The Rebirth of Private Policing*, London: Routledge.

Loader, I. (2006) "Policing, Recognition, and Belonging." *The Annals of the American Academy of Political and Social Science*, 605(1): 201–21.

Loader, I. and Mulcahy, A. (2003) *Policing and the Condition of England*, Oxford: Oxford University Press.

Logan, J.R. and Molotch, H. (1987) *Urban Fortunes*, Berkeley, CA: University of California Press.

Mason, R. (2012) "Private Companies in Hospitals, Police and Schools Are Here to Stay, says Oliver Letwin." *The Telegraph*, 1 March.

Millie, A. (2010) "Whatever Happened to Reassurance Policing?" *Policing*, 4(3): 225–32.

Morgan, R. (2012) "Crime and Justice in the 'Big Society'." *Criminology and Criminal Justice*, 12(5): 463–81.

Muir, R. and Loader, I. (2011) *Progressive Police and Crime Commissioners: an Opportunity for the Centre-left*, London: Institute for Public Policy Research.

Myhill, A. and Quinton, P. (2010) "Confidence, Neighbourhood Policing, and Contact." *Policing*, 4(3): 273–81.

Neyroud, P. (2010) "Protecting the Frontline: The Recession Dilemma?" *Policing*, 4(1): 1–3.

Povey, K. (2001) *Open All Hours: A Thematic Inspection Report on the Role of Police Visibility and Accessibility in Public Reassurance*, London: HMIC.

Prescott, J. (2012) "Police Privatisation: We Can't Let Profit Take Over." *The Guardian*, 7 March.

Reiner, R. (2010) *The Politics of the Police* (4th edn), Oxford: Oxford University Press.

Sampson, F. (2012) "Hail to the Chief? – How Far Does the Introduction of Elected Police Commissioners Herald a US-Style Politicization of Policing for the UK?" *Policing*, 6(1): 4–15.

Taylor, M. and Travis, A. (2012) "G4S Chief Predicts Mass Police Privatisation." *The Guardian*, 20 June.

Thomas, L.J. (1945) "The 'Scarecrow' Function of the Police." *The Police Journal*, 18: 298–304.

Travis, A. (2012a) "Surrey Police Shelve Privatisation Plan after G4S Olympic Failure." *The Guardian*, 12 July.

Travis, A. (2012b) "Police Privatisation Must Be Stopped, Says Lord Prescott." *The Guardian*, 5 March.

Travis, A. and Williams, Z. (2012) "Revealed: Government Plans for Police Privatisation." *The Guardian*, 2 March.

Tuffin, R., Morris, J. and Poole, A. (2006) *An Evaluation of the Impact of the National Reassurance Policing Programme*, London: Home Office.

White, A. (2010) *The Politics of Private Security*, London: Palgrave Macmillan.

Winsor, T.P. (2011) *Independent Review of Police Officer and Staff Remuneration and Conditions Part 1 Report*, London: HMSO.

Wright, O. (2012) "G4S Proves We Can't Always Rely on Private Sector, Says Minister." *The Independent*, 14 August.

Zedner, L. (2003) "Too Much Security?" *International Journal of the Sociology of Law*, 31(3): 155–84.

2 From revolution to government, from contradictions to harmony

Urban community policing in post-Deng China

Gary Sigley

Introduction

China's rise is not only challenging the geopolitical "new world order," it is also challenging the assumptions concerning the order of things. Such a bold opening claim is made knowing that China's rise is both a physical and intellectual challenge, the latter especially so for the Western academy. Simply put, Chinese modernity is unlike anything seen before, a mixture of consumer capitalism, Leninist–Marxist authoritarianism, and rich legacy of Chinese culture, consolidating the mix on an unprecedented scale compressed within a very short span of time. Attempting to describe how China is using the methods and discourse of the Western social sciences, which are now also firmly part of Chinese modernity, is a perpetual state of reflection within Chinese Studies itself. If global capitalism has a logic, then how will it play out in China's cities? If Enlightenment ideals have spread to the four corners, what impact has this had on Chinese thinking? What scope is there for Chinese forms of reasoning and social/cultural life to adapt, respond and be applied in new contexts? If urban neo-liberalism, both as an ideology and as a form of governmental reasoning and subjectivity, is on the ascendency, then should we expect to find the neoliberal subject wandering the shopping malls of Beijing?

This chapter ponders these questions through an examination of the discourse of community policing in urban China during the post-Deng period. By "post-Deng China" I refer to the period post-1992 in which the "socialist market economy" (*shehuizhuyi shichang jingji*) becomes the dominant ideological reference point as China enters a time of profound growth and transformation. It is during this period of rapid economic growth and social/cultural transformation, and great dislocation, that the party-state continues its own remarkable transformation from a hard-line Marxist–Leninist–Maoist institution in to a modern technocratic governing political party(-state) that rather than diminishing its power has invested heavily in increasing its effectiveness and capacity. Chinese texts commonly refer to this period as the "new era" [*xin shiqi*] in which one of the central challenges is to maintain and strengthen party-state authority under rapidly changing circumstances whilst adapting a mixture of old and new methods of government. The institutional and ideological transformation is captured in the notion of the party shifting from being a "revolutionary party" (*gemingdang*) to a "governing party" (*zhizhengdang*). Part of this set of changes also entails a shift heralded by the party-state since 2002 in "community construction" (*shequ jianshe*) as the foundation of government and administration in urban areas. In the wake of this general policy development "community policing" (*shequ jingwu*) has emerged as a renewed focus in terms of "security" and "stability" during this rapid transition. Yet, as we shall see, equating the Western liberal/neoliberal notion of "community" with the Chinese concept of "*shequ*" is not so straightforward. Although for the purposes of convenience "*shequ*" shall be rendered in English in this chapter as "community" its connotations differ significantly from the equivalent notion in the West. Rather than conceiving of the "community" as (semi)autonomous realm made up of self-governing citizens, in the Chinese context "community" in urban contexts is an extension of the long time view of "the masses" (*qunzhong*) as an entity largely under the direction and guidance of the party-state. This is not to suggest that there is no space in urban China for the autonomous citizen (or indeed on the flipside that there is no subject of direct intervention in the Western context). Instead it highlights that in the context of an authoritarian form of governmentality the relationship between "community/citizen" and the "party-state" is driven by factors that significantly curtail the role of citizen participation at the grass-roots.

I first outline in broad parameters the features of security in the Chinese context. This is followed by a brief overview of a "Chinese urban governmentality," introducing the reader to the growing body of research in this field. The focus is then directed towards the emergence and development of urban community policing in China. I conclude by further developing the distinctions between liberal and non-liberal forms of urban policing and suggesting some directions for future research.

"Security" in the Chinese context

As the chapters in this collection demonstrate, "security" is an important feature of writing and reasoning in contemporary urban liberal/neoliberal governmentality. The rise of the notion of "security" has rapidly expanded to cover numerous domains of liberal government (Valverde 2010: 4). It encompasses new approaches to social development (e.g. human security), international relations (e.g. food security), new technologies (e.g. surveillance cameras), new professions (e.g. private security staff), new domains (e.g. the digital domain and computer security) and new strategies (e.g. community participation). Yet as far as the Chinese party-state is concerned, the questions of security in terms of what to govern, how to govern, and for whom to govern are fundamentally different from the ways these questions are posed in Western contexts, making simplistic comparisons fraught with danger. For instance, associated with this transition from "revolutionary party" to "governing party" is the production of an enormous and diverse array of writing, and policy, on government. Nowhere is this voluminous body of "memorial literature" (*zouzhe wenxue*) more clearly visible than in the discourses and apparatuses of "security." In 2004 at the Fourth

Plenum of the Sixteenth Central Committee, recognizing the growing challenges and need for governmental reform, the party passed a "Resolution on Strengthening the Party's Governing Capacity" (*Guanyu jiaqiang dangde zhizheng nengli jianshe de jueding*) which clearly states: "We must develop a stronger sense of crisis,[1] draw experience and lessons from the success and failure of other ruling parties in the world, and enhance our governance capability in a more earnest and conscientious manner" (Zhonggong zhongyang 2004). In terms of security the resolution notes that the party and government must actively work towards "a robust social [crisis] warning system under unified leadership with well-rounded capabilities, effective and sensitive responses and rapid and efficient turnarounds that raises public security and deals [effectively] with social incidents."[2]

Security and policing are thus of paramount concern to the Chinese party-state, but in ways considerably different to those in neoliberal contexts. In a close reading of the resolution and of policy measures taken over the last two decades we can discern several important trends in "security" in China. Firstly, despite the general impression given by Western media and a more superficial view of the development of a "market economy," the Chinese party-state has not "retreated." Xie Yue, a prominent Chinese scholar on matters of social stability and security, notes:

> Generally speaking people tend to consider that in contemporary China the scope of state activity has shrunk and the capability of government (*zhengfu zhineng*) has been reduced. This is because in many areas people can see the results of state withdrawal. However, whilst government capability is being reduced [in some areas] at the same time it is selectively engaging in strengthening [in other areas]. In some fields [such as security] the state's capabilities have not shrunk, but on the contrary, have continuously expanded.
>
> (Xie 2008: 32)

Second, the production of knowledge and relationship with the institutions of the party-state are also quite different from those found within liberal contexts. The notion of "security" in China comes under the banner of "social management" (*shehui guanli*). "Social management" is a body of party-state discourse concerned with securing, policing and governing society. Indeed, as mentioned briefly above, there is a voluminous and diverse discourse on government in contemporary China. This is a large field in which the modern social sciences, especially economics and sociology (including criminology and policing studies), guided by a constantly "evolving" party-state ideology, measure, identify and discuss social issues. The party-state academy – dominated by the institutions of higher learning, party schools, and government sponsored think-tanks – is tasked with undertaking an incredible array of research projects, conferences and study sessions on how to "strengthen the party's governing capacity." There is also close interaction and frequent movement of experts to and from the "academy" and government in ways not common in Western contexts. Further, given China's size and geographical diversity there are at any moment hundreds if not thousands of grass-roots "experiments" being undertaken across the country. Thus, how problems are identified and analyzed and how policy is formed and implemented is fundamentally different compared with liberal contexts.[3]

Third, under the auspices of "social management," a broad definition of security is deployed, much broader than in the liberal case. There may be recognized limitations on what the party-state can achieve through policy under conditions of the "socialist market economy," but there is no significant conception of the limits of the party-state itself. Any notion of "civil society" in Chinese governmental reasoning is arbitrary, capricious and without a strong foundation so long as the party-state may intervene on behalf of "security" and "social management" when it sees fit to do so. The Chinese party-state polices a broad range of activities, including what we commonly associate with policing (public security, law enforcement, and so forth) and other activities which in most Western contexts, at least nominally, are regarded as the desirable limit of the state (public opinion, political association, religious practice, and human reproduction, to name a few).[4] The trials and tribulations of a changing Western liberal policing as described by Greg Martin (2011) do not apply here. "Socialist policing" is particularly "undemocratic." The policing apparatus is part of the "dictatorship of the proletariat" (that is, "party-state"), and although not often these days discussed in public within China, the Communist Party of China (CPC) retains a firm grip on both "the gun" (the military, policing, and other related public security institutions) and "the pen" (the media and cultural/ideological realm). There is no scope for civilian oversight of policing as is the case in many liberal contexts (Hyrniewicz 2011), and indeed little open discussion about the possible limitations on individual choice in the face of increasing security and policing measures.

Finally, this transformation is taking place at a time of rapid social/cultural change. Although we may be weary of hearing how incredible is China's transformation, it is nonetheless necessary to remind ourselves how staggering indeed is the scale, scope and speed of social change. In this regard, policing theorists such as Wang Zhong (2011) (People's Public Security University of China) recognize the validity of Beck's notion of the "risk society" and that China has entered such a period. Qi Dianpeng (2011: 12) likewise notes the party-state and public concern with "social order" (*shehui zhian*) and "social stability" (*shehui wending*) and the contradictions generated in attempting to achieve these objectives:

> In recent years China has entered a strange 'spiral of stability management.' That is, various levels of government are allocating vast resources to maintaining stability, and yet the quantity of social contradictions and conflict does not reduce but instead ever increases. To a certain extent China has entered the vicious cycle of 'the more efforts are made to maintain stability the less stable society becomes.'

Official Chinese government statistics reveal the growing reality of social conflict and tension. In the measurement of "mass incidents" (*quntixing shijian*), which can range from a small gathering of disgruntled workers demanding back pay to large urban demonstrations (sometimes violent) involving tens of thousands, the authorities have reason for concern. In 1994, ten thousand mass incidents were recorded. By 2004, the number had increased to seventy-four thousand, a six-fold increase (Xie Yue 2008). The number of "mass incidents" has since risen on a yearly basis with 2010 estimates surpassing ninety thousand (Freeman 2010). It is thus well recognized in China that the process of "modernization" inherently carries with it a great deal risk (*fengxian*). Indeed, the social fabric has changed so much that a perpetual theme in Chinese "social management" discourse is the challenge of adapting existing policing methods to "new conditions" (*xin xingshi*) and "new requirements" (*xin xuqiu*). It is with securing the party-state and society during a period of rapid social change/dislocation that the voluminous body of writing on "social management" is primarily concerned.[5]

The above thus constitutes a broad overview of matters of "security," "social management," and "social stability" in contemporary China. The chapter now turns to exploring how these play out in urban China.

Towards a Chinese urban governmentality: constructing a "harmonious society"

The 2012 edition of the Chinese Academy of Social Science *Blue Book on Social Development: China's Social Situation, Analysis and Forecast for 2012* declared that sometime in the same year China's urban population would cross an historic milestone to constitute more than 50 per cent of the overall population. Bearing in mind that we should take such claims with a grain of salt knowing that the measurement of what is and isn't "urban" is sometimes more a matter of administrative decree rather than rigorous academic reasoning, it is obvious even to the casual observer that China is indeed urbanizing at an extremely rapid rate. This process is having profound effects on the nature of social, cultural and economic life and will rightly be the focus of intensive research in the decades to come. Indeed the subject has already been well explored from numerous angles in the academic literature (e.g., Bray 2005; Oakes and Schein 2006).

The changing nature of the urban environment has meant government and policing also need to constantly respond to new conditions. China administratively divides the total population into either "rural" or "urban" households (*hukou*). Urban household registration has always provided more resources and benefits than rural registration. During most of the Maoist period (1949–76) and for the first decade or so of the Dengist period (1978–92), the overwhelming majority of the urban population was allocated to a "socialist work unit" (*shehuizhuyi danwei*) (Bray 2005). The *danwei* provided cradle-to-grave support for its members. Given also that population migration, especially during the Maoist period and then less so during first decade of the reform period (1978–present), was restricted, working in a *danwei* was highly desirable. For policing and security, it meant that for the most part the authorities were dealing with a fixed population dependent on the state for its livelihood, thereby creating a relatively stable and predictable set of conditions for policing strategies.

The most significant Chinese governmental strategy, in addition to routine everyday policing, was the campaign strategy of government. The campaign (*yundong*) is a key feature of Chinese governmental reasoning and practice, although its function has changed somewhat in the contemporary period (Dutton 2000). First developed during the revolutionary/civil-war period (pre-1949) the campaign subsequently became the foundation for many policy and ideological campaigns during the Maoist period. The campaign rests on the notion of the Communist Party as the vanguard relaying its "superior" policy through transmission belts (trade unions, women's federation, religious associations, work units, and so on, all under the authority of the party-state). The Cultural Revolution was an ideologically driven campaign, but there were also many campaigns focusing on much more "mundane" matters (such as social hygiene, extermination of agricultural pests, the building of dams and irrigation channels, training of militias and so on). The campaign was the party's main method of "mobilizing the masses" (*dongyuan qunzhong*). It was also a central strategy in policing that included efforts to fight crime but also class enemies and so-called "revolutionary crimes" (Dutton 2005).

During the reform period the existing measures that limited population mobility and had slowed rapid urbanization (unlike in many other developing countries) began to fail. Starting in the 1980s, and increasing significantly after 1992 when the Party embraced the notion of the 'socialist market economy', the population became ever mobile with well over a hundred million people on the move, many migrating seasonally to the eastern seaboard for work. The authorities referred to the fear of uncontrolled population movement into the cities as the "blind flow" (*mangliu*) and stepped up efforts to police and monitor the floating population (now an integral function of police work in urban areas). The party-state also began to reform the work unit system, which in many cases meant either *de facto* privatization and reorganization of state-owned enterprises. Many privileges of the old work unit system, such as subsidized housing, began to be phased out. The old walled compound communities typical of the work unit began to diversify and new communities emerged in new gated complexes and in cheaper accommodation in the zone between the city and the countryside (whilst still within, for example, Beijing municipality). Chinese writing on this transition refer to it as moving from the "*danwei*" (work unit) to "*shequ*" (community) and this has been reflected in broader governing strategies.[6]

Confronted with these social changes, security and policing strategies also began to adapt. As noted above, the authorities now had to consider policing the new rural to urban migrants and general population mobility. As crime rates rose during the reform period and new social challenges emerged, which were largely absent during the Maoist period (such as corruption, drug trafficking, gambling and prostitution), the party-state still relied on the campaign method of policing (Dutton 2000; Jeffreys 2004). The "strike hard" (*yanda*) campaigns of the 1980s and 1990s, a form of "tough on crime" campaign, were reasonably effective in terms of designated focus, but critics began to note they laid foundations neither for effective long-term policing nor for committed community participation (Qi Dianpeng 2011: 13).

In this regard, Shi Yijun (2009) discusses increasing public conflicts with police, which he sees partly as the result of the atomization of society, the rise of the individual, and a changing sense of moral values, all of which is impacting "relations between the police and the people" (*jing min guanxi*). Part of the problem lies in the rapid increase in the urban population with police numbers unable to keep up. The old system of "visiting all the families and knowing all the goings-on" (*chuang bai jia men, zhi bai jia qing*) that was the bedrock of a stable urban *danwei* population no longer works. Shi (ibid.) is critical of the lack of effective urban policing, blaming an overwhelming workload, of being caught up in "non-police" (*feijingwu*) activities (such as forced evictions, which is a sore point for many residents) all leading to a low opinion of police amongst the citizenry. The problem is exacerbated in rural regions within municipal boundaries that are undergoing rapid urbanization and experiencing influxes of rural migrants, sometimes experiencing a doubling or tripling of population within ten years (Leng Youmin 2003).

As the pace and extent of urbanization gained momentum many social issues began to steadily bubble to the surface. Society became more diverse and at any one moment social tension and conflict became more commonplace. Many of these moments are counted as the aforementioned "mass incidents" (*quntixing shijian*). In Chinese Marxist parlance, society is now brimming with "contradictions" (*maodun*). The party-state has since invested a great deal of resources in considering how to effectively deal with these challenges and create a "harmonious society" (*hexie shehui*).[7] The "harmonious society" (*hexie shehui*) strategy is the current key ideological platform of the Hu-Wen administration and is a response to the increasing social tensions, inequality and imbalances. It continues the focus on "party building" (*dangjian*), especially at the grass-roots. The CPC now has over 80 million members including many wealthy entrepreneurs. The strategy includes "social management" as well as measures meant to address growing geographical and social inequality (many initiatives have been implemented in agriculture, industry – including the creative industries such as social welfare, education and health). There is a shift in focus from achieving economic growth to also considering challenges of rapid urbanization and social change and improving livelihoods (*minsheng*) and social justice (*gongping zhengyi*) and for government to become more service orientated (*yi fuwu weizhu*).

Although not concerned with only policing and security, "harmonious society" could be said to have issues of security and social stability at its core. Indeed, in discussing "social management" and "harmonious society" Chinese texts often note the aphorism that "stability is the core concern" (*wending yadao yiqie*). Zhang and Yin (2007) refer to "harmony" as consisting of "multiple factors and contradictions" that exist in a "harmonious state of difference" (*he er bu tong*). Under the right circumstances and with the right conditions, "like the ingredients in a tasty dish" or "in the elements that combine to make efficacious Chinese medicine," even contradictions have their place in a harmonious society. In reference to Maoist notions of "handling contradictions between the people," this does not mean there will not be a need to "struggle" (*douzheng*) against certain forms of contradictions (Zhang and Yin 2007: 11). What is crucial is knowing the "degree" (*du*) of "struggle" required. That is, the amount of resources and physical force brought to bear on a specific "contradiction." In reform era China, it is held, the major form of contradiction is that of "internal contradictions among the people" which are distinct from forms of contradiction arising from "enemies" and "class struggle" (Qi Dianpeng 2011: 11).

Liu Haizhong (2011: 74) on noting the developing public consciousness and need for authorities to adequately and appropriately respond writes:

> Nowadays, the democratic, legal and rights consciousness of the people has increased like never before as has the capability of protecting self-interest. The call for social justice is also much stronger as is the demands on government. We cannot use a feudal [that is, outdated] vision and label the people, even those expressing dissent in irrational ways, as 'trouble makers.' We need to use a deep sensitivity and the legal processes to cope with demands from the masses.

The quest for security thus creates both "security" and "risk." As Valverde (2010: 4–5) notes, "Projects that seek to increase security are thus inherently unstable and contradictory, whether the contradictions arise internally or among different projects with conflicting aims (or with the same aims but working at different temporal or spatial scales)." The contradictory nature of policy formation and implementation is widely canvassed with Chinese policy discussion reminding us that policy discourse is made up of diverse voices and opinions, even with a seemingly monolithic Chinese bureaucracy.

Community policing: the continuation of the mass line

It is in this changing urban environment that development of new policies and strategies of "community policing" (*shequ jingwu*) makes its appearance in the early 2000s as a specifically guided and conceived strategy. Community policing is related closely to the reforms of the late 1990s, which recognized the importance of the local urban "community" (*shequ*) as the new focus of government (Bray 2009). It came to prominence as a new strategy in a 2002 National Meeting of Police Stations where the Public Security Ministry announced the goal of establishing a new community policing strategy nationwide by 2004 (Wang and Xu 2004).

Actively involving the community in local policing has become widespread in China. Yet rather than deploying notions of active civic engagement as one finds in the Western liberal/neoliberal context, policing officials in China such as Lü Qingxu (Nanjing Police Chief) talk about community policing through the Party metaphor of "fish and water," with the police in this case being the "fish" and the community "the water" (Lü 2001). The Chinese case is thus much more focused on "policing the community" (managing the population and household registers, developing an information network amongst the community, and so forth), rather than actually fostering active community involvement in policing other than as "eyes and ears." In this sense "community policing" is still seen and understood as a continuation of the "mass line" (*qunzhong luxian*) in which the objective is to gain the people's trust through positive service (Hou 2004: 89).[8] This is thus not participation of citizens informed by a liberal notion of civic participation and responsibility. As Bray (2005: 91) notes in his discussion of the emergence of "community" as a site of government in urban China since the mid-1990s, it was the party-state that introduced the notion of using "community" (*shequ*) to designated the lowest levels of administration in urban China (that is, the "street offices" (*jiedao banshichu*) and "resident committees" (*juweihui*)). "Community" in this sense is seen as first and foremost as an administrative entity and not as a "community of citizens sharing a common interest." The form of "community participation" here is quite limited. That is:

> ... the term 'community' was confined within a narrow and specific definition underpinned by three key characteristics: first, the nature and functions of *community* were to be determined by government; second, the *community* would perform a largely administrative role; and, finally, each *community* would have a clearly demarcated territorial space.
>
> (Bray 2009: 92)

A good example of the kind of community participation encouraged by authorities is the Chinese equivalent to "neighborhood watch." Under the joint leadership of the municipal government and police department, and closely tied to the local residents/ street committee (the lowest level of political/social/municipal administration in urban China), have established a system of "security volunteers" (*zhian zhiyuanzhe*) part of a nationwide campaign of "safe cities" (*pingan chengshi*). On any day, these volunteers are on the streets and in the residential communities of urban China. They are conspicuous in the donning of red arm bands and that more than half are over fifty. The volunteers engage in local patrols, watching the neighborhood (often sitting on stools in small groups chatting), promoting fire safety, and generally keeping an eye on the comings and goings in the community, reporting anything of consequence to the appropriate authorities. The numbers of volunteers have expanded considerably in recent years thus confirming this particular campaign as an important strategy. During normal periods only about 20 percent of the volunteers are out on patrols or neighborhood watch, but this number can expand significantly during big events such as international sporting events and party congresses. In 2009 during the celebrations of the 60th Anniversary of the People's Republic of China, Beijing "recruited" eighty thousand volunteers, up from the mere fifty thousand from the Olympics the year before (Zhongyang Zhengfu Menhu Wangzhan 2009).

As with liberal community policing initiatives, one goal is to gather local information and provide the police with more resources. Yet in the liberal context there is often the argument that community participation will enhance the citizenship monitoring of police work thus creating greater transparency, trust, and efficiency (Terpstra 2011). This dimension is almost completely absent from official writing on community policing in China (see, for example, Wang 2011). In an official document outlining the volunteer program it uses the language of the "mass line" (*qunzhong luxian*), the emphasis is on the "masses" (*qunzhong*) rather than anything to do with "citizen." Indeed the term "citizen" (*gongmin*) does not appear once. Rather, it states the objective of the campaign is to "massify" (*qunzhonghua*) public security under the "new conditions" (*xinxingshi*).

This is not to suggest that notions of "autonomy" or "self-governance" do not exist within the theory and practice of the "community" in urban China. Even during the excesses of the Maoist period, the grass-roots organizations were almost always described as "of the people." Into the reform era the party-state has actively encouraged the development of "autonomous subjects." However, in both cases any "autonomy" or "self-governance" must still come under the ultimate leadership and direction of the Communist Party of China. In contemporary China, the party-state judges the value of citizenship participation through a discourse of "quality" (*suzhi*). Citizens of "high quality" (*gao suzhi*) are generally well educated, law abiding, and healthy/hygienic (Sigley 2009; Bray 2009: 101–102). So long as they do not cross overt political boundaries, they can be trusted to govern themselves. However, citizens of "low quality" (*di suzhi*), often the rural migrant, the criminal element, the uneducated, and so forth, are instead seen to be in need of observation and management.

The flipside to the "community policing" strategy in this regard is the "urban management law enforcement" (*chengguan zhifa*). The *chengguan*, founded in 1997, is a local law enforcement agency tasked with enforcing non-criminal urban administrative regulations. It does not have the extensive powers and authority of the police. Indeed, what authority it does possess seems rather ambiguous and is often contested. The *chengguan* have offices in most urban residential areas. The officers wear uniforms that resemble security personnel, and drive vehicles that look like police cars. On the surface, they appear to be a policing authority. However, in a survey of police studies journals, the author was unable to find a single article examining the *chengguan*. Many foreign studies of policing in contemporary China also tend to overlook their significance in urban China. This may be because the *chengguan* focus on "non-criminal urban administrative regulations." This typically involves clearing the streets of vendors (who pile their wares on sheets and in boxes ready to pick up and flee at a moment's notice), removing illegal advertisements, and demolishing illegal constructions (such as a street side food stall).

The *chengguan* are notorious for aggressive exertion of authority and confiscation. A Human Rights Watch (2012) report details 150 cases of *chengguan* abuses reported in Chinese national and local media between July 2010 and March 2012. This is the Chinese party-state preferred response to the issue of "loitering" in public spaces (an effect of the decline in social welfare and real incomes forcing people (migrants, those on lower incomes, the so-called "weak social elements" (*shehui ruoshi qunti*) to earn a few yuan per day), and laid-off workers (*xiagang gongren*), all of which are seen as threats to social stability. The rise of the *chengguan* also reflects the decline of authority of the work unit (*danwei*) (which prevented members from sideline activities and had the power to withdraw privileges as a tool). These concerns are similar concerns with "public disorder" in the West described by Ranasinghe (2011). Thus, on the one hand, whilst the community based "volunteers" act as the "eyes and ears" of the masses, the *chengguan* acts as law enforcers (despite an often disputed legal status and growing record of physical abuse against the weakest members of society). Citizens of "high quality" are encouraged to "govern themselves" (*zizhi*), but this by no means implies that they should be involved in the "government of others" within their community.

Conclusion

It is highly unlikely that policing in China will in the foreseeable future ever develop anything like the community policing programs found in, for example, Chicago. As Rai (2011) explains, the Chicago Alternative Policing Strategy is a form of community policing in which policing authorities actively support and encourage residents to literally take to the streets to manage certain social issues within their community (no doubt with adverse effects for those who are the target of such forms of "community policing"). Such a community-based strategy takes community members to be citizens with a common interest and desire to be actively engaged in their own government and is a reflection of the role of civil society and civic associationalism at the grass-roots in a liberal/neoliberal society.

As I have outlined above, such a notion of the community and role of the citizen do not operate within Chinese concepts of the *shequ*. Instead of understanding citizens in the community as individuals with a right to civic participation, in China the citizen-resident is instead seen as the "eyes and ears" of the masses (*qunzhong*). The community policing strategy can thus be seen as a modified version of the famous "mass line" (*qunzhong luxian*). Policing in China has, of course, undergone considerable reform, including professionalization and specialization, over the last three decades. Yet the conceived notion of the relationship between the police and the masses as one of the "fish and the sea" seems to have not only been retained, but on the contrary, readapted to suit the pressing needs of monitoring and policing a much more complex urban environment (as seen in the "security volunteer" program).

This is not the kind of community described by Rose (1996: 331): "a new territory for the administration of individual and collective existence, a new plane or surface upon which micro-moral regulations among persons are conceptualized and administered." Rose writes that in modern liberal societies individuals "relate to themselves . . . as subjects of freedom" (Rose 1999: 42). The Chinese party-state also seeks to govern through autonomy, but it would be incorrect to call this "freedom" in any political sense. "Community" in China remains an administrative extension of the party-state. We would therefore be wise to carefully nuance any claims that "neoliberalism" as a form of governmentality is alive and well in contemporary China. On the contrary, all the evidence suggests that there are stronger Marxist–Leninist, Maoist, and Dengist forces at work that have in some places taken on the trappings of neoliberal projects but wedded these closely to the tried-and-tested strategies of the past such as the campaign.

Nonetheless, the party-state does not always have everything its own way. As we have seen above, it is well acknowledged that Chinese society and cities are becoming much more complex and difficult to govern. The party-state seeks to adapt governing strategies to suit its own objectives. In many cases, these strategies seem to be relatively successful in maintaining stability in the short term. However, as Qi Dianpeng (2011) notes, there are drawbacks to adhering to a concept of "traditional stability" in which the goal is no mass incidents. Rather, as society develops and becomes more complex, it is normal that mass incidents should arise. Qi (2011: 12) argues that authorities should shift from desiring a "situation is stable" to the "trend is stable" and put the emphasis on the overall trend. This also implies that more "genuine" forms of community participation and civic rights will continue to emerge and gradually, sometimes violently, push the boundaries of what the party-state is willing to accept in urban China.

Notes

1 In Chinese the term for "crisis" (*weiji*), often interchanged with "risk" (*fengxian*), denotes both "crisis" and "opportunity."
2 The original Chinese version of the resolution and the English synopsis are available from the author.
3 A sense of this crucial difference is captured in Leonard (2008).
4 Managing public opinion is an openly discussed aspect of policing work in China. Li Fucheng (2011: 21), a scholar in the field of policing studies, talks in a matter of fact manner about the need to direct online public opinion so as to guide it "from the irrational to the rational, from the violent to the civilized and peaceful." In particular Li is addressing specific online incidents, which in China are known as "online public opinion hot incidents" (*wangluo redian anjian yuqing*). These are incidents that through online discussion and distribution of information attract widespread social attention (encompassing a wide variety of social classes and strata) and create a common social focus, both of which are cause for concern in the party-state's agenda to "maintain stability."
5 The other side of this risk equation is the discourse of "overall national strength" (*zonghe guoli*), in which the stress is not so much on "risk" but on "competition" between nation-states and the need for China to strengthen all facets of social, cultural and economic life (Sigley 2004).
6 For an authoritative Chinese source see Sun Liping (2003). For work in English on this subject with a view towards governmentality, see Jeffreys (2009) and Sigley (2011). As well, *Mao's Invisible Hand* (Heilmann and Perry 2011) explores the continuing adaptive legacy of Maoist forms of government in the contemporary period.
7 Indeed, in another measure of how important "maintaining social stability" (*weiwen*) has become to the party-state the total budget for the security apparatus is now several billions yuan more than total military expenditure (Chen *et al.* 2011; Bandurski 2012).
8 To be fair, some writers have been critical of the community policing strategy, seeing it as "old wine in a new bottle" (Wang and Xu 2004), yet these opinions are in the minority. Part of the reason for a lack of criticism also has to do with the sheer novelty of "citizenship participation" in any form of grass-roots government in urban China. It is difficult for policing officials to conceive of how to do their work differently, especially given the central emphasis on "stability maintenance" (*weiwen*). Sociologists such as Sun Liping (2011) have discussed the need to promote "positive social management" (*jiji de shehui guanli*), one which strives for a sense of social fairness, equality, and justice.

References

Anonymous (2008) "Guanyu zuzhi kaizhan zhian zhiyuanzhe huodong de shishi fangan." Online. Available at: http://www.gzu521.com/essay/article/governmental/200804/25303. htm [accessed 6 August 2012].

Bandurski, D. (2012) "Making Sense of China's 'Public Safety' Spending." *China Media Project*, online. Available at: http://cmp.hku.hk/2012/03/07/20160/ [accessed 6 August 2012]. Bray, D. (2005) *Social Space and Governance in Urban China: The Danwei System from Origins to Reform*, Stanford, CA: Stanford University Press.

Bray, D. (2009) "'Building Community': New Strategies of Governance in Urban China." In E. Jeffreys (ed.) *China's Governmentalities: Governing Change, Changing Government*, London: Routledge.

Chen X., Xu K. and Li W. (2011) "The Public Security Accounts." *Caijing*, 5 May.

Dutton, M. (2000) "The End of the (Mass) Line? Chinese Policing in the Era of the Contract." *Social Justice*, 27(2): 61–105.

Dutton, M. (2005) *Policing Chinese Politics: A History*, Durham, NC and London: Duke University Press.

Freeman, W. (2010) "The Accuracy of China's 'Mass Incidents." *Financial Times*, 2 March 2010.

Heilmann, S. and Perry, E. (eds) (2011) *Mao's Invisible Hand: The Political Foundations of Adaptive Governance in China*, Cambridge, MA: Harvard University Asia Center: Distributed by Harvard University Press.

Hou W. (2004) "Yi shequ '10 xunluo' cujin chengshi shequ jingwu gaige." *Gongan Yanjiu (Police Studies)*, 5: 88–91.

Human Rights Watch (2012) "Beat Him, Take Everything Away: Abuses by China's Chengguan Para-Police." Online. Available at: www.hrw.org/sites/default/files/reports/china0512ForUpload_1.pdf [accessed 26 June 2012].

Hyrniewicz, D. (2011) "Civilian Oversight as a Public Good: Democratic Policing, Civilian Oversight and the Social." *Contemporary Justice Review*, 14(1): 77–83.

Jeffreys, E. (2004) *China, Sex and Prostitution*, London: Routledge.

Jeffreys, E. (ed.) (2009) *China's Governmentalities: Governing Change, Changing Government*, London: Routledge.

Leng Y. (2003) "Nongcun chengshihua jincheng zhong de shequ jingwu." *Gongan Yanjiu (Police Studies)*, 1: 50–4.

Leonard, M. (2008) *What Does China Think?*, London: Fourth Estate.

Liu H. (2011) "Quntixing shijian xianchang guanli de celue yu fangfa." *Shanghai Gongan Gaodeng Zhuanke Xuexiao Xuebao (Journal of Shanghai Police College)*, 21(4): 74–7.

Liu M. (2012) "Putting Everyone on the Map." *Global Times*, June 6, 2012.

Lü Q. (2001) "Shequ gaige yu shequ jingwu zhanlue." *Gongan Yanjiu (Police Research)*, 1: 84–6.

Martin, G. (2011) "Showcasing Security: The Politics of Policing Space at the 2007 Sydney APEC Meeting." *Policing and Society*, 21(1): 27–48.

Oakes, T. and Schein, L. (eds.) (2006) *Translocal China: Linkages, Identities, and the Reimagining of Space*, London: Routledge.

Qi D. (2011) "Qiantan weiwen siwei de zhuanbian." *Shanghai Gongan Gaodeng Zhuanke Xuexiao Xuebao (Journal of Shanghai Police College)*, 21(2): 11–13.

Rai, C. (2011) "Positive Loitering and Public Goods: The Ambivalence of Civic Participation and Community Policy in the Neoliberal City." *Ethnography*, 12(1): 65–88.

Ranasinghe, P. (2011) "Public Disorder and Its Relation to the Community–Civility–Consumption Triad: A Case Study on the Uses and Users of Contemporary Urban Public Space." *Urban Studies*, 48(9): 1925–43.

Rose, N. (1996) "The Death of the Social? Refiguring the Territory of Government." *Economy and Society*, 25: 327–56.

Rose, N. (1999) *Powers of Freedom: Reframing Political Thought*, Cambridge: Cambridge University Press.

Shi Y. (2009) "Lun jingmin guanxi jianshe zhong gongan jiguan ruanshili de peiyu." *Shanghai Gongan Gaodeng Zhuanke Xuexiao Xuebao (Journal of Shanghai Police College)*, 17(5): 33–6.

Sigley, G. (2004) "Liberal Despotism: Population Planning, Government and Subjectivity in Contemporary China." *Alternatives: Global, Local, Political*, 29(5): 557–75.

Sigley, G. (2009) "Suzhi, the Body, and the Fortunes of Technoscientific Reasoning in Contemporary China." *Positions: East Asia Culture Critique*, 17(3): 538–66.

Sigley, G. (2011) "Social Policy and Social Work in Contemporary China: An Interview with Xu Yongxiang." *China Journal of Social Work*, 4(2): 103–13.

Sun L. (2003) *Duanlie: Ershi Shiji Jiushi Niandai Yilai de Zhongguo Shehui [Cleavage: Chinese Society Since the 1990s]*, Beijing: Shehui kexue wenxian chubanshe.

Sun L. (2011) "Zouxiang jiji de shehui guanli." Online. Available at: [accessed 6 August 2012].

Terpstra, J. (2011) "Governance and Accountability in Community Policing." *Crime, Law, and Social Change*, 55(2): 87–104.

Valverde, M. (2010) "Questions of Security: A Framework for Research." *Theoretical Criminology*, 15(1): 3–22.

Wakeman, F. (1996) *Policing Shanghai, 1927–1937*, Berkeley: University of California Press.

Wang D. and Xu Z. (2004) "Yi tuixing shequ jingwu wei qiji shixian gongan gongzuo kuayueshi fazhan." *Gongan Yanjiu (Police Studies)*, 2: 37–40.

Wang Z. (2011) "Xin shiqi jianli zhian yujing de lilun yiju chanshi ji yiyi fenxi." *Shanghai Gongan Gaodeng Zhuanke Xuexiao Xuebao (Journal of Shanghai Police College)*, 21(2): 60–4.

Xie Y. (2008) "Shehui kangzheng: Guojiaxing bianqian de minjian fanying." *Dangdai Zhongguo Yanjiu*, 2: 29–35.

Zhang J. and Yin J. (2007) "Xin lishi tiaojian xia dui gongan jiceng gongzuo de sikao." *Shanghai Gongan Gaodeng Zhuanke Xuexiao Xuebao [Journal of Shanghai Police College]*, 17: 10–20.

Zhongyang Zhengfu Menhu Wangzhan (2009) "Beijingshi 80 wan zhian zhiyuanzhe jiang quanmian touru guoqing anquan baozhang." Online. Available at: http://www.gov.cn/gzdt/2009-09/16/content_1418795.htm [accessed 04 July 2012].

Zhonggong zhongyang (2004) "Zhonggong zhongyang guanyu jiaqiang dangde zhengfu zhineng." Online. Available at http://www.people.com.cn/GB/40531/40746/2994977.html [accessed 24 July 2012].

3 To know the city

Urban policing innovations in the post-Soviet Republic of Georgia

Matthew A. Light

Introduction

Following the breakup of the Soviet Union, law enforcement agencies in post-Soviet countries have had to find new ways to police urban areas. This chapter explores efforts to remake urban policing in one post-Soviet state, the Republic of Georgia. Although Georgia's police reforms are considered the most ambitious in the former Soviet Union (FSU), to date, scholars have primarily assessed their effects on levels of crime and corruption, and respect for civil rights (Bonvin 2006; Kupatadze *et al.* 2007; Scott 2007; Kukhianidze 2009; Burakova 2011; Kupatadze 2012). Elsewhere (Light forthcoming), I examine why Georgia undertook police reforms. This chapter, however, examines how they have reshaped day-to-day Georgian urban policing and police–citizen relations. It explores how the post-reform Georgian police, Civil Registry Agency (CRA), and other agencies are rebuilding their capacity to gather information about, and communicate with, urban residents. Overtly repressive Soviet methods of surveillance have been abolished in contemporary Georgia. Instead, advanced digitized record-keeping and new techniques of neighborhood policing are combined to create a unified system that enables the police to gather information about residents' location and activities. Such measures seek to make the city and its population legible to the state in radically changed political circumstances.

Georgia is located on the south slope of the Caucasus Mountains and along the Black Sea, and is famed for its mild climate, coastal and mountain scenery, and wine and citrus production. Georgia existed as an independent kingdom from the first millennium, and it was one of the first countries to adopt Orthodox Christianity. In the late eighteenth century, it was conquered by the Russian Empire, and later became a constituent republic of the USSR until independence in 1991. While most people speak some Russian, the national language, Georgian, is unrelated to Russian. Georgia's post-Soviet economic transition was difficult, and while the economy has recently grown rapidly, living standards remain far below Western European countries.

Georgia has a population of some 4.5 million, of whom over one million live in the capital and largest and richest city, Tbilisi, where most research for this chapter was conducted. Already several times larger than any other city in the country, Tbilisi grew rapidly in the post-Soviet years, as Georgians from the provinces flocked to the capital to look for work. Tbilisi has also been the site of the revolutions, protests, and other major dramas of the country's stormy post-Soviet political history, and it contains the headquarters of most government ministries, including the Ministry of Internal Affairs (MIA), which in turn controls most law enforcement agencies. Tbilisi thus holds both a unique political significance, and with its large and fluctuating population, represents a challenge for the police and related agencies seeking to monitor it.

This chapter is based on one month of field research in Georgia in August 2011 and June 2012. Sources of data include in-depth, unstructured interviews with Georgian officials, NGO activists, and others, as well as the author's field notes based on participant observation at sites, such as "Public Service Halls" discussed below. I also "shadowed" two Georgian Neighborhood Police officers for approximately two weeks as they carried out their duties in their station and with citizens – the first time a non-Georgian academic has been given such access. The chapter also draws on documentary sources, such as NGO and government reports.

Below, I first discuss Georgia's urban policing reforms in the context of Soviet and post-Soviet models of surveillance and monitoring of the urban population. I then analyze Georgia's reforms of its civil registry system and other methods of collecting and deploying information about the urban population. Next, through a case study of neighborhood policing in Tbilisi, I explore how such electronic information complements the work of Neighborhood Police to give the state more complete information about the urban population. Georgian urban policing comprises a mélange of Soviet, western, high-tech, and distinctively Georgian practices. These innovations have created more systematic ways for the state to learn about the urban population than the Soviet Union ever achieved. The conclusion assesses how these reforms fit into Georgian politics, what implications they hold for civil rights, and how applicable Georgia's urban policing model may be to other post-Soviet countries.

Georgian urban policing in Soviet and post-Soviet context

Georgia, like other post-Soviet states, is heir to the USSR's repressive surveillance over its urban population. The Soviet Union deployed enormous human and material resources to monitor cities. In particular, the Soviet regime deployed a system of mobility controls based on the internal passport and so-called *propiska*, or residence permit, which it used to restrict urban residence rights (Light 2012). Under this system, rural residents had to request special permission to leave the countryside. Only citizens holding the current residence permit were authorized to live in cities, which, in the Soviet-planned economy, enjoyed access to superior public services and consumer goods. The system was meant to ensure that citizens were employed in a state-approved workplace, and resided and received public services only where they were authorized to live. Moreover, Soviet policies further restricted people's right to live in Moscow and other major cities, including Tbilisi and other Soviet republic capitals, which typically had especially privileged living standards. These restrictions both rationed scarce urban housing and amenities, and allowed the regime to shape the urban population by filtering out undesirable potential residents, such as former convicts, dissidents, and stigmatized ethnic groups (Houston 1979; Liubarskii 1981; Shelley 1981; Zaslavsky 1982; Matthews 1993; Buckley 1995; Colton 1995).

In the USSR, the Ministry of Internal Affairs (MIA) both operated most police forces and issued internal passports and residence permits. Police could demand presentation of the passport and residence permit at any time. Thus, mobility controls were partially fused with urban law enforcement. This system gave police and intelligence services the tools to locate citizens and monitor those deemed suspicious (Moine 1997; Kessler 2001). This documentary database was supplemented by human intelligence focused on urban residents. A major component of this system was its network of informants, often coerced. For example, apartment building superintendents were required to report to police on activities in their building, including unauthorized residence (Shelley 1996: 122-23). Likewise, the police typically used denunciations to identify suspects, and used confessions, often following brutal interrogations, to close a case. As in other authoritarian regimes, sophisticated detection techniques, including crime scene, forensic, and ballistic investigations, witness interviews, and preservation of evidence were far less developed than in liberal states (Tanner 2000: 110).

Since 1989, urban policing in the former Soviet Union (FSU) has been transformed. In Russia and many other FSU states, the transition from communism led to a collapse legitimate law enforcement (Caparini and Marenin 2005; Solomon 2005). Post-Soviet policing is marred by serious corruption, including police involvement in organized crime (Varese 2001; Volkov 2002). A further problem is the unwillingness of citizens to cooperate with them. Russians and Ukrainians have become alienated from police who they regard as unresponsive, unhelpful, and corrupt – if not downright brutal and incompetent (Beck and Chistyakova 2002; Beck 2005; Beck and Robertson 2005). As the police have lost their ability to monitor flows of goods and people into cities, organized crime has also proliferated (Shelley 2003). Under Russian Presidents Vladimir Putin and Dmitri Medvedev, the regime's control over police has been reinforced, but without notable improvements in service to citizens (Taylor 2011; Solomon 2013, forthcoming).

The breakdown of the Soviet police state also has seen the degradation of Russian urban policing. As a result of the transition to capitalism, Moscow and other post-Soviet capitals have lost their role as showcases of the planned economy, and instead have become financial centers. However, they retain a highly privileged standard of living, and their appeal as destinations for migrants has only increased (Argenbright 2004). Although Russia and other post-Soviet countries have formally abolished the passport-residence permit system that restricted urban dwelling, the Russian MIA continues to issue internal passports and residential "registration." However, corruption and abuse by police and regional government officials has degraded such documentation (Schaible 2001; Light 2006, 2010). Identity documents are frequently obtained illicitly, and often contain inaccurate information. Many people do not live where they are officially registered, frequently because of bureaucratic obstructions to registration. Also, police abuse of the internal passport and registration system continues in new guises. A serious example is discrimination against ethnic Chechens and other stigmatized ethnic groups in Moscow and other major Russian cities, which often makes it impossible for them to register without paying a bribe (or at all), in turn leading to further police harassment (Light 2010). Thus, the state's capacity for legitimate data-collection and urban law enforcement has been compromised. In contrast, Georgia's innovations in human and electronic methods of gathering information demonstrate that it is possible to develop new methods of urban policing in the FSU that diverge dramatically from inherited Soviet models.

In 2003, following a disputed election, Georgia experienced a non-violent political upheaval, the "Rose Revolution," which brought to power President Mikheil Saakashvili, who had promised to tackle rampant police corruption (Wheatley 2005; Jones 2006). In addition to severe bribe-taking, graft, and extortion, some high-level officials at the Georgian MIA had become associated with Georgia's powerful organized crime groups (Kukhianidze 2009; Slade forthcoming). Once in office, Saakashvili dismissed thousands of police officers, introduced new services such as cars equipped with radios that are dispatched following citizen complaints, and promoted new methods of training, compensating, and disciplining officers (Kupatadze *et al.* 2007; Kupatadze 2012). These measures have created a police force that it is superior to nearly all its counterparts in other FSU countries in both service and integrity. Many forms of corruption have been largely eliminated.

Despite these improvements, many observers criticize the continuing lack of civilian oversight and draw attention to its putative effects. The MIA remains responsible only to its minister and President Saakashvili, who has held power since 2003 (Light forthcoming). Although police brutality has diminished substantially since the reforms, many human rights advocates claim that the MIA lacks a transparent system to address complaints. While the courts convict nearly all civilians accused of crimes (Kupatadze 2012), police are rarely prosecuted for misconduct. The police have also harshly dispersed some anti-government demonstrations.

While all these issues are important, to date relatively little research analyzes how the reformed police interact routinely with citizens in non-political, non-criminal contexts. In the next sections, I chart two new methods by which Georgian police and other agencies elicit information from and about urban residents: first, a new system of population records; and second, new neighborhood policing techniques. Together, these innovations help policing overcome the anonymity of the post-Soviet urban environment.

Reform of the Civil Registry and related information technology programs

Restructuring law enforcement following a transition from authoritarian rule involves both abolishing repressive police methods inherited from the previous regime, and creating new institutional capacities (Tanner 2000: 102). Both phenomena – abolishing old policing techniques and introducing new ones – are on display in Georgia. Thus, one important reform has stripped the MIA of authority to issue identity documents and residential registration. These responsibilities have been transferred to a new entity, the Civil Registry Agency (CRA), which along with other agencies has modernized official records of the population's civil status and residence. These innovations influence urban policing in subtle but important ways.

As noted above, in the Soviet Union and early post-Soviet Georgia, local offices of the MIA were responsible for issuing internal passports and registering citizens' place of residence. For recording births, marriages, divorces, and deaths, both the USSR and Russia have a separate service known by its Russian initials as ZAGS, or the Registry of Acts of Civil Status. Instead, since the 2003 revolution, Georgia has combined records of civil status, identity documents, and residential registration in one new entity, the CRA, created by act of parliament in 2006 as a "legal entity of public law" (LEPL) within the Ministry of Justice. LEPL status allows the CRA to set most policies autonomously and control its own funding. Thus, it collects fees from citizens and, instead of giving the proceeds to the Justice Ministry, uses them to fund its services.[1] The CRA also issues Georgians with passports for foreign travel, and foreigners with permanent residence cards and certificates of naturalization. It thus governs almost all personal status documentation.

Interviewees cite several reasons for the creation of the CRA, including the government's wish to uproot rampant corruption and improve service and record-keeping.[2] The CRA has introduced many innovations, notably the scanning and digitization of nine million records of civil status. The government has also opened "Public Service Halls" in major cities, where citizens transact official business, including registration of civil status and real estate, payment of fines, and notarization of documents.

The author visited one such hall in the Tbilisi suburb of Telavi and interviewed its director.[3] According to him, the digitization of identity and personal status documents has rendered many transactions fully paperless. Since all citizens' photographs have been digitized, one may apply for a passport or national identity card simply by sitting for a biometric digital photograph from a camera in the hall, which is then compared with the photo on file to confirm identity. For an additional fee, passports can be issued in an hour. In addition, the CRA is phasing-in a new, biometric national identity card, which will be encoded with bank and credit card accounts, as well as an "electronic signature." Thus, while Georgia remains a developing country, officials plausibly claim it has progressed further than almost any other European state in rapid, computerized government services.[4] The government plans to open public service halls in all major cities (including a giant hall under construction in Tbilisi), and provide more services, such as payment of tax dues. The ubiquity of such sites reinforces the state's capacity to collect data about the urban population, but again, without repressive surveillance.

Indeed, the CRA actually limits the powers of the police over civilians. Like nearly all Europeans, Georgians must officially register their place of residence.

But according to the representative of a Dutch NGO who helped design the CRA, the government specifically wished to remove identity and residence recording from the MIA's control and transfer this function to a civilian agency.[5] The creation of the CRA ended the Soviet conflation of law enforcement with the documentation of identity and migration and thus represents a powerful symbolic statement that the role of police is limited to preserving law and order, not controlling citizens' movement.[6] Moreover, these reforms have also changed citizens' experience of life in the city by dramatically reducing the need for identity documents. The peremptory document checks that remain widespread in Russian and some other post-Soviet cities have largely disappeared in Georgia. As a result, the attendant risk of police extortion or harassment has also diminished.[7] While foreign visitors in Moscow are advised to carry their passport with them at all times, in case the police demand them, in Tbilisi, one's passport can be safely left in the hotel, as such document checks are unknown.

Likewise, the CRA's simplified residence registration procedures also aim to reduce official abuse. Homeowners may register their residence simply by presenting their title. Non-owners, such as family members and tenants, may either register with the owner's permission, or demand registration through the depositions of two witnesses that they *actually reside* at a particular location, without having to prove their legal right to do so. Likewise, a property-owner can also de-register a former tenant or other occupant who has left the premises by filing a deposition. Thus, by giving authority over registration to a civilian agency, and emphasizing factual residence, Georgian procedures entrench a distinction between ownership and residence rights, and mere registration. This contrasts with the Soviet passport–*propiska* system, in which the MIA had to approve every application for urban residence, and with contemporary Russian practice, where the MIA still carries out residential registration, and as discussed, sometimes refused to provide it.[8] In Georgia, the police cannot give or withhold registration, and thus (unlike Russia) cannot block citizens' access to public services or employment rights (Light 2006, 2010).

In addition, these measures have actually intensified monitoring of the urban population. Before the creation of the CRA, registration and civil status recording was cumbersome (frequently requiring visits to multiple offices) and highly corrupt (frequently requiring a bribe to obtain documents), while enforcement was lax. As a consequence, citizens often simply failed to register life events, so that, for example, widespread unregistered deaths caused population estimates and lists of eligible voters to become wildly inaccurate. The government has now tightened enforcement. It requires that undertakers (funeral parlors) require presentation of a death certificate before providing their services. Likewise, services for children also now require presentation of a birth certificate. And while failure to register one's residence can lead to a small fine, the system enforces compliance mainly by requiring registration for services such as garbage collection and access to the public water supply. The new digital ID cards will also enforce registration by becoming deactivated if the holder's registration lapses.[9] Officials claim that these measures have dramatically improved registration of residence and life events.[10]

Other Georgian law enforcement and emergency services similarly harness information technology. Thus, another LEPL within the MIA is opening a national emergency call center in Tbilisi to respond to calls throughout Georgia. A single telephone number, "112," is replacing separate numbers formerly needed for different emergency services and regions. The center will serve as the dispatcher for emergency services in Tbilisi and will transfer calls to regional dispatchers elsewhere. Specialized software was developed to route calls correctly.[11] In addition, the MIA has also created an online system for citizens to report crimes and security concerns to the police (anonymously, if they wish).[12]

An even more ambitious step toward digitized law enforcement came in the "Integrated Criminal Case Management System of Georgia," informally known as "CrimCase," which was developed for the Justice Ministry by yet another LEPL. Prosecutors, police, judges, and the correctional service can access CrimCase. Its developers claim it is the first fully horizontally integrated and paperless law enforcement data management system in the world.[13] Access depends on a user's position and rank. For example, a police officer can see only files relating to cases he or she is investigating, whereas the commanding officer of a police station can see all cases in the station, and the Minister of Justice and Attorney General can see all cases in Georgia. In addition, all police officers with the status of "investigator" have access to basic data about all citizens from the CRA, including a photograph, name, date of birth, legal address, father's name, criminal record (if any), and spouse and children (if any).[14] In a further Georgian innovation, officers can access these data from "police pads," specially modified i-Pads.

To summarize, in contemporary Georgia, Soviet surveillance methods that relied heavily on overt coercion have been abolished. Instead, the state now uses technological refinement and facilitated reporting to document city residents more efficiently than ever before. The new methods of monitoring citizens have also changed how they interact with authorities in urban spaces. While reporting civil status and address changes is still mandatory, it has been redefined as no longer a police matter. In the Soviet Union, and to some extent contemporary Russia, the MIA was constantly collecting and scrutinizing identity, status, and residence information. In Georgia, such documentation has been civilianized and centralized, confined to a few specific contexts and locales (such as public service halls), and otherwise removed from daily life.

In the next section, I turn to Tbilisi police officers' day-to-day work in their neighborhoods, and in particular, their efforts to facilitate communication between police and citizens. These efforts both rely on, and complement, the advanced technologies described in this section. The goal is similar: to encourage citizens to share information.

Neighborhood policing in Tbilisi: coaxing people to talk to the state

In Georgia, major criminal investigations and routine police services for citizens are handled by local stations staffed by the "Neighborhood Police," an agency of the MIA. Saakashvili has made major investments in the Neighborhood Police, notably in their physical plant. New police stations have been built throughout Georgia. In Tbilisi alone, an MIA official claimed that of 39 current police stations, 33 had either been newly built or renovated since 2003.[15] The new stations, fitted with transparent walls intended to convey openness, are imposing modern structures. In some small towns, the police station is now the most impressive building, and even in central Tbilisi, the new stations contrast strikingly with the (sometimes dilapidated) historic buildings around them. In a further break from Soviet practice, Tbilisi neighborhood stations no longer contain the so-called *ob'yazannik* (in Russian, or "ape cage"), a holding cell still found in Russian police stations. Instead, detention has been consolidated in a few locations around Tbilisi, further separating the public service and law enforcement functions of the police. Station buildings thus present the police as ubiquitous but friendly.

With permission of the MIA, I spent approximately two weeks in June 2012 at a Tbilisi police station following two officers, whom we will call Giorgi (a lieutenant) and Gocha (a major). In such officially organized research, spontaneous observation is limited, and the researcher's presence may affect subjects' behavior.[16] However, "shadowing" Gocha and Giorgi enabled more detailed observation of how police interact with Tbilisi residents.

Much about Georgian neighborhood policing has changed since the 2003 revolution. As Gocha and Giorgi informed me, only a handful of the officers currently serving in their station were employed by the MIA before the revolution. In addition, despite the centralized organizational structure of the MIA, day-to-day operational decisions have been partially devolved to the local or at least municipal command level (Light forthcoming). Likewise, the tasks of the Neighborhood Police also reflect an attempt to refashion the police as a local presence. Gocha and Giorgi's station is located in a mainly residential district of old Tbilisi. As they proudly pointed out to me, children often play ball in the grassy square in front of the station entrance – a testament, they claim, to the harmonious relations between police and residents.

Just as their station serves a district of Tbilisi, the two officers are specifically responsible for routine service to residents of a smaller area, including both responding to calls, and interviewing new residents. My time with Giorgi and Gocha revealed that Georgian Neighborhood Police both identify new residents independently through their own work, and use CRA data for routine law enforcement and crime prevention, which Gocha referred to in Russian as *profilaktika*. The station receives periodic updates from the CRA, listing persons who have registered a new address in the district. Also, in some cases, local residents spontaneously tell police about new neighbors. The station then sends out officers to greet the new resident. During this meeting, the officer also administers a questionnaire, asking for the resident's name; his or her father's name; date of birth; place of registration; telephone number; occupation; and criminal record, car registration; and weapon registration (if applicable). These house calls are repeated annually to update the information.

I attended two such visits with Gocha and Giorgi. In one, the resident was re-interviewed in the annual house call, and the officers also verified his license for and storage of his handgun.[17] Another house call was triggered by a call from a neighbor (rather than information from the CRA). In the apartment, we found two young women who identified themselves as the owner's daughters, but said they did not reside there. Giorgi and Gocha did not administer the survey, but did offer their business cards, which list their "service" mobile phone numbers. Providing the local officer's mobile number is standard practice meant to enable residents to call the officers assigned to their block directly. Such familiarity with local officers may encourage citizens to share their security concerns with the police.

In addition, the visits allow the police to assess what Gocha described as the "operational situation": who is living in their neighborhood, what they do, and presumably, whether they are likely to cause trouble. Gocha and Giorgi emphasized they do not *enforce* residence registration. Thus, they cannot order anyone to record a change of address, or even question someone about a discrepancy between a legal address and actual place of residence. However, taken together, the CRA reporting system and police house calls reveal both where a citizen is officially registered and where in the city he or she can actually be found. In other words, Georgian police, unlike Soviet police, no longer enforce residence *controls*. And unlike Russian police, it is not their business to enforce residence *registration*. But they are still very much in the business of *knowing* where people live. Moreover, during house visits, Giorgi and Gocha also seek out residents who would be likely to cooperate with the police by reporting suspicious activities. They record such people's contact information in their private notebooks, but not in any official database. Such residents thus become in effect voluntary informants, replacing the coerced local informants, such as building managers, used by the Soviet police.

Indeed, as I observed, Gocha and Giorgi strive to cultivate informal relations with local residents. Giorgi said that he encourages residents to address him by his first name, although some preface it with the polite Georgian term *batono* (equivalent to "Mr."). Once, he and Gocha responded to a call from a householder complaining of noise from a neighboring restaurant. Upon entering the apartment, we were first ushered over to a stand holding several icons, religious images venerated by Orthodox Christians. We were invited to light candles in front of the icons, after which we were served coffee, as the officers advised the householders on options for remediating the noise problem. On another visit, the two officers had a long conversation with an elderly woman living alone who complained of unknown persons ringing her doorbell early in the morning. As Giorgi and Gocha told me afterwards, the householder's security concerns were probably not the only reason for her call: they had the impression that she simply wanted to talk.

Urban Georgians' often crowded living accommodations, and perhaps also cultural assumptions about neighborly relations, may promote this informal policing style. Tbilisi, like other post-Soviet cities, contains many "communal apartments," in which tenants share a bathroom and kitchen with others. On one visit, we found an elderly married couple living in such a communal apartment, cheek by jowl with their son's ex-wife. Tension between the ex-in laws had erupted into mutual accusations of assault, which Giorgi and Gocha had to investigate. After the usual coffee and pleasantries, they enjoined both parties to refrain from provocative acts. On another visit that I did not witness, Giorgi told me that a woman had asked him to attend a domestic disturbance – only to learn after arriving at her residence that the "disturbance" consisted of her husband returning home drunk. Although no crime had been committed, MIA policy required Giorgi to draw up an official incident report and furnish it to the complainant. He speculated that the woman called him to the scene essentially in order to shame her husband into sobriety. Thus, in urban Georgia, neighbors' relations may be both intimate and hostile, and urban police are likely to be enlisted as mediators.

An obvious question is how representative my observations are of Georgian neighborhood policing. Gocha, Giorgi, and other Tbilisi officers described house visits as standard, and gave me a copy of the questionnaire form. Anecdotal evidence, however, suggests that the policy may not be universally observed. One Tbilisi resident told me that although her local police had once interviewed her at home, they had not followed up with subsequent house calls. A resident of a town outside Tbilisi told me that she had *never* been visited by a police officer and added that such visits are not routine in her town. She also claimed that although some officers are excellent, others fall short of acceptable service standards.[18]

On the other hand, my observations of courteous and friendly officers are consistent with survey research showing that the police are the most respected public institution in Georgia. While their popularity has been attributed mainly to the elimination of graft and corruption (Transparency International 2010; Light forthcoming), perhaps helpfulness, civility, and a light touch have also paid off in public approval and cooperation. Requests for police service have increased dramatically since the reforms (Burakova 2011: 74). More recently, complaints of "domestic conflicts" increased more than six-fold between 2010 and 2011, which an MIA official attributed to a coordinated advertising campaign, cooperation with NGOs, and police outreach (Georgia (Ministry of Internal Affairs), 2012).[19]

How can we reconcile these contrasting evaluations of Georgian police work? First, just as survey data primarily reflects people's experiences of the police as service providers, my observations reveal how Gocha and Giorgi work with citizens they regard as law-abiding, and not with criminal suspects. (Indeed, the one occasion on which I was not permitted to accompany Gocha to an interview involved some persons defined as gypsies whom he was going to question in connection with a crime.) Thus, improved civilian oversight and other safeguards might be necessary not to provide good service to the public but more to protect the rights of suspects. Second, as the country's largest and richest city and capital, Tbilisi may be subject to more intensive police monitoring, or simply receive better police services, or both.

A related hypothesis, suggested by Tbilisi officers themselves, is that the house-visit system helps overcome Tbilisi's urban anonymity, but may be less valuable in smaller cities and towns.

A further question is how urban Georgians feel about police information gathering. While the residents I observed greeted Gocha and Giorgi cordially, both the house visits and "police pads" with CRA data could be seen as intrusive, even if people hesitate to share such reservations. The Tbilisi resident quoted above said that she does welcome police house calls: as she put it in Russian, "I'm not a spy." According to the officers, admitting police to one's residence to respond to the questionnaire is voluntary. But they acknowledge that residents rarely refuse such requests – Giorgi only recalled three refusals in his recent experience, out of thousands of residents he had visited. Giorgi and Gocha explained such widespread compliance by pointing to public support for law enforcement following the criminality of the 1990s and early 2000s.

While this explanation cannot be dismissed, a broader mix of factors may be at play. Thus, on the one hand, Georgians may retain Soviet assumptions about police powers: the Soviet *uchastkovyi* (local police officer) could enter a dwelling and interview the occupants at will. Or residents may simply consider it unwise to refuse such requests, especially when most people comply with them. On the other hand, the informal policing style I observed may reflect a deeper cultural propensity, rather than a Soviet-era residue.

In addition, people's willingness to talk to police may reflect confidence in their probity. As part of Saakashvili's reforms, officers are strictly prohibited from accepting even small gifts. As Giorgi put it, "You must pay for services." He claimed that accepting even a glass of wine without charge at a local restaurant is treated as bribe-taking and can result in dismissal or prosecution. Likewise, off-duty officers who are stopped for traffic violations while driving must not disclose that they work for the police, and must pay any fine they incur. (In June 2012, I learned that one high-ranking officer who violated this policy had been threatened with dismissal.) By reducing citizens' fear of extortion, such stringency may make contact with police more palatable.

To review, Georgian urban policing techniques complement the data collection of the CRA. The Neighborhood Police encourage citizen communication and responsiveness through expanding the police presence in and outreach to urban neighborhoods. The final section considers how such urban policing fits into the Saakashvili government's broader agenda, and how it fits into the post-Soviet region as a whole.

Georgian reforms: toward a post-Soviet urban policing?

Georgian urban policing is post-Soviet in several respects. First, Saakashvili's reforms reflect the political ambiguities of a post-Soviet state that has achieved spectacular administrative reforms, but not a completed democratic transition. The Georgian government aims to enhance all aspects of state efficacy – but more through centralization than democratic contestation (Jones 2006: 44–6; George 2008).

In themselves, the urban policing tools discussed here do not constitute rights abuses. Both police and civil registry reform have improved services to the public, and indeed indisputably *limited* many abuses: it is now almost inconceivable that either Neighborhood Police or CRA officials would engage in shakedowns for bribes, as are still common in Russia and many other post-Soviet countries. On the other hand, even benign methods of learning about citizens may lead indirectly to abuse, for example, if police use house calls to learn about residents' political activities.[20] And Saakashvili's government has not instituted civilian oversight mechanisms that might prevent such abuse. (As the NGO activist put it, "Police should be independent, not answerable to the minister."[21]) Thus while urban policing does not appear routinely politicized, it cannot be fully separated from other aspects of Georgia's post-Soviet political order.

Georgian urban policing also reflects broader post-Soviet social conditions. Georgia, unlike most other Soviet states, has clearly rejected important elements of Soviet urban policing. But it has also shunned the twentieth-century North American "professional" model, in which police work is highly procedural, insulated from civilians, and differentiated based on the race and class of citizens – criticisms still leveled at US police even in the age of "community policing" (Pino and Wiatrowski 2006: 68). Indeed, Georgia's efforts to create a pervasive but friendly police presence in urban neighborhoods appear somewhat similar to those of Japan (Leishman 1999). One possible interpretation of this similarity is that Georgians, and possibly post-Soviet people in general, may simply have different norms of privacy, and perhaps hospitality, from North Americans. Also, while Georgia is on average far poorer than the United States, like Japan, it lacks US cities' concentrated – and often racialized – poverty and violent crime. Giorgi and Gocha said that serious crime rates do not vary widely between Tbilisi neighborhoods, and from their perspective, routine police work is not inherently more dangerous in particular parts of the city. While Tbilisi includes substantial ethnic Armenian and Azeri communities, nearly all speak Georgian. In short, while urban police in Tbilisi operate in an environment rife with overt political conflict, it lacks the sharp social and ethnic divides of US cities. This relative homogeneity may facilitate Japan-style neighborhood policing.[22]

These similarities add to the relevance of Georgia's experience for urban policing elsewhere in the FSU. On the one hand, Georgia has already curbed official corruption. In post-Soviet countries where gross forms of everyday corruption and malfeasance remain rife, Georgian-style innovations that require elementary police probity may not yet be viable. But eliminating overt malfeasance is not enough to remedy the broader policing malaise in the FSU. Rather, the yawning chasm of mutual mistrust between citizens and police must somehow be bridged. To address this problem, Georgia has both removed the most repressive features of urban policing and substituted other methods likelier to induce citizens' disclosure and compliance. The challenge for other states in the FSU is not how to make post-Soviet police less corrupt, but how to develop new models of policing viable in post-Soviet urban conditions.

Notes

1 Interview with Mamuka Samkharadze, director of passport and population division, CRA; and Valeri Keshilashi, management and IT consultant, Tbilisi, August 5, 2011.
2 Interview with Samkharadze and Keshilashi; interview with Andro Gigauri, Ministry of Justice, Tbilisi, August 11, 2011.
3 Interview with Givi Chanukvadze, director, Public Service Hall, Telavi, Georgia, June 22, 2012.
4 Interview with Samkharadze and Keshilashi.
5 Interview with Levan Tsutskiridze, Tbilisi, August 12, 2011.
6 Interview with Gigauri.
7 Likewise, Georgian drivers are no longer required to carry their license when operating a vehicle. According to Giorgi (a police officer introduced in the next section), this policy prevents the police from extorting a bribe from drivers caught without their license.
8 Interview with Samkhiradze and Keshilashi.
9 The cards also contain the holder's fingerprints, so that once every Georgian citizen has received a card, there will be a national fingerprint database. Interview with Chanukchadze.
10 Interview with Tsutskiridze.
11 Interview with Mamuka Komakhia, director, MIA LEPL "112," Tbilisi, June 17, 2012.
12 Interview with Nato Javakhashvili, deputy head of information center, Department of Information and Analyses, MIA Georgia, Tbilisi, June 19, 2012.
13 Interview with Eka Bagaturia, head of software department, LEPL "Smart Logic"; and Shalva Saghirashvili, Head of Analytical Unit, Prosecutor's Office of Georgia; Tbilisi, June 21, 2012.
14 This system was demonstrated to me by a Georgian police officer, Keti, who used her own profile as an example. She noted during the demonstration that the system logs each use of citizens' data, and officers can be required to account for their use of the database.
15 Personal communication from Gela Kvashilava, acting director, Analytic Department, MIA, July 17, 2012 (by e-mail).
16 The station and officers were selected by the MIA. As I requested, the officers speak Russian, which we used to communicate. I was not given any instructions from the MIA or the officers limiting my questions to them.
17 Handguns must be licensed, stored (dismantled) in an approved safe, and presented for inspection at the demand of the police.
18 Interview with NGO activist, Tbilisi, June 21, 2012
19 Interview with Javakhashvili.
20 Thus, police have recently seized a number of satellite television dishes, which opposition activists allege was meant to prevent the owners from receiving oppositional broadcasts; see http://www.rferl.org/content/georgia-police-seize-satellite-dishes/24622670.html.
21 Interview with NGO activist.
22 There are regions of the country with substantial Armenian and Azeri populations, some of whom do not speak Georgian. More research is needed to investigate differences in police work these ethnic minorities, as well as others, such as Gypsies, who in the post-Soviet region are frequently stigmatized.

References

Argenbright, R. (2004) *Post-Industrializing Moscow: City and Oblast.* Boston: American Association for the Advancement of Slavic Studies, December 5.
Beck, A. (2005) "Reflections on Policing in Post-Soviet Ukraine: A Case Study of Continuity." *The Journal of Power Institutions in Post-Soviet Societies*, Issue 2. Online. Available at: http://pipss.revues.org/294.

Beck, A. and Chistyakova, Y. (2002) "Crime and Policing in Post-Soviet Societies: Bridging the Police/Public Divide." *Policing and Society,* 12(2): 123–37.

Beck, A. and Robertson, A. (2005) "Policing in Post-Soviet Russia." in W.A. Pridemore (ed.) *Ruling Russia: Law, Crime, and Justice in a Changing Society.* Lanham, UK: Rowman & Littlefield.

Bonvin, B. (2006) "Public Security in Georgia and the Region Bordering Abkhazia: Revisiting Some Received Ideas." Geneva: Transnational Crime and Corruption Centre, Caucasus Office.

Buckley, C. (1995) "The Myth of Managed Migration: Migration Control and Market in the Soviet Period." *Slavic Review,* 54: 896–916.

Burakova, L. (2011) *Pochemu u Gruzii poluchilos,* Moscow: United Press.

Caparini, M. and Marenin, O. (2005) "Crime, Insecurity and Police Reform in Post-Socialist CEE." *The Journal of Power Institutions in Post-Soviet Societies,* Issue 2. Online. Available at: http://pipss.revues.org/330.

Colton, T.J. (1995) *Moscow: Governing the Socialist Metropolis,* Cambridge, MA: Harvard University Press.

George, J.A. (2008) "Minority Political Inclusion in Mikheil Saakashvili's Georgia." *Europe-Asia Studies,* 60(7): 1151–75.

Georgia (Ministry of Internal Affairs) (2012) *Domestic Violence, Domestic Conflicts, and Juveniles.*

Houston, C.J. (1979) "Administrative Control of Migration to Moscow, 1959–75." *Canadian Geographer,* 23(1): 32–44.

Jones, S. F. (2006) "The Rose Revolution: A Revolution Without Revolutionaries." *Cambridge Review of International Affairs,* 19(1): 33–48.

Kessler, G. (2001) "The Passport System and State Control over Population Flows in the Soviet Union, 1932–1940." *Cahiers du monde russe,* 42: 477–503.

Kukhianidze, A. (2009) "Corruption and Organized Crime in Georgia Before and After the 'Rose Revolution'." *Central Asian Survey,* 28(2): 215–34.

Kupatadze, A. (2012) Explaining Georgia's Anti-corruption Drive. *European Security,* 21(1): 16–36.

Kupatadze, A., Siradze, G. and Mitagvaria, G. (2007) "Policing and Police Reform in Georgia." in L. Shelley, E.R. Scott and A. Latta (eds) *Organized Crime and Corruption in Georgia,* London: Routledge.

Leishman, F. (1999) "Policing in Japan: East Asian Archetype?." in R. Mawby (ed.) *Policing Around the World: Issues for the Twenty-first Century.* London: Routledge.

Light, M. (2006) *Regional Migration Policies in Post-Soviet Russia: From Pervasive Control to Insecure Freedom.* Ph.D. thesis, Yale University.

Light, M. (2010) "Policing Migration in Soviet and Post-Soviet Moscow." *Post-Soviet Affairs,* 26: 275–313.

Light, M. (2012) "What Does It Mean to Control Migration? Soviet Mobility Policies in Comparative Perspective." *Law and Social Inquiry,* 37(2): 395–430.

Light, M. (Forthcoming) "Police Reform in the Republic of Georgia: The Convergence of Domestic and Foreign Policy in an Anti-Corruption Drive." *Policing and Society.*

Liubarskii, K. (1981) "Istoriia razvitiia pasportnoi sistemy v SSSR i ogranicheniia prava na svobodnyi vybor mesta zhitel'stva vnutri strany." In L. Lipson and V. Chalidze (eds) *Papers on Soviet Law.* New York: Institute on Socialist Law.

Matthews, M. (1993) *The Passport Society: Controlling Movement in Russia and the USSR,* Boulder, CO: Westview Press.

Moine, N. (1997) "Passeportisation, statistique des migrations et controle de l'identite." *Cahiers du monde russe,* 38(4): 587–600.

Pino, N. W. and Wiatrowski, M. D. (2006) "Policing and Police Reform in the US: Adequate for Export?" In N. Pino, and M. Wiatrowski (eds) *Democratic Policing in Transitional and Developing Countries.* Aldershot, UK: Ashgate.

Schaible, D.S. (2001) "Life in Russia's 'Closed City': Moscow's Movement Restrictions and the Rule of Law." *New York University Law Review,* 76(1): 344–73.

Scott, E. (2007) "Georgia's Anti-corruption Revolution." In L. Shelley, E. Scott, and A. Latta (eds) *Organized Crime and Corruption in Georgia.* London: Routledge.

Shelley, L.I. (1981) "Internal Migration and Crime in the Soviet Union." *Canadian Slavonic Papers,* 23: 77–87.

Shelley, L.I. (1996) "Criminal Kaleidoscope: The Diversification and Adaptation of Criminal Activities in the Soviet Successor States." *European Journal of Crime, Criminal Law and Criminal Justice,* 4(3): 245–56.

Shelley, L. (2003) "The Challenge of Crime and Corruption." in S. Wegren (ed.) *Russia's Policy Challenges: Security, Stability, and Development.* Armonk, NY: M.E. Sharpe.

Slade, G. (Forthcoming) "Status Anxiety: Why the 'Georgian Mafia' Disappeared." *Law and Society Review.*

Solomon, P.H., Jr. (2005) "The Reform of Policing in the Russian Federation." *The Australian and New Zealand Journal of Criminology,* 38(2): 230–40.

Solomon, P.H., Jr. (Forthcoming 2013) "Courts, Law and Policing Under Medvedev: Many Reforms, Modest Change, New Voices." In L. Black and M. Johns (eds) *Russia After 2012.* London: Routledge.

Tanner, M. S. (2000) "Will the State Bring You Back In? Policing and Democratization." *Comparative Politics,* 33(1): 101–24.

Taylor, B. D. (2011) *State Building in Putin's Russia: Policing and Coercion After Communism,* Cambridge: Cambridge University Press.

Transparency International (2010) *Global Corruption Barometer.* Online. Available at: www.transparency.org

Varese, F. (2001) *The Russian Mafia: Private Protection in a New Market Economy,* Oxford: Oxford University Press.

Volkov, V. (2002) *Violent Entrepreneurs: The Use of Force in the Making of Russian Capitalism,* Ithaca, NY: Cornell University Press.

Wheatley, J. (2005) *Georgia from National Awakening to Rose Revolution: Delayed Transition in the Former Soviet Union,* Aldershot, UK: Ashgate.

Zaslavsky, V. (1982) *The Neo-Stalinist State: Class, Ethnicity, and Consensus in Soviet Society,* Armonk, NY: M.E. Sharpe.

4 Policing-centered community cohesion in two British cities

Don Mitchell, Kafui Attoh, and Lynn A. Staeheli

Introduction

The riots that wracked English cities in the summer of 2011 caught many people off guard. As one Manchester city employee – whose job focused on community safety – wrote in an email on the day after that city's hottest night: "Yes [it is] quite ironic after my confidence around community cohesion last week." This employee was fairly sure, however, that the riots in his city represented more "a new tactic for criminals to steal than a major rift in society. Given the experiences of the 1980's this is a strangely reassuring conclusion as it seems like we can deal with that." Indeed, he wrote, "Manchester's most famous crime fighter PC Rain came to our assistance last night and things seem to have settled (touch wood)" (email, 11 August 2011).[1] The riots, in this employee's view, were epiphenomenal, to be dealt with through standard crime suppression and public order techniques and not a threat to the new kind of community built over the previous two decades. This kind of community had been *defined and constructed through* community policing. Community cohesion, as our correspondent used the term, might best be understood as *policing-centered* community cohesion. Policing-centered community cohesion is a normative (and contested) project whose contours deserve further inquiry.[2] Our goal in this chapter is to contribute to such inquiry by examining some of the practices and ideologies of policing-centered community cohesion as they have been worked out in two British cities: Glasgow and Manchester.

Community cohesion and community policing

"Community cohesion" became a mantra in Britain in the last decade (Ratcliffe 2012), particularly in the wake of the 2001 riots in Oldham, Bradford, and Burnley. The term typically refers "to situations in which individuals are bound to one another by common social and cultural commitments" (Lynch 2001: 70). It connotes cohesion both *within* specific communities (or what used to be called "subcultures," e.g. "white working class;" "Asian immigrant;" "Muslim"), and *between* such communities within a neighborhood, city, or region. The policy discourse that grew around the concept of community cohesion, as Ratcliffe

(2012: 274) notes, "overly ethnicizes" it, and tends to use discourses of community cohesion to smooth over economic inequalities and social exclusions. Class did enter the discussion, but usually in relation to ethnicity. In much of the official discourse of community cohesion, Muslim communities were presented as too cohesive (and thus not well integrated) while white working class communities were presented as not cohesive enough (Ratcliffe 2012: 265).

The way our Manchester correspondent used community (both in correspondence and in an interview: M35[3]), however, suggests that among urban managers it is understood more loosely as an indicator of a well-functioning, even secure community, in which residents seem to be relatively content, while crime and antisocial behavior are extraordinary to – rather than formative of – social life. Such a broader sense of community cohesion accords with the definition of community cohesion offered in the Home Office's (2001) report issued in the wake of the 2001 riots (The Cantle Report). This report followed Forrest and Kearns (2000; Kearns and Forrest 2000) in arguing that "community cohesion" consisted of several identifiable "domains":

- Common values and a civic culture: common aims and objectives; common moral principles and codes of behaviour; support for political institutions and participation in politics.
- Social order and social control: Absence of general conflict and threats to the existing order; absence of incivility; effective informal social control; tolerance, respect for differences, inter-group co-operation.
- Social solidarity and reductions in wealth disparities: Harmonious economic and social development and common standards; redistribution of public finances and opportunities; equal access to social services and welfare benefits; ready acknowledgment of social obligations and willingness to assist others.
- Social networks and social capital: high degree of social interaction within communities and families; civic engagement and associational activity; easy resolution of collective action problems.
- Place attachment and identity: strong attachment to place; intertwining of personal and place identity.

(Home Office 2001: 13)

This sense of cultural cohesion, we suggest, is central to the project of community policing in Britain.

"Community policing" is also a mantra, perhaps the dominant mode of contemporary policing in Britain (as around the world: Wisler and Onwudiwe 2009), at least ideologically. Since the 1980s, theories, and to some degree practices, of community policing have replaced the "professional model" that dominated policing for much of the twentieth century. Yet, "community policing" is "a remarkably amorphous term" (Herbert 2001: 448) and highly varied on the ground. Generally, it incorporates the following: a focus on problem-oriented policing (which pays attention to the context of crimes, not just the crimes themselves, and thus which also includes coordination of efforts with other agencies); the creation of neighborhood beats, often walked on foot, frequently by specifically designated "problem-solving officers" and, as is the case in England, limited-authority "police community support officers"; the encouragement of community involvement in both crime prevention and in setting priorities for neighborhood policing (through frequent community meetings, the development of "Key Individual Networks" – networks of police informants and communication conduits (Ottiwell 2008)); an emphasis on social order and the prevention of disorder (both in everyday life and in moments of protest); a related focus on enhancing "quality of life" and punishing acts that are understood to diminish it (focusing on "broken windows"); and an effort to reduce people's "fear" of crime and to provide "reassurance."

The rise of community policing is bound up with the range of changes in governance that have marked neoliberalism (Raco 2007; Scranton 2004) and is part of a process that Helms (2007: 290, see also Johnston 2003; Jones and Newburn 2002) calls "the pluralization of policing" in which professional police are joined by neighborhood wardens, private security guards, and Business Improvement District-paid "ambassadors" (see Lippert 2012; Sleiman and Lippert 2010). This is why we refer to policing-centered community cohesion (as opposed to police-centered community cohesion): it is the *act* of policing that is important, more than the organization doing it (also see Berg, this volume).

As Barlow and Barlow (2009: 168) make clear, however, whatever "dramatic changes have occurred in the rhetoric of policing [and its practices], the fundamental role of the police in society has not changed." That role remains "to maintain the social order" and, largely, "to preserve the status quo in relations of power" – essentially the second of the community cohesion domains. Community policing, we will show, is now a key component of this effort toward order maintenance. It is also a means of placing policing – "the regulation and control of a community" as the *Shorter Oxford English Dictionary* defines "police" in the first instance – at the center of all the domains, from instilling common values to encouraging place attachment (Oxford University Press 2002: 2266). It is part of an evolution of policing that places the police at the center of society, not just vouchsafing its security, but producing it in a particular form. The rise of community policing is thus part of the development of a "total policing model" within which the public police serve as a "control hub" and coordinate "a number of different strategies to tackle local problems" (Harrington and Millie 2006: 153; Ericson and Haggerty 1997; Innes 2004; also see Eick, this volume). In addition to different strategies that focus on policing as such, the police and police-related agencies in numerous cities (including Glasgow and Manchester) coordinate other programs, ranging from planning defensible space, to assisting with immigrant or asylum-seeker resettlement, to assuring the delivery of key services such as garbage collection, all with the goal of providing reassurance that social order – community cohesion – is being created and maintained. In the process, community policing defines what community *is*.

The problem of community

In the literatures on community cohesion and community policing, "community" is rarely defined. In the latter, especially the literature that seeks to promote and analyze the effectiveness of community policing strategies, the complexity of the term is frequently admitted – e.g. "there are many problems in defining 'community'" (Herrington and Millie 2006: 160, n9) – but that complexity is held in abeyance, and, typically, a spatial placeholder is introduced: "neighborhood," "locality," "bounded area." Neither the question of who constitutes "the community," nor what power relations may shape it, tends to be asked (a critical exception is Ericson and Haggerty 1997, especially Ch. 9). The effect both in the policing literature and more widely in society, as Steve Herbert (2006: 3–4, following Bell and Newby 1974) argues, is that "community" functions as a "god word" before which we genuflect in lieu of examining it critically. Community (and community cohesion) is understood to be a desired good.[4] It is seen, as Miranda Joseph (2002) has shown, as an almost unalloyed good, a romantic idea that somehow stands against, if within, modern society, giving form to inchoate desires for belonging and for place, even as it eludes coherent definition.

"Community," as undefined as it is, nonetheless is the locus of "community policing," and so Herbert (2006: 4) asks:

> What does it mean to involve something called the "community" in [policing]? What does this community look like? What is it, actually? Can distressed neighborhoods be accurately described as communities? If so, on what basis? Can they organize in any coherent, representative, or effective fashion? ... And even if a community can be legitimately named, effectively organized, and accurately represented, just how can it interact with state agencies such as the police?

These are important questions. But for an analysis of the practices of policing-centered community cohesion, they are slightly askew, since they assume a "community" apart from police and policing, definable and distinct, and thus (as difficult and as fraught as the process may be) potentially able to interact as an entity with the police. They also assume that the emptiness of the signifier "community" is a problem, rather than central to the whole project of producing community cohesion. The "emptiness" of "community" is not so much a problem as an opportunity: "community is contested, struggled over" (Staeheli 2008: 7), both as a concept and as a reality of lived life. In that struggle, community is defined, given shape, its relations of power settled (if not permanently, at least fairly solidly). As powerful as the concept is ideologically, as with other keywords of social life like "culture" (Mitchell 1995), there is no such thing as community in an *a priori* sense; it is formed in process, the reified result of social struggle. Community *is* a product of the struggles that go into its making.

Community cohesion is, in this view, a function of struggle over and in community, and especially the ability to win the struggle to define community itself.

The lack of definition of "community" in community cohesion and community policing literature (and practice) can be understood, therefore, as to some degree strategic. By holding definitions of "community" in abeyance, the meaning (and actuality) of community can be (and is) produced in the practices of policing. Increasingly, it is produced by putting policing at the heart of efforts to transform the conditions that shape social life and interaction on the ground. As Rose (1999: 249–50, quoted in Helms *et al.* 2007: 271) argues:

> Community is not simply the territory within which crime is to be controlled; it is itself a means of government: its ties, bonds, forces, and affiliations are to be celebrated, encouraged, nurtured, shaped, and instrumentalized in the hopes of enhancing the security of each and all.

As is well known, government (or these days "governmentality") produces subjects and does not merely govern society, but gives it structure in the first place. Community policing has likewise become the means by which community is given form, given definition, and made to *cohere*, both through the transformation of urban landscapes and through the transformation of peoples' collective and individual bases for social life.

Policing does so by defining common values and deciding who and what behaviors transgress them; it does so through creating new hubs, with the police at the center, around which civic culture is made to revolve. Through policing, people become attached to place (or are expelled from it) and shape their identities (even if in opposition to dominant modes of policing), and social networks are strengthened or interrupted. Even problems of social solidarity and inequality are attacked, in manners now consistent with a policed society. For example, access to subsidized housing is tied to behavioral contracts. All of this is centered on the primary goal of maintaining social control and minimizing "threats to existing order." That is the ideal.

But "community is contested, struggled over" (Staeheli 2008: 7), and community policing is "amorphous" and incomplete in implementation in most jurisdictions. So what does the practice of policing-centered community cohesion look like on the ground? To what degree is policing-centered community cohesion a reality?

Policing-centered community cohesion in two cities

Glasgow

Britain has taken seriously the argument that the problem of crime is not *only* a problem of crime and has instituted community policing as a part of a much more comprehensive program of social service provision and cultural change. While it is described as a "joined up" approach (G16; Helms 2007), it seems that "the community" is often not meaningfully involved in the project of community policing or developing community cohesion. In the Govanhill area of Glasgow, for instance, every weekday "the police go, the fire service go, the council representatives go, the local housing association go" to a place called the Hub, where they meet with the local beat officer for a

> partnership meeting [that is] basically a problem-solving group. We take a look at what's happened in the last 24 hours in that area, and if there's things that we think are relevant for our partners to be involved in, we'll do information sharing and try and do problems solving around that.
>
> (G16)

In addition to police, fire, and the housing association, attendees include representatives from the city council, community planning, code enforcement, environmental health, the education department, the Govanhill Law Center, the private landlord registration team, and Glasgow Community Safety Services (about which more soon) (G22.1). Before there was the Hub, according to a police officer,

> we had difficulty knowing who to contact with a particular difficulty, but with the Hub ... we can pass our difficulties onto [the police coordinator] who can then take it straight to the correct department ... as opposed to us trying to track it down through a million different numbers to try to find the right person to speak to. ... [And] it allows other associations or other partners to bring information to the police that maybe wouldn't always be brought to the police's attention.
>
> (G22.2)

This arrangement pushes communities to the margins, and centers the role of policing in creating cohesive communities. According to the officer quoted above, "No residents go to that meeting [at the Hub], because it's a partnership meeting." Resident input is instead garnered through monthly community councils where "we [Strathclyde Police] go along and do an input in relation to what the crime statistics look like" (G16). After the meeting, a group might "visit a local resident, or somebody who's got antisocial behaviors [and] do a partnership visit to them and speak to them about the antisocial aspects of what's been happening" and perhaps develop a further intervention such as "an acceptable behavior contract" as part of their tenancy agreement with their housing association. These partnership visits are meant to provide reassurance: "the biggest thing in community policing is public reassurance, reassuring the public about what we're doing" (G16); "public reassurance is the big push for Strathclyde [Police]" (G28); "public reassurance, that's the buzzwords" (G22.2). According to a police officer,

> since last October [2010] we have more community officers on the street, and they are very visible, providing public reassurance. And basically we have had feedback directly from members of the community saying "I feel safe to be out and about because I know the police are roundabout the area."
>
> (G22.1)

Who is being reassured – which members of the community – is not clear; nor is it clear what they are being reassured *about*.

Indeed, not all Glasgow residents are so easily reassured, as the officer just quoted acknowledged. Those who exist beyond the bounds of police-defined civic community are often hostile to the growing police presence (G22.1). More pointedly, for one young activist, it is important to remember that "while the state exists as it does, under capitalism, and you've got inequality, the role of the police is to maintain social peace in a society, where there is inequality and injustice." In Glasgow, he says,

> now, when there's starting to be protests and organizations built up in opposition to what's happening, the police are primarily being used to crush protests and imprison activists . . . . It's not just specialist groups of police officers which are involved in public order; it's more and more police officers from community policing teams that are undergoing public order training, anti-terror training. So your friendly community policeman the next day could be wearing riot gear and battering you in a protest. There's not this division any more. It's a paramilitary force.
>
> (G20.1)

Neither this activist, nor his comrades, deny that crime is a real problem, but they also argue that policing is class-based and class-biased.

> I don't think there is any denying the fact that you need to police . . . . But people are frustrated because look at how many resources and hours have been poured into harassing and attacking us [protesters] in Govanhill and everyone knows the heroin and drug dealing and the rest that's going on, and it seems to be untouched. Some landlords rent flats for £800 a month without electricity or toilets. That's the real problem in the community, yet they're out after us.
>
> (G20.1)

His colleague added:

> If you go into a working class area … and you ask the people who phone the police … if the police are effective in controlling crime. The people we spoke to say no, whenever they're called up to actually do their job, they're not there. They arrive a lot later in poorer areas for emergencies. They're called from Newton Mearns or other prosperous parts of Glasgow. It's a class issue. The police are an arm of the state and they represent a government and a system that's protecting the interest of the minority at the expense of the people in Govanhill and all over. So if relations were toasty with the police, we'd be more happy than anyone.
>
> (G20.2)

Community cohesion in this view is a class project aimed at protecting the current order, such that groups that meet at the Hub:

> that are supposedly independent, that supposedly represent the interests of local people in Govanhill, they are really there to maintain social control. They are collaborating with the Strathclyde Police. The Govanhill Housing Association, with Glasgow Labour [city] council, being the fundamental organizations that are maintaining the problems in Govanhill. ... These are the organizations that are supposed to represent local people and yet they participate in controlling the area and making sure that nothing gets out of hand, that there's no real change.
>
> (G20.1)

For all the talk of "partnership" in community policing discourses (Herbert 2006), in Govanhill such partnerships explicitly exclude community members. In the view of these activists, the Hub model of partnership represents the epitome of what ails the community, and thus is an impediment to real community cohesion.

Indeed, in the view of some, Govanhill is not a particularly cohesive place. A primary concern of at least some residents is that large groups of Slovakians and other recent immigrants gather on street corners. In the words of one police officer, for some in the neighborhood, "it's pretty intimidating, and [they ask] why are the police not moving them away. ... It's a difficult nut to crack ... We don't want to move people who are not doing anything wrong, we don't have legislation to do that" (G16). The key, he argues, is "education." Police need to instill the common codes of behavior, tolerance, and respect for difference that are the hallmarks of community cohesion; they need to define the behaviors appropriate for inclusion in the community. He goes on to note that this is not entirely a community policing issue: it is something to be solved "socially." But there are steps the police, working through the Hub can do, such as speak

> to the local council ... about the street furniture, for instance, because there's one particular area where people like to gather, and it's a very wide corner, and it's got a kind of barrier along the side, which people like to sit on. It almost encourages people to gather at that point.
>
> (G16)

He also says that "quite a few people in the local community would like us to consider" employing a provision in the Scottish antisocial behavior legislations that empowers police to issue "group dispersal" orders. It is a sweeping power, not to be issued "without a great deal of thought:" "If anybody is walking about in a group of two or more they can be arrested and charged under this legislation" (G16).

The young Govanhill activists have been served with something like this order – an "undertaking," the police called it, that they were forced to sign as a condition of release from jail after being arrested in the wake of a series of protests – which

> banned us from entering certain streets in Glasgow city center. It banned us from entering Glasgow University campus. They gave that ban even to students who were at Glasgow University, so they couldn't enter their own campus. Even more extraordinary, it had a line about 'You are not allowed to assemble with two or more people for the purpose of a demonstration,' which would seem to counter the human rights act and freedom of assembly.
>
> (G20.1; on banning, see also Palmer and Warren, this volume)

It is also an essential tool in the police's arsenal for directing both the formation and the interdiction of the social networks (and "social capital") that make for community cohesion. It is a means of assuring such formations are structured on the state's terms (however capacious those terms may or may not be).

Antisocial behavior orders and "undertakings" are typically the jurisdiction of the Glasgow Community and Safety Services (GCSS), "an arms-length external organization ... set up by the local government and Strathclyde Police" in 2006. It is "wholly owned by the council and police" to coordinate efforts to make people "feel safe and secure within their communities [by] respond[ing] to antisocial behavior, crime, and disorder" (G28). The GCSS is rooted in broken-windows theory (also see Berg, von Mahs, and Palmer and Warren, this volume), which the Strathclyde Police have "always worked to, from the 80s right through" and the issuance of antisocial behavior orders is a central tool in the GCSS kit, though, an employee with the organization says, it always asks before issuing one, "is there anything we can do to assist [you] to stop doing that behavior"? GCSS relies heavily on the use of community enforcement officers – "the other uniformed officers" – to "issue fixed penalty notices for dog fouling, litter, that type of thing," to "provide reassurance," and to "gather community intelligence." GCSS operates an extensive network of fixed and mobile CCTV. It coordinates Crime Prevention through Environmental Design (CPTED) analyses and improvements. And it deploys "hot spot intervention teams" – "youth diversionary staff with ... mobile football pitches" that can be quickly set up (in consultation with community organizations) as a form of "preventative work." This last intervention is designed "to keep them [youth] from hanging about in the streets" (G28).

The Hub and the GCSS represent steps in the implementation of a "total policing" model in Glasgow. With the police at the center, this model relies heavily on "civilian" workers – ranging from social workers and code enforcers employed by the council (or its private contractors), to housing association employees, to community wardens with limited, but still significant police and enforcement powers. It places "problem solving" at its heart. But community involvement seems largely restricted to legislated "community consultation," monthly "greetin' meetings" (G28) ("greetin'" is Scottish for "crying"), annual community surveys conducted in neighborhood shopping centers, and "doing an input" on crime statistics at local council meetings (G16; G29). Such meetings provide only limited opportunities for community input, and it is not clear whether or how such input is incorporated into planning for and practices of policing and community cohesion. In Glasgow, policing-centered community cohesion is an incomplete project. It is incomplete both for this immediate reason and because of its failure to overcome distrust of those who believe, like the activists quoted above, that policing-centered community cohesion is little more than a class project aimed at maintaining a fundamentally unjust status quo.

Manchester

Managed through GCSS, Strathclyde Police and the Glasgow City Council rely heavily on community wardens as part of their total policing model. Wardens there are an important part of reassurance policing (see also Helms 2007; Barker and Crawford this volume). In Manchester, as in England more broadly, wardens, as well as Community Safety Teams (M28) are supplemented by Police Community Support Officers (PCSOs), who "often end up doing many of the same jobs as a police officer," but who "don't have the power of arrest." They wear uniforms similar to those worn by constables – only the color of their hatbands and sometimes their T-shirts are different – and act as "the eyes and ears of the police" while engaging in problem solving, "and obviously commensurately the[ir] salary is lower than the police officers." For some officers and for the Police Federation, there are concerns that the use of PCSOs at a time when the Greater Manchester Police (GMP) force is shrinking due to budget cuts (see Barker and Crawford this volume) is "conning the public; it fools the public into thinking there are more officers about." Yet even those skeptical of the introduction of PCSOs, one officer (himself skeptical) told us,

> would have to accept that the community likes its community support officers, the local councilors like community support officers, and albeit the results they get in terms of detecting crime are low, as a public reassurance [the results] are high.
>
> (M12)

Moreover, PCSOs "can be an effective deterrent against crime ... 10 years down the road" because of the work they do with youth (M12). PCSOs are, it seems, critical to efforts at instilling community cohesion in Manchester over the long haul.

But as in Glasgow, community cohesion is contested, especially when the organizing principle of policing is "reassurance." Questions of *who* constitutes the community rise to the fore. Similar to the Scottish city, Manchester has seen an influx of new immigrants: Roma, Slovaks, Poles, and others from the eastern edges of the European Union. South of City Centre in the Levenshulme and Gorton South areas, according to one police officer,

> there was a lot of pride in the area and suddenly you had an influx from the Roma community. They settled here because it was cheap, affordable, private property rental available. So all of a sudden you've got this different culture arrive, and arrive en masse. What happened was you ended up with a community within a community, who didn't feel the need to integrate. They've always been self-sufficient; they've always had to look after themselves.[5]
>
> (M22)

What seemed to upset many members of receiving communities was that Roma (especially men) tended to hang out on the streets in relatively large groups, sit in the parks and speak a foreign language, spit sunflower seed shells (the mess this made was mentioned in several interviews), and, especially, their failure to "use the [rubbish] bins" (M22; also M2, M12, M25).

The police and police-affiliated people we interviewed all agreed that none of these behaviors attributed to Roma were illegal or even anti-social. But some residents found "large groups, sometimes 30, 40, 50 men, all taking loudly and spitting seeds" to be intimidating because the groups "wouldn't move to the side" and pedestrians

> had to walk around them into the road or cross over the road, and this sort of thing caused a lot of conflict. People started to think they're ignorant. Now, it wasn't so much that they were ignorant, it was just that … they didn't realize [the norms of Mancunian culture].
>
> (M22)

At issue was "how they use the street, how they use public space" (M22). For police in Manchester it seems (judging by how much this issue came up in our interviews, largely unprompted), the arrival of large populations of Roma and Eastern Europeans presented the city with a classic case for problem-solving-oriented community policing: the behaviors at issue were not illegal, were rooted in deep differences within place, and seemed to have a significant impact on (some people's) quality of life. Roma behavior became the subject of a series of meetings with people "up in arms about the behavior of members of that community" (M22). Their presence not only focused attention on urban public space behavior, but implicated the role of private landlords (and to some degree housing associations), and required an examination of city services (like garbage collection) and particularly education (on both sides) geared towards "chang[ing] people's habitual activity" (M35).

The problem-solving officer for the area – an award winner who was mentioned as being among the best by many of our interviewees – worked closely with the local Member of Parliament. He coordinated his efforts with a local agency too, which had developed a "mentorship program" geared towards helping Roma better negotiate dominant English and Mancunian culture (its director was adamant that she was uninterested in seeing the Roma assimilate, if that meant them losing their own culture: M25). The officer also helped to create "multiagency patrols" whose members could meet a family and, as one patrol member told us,

> introduce them to Ross [about whom] we said, 'This is the bin man.' Ross isn't really the bin man, but he deals with the environment, and that was the best way of describing him. And he [Ross] was [then] able to knock on the door and say, 'Do you know what day your need to put your bin out? You put it out on Tuesday.'

But because the families are "highly mobile, we get new families all the time, so the education can never stop" (M25). Police are at the *center* of these educational efforts, coordinating them, explaining to residents their value, constructing a framework through which a more harmonious community might be instilled.

The problem-solving officer thinks this sort of joined up or multiagency work is crucial and seeks always to promote it. When he meets with the community, he typically brings with him "a partner [to speak] about a project they are working on," or he asks "a member of the community to speak about why they love" their neighborhood. He will seek out community input because

> I think if people can tell you what the problems are and you can address them, they'll feel better, and then the quality of life increases automatically. But, "people expect a lot, and the more that you do, the more people expect. The more we keep pushing the boundaries to improve and improve, people want everything and more.
>
> (M22)

He related a story of a recent meeting when community members were given a chance to raise what they thought were significant problems in their neighborhood, and all that came up were small traffic problems. "So I am thinking, 'That's not bad'" (M22). Yet there are limits:

> I'll be honest with you. I've got to be clear on this, because I've always said to the force: "I am not going to a meeting with three people and they want to tell me that dog fouling is a big issue." Dog fouling isn't going to be an issue with me, because I am going to pass it on to someone else to dismiss it, because I ain't working on dog fouling. ... I'm not doing anything with that. Because I've got stuff that is going to affect people, which is antisocial behavior. ... So this priorities business, you've got to be clear, really. I'm not going to these meetings saying, 'Whatever you tell me now, I'm going to put on a website and say, these are the priorities.' No. ... People would think I've lost my pot.
>
> (M22)

The minor issues, and even larger ones like the question of Roma integration, are handled by PCSOs under this officer's command; he reserves police constable (PC) time for "the crime stuff," though typically, PCs, PCSOs, and traffic wardens work as teams – "a joint approach to it" (M22) – on the understanding that there is an organic relationship between minor issues (like dog fouling, traffic worries, and failure to use the bins) and larger crimes like burglary and assault.

Broken-windows policing is thus essential to this joint approach in Manchester, which is at the heart of the kind of "robust policing" that "improves an area." To support robust policing and community buy-in, Manchester relies extensively on the use of KINs (Key Individual Networks): people "we can pump out information to" (M22), but also "people that don't need to come to [community] meeting[s], but who the police and partners visit regularly, speak to and then ask for input back from … to share intelligence" (M35). KINs can be extensive:

> We've got 683 streets in Gorton South. We've got people on every single street who work with us on stuff. So now there are about 1,200 signed up to make the place better, to give us information, exchange information, and there's nowhere else in the country with all that buy-in.
>
> (M22)

Total policing implies total involvement of the public. As this officer's comments make clear, however, it does not involve a commitment on the part of the police to act at the behest of the community. The police reserve the right to decide how or whether information is used.

Nonetheless, total policing has its effects. Through such efforts, crime has been reduced dramatically on this officer's patch. By his accounting, antisocial behavior has been reduced by 40 percent, robbery by 47.5 percent, and vehicle crime by more than 30 percent,[6] mostly though a targeted program of "offender management":

> We look at who are our main offenders in a particular [area]. For instance, across those three wards [indicating to a map], there are 20 main offenders that we've identified as being responsible for the majority of the crime. … If an offence takes place we know who the key people are in the area, where they live, what the escape routes are, so that we can deploy our resources as effectively as possible. We have patrol plans, so we know what the temporal analysis says about where the problems are time-wise, and then obviously location. There's cold calls on all the offenders, so all 20 offenders will get visited within the course of that operation to see what they're wearing, what they're doing, who they're with. That intelligence will be submitted that same day.
>
> (M22; also M33)

One of the places that the intelligence is submitted is Greater Manchester Against Crime (GMAC), the central clearinghouse for police intelligence. Besides broken-windows policing in general and a focus on "signal crimes" more particularly,[7] GMAC roots its analyses and actions in Routine Activity Theory (see Felson 1994), the idea that "offenders predominantly are not clever people. They're lazy. They do not transgress much beyond where they live" (M33). Assuming this, if GMAC notes a burglary in an area, then

> within 24 hours, officers need to be letting the people know in that area there has been a burglary so they can review their crime prevention strategies. Are your windows closed, your alarm working, your dog signs there, your bushes trimmed?
>
> (M33)

Similar strategies are deployed for antisocial behavior, focusing resources on the specific areas, the confined geographical spaces (as determined by GMAC) where it is the biggest problem. Though not as easily mapped, nor necessarily as focused as crimes like burglary, "this is what antisocial behavior looks like. The clusters tend to be smaller than other clusters, so what we try to do then is bring the clusters together to get a priority area" where the police and other agencies

> direct the resources, collect the information, present it back, enable you, as a senior officer, to have a look at this ... and say, "I want all these" ... [and] start to own each one of these [areas] and start to put a tactical plan together in partnership with others.
>
> (M33)

GMAC might "tag the top five" problem areas "because we recognize, if we actually lance the boil in that really chronic area, we are going to have an impact." The data-driven, information-heavy work of GMAC is central to the practice of community policing in Manchester. However, according to someone who works with a Roma mentoring program as well as on antisocial behavior issues, "what works is the drip, drip slow approach. Anybody that does any work on interaction and community cohesion, basically, it's employment and meaningful contact" (M25). The advantage of team-based, problem-solving community policing, of working through organizations like GMAC as well as the city council-operated Crime and Disorder Partnership (which focuses on "preventative stuff" and which after the police have "deal[t] with the stuff on the day and sort of walk[ed] away again" [because of the limits to policing as social work], can "go in and just try to hold the line") and of taking "the priorities business" seriously is that there can be a sustained effort at community regeneration, improving quality of life and promoting community cohesion (M35). Together, city agencies and especially the police have not just a

> traditional enforcement role, but equally, there is a sort of pastoral role as well that they undertake. And that pastoral role is a concern for individuals, particularly for individuals where there is a potential route out of either the life they're in [or] the criminality their involved in, whatever their age is.
>
> (M2)

Community policing implies police-centered attention to all the domains that constitute community cohesion. It does not, however, seem to imply attention to concerns of all the members of the community itself.

Whatever the depth of attention, no matter the degree to which deeply committed police officers involve the community either through public meetings or KINs, there is no doubt that antagonism between police and public remains an important aspect of policing in Manchester – after all the city has given out anti-social behavior orders banning certain individuals from using the word "grass" (snitch) (M35) – and there is no doubt that the traditional roles of policing (responding and arresting, as well as crowd control at demonstrations) remains important. But, more so than in many other cities, GMP and its partner agencies seek to place themselves not against community, and not at the behest of community, but at the center of community. Community cohesion is a policing-*centered* project.

Conclusion

In the view of at least some of those interviewed who are connected to community policing efforts in Manchester, the range of interventions, from deploying PCSOs to clearing data through GMAC, from working in problem-solving teams to paying close attention to environmental design (in Manchester, new housing developments have to be vetted by GMP to assure they meet CPTED standards: M33, M35) has indeed been effective in promoting community cohesion. Crime still happens and social upheaval is not absent. But that it can be dealt with by targeted enforcement and even "PC Rain" without fraying the social fabric – without creating "a major rift in society" – is not only reassuring, but proof of the effectiveness of placing policing at the center of community. It comes close to replicating, and maybe even improving on, what one GMAC official remembered as the "community intelligence" that marked tight-knit neighborhoods "in the 60s and 70s," when women less frequently worked away from home – a world, in his view, in which local people produced their own modes of security and safety as much as they relied on the police (M33). That world (if it ever existed) cannot be replaced (and this officer was clear that it should not be), but through intelligent community policing, what was valuable in it – its tight-knit quality, its cohesion – could be, and is. Policing-centered community cohesion is promoted by placing policing at the center of the domains that define it, installing force (the force of law as well as the legitimate use of violence) behind those modes of informal social control it finds acceptable, behind efforts to educate towards a certain model of tolerance, inclusion, and indeed assimilation, and installing the police themselves at the center of the hub of activities through which questions of social inequality and social service provision are to be addressed.

Yet it does all this only by excluding from this tight-knit world those people and behaviors that *authorities* – or more powerful members of the community – determine to be outside acceptable norms (such as gathering in large groups outside to socialize and spitting sunflower seeds) or to threaten the established social order (such as protesting, especially against the police themselves). In the process of creating community cohesion, it defines community itself and establishes its limits.

Notes

1 The research reported here is part of a larger project entitled, "Public Life and Democracy in the United States and United Kingdom," sponsored by the National Science Foundation (BCS-0852442 and BCS-0852455). The authors alone are responsible for all interpretations.
2 As geographers we are, of course, interested in the spatiality of community and the spatial practices of policing. As this chapter makes clear, however, the way in which "community" and "community cohesion" is framed as a (usually covert or unacknowledged) *spatialized discourse* is crucial to the practice of policing-centered community cohesion. Since "community" is rarely defined, its presumed spatial boundaries – the neighborhood – comes to stand in for it, Methodologically and strategically, we think it is important to allow this spatialized discourse to emerge over the course of this chapter, as it did in our interviews, rather than present it artificially upfront, especially since, while our account is deeply spatial, at the same time our concern is not only with the spatial – our research is necessarily interdisciplinary – but instead with the way the spatial intersects with and gives form to other forms of practice and discourse.
3 Citations to interviews in the text are given by city code (M: Manchester; G: Glasgow) and number. Details of the interviews are provided in the reference list.
4 A caveat: an appendix to the Cantle report (Lynch 2001) *does* at least raise the question as to whether community cohesion is indeed a good, and the report itself talks approvingly of a Canadian penchant for understanding "social cohesion" as never something already achieved, or necessarily achievable, but to be worked on.
5 The language of "community within a community" and "self-sufficiency" echoes exactly the Cantle Report's concern that too many immigrants in the UK were leading "parallel lives" to their "native" counterparts.
6 These figures accord with data quoted by employees of GMAC (M33).
7 The concept of signal crimes refers to those crimes and antisocial behaviors that lead to fear, disengagement with the community and built environment, and so forth on the part of neighborhood residents, and is a central element of reassurance policing.

Interviews

Glasgow

G16, Stratchclyde police inspector, 2 November 2011
G20.1, G20.2 Two political activists, Govanhill, 3 November 2011
G22.1, G22.2, Two Strathclyde community police officers, 7 November 2011
G28, GCSS employee, 10 November 2011
G29, Strathclyde police officer, 10 November 2011

Manchester

M2, Salford City Council employee, 3 June 2011
M12, GMP police inspector, 10 June 2011
M22, GMP Problem-solving officer, 20 June 2011

M25, Community center employee, 22 June 2011
M28, GMP officer, 24 June 2011
M33, GMAC employee, 27 July 2011
M35, Manchester city council employee, 29 July 2011

References

Barlow, D. and Barlow, M. (2009) "Community Policing in the United States: Social Control Through Image Management." In D. Wisler and I. Onwudiwe (eds) *Community Policing: International and Comparative Perspectives.* Boca Raton, FL: CRC Press.

Bell, C. and Newby, H. (1974) *Community Studies: An Introduction to the Sociology of the Local Community,* New York: Praeger.

Ericson, R. and Haggerty, K. (1997) *Policing the Risk Society*, Oxford: Oxford University Press.

Felson, M (1994) *Crime and Everyday Life: Insight and Implications for Society*, Thousand Oaks, CA: Pine Forge Press.

Forrest, R. and Kearns, A. (2000) "Social Cohesion, Social Capital, and the Neighbourhood." Paper presented to the ESRC Cities Programme Neighbourhood Colloquium, Liverpool, 5–6 June.

Harrington, V. and Millie, A. (2006) "Applying Reassurance Policing: Is It 'Business as Usual'?" *Policing and Society*, 16(2): 146–63.

Helms, G. (2007) "Municipal Policing Meets the New Deal: The Politics of a City-Centre Warden Project." *European Urban and Regional Studies*, 14(4): 290–304.

Helms, G., Atkinson, R. and MacLeod, G. (2007) "Editorial: Securing the City: Urban Renaissance, Policing and Social Regulation." *European Urban and Regional Studies*, 14(4): 267–76.

Herbert, S. (2001) "Policing the Contemporary City: Fixing Broken Windows or Shoring Up Neo-Liberalism?" *Theoretical Criminology*, 5(4): 445–66.

Herbert, S. (2006) *Citizens, Cops, and Power: Recognizing the Limits of Community,* Chicago: University of Chicago Press.

Home Office (2001) *Community Cohesion: A Report of the Independent Review Team,* London: Home Office.

Innes, M. (2004) "Reinventing Tradition? Reassurance, Neighborhood Security and Policing." *Criminal Justice,* 4(2): 151–71.

Johnston, L. (2003) "From 'Pluralisation' to 'the Police Extended Family': Discourses on the Governance of Community Policing." *International Journal of the Sociology of Law*, 31: 185–204.

Jones, T. and Newburn, T. (2002) "The Transformation of Policing? Understanding Current Trends in Policing Systems." *British Journal of Criminology*, 42(1): 129–46.

Joseph, M. (2002) *Against the Romance of Community*, Minneapolis: University of Minnesota Press.

Kearns, A. and Forrest, R. (2000) "Social Cohesion and Multilevel Governance." *Urban Studies*, 37(5–6): 995–1017.

Lippert, R. (2012) "'Clean and Safe' Passage: Business Improvement Districts, Urban Security Modes, and Knowledge Brokers." *European Urban and Regional Studies*, 19(2): 167–80.

Lynch, R. (2001) "An Analysis of the Concept of Community Cohesion." Appendix C in *Community Cohesion: a Report of the Independent Review Team* (London: Home Office).

Mitchell, D. (1995) "There's No Such Thing as Culture: Towards a Reconceptualization of the Idea of Culture in Geography." *Transactions of the Institute of British Geographers*, 20(1): 102–16.

Ottiwell, D. (2008) "Memorandum Submitted by David Ottiwell, Greater Manchester Community Safety Partnership Team." In House of Commons, Justice Committee, *Cutting Crime: The Case for Justice Reinvestment*, online. Available at: http://www. publications.parliament.uk/pa/cm200910/cmselect/cmjust/94/94we05.htm.

Oxford University Press (2002) *Shorter Oxford English Dictionary,* Vol. 2 (5th edn), Oxford: Oxford University Press.

Raco, M. (2007) "Securing Sustainable Communities: Citizenship, Safety and Sustainability in the New Urban Planning." *European Urban and Regional Studies*, 14(4): 305–20.

Ratcliffe, P. (2012) "'Community Cohesion': Reflections on a Flawed Paradigm." *Critical Social Policy,* 32(2): 262–81.

Rose, N. (1999) *Powers of Freedom*, Cambridge: Cambridge University Press.

Scranton, P. (2004) "Streets of Terror: Marginalization, Criminalization, and Authoritarian Renewal." *Social Justice*, 31(1–2): 130–58.

Sleiman, M. and Lippert, R. (2010) "Downtown Ambassadors, Police Relations and 'Clean and Safe' Security." *Policing and Society,* 20(3): 316–55. Staeheli, L. (2008) "Citizenship and the Problem of Community." *Political Geography*, 27(1): 5–21.

Wisler, D. and Onwudiwe, I. (eds) (2009) *Community Policing: International and Comparative Perspectives*, Boca Raton, FL: CRC Press.

Part II

New modes of urban policing and governance

5 Zonal banning and public order in urban Australia

Darren Palmer and Ian Warren

Introduction

Australian governments of various ideological persuasions at local, state, territory and federal levels have introduced a range of zonal governing techniques to manage the flow of people in urban spaces. Despite the impetus for open movement within nations or larger regional groupings, such as the European Union, considerable governmental effort has been directed towards managing public order through the practice of geographic exclusion. Zonal regulation allows police and authorized private security personnel to undertake enhanced population surveillance, summary justice and exclusionary practices within a declared urban geographic region and formally ban those engaging in disorderly activity. We examine this process in the Australian state of Victoria by using Zedner's (2010: 391–94) conception of "enemy criminal law." As a form of enemy criminal law, zonal regulation adopts property, administrative and contractual governance principles to augment conventional methods of urban securitization. This approach to maintaining public order requires new forms of mass population surveillance to enforce zonal bans in designated public places.

To date, most discussions of banning and related forms of mass surveillance focus on national border control and identity authentication procedures. This logic now permeates many localized forms of regulation that aim to promote greater urban security. This chapter describes the legal right to ban "undesirable" individuals and groups from entering or using certain "major-event areas" and "designated entertainment zones" in the state of Victoria. These zones are exemplars of the contemporary public order maintenance revolution in Australia that legally authorizes the convergence of public and private policing functions and the use of mass population screening to ensure selective and unimpeded population flows. This chapter then goes on to explain how computerized surveillance and identity verification technologies have become necessary yet problematic methods of enforcing zonal bans.

Managing urban space through zonal bans

Since the mid-1990s, extensive reforms to public order laws throughout Australia highlight a broader cultural intolerance of disorder that mirrors developments in the United Kingdom (Young 1998), Germany (Belina 2007), the Netherlands (Schuilenburg 2012), the United States (Beckett and Herbert 2010) and Canada (Hermer and Mosher 2002). New configurations of criminal law challenge the ideal of social inclusion by protecting selective and desirable commercial flows, particularly in large inner-urban housing redevelopment and entertainment precincts. Those visibly affected by illicit drug addiction, the homeless (Blomley 2010), beggars, the mentally infirm, antisocial youth (Crofts 2011; Crofts and Witzleb 2011) and drunken male "thugs," "hoons," or "yobbos" (Palmer *et al.* 2012: 306) are subject to a tighter array of behavioral controls and related surveillance practices designed to preempt and eliminate public disorder from urban space. While it is debatable whether these developments are part of a coordinated policy transfer process designed to control urban crime (Newburn and Jones 2007; Jones and Newburn 2007), extensive reforms to criminal, major-event and liquor licensing laws that incorporate zonal banning are now common forms of bio-political securitization in most major Australian cities. Such reforms promote the idea that public order can be maintained by excluding dangerous or troublesome individuals from designated commercial and entertainment areas. By extension, zonal bans allow for enhanced human and electronic surveillance to monitor population flows and exclude dangerous or troublesome populations (Schuilenburg 2012; Mattelart 2010; Aas 2011).

The current "governmentality of unease" that endorses "profiling and containing … mobility" (Bigo 2011: 47; Aas 2011) adapts the logic of immigration control to prevent "noncitizens" from accessing goods or services provided by national governments (Zedner 2010: 381). As the "logic and language" of national citizenship restrictions "seep into domestic crime control" policies, a growing number of publicly visible "irregular citizens" (Zedner 2010: 381) are considered to warrant increased enforcement scrutiny for disrupting or blocking legitimate urban population flows. Enhanced criminalization and police enforcement powers that incorporate preemptive "broken windows" philosophies (Belina 2007; 2012; Lippert 2012; Crawford 2006) focus attention on the overtly visible signs of urban decay in one of two ways. Either they rezone "deviant industries," such as legal brothels, into outer suburban industrial enclaves (Crofts 2007: 4), or they ban people from entering a growing range of urban residential and commercial spaces. Although the state has always had the power to enact regulatory offences that tinker with accepted due process requirements under the criminal law (Hildebrandt 2009), heightened social concern about preventing urban crime signals a public order maintenance revolution that enables police and authorized security personnel to ban people from a growing range of designated public spaces.

Zonal banning is a form of "enemy criminal law" (Zedner 2010). As Crawford (2003; 2011b) indicates, many recent public order laws invoke private property and contractual law obligations in an emerging branch of exclusionary quasi-criminal law that targets antisocial behavior (Schuilenburg 2012). These modes of criminalization delineate basic citizenship rights through a merit-based philosophy that rewards compliance with socially desirable forms of behavior. At the same time, hybrid criminalization targets "presumptive enemies," by allowing the state and authorized private entities to "... punish prospectively in a bid to prevent future harms; ... [impose] disproportionate sanctions in the name of security; and ... [depart] from conventional procedural protections" (Zedner 2010: 391).

Enemy criminal law also involves the "fluid interpenetration of ... residual security [measures involving] ... state, municipal, private and voluntary policing" activities (Crawford 2006: 111). Because the re-active investigative focus of the public police is considered inadequate in dealing with insecurities about crime (Crawford 2003), urban governance has evolved to incorporate a growing amalgam of public order strategies. Any blockages "to the idealistic vision of a pubic [*sic*] sphere and space that is open to everyone" increases the demand for laws enabling the "exclusion and expulsion" of undesirable individuals (Belina 2012: 20). Therefore, the power to ban is directly linked to the right to access protective enforcement services based on a citizen's social standing, appearance or "economic utility" (Zedner 2010: 394). As urban security becomes a publicly sanctioned "club good" (Crawford 2006), preemptive forms of social exclusion that target visible signs of urban disorder gain increased social acceptance. Lippert's (2012) examination of Business Improvement Districts (BIDs) that aim to encourage "clean and safe" urban commercial passage by eliminating crime, low-level disorder, vagrancy and begging in Toronto, demonstrates how this form of securitization involves selective collaborations between diverse business, policing, municipal and security industries. In Crawford's terms, these and many other urban crime prevention strategies

> ... are more frequently provided by and through collective 'club' arrangements, often with implications for the experience of public policing, which is left to manage ... crime and disorder displacement, and to police the bad risks excluded from club membership.
>
> (Crawford 2006: 121)

Increased fixed penalties, strict liability offences, incentives to plead guilty and other procedural adaptations to the criminal law (Ashworth and Zedner 2008) are all linked to the "territorialization of urban governance through the construction of differential 'zones' of security governance" (Crawford 2011b: 3). Recent Australian public order laws reflect these trends by enabling state government Ministers or unelected bureaucrats to classify a particular geographic region as a "designated area" (*Liquor Control Reform Act* Vic 1998 Part 8A). Once this designation is made, police and security personnel can implement various preemptive securitization measures to deal with crime and public disorder. Our term "zonal regulation" distinguishes these approaches to urban securitization from conventional criminal and summary offence laws that apply uniformly within each jurisdiction. Although Crawford does not define the term "zones," we believe it incorporates the preemptive "language and logic" of "enemy criminal law" (Zedner 2010) by regulating public "incivilities" (von Hirsch and Simister 2006) through the power to ban. Zonal regulation also incorporates the graded structure of various banning, barring and exclusion provisions currently in force in Victoria and several other Australian states that equate "physical presence with social harm" (Belina 2012: 21).

Major-event sites and nightclub precincts are the main settings where temporary zonal bans can be implemented to enhance urban security. Extended bans can also be imposed by authorized persons or their agents, or through court orders. We consider the convergence of these zonal banning policies (Bennett 1991) to be tied to the "long-term social processes and public acceptance of the routines of surveillance" that permeate contemporary urban life (Bigo 2011: 47; Monahan 2011). Zonal bans either expressly or tacitly endorse the expansion of "open-street" CCTV networks, identification scanning, automated and ticketing systems and the use of portable X-ray devices to prevent unauthorized individuals and items, such as weapons or drugs, from entering a designated zone. These population screening technologies are essential to enforce zonal bans and the accompanying system of fixed penalties (Ashworth and Zedner 2008: 26–8) under a "simulated" order maintenance "demerit point" framework (O'Malley 2010: 801–3). These surveillance measures are not necessarily incompatible with individual privacy, due process or other important citizenship rights (Hildebrandt 2009; Solove 2011; Lips *et al.* 2009; Aas 2011). Nevertheless, their alignment with several major inner-city redevelopment projects seems to equate urban security with the power to ban undesirable "others" through "enemy criminal law." By extension, as zonal regulation in declared public areas increasingly draws from approaches to security governance adopted in enclosed "mass private" spaces (Palmer and Whelan 2007: 401–2), new forms of mass population surveillance appear essential to contemporary order maintenance and law enforcement.

Below we describe a link between an extensive urban renewal program in the City of Melbourne and the incremental expansion of zonal banning laws in Victoria's major-event sites and night-time economies. Since the early 1990s, the attempt to eliminate disorderly and antisocial conduct through the gradual expansion of public order laws has produced a convergence of public policing and security functions at major-event sites and licensed venues. While various alcohol supply (Victorian Auditor-General 2012), anti-violence (Drugs and Crime Prevention Committee 2010) and public surveillance measures (VLRC 2010) have had mixed effects in reducing crime and disorder, zonal banning has been relatively immune from critical public debate in contemporary Australia. Our discussion views zonal banning as a key dimension of "enemy criminal law" that simultaneously reinforces the commercial appeal of revitalized inner-city entertainment areas and heightened public insecurities over groups of young "hoons," "yobbos," and "underage drinkers" attending these areas *en masse* (Palmer *et al.* 2012). In addition, the use of legal provisions derived from private property law to maintain public order adds legitimacy to contentious mass population surveillance measures aimed at enhancing security in a growing range of urban exclusion zones (Blandy and Sibley 2010). Whether this approach to urban securitization genuinely reduces crime, antisocial behavior or alcohol-related harm within or beyond Victoria's designated areas remains conjectural.

The City of Melbourne and its major-event venues

As with most Australian cities, Melbourne has experienced considerable growth since the late 1980s. The Central Business District (CBD) is a 2.7 square-kilometer grid governed by the City of Melbourne and surrounded by a 37.6 square-kilometer ring of inner suburbs (City of Melbourne 2012a). A glut of vacant office space during the 1990s led to an extensive urban regeneration strategy designed to produce a "resurgence in inner-city living" (City of Melbourne 2009: 3). Between 2001 and 2008, the CBD and immediate surrounds experienced an annual residential population growth of 13 percent (City of Melbourne 2009: 3). "Hoddle's Grid," a rectangular series of inner-city thoroughfares and laneways designed in 1837 by colonial surveyor Robert Hoddle, now has a stable residential population of around 18,000 and the largest proportion of dwellings, retail establishments, offices and employment opportunities in the municipality. Close to 50 percent of the CBD demographic comprises young professionals or university students aged between 20 and 24 years, who were born abroad, live in high-rise apartments that increasingly permeate the city's landscape and have a relatively low average individual income of under A\$500 per week (City of Melbourne 2009: 3-5). While tensions between preserving the city's architectural heritage and future commercial, residential and retail development are ongoing (City of Melbourne 2012b), the Council estimates by 2021 the CBD population will reach 30,000.

The CBD renewal was prompted by the extensive corporate land development in the neighboring Docklands area. In 1991, the Docklands Authority was created by the Victorian state government to transform the southern tip of the CBD from "an industrial wasteland ... into a modern residential, commercial and visitor destination in the heart of Melbourne" (Melbourne Docklands 2012a). Historically this area was undeveloped marshland, but later attracted heavy agricultural industries, such as abattoirs and bone grinders, before becoming Melbourne's major port district in the 1880s (Melbourne Docklands 2012b). From the early 1970s, changes to shipping arrangements rendered the land derelict until the Victorian Urban Development Authority was given the legal mandate to "develop the docklands area, to promote and encourage the involvement of the private sector in that development ... [and] to ... promote measures to encourage people to live and work in the area" (*Docklands Authority Act* 1991 s. 10).

After 15 years of sustained construction, the governance of Docklands was transferred to the City of Melbourne in July 2007. By 2010, 75.6 percent of the total 3.5 square kilometers of reclaimed land comprised "(p)arking, office, residential accommodation ... transport/storage ... retail, indoor entertainment and industrial" facilities (City of Melbourne 2011: 2–3). Demographic indices reveal the residential population of 3,940 is more affluent compared with other surrounding municipalities (City of Melbourne 2006: 10–13). By 2009, population rates were increasing by 55 percent annually and it is estimated 16,000 people will live in this high-rise suburb on the CBD's fringe by 2031 (City of Melbourne 2011: 7). Docklands also attracts considerable domestic and international tourist flows and a daily influx of up to 40,000 workers in various banking, business and service industries, while 127 cafes, restaurants and bistros and 12 bars accommodate up to 20,000 patrons (City of Melbourne 2011: 18). Southern Cross Station separates the CBD and Docklands, which is the main transit-point for all Victorian suburban and regional train services. Several internationally renowned sporting facilities are readily accessible by rail, tram or a short walk through Melbourne's well-tended inner-city parks.

Official crime statistics are a notoriously poor measure of urban insecurity. Nevertheless, it is worth noting that reported levels of serious interpersonal crime in the Melbourne Local Government Area (LGA) are negligible compared with most outer suburban and regional areas. Between 1 July 2009 and 20 June 2011, Victoria Police statistics recorded a 30–40 percent decline in all public order offence categories in and around the CBD (Victoria Police 2011a: 19). Victoria Police claim these reductions are due to the implementation of new on-the-spot fine and banning powers within the CBD and Docklands designated areas (Victoria Police 2011c: 5). We analyze the merits of these claims below. However, one notable feature of these reforms is their close resemblance to enhanced security arrangements introduced for the Melbourne 2006 Commonwealth Games. Despite limited evidence of widespread disorder, these order maintenance provisions apply to all major events held at Melbourne's sports and entertainment venues.

Zonal bans and major events

Although recent "security-focused policies" at major-event venues might bear similarities to those introduced in other urban environments, they also retain a peculiarly site-specific focus that caters to distinct patron dynamics and order maintenance requirements (Warren 2003; Warren and Hay 2009). However, when viewed as "mass private" spaces (Crawford 2006: 125; Palmer and Whelan 2007) that are connected to other elements of urban governance, new legal, policing and security initiatives appear to lose their site-specific character. The increasing standardization of event management and public order law reforms that apply in and around major-event venues is a symptom of this issue. In Victoria, widespread reforms first introduced to regulate the Melbourne 2006 Commonwealth Games now extend to all major domestic sporting and entertainment venues.

Prior to the 2006 Commonwealth Games, the prevailing regulatory model at major-event sites combined summary and criminal law provisions with site-specific by-laws enabling police and authorized venue agents to eject people for untoward behavior. Subcontracted private security personnel and venue stewards had equivalent powers to deny entry or evict patrons if there were "reasonable grounds that the person has committed or is attempting to" contravene any venue regulations (Warren 2003: 183–4). Historically, most major-event venues adopted similar trespass powers, but statistics for the Melbourne Cricket Ground (MCG) indicate these provisions were used sparingly (Warren 2003).

In the build-up to the Melbourne 2006 Commonwealth Games, the *Major Events (Crowd Management) Act* (2003) adapted key elements of the MCG by-laws to cover any domestic or international event at Docklands Stadium, the Melbourne Sports and Aquatic Centre, the National Tennis Centre, Olympic Park, the State Netball and Hockey Centre and the Phillip Island Grand Prix circuit. These provisions could be extended by the relevant Minister to cover any additional events that warranted this designation "in the public interest" (*Major Events (Crowd Management) Act* 2003 s. 5). Specified offences included refusing to undergo a compulsory bag or body search before entering a venue, failing to surrender prohibited items, such as "animals (other than ... a guide dog)," "laser pointers," and "distress signals" (*Major Events (Crowd Management) Act* 2003 ss. 9–13), or unauthorized entry onto a managed playing surface. An "authorized" security guard or crowd controller registered under Victoria's private agent's licensing system (*Major Events (Crowd Management) Act* 2003 s. 25) could impose an immediate 24-hour ban for any of these offences and fines of up to A$6,000 (*Major Events (Crowd Management) Act* 2003 ss. 14–15). Police could also issue on-the-spot infringement notices for any venue offences, while both police and authorized officers could impose fines exceeding A$2,000 for the infringement of a 24-hour ban (*Major Events (Crowd Management) Act* 2003 ss. 16; 18–24). Magistrates could impose extended bans against offenders found to have trespassed on a playing surface or who refused to comply with an order to leave a venue (*Major Events (Crowd Management) Act* 2003 s. 17). A breach of these zonal bans could lead to fines exceeding A$6,000, but the number of fines imposed under these provisions is not publicly available.

Further reforms introduced in 2009 expanded the ministerial discretion to add new events to these provisions based on their size and economic significance (*Major Sporting Events Act* 2009 ss. 9–10). All order maintenance powers were also extended to cover adjoining "event areas." Table 5.1 outlines fourteen major public order offences and their accompanying penalties under the 2011–12 fine tariffs (*Major Sporting Events Act* 2009 ss. 83–84; 90). Police can now issue mandatory 24-hour zonal bans and on-the-spot infringement penalties of up to A$735 for all public order offences (*Major Sporting Events Act* 2009 s. 91), while court-imposed bans can be issued for up to five years and lead to a maximum A$14,648.40 fine if a person is found at or in the vicinity of a specified event (*Major Sporting Events Act* 2009 ss. 86–87). Several ambush-marketing provisions have also been introduced to protect exclusive brand insignia, television, sponsorship and ticketing arrangements (Warren 2002). These reforms enable police and authorized officers confiscate property associated with any proven offences and issue fines of up to A$100,000 against individuals or A$600,000 against corporations (*Major Sporting Events Act* 2009 ss. 43–44; 54–60; 117; 125; 137–50; 166; 170–82).

Table 5.1 Major sporting event public order offences and penalties

Offence and section	Fine (dollar rate 1 July 2011– 30 June 2012)
Possession of a prohibited item (s. 62)	20 penalty units ($4,882.80)
Possessing lit distress signals or fireworks (s. 63)	30 penalty units ($7,324.20)[a]
Throwing lit distress signals or fireworks (s. 64)	40 penalty units ($9,765.60)
Possession of unlit distress signals or fireworks (s. 65)	20 penalty units ($4,882.80)[a]
Possession of alcohol not purchased in event venue or area (s. 66)	20 penalty units ($4,882.80)
Entry into sporting competition space (s. 67)	10 penalty units ($2,441.40)[a] 60 penalty units for disrupting the event ($14,648.40)
Throwing or kicking projectiles (s. 68)	20 penalty units ($4,882.80)[a]
Damaging or defacing property in and around an event area (s. 69)	20 penalty units ($4,882.80)[a]
Damaging flora in or around an event area (s. 70)	20 penalty units ($4,882.80)[a]
Blocking stairs, exists or entries (s. 71)	10 penalty units ($2,441.40)
Climbing a fence, barrier or barricade (s. 72)	10 penalty units ($2,441.40)
Obstructing the view of a seated person (s. 73)	10 penalty units ($2,441.40)
Climbing the roof or parapet of a building (s. 74)	10 penalty units ($2,441.40)
Refusing to leave or re-entering a venue within 24-hours (s. 85)	20 penalty units ($4,882.80)[a]

Source: *Major Sporting Events Act* 2009 ss. 62–74; 85.

a Also subject to an on-the-spot infringement notice issued by police.

Palmer and Whelan's (2007) interviews with Victoria Police and subcontracted security personnel working at the 2006 Commonwealth Games reveal the 2003 reforms shifted the dynamics of public order maintenance in and around designated event sites. As "the number of private security firms rostered to these events" increased, venue managers routinely hired a special "risk manager" to oversee all security activities (Palmer and Whelan 2007: 410, 412). Rather than requesting the Victoria Police to provide equivalent oversight and "beat policing" services, this contractual model was considered more "cost effective" (Palmer and Whelan 2007: 410, 412–3). Even with enhanced discretion to implement on-the-spot fines, zonal bans or to formally prosecute under summary offence legislation, the contractual securitization model ensures the public police only retain a marginal "back up" order maintenance role. Further, these provisions now apply to an extended zone surrounding a growing number of designated venues administered by venue managers who subcontract all major coordination and operational functions to private specialists. While the classification of many spontaneous forms of crowd behavior as offences generates concerns over the cultural sanitization of Australia's major sporting events

(Taylor and Toohey 2011), the legal authorization of a punitive and highly discretionary fine and ban enforcement structure effectively privatizes a growing
zone of public space in and around Melbourne's major-event sites. This approach
to public order maintenance integrates the pre-emptive logic of "enemy criminal
law" under a user-pays proprietary and contractual securitization framework,
which remains largely immune from the supervisory and judicial oversight
requirements that apply to public policing activities. Moreover, records of privately enforced fines and zonal bans are protected by trade secrecy provisions
common to most privately negotiated security contracts.

Designated alcohol-free zones

Historically, local governments could enact by-laws enabling police or municipal officers to enforce provisions designed to protect community infrastructure,
such as public roads, sewerage, trains and dance saloons (Collins and Ellis
1933). These regulations also delineated various public spaces, such as parks, as
"alcohol-free zones" or "dry areas" that had bearing on law enforcement activities (Webb *et al.* 2004: 2–6). The actual conduct of individuals contravening
these regulations was ultimately a matter for the courts to decide if police issued
a summary charge.

After the state government deregulated venue licensing in the mid-1980s, public
anxieties over the extent of alcohol-related violence and disorder throughout
Victoria increased markedly. Market forces attracted several large nightclubs at the
south end of Melbourne's CBD, which generated many governmental and independent inquiries into liquor supply and venue security (Department of Justice
2009; Drugs and Crime Prevention Committee 2010; Zajdow 2011). In 2007,
zonal bans were introduced to counter persistent concerns over rising violence and
antisocial conduct in many Victorian nightclub precincts. Zonal regulation in the
night-time economy mirrors the *Major Sporting Events Act* by enabling police and
registered security personnel to evict people from private venues and public spaces
considered by the Liquor-Licensing Minister to justify additional securitization.
Similar zonal bans can be authorized under voluntary Liquor Accord agreements
between licensed venue managers, police and local councils (*Liquor Control
Reform Act* Vic 1998 s. 146A-D). However, the use of "enemy" criminal law to
maintain "public safety and public order" (*Liquor Control Reform Act* Vic 1998 s.
148I(6)) within the liquor-licensing structure exposes a new generation of presumptive enemies to a greater array of punitive, preemptive and discretionary
enforcement and surveillance measures.

Ministerial directives are based on evidence of any alcohol-related disorder
within a proposed area provided by the Victoria Police or the Victorian
Commission for Gambling and Liquor Regulation (*Liquor Control Reform Act*
Vic 1998 s. 147). Zonal banning currently applies in thirteen "designated" areas
throughout Victoria. A zonal designation can be appealed by a local authority and
scrutinized in court (see *Liquor Control Reform Act* Vic 1998 s. 148), but this has
yet to occur in Victoria. Most designated zones outside the Melbourne CBD and

Docklands are inner-metropolitan suburbs or regional cities with high concentrations of licensed venues (see Victorian Commission for Gambling and Liquor Regulation 2012).

Police may ban any individual who does not normally reside in a designated zone for up to 72 hours for drunk and disorderly behavior, using threatening language, possessing unlawful weapons, willful property damage or serious violent and sexual assaults (*Liquor Control Reform Act* Vic 1998 ss. 148B(6)-(7); Schedule 2). A court can extend a short-term ban if the offence is proved and carries an imprisonment term of less than 12 months (*Liquor Control Reform Act* Vic 1998 s. 148I). Breaches detected by police can lead to mandatory eviction from a specified area or declared zone and fines exceeding A$7,000 (*Liquor Control Reform Act* Vic 1998 ss. 148J-L). Supplementary "barring" powers can also restrict entry within a 20-meter zone surrounding any licensed venue in Victoria. Barring orders are determined on a sliding scale ranging from one to six months depending on a person's previous offence history. These powers apply if police, venue managers or their agents believe a person's intoxication or "drunk, violent or quarrelsome" behavior presents a risk to themselves or others (*Liquor Control Reform Act* Vic 1998 s. 106D). A barred person detected within the 20-meter zone is subject to fines of over A$2,000 (*Liquor Control Reform Act* Vic 1998 s. 106J).

Table 5.2 demonstrates that between June 2009 and June 2010, police were quite willing to impose short-term zonal bans in the Melbourne LGA. Table 5.3 indicates that while over 80 percent of people receiving short-term and extended court-ordered zonal bans were young men aged between 15 and 34 years, there were only 32 detected contraventions of short-term orders between 1 July 2009

Table 5.2 Banning notices in Victorian designated areas, 2009–10 and 2010–11

Designated area	2009–10	2010–11
Bendigo[a]	14	8
Ballarat[a]	58	64
Frankston	11	6
Geelong[a]	5	15
La Trobe	20	5
Melbourne	1,697	681
Port Phillip	2	14
Shepparton[a]	8	15
Prahran	30	18
Warrnambool[a]	1	17
Yarra	21	7
Totals (n = 2,717):	1,867	850

Source: Victoria Police (2011b).

a Denotes regional cities with populations under 200,000.

Table 5.3 Age distribution of first bans and first exclusion orders, Victoria 2009–10 and
           2010–11

Age group	Bans			Exclusion orders		
	2009–10	*2010–11*	*Subtotal*	*2009–10*	*2010–11*	*Subtotal*
10–14	7	3	10	0	0	0
15–34	1,582	736	2,318	42	65	107
35–50+	175	83	258	8	8	16
Unspecified	8	9	17	0	0	0
Totals:	1,802[a]	831	2,633[a]	50	73	133
	(1,772)		(2,603)			

Source: Victoria Police (2011b).

a A calculation error of 30 cases appeared in the original source (correct figures in brackets).

and 30 June 2011 (Victoria Police 2011b). However, the 40 percent decline in the
number of banning orders issued in Melbourne in this two-year period coincides
with several additional discretionary fine enforcement powers under revised summary offence laws.

"Move-on" powers are a type of dispersal order enabling police to immediately
evict people from public spaces for conduct deemed to be an actual or potential
"breach of the peace" that might damage property or cause physical injury to
another person, or that is considered "a risk to public safety" (*Summary Offences
Act* Vic 1966 s. 6(1)). Failure to comply with a "move-on" directive can lead to
an automatic A$244 infringement notice and a 24-hour zonal ban from the area
where the offence occurred (*Summary Offences Act* Vic 1966 ss. 6; 60AA-AB).
On-the-spot penalties can also be issued for public disorder, "riotous, indecent,
offensive or insulting" behavior and using "profane, indecent, obscene" or
"insulting language" in a public place (*Summary Offences Act* 1966 s. 17(1);
Victoria Police 2011c: 5). These offences can lead to fines ranging from almost
A$2,500 and up to two months imprisonment for a first offence, to over A$6,000
and up to six months imprisonment for a third offence. Between 1 July 2008 and
30 June 2011, 21,587 of these infringement notices were issued in Victoria. Table
5.4 also indicates that penalty notices under the less severe "move-on" powers are
readily invoked to deal with public drunkenness both within and outside declared
liquor-control zones.

There is no doubt that heavier on-the-spot penalties and broader definitions of
conventional public order offences that enhance police enforcement discretion
and restrict the scope of judicial review are the main hallmarks of "enemy criminal law." The punitive impact of these reforms is especially magnified by the
graded fine and imprisonment structure for repeat offenders. However, the zonal
securitization component (Crawford 2011a) adds a further dimension to the
enemy criminal law thesis. As short-term and extended bans can be implemented
in areas surrounding private venues and where move-on powers have been

Table 5.4 Public order infringement notices, 16 December 2009 to 30 June 2011

Offence	16 Dec 09– 30 June 10	2010–11	Totals
Contravention of move-on directive	249	362	611
Drunk in a public place	8,031	13,366	21,397
Drunk and disorderly in a public place	517	618	1,135
Disorderly behavior in a public place	178	182	360
Totals:	8,957	14,528	23,485

Source: Victoria Police (2011c: 48).

invoked, an increased range of penalties specifically targets zonal infringements. As with major-event regulations, these liquor-control and summary move-on powers are silent on how the zonal banning requirements are to be enforced. Our view is these laws tacitly create a new offence of "unauthorized presence" (Belina 2012) that enables new mass population screening methods to permeate the contemporary urban order maintenance landscape. While the effectiveness of this form of urban securitization remains largely speculative, zonal regulation governs urban mobility through a contemporary variant of the "pass law" system (Cohen 1992: 187). In fact, it seems virtually impossible to enforce the graded banning measures in Victoria without the introduction of networked mass surveillance and identity verification technologies amongst public, private and municipal law enforcement agencies.

Technology, protective policing, and zonal banning

As identity authentication is central to the power to ban persons within any geographic zone, cheaper portable and networked identity-recognition systems can streamline the administration of fines and short- or longer-term zonal prohibitions. Australian major-event venues have yet to adopt contentious facial recognition technologies (Schimmel 2011). However, electronic turnstiles activated by ticket scanners are installed at all major-event sites to regulate patron entry before mandatory security checks are undertaken for alcohol, weapons and other contraband items. These mechanized processes have been a standard method of entry into most closed or cordoned open-air major-event venues in Melbourne since the 2006 Commonwealth Games.

The incorporation of these surveillance measures in the CBD and Docklands zones has already begun. A mandatory "smartcard" transport ticketing system first proposed in 2002 (Victorian Ombudsman 2011) is now fully operational on all suburban rail and tram networks. Police have also deployed portable walk-through scanners at Southern Cross and other major inner-city railway stations to randomly screen rail users attempting to enter inner-Melbourne with unlawful weapons (O'Connell 2012). Preventing access to these designated areas by foot, tram or private cars appears more difficult. However, Automatic Number Plate recognition systems and tollway scanners are deployed on many of Melbourne's major road networks. In the future, any combination of urban zonal delineations and existing or new security technologies (Loader *et al.* 2010) may enhance mass population surveillance to create a digital securitization enclosure within the CBD, Docklands and neighboring suburbs.

The adoption of mass surveillance technologies by private businesses to mitigate the risk of liquor-control violations is also accelerated by venue-specific bans. Many venue managers have installed computerized systems requiring all patrons to have ID documents or fingerprints scanned as a condition of entry. Patron data can then be networked to equivalent systems used at other venues within a designated zone and by police to identify "flagged" or banned individuals (Palmer *et al.* 2011, 2012). Lengthy queues at venue entrances mean it is often impractical to scan all patrons (Palmer *et al.* 2012). However, there is virtually unanimous trust in the capacity of computerized ID verification systems to deter violent and antisocial behavior in designated zones. According to the following crowd controller interviewed[1] in 2011, ID scanners are considered important in enforcing a venue or zonal ban:

> I tend to pull someone aside if they have been banned and I just have to talk to them and tell them this is how it is. 'You keep going, you'll be banned for a lot longer' ... [Our venue is] the place to be on a Saturday night at the moment and it hurts them when they rock up and their friends are there and they can't get in.

Most Australian states have introduced new risk-based venue-licensing schemes (Department of Justice 2009), accompanied by proposals for license fee discounts (Law, Justice and Safety Committee 2010) and "affirmative defences" (Cross 2005: 404) for proprietors who install new surveillance technologies to enhance venue security. All licensed premises in Victoria are legally required to install high-resolution digital CCTV cameras to minimize disorder at entry points and on adjoining public walkways (VLRC 2010). Such legislatively mandated incentives normalize mass computerized forms of securitization, which reinforces the acceptance of zonal banning as a key method of promoting good order by constraining urban mobility.

Outside the Melbourne CBD and Docklands, routine approaches to public order maintenance are also shifting with the introduction of state-employed Protective Services Officers (PSOs). These quasi-police officers (Crawford 2006: 134–5) have a specific mandate to combat "crime and anti-social behavior," including vandalism, loitering and illicit drug dealing or use in various designated crime "hot spots," such as railway stations, other transport hubs and adjoining car parks (*Justice Legislation Amendment (Protective Services Officers) Act* 2011; *Police Regulations* 2003 reg. 64). PSOs can enforce move-on powers, detain people for public drunkenness or serve on-the-spot infringement notices for "riotous, indecent, offensive and threatening" behavior (*Summary Offences Act* 1966 ss. 6; 15; 60AA). This extension of summary offence powers replicates the fusion of private and public policing functions at major-event venues. PSOs also have legal powers to demand a person's name and address, issue infringement notices for transport ticketing, disorder and weapons offences, and detain the mentally ill or those with outstanding warrants. Such identity authentication powers can enhance the enforcement of preemptive bans in designated inner-urban zones, and provide a day-to-day enforcement complement to periodic "stop-and-search" blitzes ordered at the discretion of the Chief Commissioner of Police on Melbourne's suburban rail network (Office of Police Integrity 2012: 26–7) and roads (Ainsworth 2012).

However, the lack of integration of these securitization developments has been widely criticized. An independent review of information communication technologies (ICT) deployed by Victoria Police recommended a centralized administrative structure to rectify several "information management and security" failures (KPMG 2009: 2). A subsequent independent investigation into seven major ICT projects across various public sector bureaucracies identified a consistent pattern of inadequate "leadership, accountability and governance, planning, funding, probity and procurement, (and) project management" (Victorian Ombudsman 2011: 15). Of particular concern was the protracted upgrade to Victoria's crime database, which lacked "a clear vision for modern policing" and failed to generate the necessary "organizational transformation from a paper-based organization to an electronic organization" (Victorian Ombudsman 2011: 66). A further report into the use of "stop-and-search" powers to control prohibited weapons found significant police intelligence gaps resulted in the selective targeting of ethnic minority youths in "designated areas" (Office of Police Integrity 2012: 26–8). Suggestions that this problem can be overcome by allowing all people to be "stopped and searched equally" (Office of Police Integrity 2012: 8) demonstrate how mass population surveillance has become normalized in contemporary urban life (also see Bigo 2006), while reinforcing the political and public acceptance of zonal banning as an effective public order maintenance strategy.

Conclusion

The "logic and language" of zonal banning as a key element of urban securitization is enmeshed within broader patterns of inner-city redevelopment. Through the adaptation of private property law principles, public order maintenance is increasingly subject to dominant market and commercial approaches to managing signs of disorder that are considered to block free and unimpeded passage through designated areas (Lippert 2012; Blomley 2010). As more public spaces are governed by this security logic, those who disrupt legitimate commercial flows can simply be removed from sight. However, zonal regulation is also part of several contingency laws that require new forms of identity validation to preserve order in Australia's cities. Any countervailing rights to privacy, free movement and presence in an increasingly fluid multi-agency law enforcement context are yet to be reconciled under this approach to "enemy criminal law" that promotes urban securitization through more intensive zonal regulation.

Note

1 Criminology Research Council Grant 42/08-09 funded the research on ID scanners documented in this chapter. The analysis presented in this chapter is that of the authors and does not necessarily represent the view of the Criminology Research Council. The authors sincerely thank Emma McFarlane for her diligence in conducting and transcribing the key stakeholder interviews for this project.

References

Aas, K.F. (2011) "'Crimmigrant' Bodies and Bona Fide Travellers: Surveillance, Citizenship and Global Governance." *Theoretical Criminology*, 15(3): 331–46.

Ainsworth, M. (2012) "Weapons Targeted in Police Stop and Search." *Herald Sun,* 13 July. Online. Available at: http://www.heraldsun.com.au/news/true-crime-scene/weapons-targeted-in-police-stop-and-search/story-fnat7jnn-1226425050249 [accessed 13 July 2012].

Ashworth, A. and Zender, L. (2008) "Defending the Criminal Law: Reflections on the Changing Character of Crime, Procedure and Sanctions." *Criminal Law and Philosophy*, 2(1): 21–51.

Beckett, K. and Herbert, S. (2010) *Banished: The New Social Control in Urban America*, New York: Oxford University Press.

Belina, B. (2007) "From Discipline to Dislocation: Area Bans in Recent Urban Policing in Germany." *European Urban and Regional Studies*, 14(4): 321–36.

Belina, B. (2012) "Ending Public Space As We Know It." *Social Justice*, 38(1–2): 13–27.

Bennett, C.J. (1991) "What is Policy Convergence and What Causes It?" *British Journal of Political Science*, 21(2): 215–33.

Bigo, D. (2006) "Security, Exception, Ban and Surveillance." In D. Lyon (ed.) *Theorizing Surveillance: The Panopticon and Beyond*, Abingdon, UK: Routledge.

Blandy, S. and Sibley, D. (2010) "Law, Boundaries and the Production of Space." *Social and Legal Studies*, 19(3): 275–84.

Blomley, N. (2010) "The Right to Pass Freely: Circulation, Begging, and the Bounded Self." *Social and Legal Studies*, 19(3): 331–50.

City of Melbourne (2006) *SEIFA (Socio-Economic Indexes for Areas) 2006: City of Melbourne Small Area – Docklands,* Melbourne: City of Melbourne. Online. Available at: http://www.melbourne.vic.gov.au/AboutMelbourne/PrecinctsandSuburbs/suburbprofiles/Documents/SEIFA2006CityofMelbourneDocklands.pdf [accessed 22 June 2012].

City of Melbourne (2009) *Melbourne Small Area Economic and Demographic Profile*, 2nd edn, Melbourne: City of Melbourne. Online. Available at: http://www.melbourne.vic.gov.au/AboutMelbourne/PrecinctsandSuburbs/suburbprofiles/Documents/Economic_and_Demographic_Profile_Melbourne_2008.pdf [accessed 12 June 2012].

City of Melbourne (2011) *Clue™2010: Census of Land Use and Employment: Docklands Small Area Report,* Melbourne: City of Melbourne. Online. Available at: http://www.melbourne.vic.gov.au/AboutMelbourne/Statistics/CLUE/Documents/CLUE_2010_SMALL_AREA_REPORTS_DOCKLANDS.pdf [accessed 22 June 2012].

City of Melbourne (2012a) *Melbourne's Precincts and Suburbs*, Melbourne: City of Melbourne. Online. Available at: http://www.melbourne.vic.gov.au/AboutMelbourne/PrecinctsandSuburbs/Pages/Melbourneprecinctsandsuburbs.aspx [accessed 21 June 2012].

City of Melbourne (2012b) *Planning Scheme Amendment C186 – Central City (Hoddle Grid) Heritage Review*, Melbourne: City of Melbourne. Online. Available at: http://www.melbourne.vic.gov.au/BuildingandPlanning/Planning/planningschemeamendments/Pages/AmendmentC186.aspx [accessed 21 June 2012].

Cohen, S. (1992) *Against Criminology*, New Brunswick, NJ: Transaction Publishers.

Collins, J. and Ellis, A. (1933) *Collins and Meaden's Local Government Law and Practice*, (2nd edn), Melbourne: The Law Book Co of Australasia Ltd.

Crawford, A. (2003) "'Contractual Governance' of Deviant Behavior." *Journal of Law and Society*, 30(4): 479–505.

Crawford, A. (2006) "Policing and Security as 'Club Goods': The New Enclosures?" In J. Wood and B. Dupont (eds) *Democracy, Society and the Governance of Security*, Cambridge: Cambridge University Press.

Crawford, A. (2011a) "International and Comparative Criminal Justice and Urban Governance." In A. Crawford (ed.) *International and Comparative Criminal Justice and Urban Governance: Convergence and Divergence in Global, National and Local Settings*, Cambridge: Cambridge University Press.

Crawford, A. (2011b) "From the Shopping Mall to the Street Corner: Dynamics of Exclusion in the Governance of Public Space." In A. Crawford (ed.) *International and Comparative Criminal Justice and Urban Governance: Convergence and Divergence in Global, National and Local Settings*, Cambridge: Cambridge University Press.

Crofts, P. (2007) "Brothels and Disorderly Acts." *Public Space: The Journal of Law and Social Justice*, 1(1): 1–39.

Crofts, T. (2011) "The Law and (Anti-Social Behavior) Order Campaign in Western Australia." *Current Issues in Criminal Justice*, 22(3): 399–414.

Crofts, T. and Witzleb, N. (2011) "'Naming and Shaming' in Western Australia: Prohibited Behavior Orders, Publicity and the Decline of Youth Anonymity." *Criminal Law Journal*, 35(1): 34–45.

Cross, J.T. (2005) "Age Verification in the 21st Century: Swiping Away Your Privacy." *The John Marshall Journal of Computer and Information Law*, 23(2): 363–410.

Department of Justice (Victoria) (2009) *Liquor Control Reform Regulations: Regulatory Impact Statement*, Melbourne: Department of Justice.

Docklands Authority Act, Victoria, 1991.

Drugs and Crime Prevention Committee (2010) *Inquiry into Strategies to Reduce Assaults in Public Places in Victoria*. Melbourne: Government Printer for the State of Victoria.

Hermer, J. and Mosher, J. (eds) (2002) *Disorderly People: Law and the Politics of Exclusion in Ontario*, Halifax, NS: Fernwood Publishing.

Hildebrandt, M. (2009) "Justice and Police: Regulatory Offences and the Criminal Law." *New Criminal Law Review*, 12(1): 43–68.

Jones, T. and Newburn, T. (2007) "Learning from Uncle Sam? Exploring U.S. Influences on British Crime Control Policy." *Governance: An International Journal of Policy, Administration, and Institutions*, 15(1): 97–119.

Justice Legislation Amendment (Protective Services Officers) Act, Victoria, 2011.

KPMG/Commissioner for Law Enforcement and Data Security (2009) *Review of Information Governance within Victoria Police Force: Final Report*, Melbourne: KPMG. Online. Available at: http://www.cleds.vic.gov.au/content.asp?Document_ ID=20804 [accessed 11 May 2012].

Law, Justice and Safety Committee (2010) *Inquiry into Alcohol-Related Violence: Final Report*, (74), Brisbane: Legislative Assembly/Law, Justice and Safety Committee.

Lippert, R. (2012) "'Clean and Safe Passage': Business Improvement Districts, Urban Security Modes and Knowledge Brokers." *European Urban and Regional Studies*, 19(2): 167–80.

Lips, A.M.B., Taylor, J.A. and Organ, J. (2009) "Identity Management, Administrative Sorting and Citizenship in New Modes of Government." *Information, Communication & Society*, 12(5): 715–34.

Liquor Control Reform Act, Victoria, 1998.

Loader, I., Goold, B. and Thumala, A. (2010) "Consuming Security?: Tools for a Sociology of Security Consumption." *Theoretical Criminology*, 14(3): 3–30.

Major Events (Crowd Management) Act, Victoria, 2003.

Major Sporting Events Act, Victoria, 2009.

Mattelart, A. (2010) *The Globalization of Surveillance*, Cambridge: Polity.

Melbourne 2006 XVIII Commonwealth Games (2006) *Commonwealth Games Athletes' Village*, Melbourne: Melbourne 2006 XVIII Commonwealth Games. Online. Available at: http://www.melbourne2006.com.au/Getting+Involved/About+the+Games/Games+Village/#res [accessed 24 June 2012].

Melbourne Docklands (2012a) *Docklands Second Decade*, Melbourne: Places Victoria. Online. Available at: http://www.docklands.com/cs/Satellite?c=VPage&cid=1276756244081&pagename=VicUrban%2FLayout&site=Docklands [accessed 21 June 2012].

Melbourne Docklands (2012b) *History and Heritage*, Melbourne: Places Victoria. Online. Available at: http://www.docklands.com/cs/Satellite?c=VPage&cid=1182927624507&pagename=Docklands%2FLayout [accessed 21 June 2012].

Monahan, T. (2011) "Surveillance as Cultural Practice." *Sociological Quarterly*, 52(4): 495–508.

Newburn, T. and Jones, T. (2007) "Symbolizing Crime Control: Reflections on Zero Tolerance." *Theoretical Criminology*, 11(2): 221–43.

O'Connell, B. (2012) "Police Arrest 16 During Weapons Crackdown at Southern Cross Station." *Sunday Herald Sun* 19 May. Online. Available at: http://www.heraldsun.com.au/news/police-arrest-16-during-weapons-crackdown-at-southern-cross-station/story-e6frf7jo-1226360952281 [accessed 19 May 2012].

Office of Police Integrity (Victoria) (2012) *Review of Victoria Police Use of 'Stop and Search' Powers*, Melbourne: Office of Police Integrity. Online. Available at: http://www.opi.vic.gov.au/index.php?i=16&m=8&t=1 [accessed 21 June 2012].

O'Malley, P. 2010. "Simulated Justice: Risk, Money and Telemetric Policing." *British Journal of Criminology*, 50(5): 795–807.

Palmer, D. and Whelan, C. (2007) "Policing in the 'Communal Spaces' of Major Event Venues." *Police Practice and Research*, 8(5): 401–14.

Palmer, D., Warren, I. and Miller, P. (2011) "ID Scanners in the Night-Time Economy." *IEEE Technology and Society Magazine*, 30(3): 18–24.

Palmer, D., Warren, I. and Miller, P. (2012) "ID Scanning, the Media, and the Politics of Urban Surveillance in an Australian Regional City." *Surveillance and Society*, 9(3): 293–309.

Police Regulations, 2003, Victoria.

Schimmel, K.S. (2011) "From 'Violence-Complacent' to 'Terrorist-Ready': Post-9/11 Framing of the US Superbowl." *Urban Studies*, 48(15): 3277–91.

Schuilenburg, M. (2012) "The Securitization of Society: On the Rise of Quasi-Criminal Law and Selective Exclusion." *Social Justice*, 38(1–2): 73–89.

Solove, D.J. (2011) *Nothing to Hide: The False Tradeoff Between Privacy and Security,* New Haven, CT: Yale University Press.

Summary Offences Act, 1966, Victoria.

Taylor, T. and Toohey, K. (2011) "Ensuring Safety at Australian Sport Event Precincts: Creating Securitized, Sanitized and Stifling Spaces?" *Urban Studies*, 48(15): 3259–75.

Victoria Police (2011a) "Crime Statistics by LGA (Local Government Area) 2009/2010–2010/2011." In Victoria Police Homepage, Melbourne: Victoria Police. Online. Available at: http://www.police.vic.gov.au/content.asp?a=internetBridgingPage&Media_ID=72178 [accessed 22 June 2012].

Victoria Police (2011b) *Liquor Control Reform Act 1998: 2010–11 Report by the Chief Commissioner Victoria Police, Section 148R Banning Notices and Exclusion Orders*, Melbourne: Victoria Police.

Victoria Police (2011c) *Crime Statistics: 2010–2011*, Melbourne: Victoria Police. Online. Available at: http://www.police.vic.gov.au/content.asp?a=internetBridgingPage&Media_ID=72176 [accessed 22 June 2012].

Victorian Auditor-General (2012) *Effectiveness of Justice Strategies in Preventing and Reducing Alcohol-Related Harm*. Melbourne: Victorian Government Printer. Online. Available at: http://www.audit.vic.gov.au/publications/20120620-Alcohol/20120620-Alcohol.pdf [accessed 13 July 2012].

Victorian Commission for Gambling and Liquor Regulation (2012) *Designated Areas*, Melbourne: Victorian Commission for Gambling and Liquor Regulation. Online. Available at: http://responsiblealcohol.vic.gov.au/wps/portal/rav/community/initiatives/designated_areas [accessed 23 June 2012].

Victorian Law Reform Commission (VLRC) (2010) *Surveillance in Public Places: Final Report*, (18), Melbourne: Victorian Law Reform Commission. Online. Available at: http://www.lawreform.vic.gov.au/wps/wcm/connect/justlib/law+reform/home/completed+projects/surveillance+in+public+places/lawreform+-+surveillance+in+public+places+-+final+report [accessed 1 November 2010].

Victorian Ombudsman (2011) *Own Motion Investigation into ICT-Enabled Projects*, Melbourne: Victorian Government Printer. Online. Available at: http://www.ombudsman.vic.gov.au/resources/documents/Investigation_into_ICT_enabled_projects_Nov_2011.pdf [accessed 9 March 2012].

von Hirsch, A. and Simister, A.P. (eds) (2006) *Incivilities: Regulating Offensive Behavior*, Oxford: Hart Publishing.

Warren, I. (2002) "Governance, Protest and Sport: An Australian Perspective." *Entertainment and Sports Law Journal*, 1(1): 67–94.

Warren, I. (2003) *Football, Crowds and Cultures: Comparing English and Australian Law and Enforcement Trends*, Sydney: Australian Society for Sports History.

Warren, I. and Hay, R. (2009) "'Fencing Them In': The A-League, Policing and the Dilemma of Public Order." *Soccer and Society*, 10(1): 124–41.

Webb, M., Marriott-Lloyd, P. and Grenfell, M. (2004) "'Banning the Bottle': Liquor Bans in New Zealand." Paper presented at the Third Australasian Drug Strategy Conference, Alice Springs, NT, 4-6 May. Online. Available at: http://www.ndp.govt.nz/moh.nsf/pagescm/1047/$File/banningbottleliquorbans.pdf [accessed 18 August 2010].

Young, J. (1998) "From Inclusive to Exclusive Society: Nightmares in the European Dream." In V. Ruggiero, N. South, and I. Taylor (eds) *The New European Criminology: Crime and Social Order in Europe*, Abingdon, UK: Routledge.

Zajdow, G. (2011) "Outsourcing the Risks: Alcohol Licensing, Risk and the Making of the Night-Time Economy." *Current Issues in Criminal Justice*, 23(1): 73–84.

Zedner, L. (2010). "Security, the State and the Citizen: The Changing Architecture of Crime Control." *New Criminal Law Review*, 13(2): 379–403.

6 Polychrome policing in German cities

Extending the state's monopoly on the use of force

Volker Eick

Introduction

Since May 2011, yellow stickers have covered the front yards in the more affluent neighborhoods of Bremen, Germany's tenth largest city, with 550,000 residents. The stickers read *Watch out! Vigilant Neighbours*, and are part of a coordinated federal and state crime prevention programme in urban areas across the country. A few streets away, a local bank and the police promote 'Assault protection through DNA' (Selecta 2011). This model project, run by the police and a high-tech company, provides citizens with artificial DNA to mark their valuables.[1] The police, the bank and the company providing the DNA also manage the local crime prevention council.

In March 2012, an 18-year-old youngster deployed as a 'neighbourhood guard' by a private security company was stabbed to death in one of Berlin's poorest neighbourhoods in the Neukölln district (Schröder *et al.* 2012). He had recently become a 'neighbourhood assistant' with a non-profit specializing in (re)integrating the long-term unemployed into the labour market. Here as elsewhere in Germany, 'the police provided training' to him when he was with his first employer, the non-profit contractor (Weeber and Partner 2012: 26).

Not only are there many stakeholders involved in policing urban Germany, as the examples above show, but the landscape of 'the police extended family' (Johnston 2003) also introduces new forms of cooperation, co-optation, competition and contestation (Eick 2011b, 2012). With reference to the different colours of the uniforms (state police) and working clothes (private security contractors and non-profit-guided long-term unemployed), this chapter employs the term *polychrome policing*. It is consonant with both Williams' (2007) 'enemies in blue' and Koplow's security personnel 'tangled up in khaki and blue' (2005) and captures the vast array of state and non-state security contractors that some scholars have tried to subsume under 'plural policing' (Bayley and Shearing 1996; Jones and Newburn 2006; Brodeur 2010).

With a focus on the policing networks that have emerged in German cities, this chapter focuses on the respective roles of the police, private security contractors and third-sector organizations providing non-profit policing in cities. By investigating what the federal and state governments call Germany's new 'security architecture' (Ständige Konferenz 2009; see below) the chapter develops three arguments. First, the commercialization of policing since the 1980s and its counterpart, the neocommunitarian variant (Jessop 2002) organized by non-profits since the 1990s, can only be grasped within the context of emerging neoliberalization and its variations: neostatism, neocorporatism and neocommunitarianism since the mid-1980s. Second, it is misleading to understand the rapid growth and influence of commercial security providers as undermining the state monopoly on the legitimate use of force. At least in the German case, as shaky as its 'security architecture' might be (Eick 2011b), it entails an extension of this monopoly. Cities under neoliberal command are key sites for this enlargement. Third, insights from different disciplines provide a broader understanding of the aims, practices, and impacts of SOS policing (*Sauberkeit, Ordnung, Sicherheit*), that is, the enforcement of cleanliness, order and security in German cities against 'undesirables' and in favour of a so-called 'sustainable' neoliberalism.

Grand pictures, small images

Grand pictures of control and punishment have their merits as they illustrate defining features of current societies and also help us better understand tendencies within the most advanced capitalist nation states. The respective endeavours of scholars such as Garland (2001) and Wacquant (2009) to analyse policing and crime fighting strategies are significant, but this chapter holds that 'they do it differently in Minnesota' (Daems 2009), that is, there are local varieties evident in different cities (Kreissl and Ostermeier 2007). That said, this chapter is inspired by an empirically informed regulation approach and by a focus on what is known as 'actually existing neoliberalism' (Brenner and Theodore 2002). Neoliberalism as an ideology is defined here as a set of political discourses that reconfigure liberal conceptions of freedom, the individual, the market and the non-interventionist state, rejecting both egalitarian liberalism and the Keynesian welfare state. Yet neoliberalism is also a practice. As such, neoliberalization promotes market-led economic and social restructuring. In the public sector this involves processes such as privatization and liberalization, while the residual public sector and the non-profit sector are confronted with the imposition of commercial criteria. For the urban environs, neoliberalization entails the marketing of 'cities as entrepreneurs' competing in a glocal[2] market within which 'security' and policing transform into economic assets; it also entails the privatization of public space and of public services. Neoliberalization further supports free trade and capital mobility in a global economy that involves as dominant trends of financial deregulation, flexibilized labour, a respective 'enabling state' policy to promote neoliberalism, and cities as 'headquarters' for glocal businesses.

While neoliberalization implies the destruction of Fordist–Keynesian amenities, institutions and agreements (Peck and Tickell 2002), neoliberalization also implies the establishment of new institutions and practices or cooptation of existing ones with the goal of reproducing neoliberalism in the future. On the urban scale, that might lead to government-business consortia, to legislative amendments initiating workfare policies, or to different types of public–private partnerships, police–private partnerships included.

Peck and Tickell (2002) have argued that neoliberalization consists of three phases: a proto-phase (from the 1970s onwards), a roll-back phase (through the 1980s) and a roll-out phase (beginning in the early 1990s). However, Jessop (2002) remarks that four key features allow for a differentiation between the Keynesian welfare state and what he terms a Schumpeterian workfare post-national regime (SWPR). First, there is promotion of international competitiveness and socio-technical innovation through supply-side policies. Second, there is sub-ordination of social policy to economic policy. Third, there occurs a growing importance of local, regional, and supranational levels of governments. Finally, there is increasing reliance on partnerships, networks, think tanks, consultation, negotiation, and other forms of (reflexive) self-organization.

It is beyond this chapter's scope to recount Jessop's arguments on SWPR and its 'others' (neoliberalism, neostatism, neocorporatism, neocommunitarianism).[3] However, to understand changes in urban policing in Germany since the early 1980s, it is worthwhile highlighting two further arguments Jessop made. First, in line with other scholars (e.g. Leitner *et al.* 2007), he argued neoliberalism is only one of four variants of SWPR and that these 'different strategies may be pursued on different scales' to promote international competitiveness. Second, he argued such promotion coheres with implications for the urban level, 'where key issues of competitiveness, labour market flexibility, and social policy intersect, and where new supply-side orientations may permit differential economic and social policies' (Jessop 2002: 463–4; cf. Harvey 1989).

Indeed, from the 1990s onwards cities began to play a decisive role in politics and economics on the one hand functioning as 'nodes' in a hierarchically organized global network, on the other stimulating competition within their respective city borders. Intensified inter- and inner-urban competition resulted in the emergence of multiple neoliberalisms. In times of glocalized neoliberalization, the most important goal of today's urban policy is to mobilize city space as an arena of market-oriented economic growth. Roll-out neoliberalism has established some flanking mechanisms and modes of crisis displacement such as local economic development policies and community-based programmes – including crime prevention schemes – to elevate social exclusion. It has introduced new forms of coordination and inter-organizational networking among previously distinct spheres of local state intervention, so that social, political and ecological criteria have become intertwined and redefined in an attempt to promote economic competitiveness and 'security'. Social infrastructures, political culture, and law and order in the city are thus transformed into economic assets.

Policing between market and community

During the roll-out phase of neoliberalization in the 1990s, new discourses on reforms (dealing with welfare dependency, crime and disorder, community regeneration, social capital, new public management) and new institutions and modes of delivery such as integrated area development, civic engagement, public–private partnerships, urban regeneration and social workfare emerged. Today, large numbers of non-state actors are involved in these fields, including in policing. Together they lead to different forms of urban governance (Harvey 1989). The sale of urban space and the respective images have become as important as the measures to keep down-town areas and event spaces 'sober' and free of 'undesirables' and of what was once known as 'dangerous classes' (Morris 1994) and 'social junk' (Spitzer 1975), includ-ing youth, homeless people, beggars, drunkards, and street sex workers (Mitchell 2003; Beckett and Herbert 2010).

Jessop (2002: 460) claims neoliberalism can be contrasted 'with three other ideal-typical strategies'. This chapter exploits Jessop's aforementioned 'configu-rations' to critically investigate current strategies and tactics of cooperating *and* competing policing entities in urban space and of urban populations in Germany. My aim is to provide a broader picture of the state polices' attempts to cope with the emerging neoliberalization; of the commodification of policing services by private security companies; and of the respective quasi-policing by non-profits that goes beyond of what Jason-Lloyd (2003: xv) described as 'the increasing use of civilians who have been given special powers under statute for the perfor-mance of specific public protection duties' in the UK.

Moss-green and mustard-yellow police

Due to demographic change, the decline of farm production as labour intensive industry, and rural flight in Germany, the *Länder* (or state) administrations decided to largely withdraw police from the countryside beginning in the mid-1990s (in turn, police are replaced by technological means and by private security; cf. Eick 2006). State policing today is thus an urban business. Unlike other public services, there was no roll-back neoliberalism within the police – the number of police offic-ers (roughly 270,000), their status as civil servants,[4] their wages, and their working conditions have remained comparatively stable through the 1990s until 2006. That year, the so-called Federalism Reform devolved significant parts of the public sec-tor's legal regulation to the *Länder*. Thus, wage differentiation occurred (unequal pay for equal work), career advancement and training policies diverged (Briken *et al.* forthcoming), and outsourcing to private security contractors occurred (Eick forthcoming). Further, in adjusting to perceived new challenges, new strategies and tactics were rolled out.

A telling example concerns police uniforms. Only with police reform in 1972 did German governments seriously attempt to provide state police with the same uniforms in moss-green and mustard-yellow colours. Before that time, police uni-forms were as colourful as rag-rugs (Hackspiel-Mikosch 2011). From the beginning, the new uniforms were contested. While for some they were a 'manifestation of a democratic police force', for others they were the ugliest uniforms in Europe (Käppner 2004). Even though the uniforms were said to be high-end technology, according to the police unions, they lacked acceptance because they were said to be 'impractical' (Tetzner 2008). The debate went on, but in 2004 the Federal Minister of the Interior, Otto Schily, not only decided to rename the Border Police the 'Federal Police'[5] – a really *serious* affront against German federalism – but also to clothe them in blue without prior consultation with the 16 *Länder* Ministers of the Interior. While the *Länder* protested in vain against Schily's decision to undermine what they perceived as the greenish 'unity of uniforms', the police unions also complained without success against his second gambit: inviting the private security company *Bahnschutz Gesellschaft* (*BSG*), in charge of securing Germany's railway stations, to change their working clothes to match the uniforms of the Federal Police (Holecek 2006).

What was at stake here was neither a re-invention of Goethe's theory of colour (Lauxtermann 1990) regarding police uniforms, nor the disturbing fact that all German police uniforms are produced in Belarus (Deutsche Welle 2005). Instead, what was at stake was the blue uniform as the first expression of the attempt to give the Federal Police a distinct role and, by so doing, claiming a larger role for the 40,000 federal police officers against the 230,000 *Länder* police forces and the respective ministers. Further, the federal police became the first police force to officially cooperate with the private security industry on a contract basis.

This example is the *pars pro toto* for dominant trends within the German police apparatus since the mid-1970s. A pervasive centralization of police forces (and intelligence services) removes restrictions deployed by the allied forces after World War II. The Federal Police have significantly grown in numbers and responsibilities, especially since 1992. Along the same line, a primacy of the executive authority (against the legislature and judiciary) intensified and includes the *de facto* merging of police and intelligence services. Thus, it turns the post-war argument against the Gestapo upside down as the argument now goes: *because* police and intelligence services should remain different organizations with different tasks according to the Constitution, their cooperation is now even more necessary. At the same time, police work and intelligence service work began to be patterned after one another. Further, law enforcement agencies redefined urban incivilities into crime, and urban municipalities introduced their own local police forces on the beat (again, with their own uniforms and a plethora of colours). Neither is the latter (who are called municipal public order offices, or *Ordnungsämter*) nor the state police referred to as 'local police' in Germany, even though both work on the local scale. However named, Federal Police, state police and *Ordnungsämter* have developed an urban focus (Busch *et al.* 1988; Eick 2006).

Patterning police work and intelligence service work after one another, policing in Germany evolved into what Ericson (2007) called 'precautionary logic': when groups become subject to surveillance and sanction not on the basis of any act they have committed but on the basis of what they might do or could become. This is true for crime prevention by the police on the beat, but it is also evident in the sophisticated technological devices increasingly utilized by the police (for instance, the 'dragnet investigation' of the late 1970s, or the 'Federal Trojan' of the mid-2000s).[6] Further, an intensified orientation towards proactive crime prevention (including the selective integration of other policing stakeholders and the citizenry by responsibilization and economical means) became popular and includes police–private partnerships.

Public administration not only identified new policing stakeholders but also selected new 'targets' within the entrepreneurial city. By the late 1980s, the organizational specialization of the police apparatuses (federal, state, local), for example regarding certain ethnic groups and urban spaces, was already a widespread phenomenon in German cities. For example, the Berlin police alone saw the emergence of more than 20 Operative Groups (OGs) along ethnic and spatial lines. OGs were released from administrative work and were made responsible for patrolling the streets on their own without any control by superiors.[7] Parts of this roll-out, though, have been rolled back in the early 2000s in that the OGs were reintegrated into the bureaucratic structure of the ordinary police apparatus; in turn, policing along ethnic and spatial lines did not vanish but became institutionalized. Further, each of the six police departments in Berlin now has a specialized force targeting youths, the OG 'Youths Investigation Team' and a respective team focusing on non-Germans, the 'Working Group Integration and Migration' (AGIM) responsible for deporting 'illegal' migrants and for infiltration ethnic communities marketed as crime prevention. One additional team was established targeting graffiti in 1994, and for the Federal Police racial profiling became legal in trains and on railway stations in February 2012 (Verwaltungsgericht Koblenz 2012).[8]

As for the question of neoliberalization in terms of responsibilities and duties of the police, the state as such did not retrench. Rather, the federal scale (nation state) gained more importance in policing. The aforementioned adjustments of the police apparatus reacted to perceived new conditions and stakeholders and developed respective tactics und police units (Eick forthcoming). While tactical responses to the new stakeholders – private security contractors started to grow significantly in the 1980s (see below) – ranged from sheer neglect, tacit admission and strict suppression to forms of guidance, support and participation, neither police nor ministries developed any strategy to respond to the growth of private security contractors until the late 1990s (Eick 2011b).

Inasmuch as advocates of neoliberalism claim that public financial, administrative and human resources are limited and respective limitations in productivity are to be addressed, politicians tried to apply strategies such as human resource management (HRM), lean production, and new public management (NPM) to the police (Ritsert and Pekar 2009) but failed – except for further centralization – due to strong unions. Instead, attempts to make wage labour in security provision more productive, neoliberal 'security governance' to an increasing extent opened up to delivery by 'third parties' (Buerger and Mazerolle 1998). These include the corporate sector (private security contractors), non-profit organizations ('SOS Sentinels' financed through the public employment offices), and the voluntary sector (e.g. neighborhood watch) – all of them, except private security contractors, only marginally, or not at all, have been involved in security provision before. The participation of these stakeholders is a consequence of the intensified commodification of urban space, which reflects an understanding of 'security' as a commodity. However, the valorization of urban space, its citizens, and of 'security' occurs within a state-bound setting. The extension of what might be called an 'urban policing family' is undeniable, but *only* the police have legal standing to overpower resistance to their intervention in *any* situation.

State-run (bureaucratic), for-profit (commercial) and non-profit (brokering) policing stakeholders convey the 'pluralization of policing' on all scales – globally, nationally, regionally and locally. In so doing, for-profit and non-profit stakeholders helped to extend the scope and scale of policing (Eick 2012) while it is exclusively the police whose use of force is 'unlimited in its scope' (Brodeur 2010: 113). Public police emerged from private forms of policing during Feudalism and became prevalent with urbanization and industrialization. Given the character of policing today in all its shapes, one might even speculate about current urban policing as 'neo-Feudal'. The next section discusses the expansion of the commercial security industry and the new roles that security contractors perform in German cities.

Black sheriffs

In recent years, Germany saw a mushrooming of private security providers. They have grown in numbers since the mid-1980s and have conquered public urban space with a view to gaining profits from the 1990s onwards. The scope of non-profits is defined by the extremes of armed militias protecting the eastern borderland of Germany against 'aliens' and the so-called crime prevention schemes which are organized, on the one hand, by concerned middle-class burghers and, on the other, by non-profit organizations creating labour market (re)integration schemes for the long-term unemployed. Commercial security contractors, by contrast, range from ordinary guards to high-end security consultants (Briken 2011b).

Statistics divide the German commercial security industry into three particular markets: mechanical, electronic security, and security services. In 2010, the respective annual turnovers amounted to €2.0 billion (mechanical security), €3.4 billion (electronic security) and €4.6 billion (services), the latter encompassing 3,700 commercial security companies with a workforce of about 170,000 employees (BDSW 2011).

Not all private security provision is commercial, or for-profit, policing though. Therefore an additional differentiation may be helpful. In line with Nogala (1995: 250), who notes that 'commercial security companies ... owe their existence to a firmly profit mongering', I argue that security companies are not 'private' but 'commercial', i.e. concerned about profits and market shares. 'Private', to the contrary, are those initiatives that are not primarily interested in generating profits, such as militias, non-profits, and crime prevention schemes in all their shades (Kury 1997; Eick 2011b, 2012). If there is talk about 'privatization' with regard to the security industry it is essentially about commercialization and commodification of 'security promises' (Nogala 2005: 252).[9] The next section focuses on security services and the subsequent section provides empirical detail on working conditions of private security guards.

While the first German commercial security company (CSC) was founded in 1901, the industry has enjoyed significant growth, in particular since the mid-1980s and early 1990s (BDSW 2011; Briken 2011b; cf. Table 6.1).

Table 6.1 Commercial security industry in Germany (1974–2011)

Year	Companies	Turnover (million euros)	Employees
1974	300	314	47,400
1984	400	507	61,700
1990	600	1,200	105,000
1997	1,697	2,610	121,000
2000	2,065	3,380	140,000
2004	2,570	3,930	172,000
2007	3,430	4,290	177,000
2011[a]	3,700	4,820	175,000

Source: own account.

Note
a Estimates.

The industrial structure of Germany's commercial security industry comprises small-to-medium enterprises, and of the 3,500 companies in 2009, 2,700 have had less than 20 employees. Of the remaining 800, only 3 per cent employed more than 500 workers, while the 10 biggest players had a workforce of about 51,000 (30 per cent of the total workforce), representing an 'oligopolistic market' (Eick 2006: 70). According to the latest numbers, the 10 largest companies, in 2010, employed 53,000 security guards with an annual turnover of roughly €1.6 billion (34.8 per cent of the total turnover in this industry), an increase of 5.9 per cent compared with 2009 (Lünendonk 2011). Noteworthy is that, of the 171,000 employees within the industry in 2010, more than 50,000 did not hold contracts subject to social insurance contributions (Briken 2011b; Eick forthcoming). The constant growth of CSCs and employees alike does not stem from a growing demand for a 'feeling of security' throughout the populace (Klimke 2008). Rather, the growth results from a redefinition of 'core tasks' by both commercial enterprises and state institutions (Bachmann and Braun 2011), influenced by neoliberalism. The respective concepts promise increased efficiency through restructuring and entail as their leitmotifs 'outsourcing' and 'governance'. While the meaning of the term 'governance' is contested (Offe 2009; Davies 2011) 'policing below and beyond the state' (Eick 2011a) is deemed a precondition for effective policing in urban settings. Cooperation between state- and non-state actors in order to produce 'security' is the *sine qua non* of urban policing today.

Aside from cash-handling services, crowd management (event security), monitoring and alarm receiving, security consultancy and training, and guarding (military facilities, for example, have been guarded by commercial security contractors since 1918), all of which are well-known security services provided by commercial security contractors for decades, there are also new services that have emerged only in the last few years:

- City Points/City Patrols;
- counter-piracy operations;
- electronic surveillance;
- facility management;
- intelligence;
- labour market (re)integration;
- manhunt (Siemens, Telekom);
- military services;
- neighbourhood management;
- pollution control (ranger);
- pre-deportation detention;
- prison management;
- psychiatric clinics;
- public transport;
- video surveillance.

Noteworthy are so-called City Points; here, in addition to commercial City Patrol teams, quasi-police stations are built by private security contractors on public spaces such as pedestrian zones, in front of shopping malls and apartment blocks. They function as contact points for the police and the public and allow, for the first time ever, for a *permanent* presence of private security in the city.

The pluralization of policing was nicknamed the 'extended police family' in the UK more than 10 years ago (Home Office 2001: 6) but is referred to as the new 'security architecture' by the current German government (Ständige Konferenz 2009). Though advertised as a new development, it is more like a cream topping for commercial security contractors as they are now also *officially* part of a formerly strictly state-run 'market'. Accordingly, the 2008–09 update of the programme *Innere Sicherheit* (Internal Security) reads: 'the companies encompassing the service sector spectrum of private security are an important component of the security architecture' (Ständige Konferenz 2009: 25).

By the time the Internal Security programme was updated, neither the federal nor the state governments had a clue of how many cooperations the police have established with private security providers. Results of an evaluation published by a subcommittee of the Interior Ministers' Conference in April 2011 (cited in Eick 2012) identified 32 cooperation agreements between the federal and state police with 123 CSCs in 10 of the 16 *Länder* and with the Federal Police. In addition, 18 contracts have been signed by the Federal Association of the Security Industry (BDSW), the largest lobby organization of German commercial security contractors, with 12 local and federal police administrations and with six municipal offices of the interior.

Beyond these police–private cooperations, commercial security contractors also commenced operations with the retail industry in public and/or semi-public space, among them about 20 security agreements in Germany's Business Improvement Districts (BIDs), an estimated 150 City Patrols in cooperation with the business community in inner cities, and roughly 200 security contracts with the public and private real-estate industry. These latter private–private cooperations reflect the tendency to privatize public space and to 'secure' its profitability by commercial means. The 'shop floor' of the entrepreneurial city not only comprises retail and real-estate personnel but operates in conjunction with the respective 'plant security'. However, another form of private police emerged in German cities, adding even more colours to policing: a non-profit police.

Yellow angels, green cops and red devils in the city

The last two decades have seen the intensified creation and deployment of new for-profit and non-profit policing forces in public urban space in Germany, the latter employing long-term unemployed in workfare schemes while instructing them how to tackle what they and the local administrations perceive as disorder, incivilities and 'undesirables'. The emergence of these new policing agencies is to be explained by new urban development strategies that seek to rejuvenate hitherto neglected parts of the respective cities under the headline of a 'socially integrative city' (Eick 2011a). Disturbingly, the variegation of policing agencies in the fields of cleanliness, safety and security does not come with any regulation. Structures and activities of the new security forces are as diverse and unregulated as their working clothes are colourful.

A list of these would include 'SOS sentinels' and militias, neighbourhood watch and crime prevention schemes with or without the support and/or participation of the police, civil wardens, and organizations such as the Guardian Angels (Eick 2006; Pütter 2006). It further encompasses long-term unemployed mobilized in workfare schemes based on the so-called German Hartz IV laws (Knuth 2009) who are to provide SOS services as the so-called 1-Euro-Jobbers[10] in projects that are deployed under fancy names, mirroring neocommunitarian endeavours, such as *Ortsdiener* (place servants), *Spielplatzkümmerer* (playground attendants), *Wohngebietsaufsichten* (residential neighbourhood supervisors), *Rote Teufel* (Red Devils) in Berlin; *Gelbe Engel* (Yellow Angels) in Stuttgart and *Grünpolizei* (Green Cops) in Frankfurt. Their tasks include notifying landlords and the police about graffiti; the removal of graffiti; ensuring that dogs are kept on leashes in private and public city parks; enforcing the no-alcohol by-laws in parks and on squares; and even the control of stationary traffic (Eick 2011a; 2012). Further, long-term unemployed are engaged as school and schoolyard attendants, as school-run escorts, as park inspectors, as supervisors of residential areas and playgrounds; in addition, they control underground parking lots, enforce public green space by-laws, are available as contact persons in emergency and conflict situations, and pay heed to cleanliness (Eick 2011a). While the North American and British 'hosts' and 'ambassadors' tend to focus on guiding of and providing information to tourists, foreigners, or newcomers in the respective cities, the focus of their German counterpart is explicitly on policing the urban poor. This form of policing is meant, from the perspective of the public administration, to complement the state-led and private securitization of the city.

The additional downside is that such jobs are not subject to social insurance contributions; are not labour contracts but rather allowances; and only pay between one and two-and-a-half euros per hour. These jobs, according to the non-profit labour law, should not replace regular jobs and have to be additional –such jobs are meant to extend the low-wage sector. Further, there is a trend of deploying urban poor as quasi police forces to police themselves, which I have called 'the poor policing the poor' (Eick 2003). As a group of leading Christian Democrats made clear in 2011, a neocommunitarian approach to policing in 'disadvantaged' neighbourhoods is embraced:

> In neglected neighbourhoods crime is more likely to grow than in neighbourhoods where local residents feel at ease. Therefore, "district runners" or "neighbourhood guards" should care for those parts of town identified as those with special developing needs [but] without holding sovereign powers ... Ideally being at home in their operational area, they know the miseries of the local residents and enjoy far more trust compared to someone "from office".
>
> (Gröhe *et al.* 2011: 26)

This trend is in line with the current strategy of the Job Centers, the public employment service for the long-term unemployed, as the following statement of the Berlin head of the employment service clarifies: 'Life is not all guns and roses' for long-term unemployed, and 'for me vacancies in the private security industry and cleaning business are a no go for the Job Centers' (Wagon 2012: 15). This is just one example of the many paradoxes that go with the fetishism of 'security' – it ought to be of highest value for the urban environs and their citizenry but at the same time neither necessitates meaningful qualification for its provision nor acceptable working conditions, let alone decent wages. Policing the neoliberal city in the twenty-first century is characterized by overbidding and undercutting the fetish of 'security', which undermines the common good that should be the centrepiece of any city: well-being.

Conclusions

This chapter provided a glimpse of what polychrome policing is about in German cities. It did so by starting from a socioeconomic understanding of recent capitalist development and by drawing insights from a regulation approach. Relating these insights to policing in Germany since the 1980s, it turns out that two key features of neoliberalism – the promotion of free competition (liberalization) and the sell-off of the public sector (privatization) – did not apply to the state police in Germany until recently. Privatization of law enforcement indeed does occur in the form of outsourcing of previously restricted public functions to for-profit entities, but did not lead to a decline of state police forces. Rather, the opposite is true, and in particular the Federal Police grew significantly in numbers and influence (Eick 2012 forthcoming; cf. Loveday 1999: 142–146 and Manning 2008: 29–34 for the USA).

Two other neoliberal features do apply, at least in part. First, the reduction of the role of law (and the state as its guarantor) is obvious as the primacy of the executive powers against the judiciary and the mingling of intelligence services and police forces clearly show. This is not to say that the (national) state loses its influence. In fact, and in line with the difference between neoliberalism (ideology) and neoliberalization (praxis), this move helped to extend the role of the state and thus its monopoly on the legitimate use of force.[11] This is true for urban policing particularly as cities are increasingly understood as and run like 'companies'. Current urban neoliberalization is a form of state-led commodification of the city, and commodities demand a particularly patterned form of 'security'. Inasmuch as the state never was the *sole provider* of security, it is also the case that the number of non-state policing entities increased during the last 30 years. At least for urban policing, and in particular for policing public space, the state remains as the *sole arbitrator* on security. Legal and administrative regulation of security provision by private security contractors might be incomplete or by and large non-existent (as is the case in Germany where no private security law exists; cf. Eick 2011b), and the topic of 'security' is not mentioned in any meaningful way for non-profit policing (it is dubbed and concealed with the term 'labour market integration'; cf. Eick 2012). But this vast *grey* area of unregulated policing is left blank by the state on purpose, as it allows for variegated forms of urban policing on a case-by-case basis differing from place to place. Though orchestrated by the state, flexible, even 'fluid' policing as regards legal regulation is a precondition for urban neoliberalization.

Second, as shown by attempts to deploy NPM and other management techniques within the police apparatuses (federal, state, municipal) – even though successfully resisted by the police unions until recently – 'market proxies' in the residual public sector have been institutionalized (Briken *et al.* forthcoming). In the absence of a real 'product' or 'market', for the police this leads to the task to be more 'efficient' and also to more sensitive service delivery to their 'customers' (Briken 2011a; Neocleous 2011; Eick forthcoming). Nevertheless, state, or public, police explicitly remain as 'state business' complemented by private security contractors. At the same time, a neocommunitarian approach from within the police apparatus, supported by politicians, translates into a particular form of 'empowerment' – demanding self-policing initiatives and neighbourhood watch schemes from the urban populace. Meanwhile, private security companies are 'invocated' by the state as both part of the 'civil society' and of the new state-led 'security architecture'. The security industry translates this invitation into the extension of a profitable market.

Geographically inspired studies and ethnographic research allow for an understanding of the different approaches of the polychrome policing stakeholders and reveal that SOS policing does *not* resemble a spatial division of labour. State police is *not* solely focusing on 'high policing' (Brodeur 2010) but remains omnipresent in the urban environs. Commercial security contractors do *not* fill 'gaps' but exploit and invent business opportunities wherever possible. It is only the non-profit police that are, for the moment, *not* broadening their spatial footprint but are confined to 'disadvantaged' urban areas. Together, they form the branches of an urban army either armed or unarmed but ready for policing the decisive commodity of the twenty-first century, the city.

To paraphrase Shakespeare, 'there is nothing rotten in the state of Germany'. State police still advertise for a private high-tech company and the 18-year-old Yussef in Berlin-Neukölln is still dead. Max Weber's state monopoly on the legitimate use of force is still in place. Germany further elaborates its shaky foundation for a new 'security architecture'. And for those who are losing track in the face of black, blue, green, red, and yellow working clothes and uniforms in the name of 'security' there is some relief. When it comes to policing political dissent, German cops are reliable – they appear in anthracite-black riot gear.

Notes

1 The DNA-coded spray remains for weeks on items and on those touching them, is visible under ultraviolet light only, and allows police officers on the beat to identify the substance with special lights. Current research though revealed that also this 'promise of security' turned out to be hollow (Schulz 2012).
2 'Glocal' means at once global and local.
3 The key features of *neoliberalism* are: liberalization, deregulation, privatization, market proxies in residual public sector, internationalization, and lower direct taxes; for *neostatism*: from state control to regulated competition, guide national strategy rather than plan top-down, auditing performance of private and public sectors, public–private partnerships under state guidance, neo-mercantilist protection of core economy, and expanding roles for new collective resources; for *neocorporatism*: rebalance competition and cooperation, decentralized 'regulated self-regulation', widening the range of private, public, and other 'stakeholders', expanding the role of public–private partnerships, protecting core economic sectors in open economy, high taxation to finance social investment; for *neo-communitarianism*: deliberalization, empowerment, socialization, emphasis on social use-value and social cohesion, fair trade not free trade, redirecting taxes – all of this to be understood as ideal types that 'involve thought experiments, not . . . some normative ideal or other' (Jessop 2002: 460).
4 More than 98 per cent of police officers are employed as civil servants (*Beamte*). Only a minority – working as guards for embassies, public buildings and regulating traffic in Bremen and Hesse – are employed as public sector workers (*Angestellte*).
5 Until the early 1990s, the Border Police were only responsible for protecting the German borders (including harbours and airports) and supporting the state police under particular circumstances (such as mass demonstrations, riots). In 1992, policing of border *areas* (random police checks) and of inner-cities (intensified police presence in urban space as part of the program "Operation Safety Net" starting in 1994), and the protection of railways and railway stations was taken over from state police and the former railway police in both East and West Germany.
6 The *Bundestrojaner*, or Federal Trojan, is a term for spyware used by German law-enforcement agencies against private computers, similar to the US CIPAV system (Computer and IP Address Verification). The Trojan can be implemented through spyware, through existing 'backdoors' and even download-contamination; it should be noted though, as Manning (2008) showed, that not all IT changes police practice.
7 Such OGs are called 'RumBa' (for Rumanian gang crime/Rum*änische* Ban*denkriminalität*), OG 'Jugo' (for persons originating from former Yugoslavia), and OG 'Schwarzafrika' (sub-Saharan Africans). As for the spatial specialization, OGs are known along the names of districts, subways and parks (Flakin 2010; Eick 2012).

8 In October 2012 though, the Administrative Appeals Tribunal nullified this decision (Adam 2012).
9 Nevertheless, within this chapter, the terms "private" and "commercial" are used interchangeably but will be explicated whenever necessary.
10 Part of the new workfare measures under Hartz IV are the so-called 1-Euro Jobs – employment relationships for long-term unemployed that are not labour contracts but just allowances; until recently, they not only were to be *zusätzlich* (i.e. they should not lead to the replacement of regular workers who have the same position with – if at all – tariff wages) but in the public interest and to serve the public good (*gemeinnützig*). The latter was abolished in 2011.
11 Interestingly, the same applies to the current fight against sea piracy. Given that another feature of neoliberalism is internationalization, or the free inward and outward flow of capital, goods, services and (to a limited extent) persons, securing the "supply chain" is of high importance – the German government though does neither protect its merchant fleet by the military (as this is against the Constitution) nor by the Federal Police (as the law would suggest) but decided to outsource the protection of its fleet to private security contractors. Again, this does not undermine the state monopoly of force, but allows for less democratic control by and a lack of transparency for the parliament (Eick 2011c).

References

Adam, S. (2012) *Kontrolle wegen der Hautfarbe verstößt gegen das Grundgesetz*. Online. Available at: http://tinyurl.com/bz7gqxv [accessed 23 November 2012].

Bachmann, R. and Braun, S. (2011) "The Impact of International Outsourcing on Labour Market Dynamics in Germany." *Scottish Journal of Political Economy*, 58(1): 1–28.

Bayley, D.H. and Shearing, C.D. (1996) "The Future of Policing." *Law & Society Review*, 30(3): 585–606.

BDSW (2011) *Statistiken im BDSW*. Online. Available at: http://tinyurl.com/7o6a3uc [accessed 23 August 2012].

Beckett, K. and Herbert, S. (2010) *Banished*, Oxford: Oxford University Press.

Brenner, N. and Theodore, N. (2002) "Cities and the Geographies of 'Actually Existing Neoliberalism'." *Antipode*, 34(3): 349–79.

Briken, K. (2011a) "Suffering in Public?" *Social Justice*, 38(1–2): 128–45.

Briken, K. (2011b) *Produktion von 'Sicherheit'?* Düsseldorf: Hans-Böckler-Stiftung.

Briken, K., Gottschall, K., Hils, S., Kittel, B., Streb, S. and Tepe, M (forthcoming) *The State as Employer*, Basingstoke: Palgrave MacMillan.

Brodeur, J.-P. (2010) *The Policing Web*, Oxford: Oxford University Press.

Buerger, M.E. and Mazerolle, L.G. (1998) "Third-party Policing." *Justice Quarterly*, 15(2): 301–27.

Busch, H., Funk, A., Kauß, U., Narr, W.-D. and Werkentin, F. (1988) *Die Polizei in der Bundesrepublik Deutschland*. Frankfurt a.M.: Campus.

Daems, T. (2009) "Book Review on: Hess, H., Ostermeier, L. and Paul, B. (eds) (2007) Kontrollkulturen." *Theoretical Criminology*, 13(2): 262–65.

Davies, J.S. (2011) *Challenging Governance Theory*, Bristol: Policy Press.

Deutsche Welle (2005) *German Police Uniforms Made in Belarus*. Online. Available at:http://tinyurl.com/c6somqb [accessed 23 August 2012].

Eick, V. (2003) "New Strategies of Policing the Poor." *Policing & Society*, 13(4): 365–79.

Eick, V. (2006) "Preventive Urban Discipline." *Social Justice*, 33(3): 66–84.

Eick, V. (2011a) "Policing 'Below the State' in Germany." *Contemporary Justice Review*, 14(1): 21–41.

Eick, V. (2011b) "Germany's New 'Security Architecture." *Social Justice*, 38(1–2): 140–57.

Eick, V. (2011c) *A Charter for Boarding*. Online. Available at: http://tinyurl.com/95l45zb [accessed 23 August 2012].

Eick, V. (2013) "Ein pazifiziertes Berlins?" In A. Holm (ed.) *Reclaim Berlin*, Berlin: Assoziation A.

Eick, V. and Briken, K. (ed.) (Forthcoming) *Urban Security*, Ottawa: Red Quill Books.

Ericson, R.V. (2007) *Crime in an Insecure World*. Cambridge: Polity Press.

Flakin, W. (2010) "Are you Living in a Danger Zone?" *Ex-Berliner*, 7: 18.

Garland, D. (2001) *The Culture of Control*, Chicago: University of Chicago Press.

Gröhe, H., Mohr-Lüllmann, R., Henkel, F., Roth, P. and Elbers, D. (2011) *Politik für die Stadt der Zukunft*, Berlin: CDU.

Hackspiel-Mikosch, E. (2011) "Vom bürgerfreundlichen Grün zum respekteinflößenden Blau." In S. Wiggerich and S. Kensy (eds) *Staat – Macht – Uniform*, Stuttgart: Franz Steiner.

Harvey, D. (1989) "From Managerialism to Entrepreneurialism." *Geografiska Annaler*, 71B: 3–17.

Holecek, R. (2006) *"Bundespolizei im Berliner Hauptbahnhof nimmt es mit 300.000 Reisenden auf"* (8 June). Online. Available at: http://tinyurl.com/c482zvm [accessed 23 August 2012].

Home Office (2001) *Policing a New Century*, London: HMSO.

Jason-Lloyd, L. (2003) *Quasi-Policing*, London: Cavendish.

Jessop, B. (2002) "Liberalism, Neoliberalism, and Urban Governance." *Antipode*, 34(3): 452–72.

Johnston, L. (2003) "From 'Pluralization' to 'The Police Extended Family'." *International Journal of the Sociology of Law*, 31: 185–204.

Jones, T. and Newburn, T. (eds) (2006) *Plural Policing*, New York: Routledge.

Käppner, J. (2004) "Froschgrün und Schilyblau." *Süddeutsche Zeitung* (20 October).

Klimke, D. (2008) *Wach- und Schließgesellschaft Deutschland*, Wiesbaden: VS.

Knuth, M. (2009) "Path Shifting and Path Dependence." *International Journal of Public Administration*, 32(12): 1048–69.

Koplow, D.A. (2005) "Tangled up in Khaki and Blue." *Georgetown Journal of International Law*, 36(3): 703–808.

Kreissl, R. and Ostermeier, L. (2007) "Globale Trends und lokale Differenzen." *Kriminologisches Journal*, 39: 137–51.

Kury, H. (ed.) (1997) *Konzepte Kommunaler Kriminalprävention*, Freiburg/Brsg.: Edition Iuscrim.

Lauxtermann, P.F.H. (1990) "Hegel and Schopenhauer as Partisans of Goethe's Theory of Color." *Journal of the History of Ideas*, 51(4): 599–624.

Leitner, H., Peck, J. and Sheppard, E. (2007) *Contesting Neoliberalism*, New York: Guilford.

Loveday, B. (1999) "Government and Accountability of the Police." In R. Mawby (ed.) *Policing Across the World*, London: UCL Press.

Lünendonk GmbH (2011) *Führende Sicherheitsdienstleister in Deutschland*, Kaufbeuren: Lünendonk.

Manning, P.K. (2008) *The Technology of Policing*, New York: NYU.

Mitchell, D. (2003) *The Right to the City*, New York: Guilford.

Morris, L. (1994) *Dangerous Classes*, London: Routledge.

Neocleous, M. (2011) "Security as Pacification." In M. Neocleous and G. Rigakos (eds) *Anti-Security*, Ottawa: Red Quill Books.

Nogala, D. (1995) "Was ist Eigentlich so Privat an der Privatisierung Sozialer Kontrolle?" In F. Sack *et al.* (eds), *Privatisierung staatlicher Kontrolle*, Baden-Baden: Nomos.

Offe, C. (2009) "Governance: An 'Empty Signifier'?" *Constellations*, 16(4): 550–62.

Peck, J. and Tickell, A. (2002) "Neoliberalizing Space." *Antipode*, 34(3): 380–404.

Pütter, N. (2006) *Polizei und kommunale Kriminalprävention*, Frankfurt a.M.: Verlag für Polizeiwissenschaft.

Ritsert, R. and Pekar, M. (2009) "New Public Management Reforms in German Police Services." *German Policy Studies*, 5(2): 17–47.

Schröder, T., Schmalz, A. and Hemme, I. (2012) "Jussef el-A. starb nach einem Fußball-Streit durch einen Messerstich." *BZ* (10 March). Online. Available at: http://tinyurl.com/873tmbu [accessed 23 August 2012].

Schulz, A. (2012) "Vom 'Wundermittel' künstliche DNA." *Berliner Behörden Spiegel*, 28(11): 50.

Selecta (2011) "Diebstahlsschutz durch DNA." *Die Sparkasse Bremen* (12 October). Online. Available at: http://tinyurl.com/8283dxq [accessed 23 August 2012].

Spitzer, S. (1975) "Toward a Marxian Theory of Deviance." *Social Problems,* 22(5): 638–51.

Ständige Konferenz der Innenminister und -senatoren der Länder (eds) (2009) *Programm Innere Sicherheit. Fortschreibung 2008/2009*, Potsdam: IMK.

Tetzner, M. (2008) "Grünes Licht für Blau?" *Deutsche Polizei*, 54: 6–11.

Verwaltungsgericht Koblenz (2012) "*Identitätsfeststellung eines Zugreisenden.*" Online. Available at: http://tinyurl.com/crq9j5o [accessed 23 August 2012].

Wacquant, L. (2009) *Punishing the Poor*, London: Duke University Press.

Wagon, D. (2012) "Das Leben ist kein Ponyhof." *Berliner Zeitung* (25 July): 15.

Weeber and Partner (2012) *Integriertes Handlungs- und Entwicklungskonzept Weiße Siedlung Dammweg 2012*, Berlin: ms.

Williams, K. (2007) *Our Enemies in Blue*, Cambridge, MA: South End Press.

7 Rescaling security strategies

State tactics and citizen responses to violence in Mexico City

Diane E. Davis and
Guillermo Ruiz de Teresa

Introduction: the spatial dynamics of policing and security

Many cities of the developing world are facing growing urban violence and insecurity (Moser 2004; Rotker 2002). These developments are evident in rising rates of homicide, robbery, assault, and kidnapping, as well as contraband-related violence (often involving drugs or guns). In the most violence-prone cities, police corruption and impunity have contributed to public insecurity, helping produce outposts of urban violence in which organized gangs involved in illegal activities, ranging from drugs and guns to knock-off designer products, are as powerful as – or in competition with – police and military. These conditions are pervasive across Latin America and the Caribbean, where organized gangs equipped with arms and advanced technologies for protection and detection against law enforcement raids have blatantly attacked police, military, and citizens who report gangs to authorities. Many organized crime groups have become the functional equivalent of mini-states by monopolizing the means of violence and providing protection and territorial governance in exchange for citizen allegiance, whether coerced or freely given (Davis 2010). Their capacities derive partly from the state's longstanding absence from these geographical areas, with years of infrastructural and policy neglect having reinforced poverty in ways that have made local residents open to the protection offered by gang leaders (Arias 2006).

Just as significantly, these dynamics can weaken national states and empower criminal forces whose blatant disregard for rule of law, democratic governance, and human rights can further destabilize cities, thus driving the vicious cycle. Both local and national authorities are facing governance challenges because the acceleration of violence and crime has in certain cases pushed citizens to take justice and governance measures into their own hands through vigilantism. Even in those countries where citizens are not yet resorting to such measures, governments are finding their legitimacy eroding. Larger numbers of armed actors in the most "fragile cities" of the global south marshal weapons and other coercive means that can parallel, if not exceed or undermine, those of the nation-state (Muggah and Savage 2012). This further reduces state legitimacy, for two reasons. First, citizens give up hope that governments can stem the tide of disorder. Second, such developments motivate states to use militarized tactics to combat civilian armed actors – ranging from the deployment of the military to more routine forms of police violence – that can further alienate the affected communities from the state (Graham 2010).

Complicating this situation is the fact that in these cities violence often stems from illegal or illicit trading in drugs, guns, and other contraband that involves large capital transactions. This has made it relatively easy for violence entrepreneurs and other non-state armed actors to bribe the state's own coercive agents, thereby reinforcing networks of impunity and a lack of accountability that further test the state's legitimacy and its coercive capacity to restore order. For these reasons many urban residents have held little trust in the state, particularly police and the justice system. In response, disenfranchised citizens may feel compelled to take matters into their own hands – either through vigilante acts or, more commonly, by hiring private security guards who act on behalf of individuals and communities but not the larger public, or even at times by siding with the local organized criminals in return for protection. Either way, state capacity and legitimacy decline even as individual and more privatized forms of protection or coercion become the norm, a situation that serves as a breeding ground for ongoing violence.

That organized crime or illicit activities are embedded in everyday urbanism in Latin America has made crime-fighting and reduction of violence major challenges for state authorities. This is because narco-trafficking is usually situated in transnational networks, but relies on nodes and strategic spatial locations in the city to flourish. Its dual character – operating both locally and transnationally – means that both police and military must coordinate their efforts, an organizational challenge for most states. Further limiting crime-fighting capacity is the fact that actors involved in smuggling direct their efforts towards keeping the state out of those key "hot spots" within the city where illicit activities tend to flower. To do so, organized criminal groups use violence to monitor or restrain the state's entry to – and citizens' movement in – those urban spaces where control of markets is key to economic success. Criminals thus invest social, political, and economic resources into efforts to spatially dominate the neighborhoods, streets, or corridors of urban space where their activities unfold.

It is the will and capacity to control space locally while operating transnationally that gives organized criminal cartels, mafia, smugglers, or other pirating forces their greatest coercive and accumulative power (Davis 2009). Yet these same dynamics make policing difficult, especially if it is not well-coordinated across multiple scales of crime-fighting. The extent to which states are effective in policing criminal activities at all territorial or spatial scales will thus determine both the local and national security situation.

In this chapter, we critically examine the spatial dynamics of security policy in an environment of chronic, drug-related violence, considering the implications for state authority and urban life. We start from the premise that the state's capacity to police urban space – and criminal activities within it – is the key to security, particularly in the struggle against organized crime. We frame our understanding of security in debates about the rescaling of state power (Brenner 2004), but contribute to this literature by asking under what conditions the rescaling of state power takes the form of alternative spatial strategies of policing devolved down from the nation to the city, to the neighborhood, and even the street. Using a quasi-ethnographic account of social, spatial, and institutional conditions in Mexico City and its most violent neighborhoods, and later contrasting this experience to that of urban policing strategies in Rio de Janeiro, we ask what social or spatial conditions enable or constrain local authorities' capacities to offer security at the neighborhood scale. The approach we use combines methods and insights from various disciplinary vantage points, including those concerned with urban governance, cultural history (in terms of community), geography (in terms of spatiality), sociology (in terms of resistance), and the law. We not only show that security must be understood as a negotiated process involving citizens and the state in a delimited territorial space. We also demonstrate that the state's power to securitize key locations in the city is iteratively constructed through contestation within and among citizens, criminals, and local authorities, with these interactions mediated by urban cultural history, concepts of community, and the law. The chapter concludes with an assessment of whether the decision to pursue a more spatially targeted strategy of security has brought success, not merely in crime-fighting but also in affirming state power and legitimacy.

Our aim is to further illuminate twenty-first-century transformations in policing and security practices, at least in countries struggling with chronic drug-related violence. Historically, scholars have identified the state's efforts to impose social order and create mechanisms for internalizing such goals among individual citizens as most successful when individuals accept the legitimacy of national authority. In a departure from this presupposition, our research suggests that the local scale remains the most important terrain for reinforcing security and grounding state legitimacy, at least in situations of chronic violence. We argue that the state's imposition of spatial control and social order in delimited urban spaces provides the basis for a new social contract between citizens and the state built around spatial control of targeted spaces as much as through policing. Such strategies not only help legitimize locally negotiated state authority at the expense of national state authority in ways that challenge traditional scales of sovereignty; they also give the state options for providing security through control of urban properties in ways that directly bypass the police as the key agents of the state and its security apparatus. Thus security is transformed from a social and political project in which police are the key coercive force, to a spatial project in which the police are much less relevant and where citizens and local authorities directly negotiate modes of security through contention over given urban territories and neighborhood sites.

Drug violence in Mexico: a problem for the local or national state?

In Mexico, accelerating urban violence has continued for more than a decade, owing to the dramatic expansion of the drug trade and its empowerment of organized criminal cartels and narco-traffickers (United Nations 2008). In 2006, Mexico's President Felipe Calderon launched a full-fledged war against the narcos, strategically deploying military troops throughout the country. Many of these efforts were focused on the US–Mexico border, a key territory in the illicit drug trade. This strategy itself was part of a larger military initiative to control entry into and exit from the country as a plan to secure the entire national space. The Calderon government chose this strategy because it recognizes that cartels control market routes, and has been fighting to claim "ownership" of them given that profit margins owe to the capacity to control entry points into the USA.

Calderon's efforts have had minimal gains from the vantage point of cities. As Calderon's six-year term comes to an end, Mexico still hosts 13 out of the 50 most violent cities in the world, with its most violent, Ciudad Juarez, reporting 229 murders per 100,000 inhabitants (Consejo Ciudadano 2010). With drug cartels violently fighting back against Calderon's militarized strategy, bringing civilians into the range of battle, there has been little room for negotiations within and between cartels and the state, allowing the drug trade to continue. At the same time, changes in the nature and access to the US market have shifted the spatial dynamics of the drug trade. With military activity at the border, smugglers have turned their sights to local markets, seizing new territories and seeking to establish control over urban spaces linked to Mexican consumer markets. The battle over turf in Mexico's cities is part of what drives up rates of urban violence, evidenced by intra and inter-cartel battle in cities – like Monterrey – where armed gangs have occupied freeways and closed down points leading in and out of the city (Milenio 2012).

For drug smugglers the challenge is no longer just how to transport drugs more efficiently, but how to establish boundaries of consumer markets in contested urban environments. Some of this is a byproduct of shifting market activities unrelated to the problems with border crossing. Social trends and shifts in the economy over the last decade created more demand for synthetic drugs within the US market. Subject to slow business cycles, cocaine that flowed through Mexico towards the north became trapped in a depreciated economy and sellers were forced to find new consumers. These changes in consumer preferences shifted the spatial terrain of drug operation: from transport infrastructure, ports and border crossings, to any urban environment where new markets could be found or formed. This process proves to be symptomatic of a country that morphs from being mostly a transit territory into a consumer market. In addition, the government was not prepared for an increase in drug addiction or youth gang-related activities. Having undertaken a national war against organized crime, the state was caught unaware as *narcomenudeo* – small scale, street-level drug trafficking – surged.

By 2010, street-level drug retailing had positioned itself as one of the most profitable illegal businesses in Mexico. This small-scale sector showed profits of more than one billion dollars, and was responsible for national consumption rates totaling close to 500 tons of drugs per year.[1] Figures confirm that in the last decade, problems of drug-related violence in Mexico have trickled down from the national to the urban scale in the form of *narcomenudeo*, in ways that have transformed the urban landscape (Proceso 2010). The relationship between drugs and their consumers, as in any retail trade, is about location and accessibility. This also explains why former "middlemen" for the traffickers are now members of cartels, capable of bringing significant profits by conquering neighborhood territories through extortion, threat, or actual control of real estate. Whether by claiming public hubs of consumption, such as bars, occupation of actual storefronts, or by engaging informal vendors in their service, large swathes of urban territories are becoming identified as outside state control and in the hands of drug traffickers. In cities where this reality is contested by either urban residents or the state, the edges of these so-called "no man's lands" are generating high degrees of violence and insecurity.

Narcomenudeo in Mexico City: can the local state make a difference?

Given the evidence of increasing violence linked to *narcomenudeo* in Mexico's cities (Molzahn *et al.* 2012), it is surprising that the country's largest and most economically vibrant city stands as an exception. Mexico City is no longer one of the top fifty most dangerous Mexican cities, despite the fact that much of the original violence in the 1990s concentrated there (Davis 2006; 2007). Since Calderon initiated his national anti-crime and security strategy, Mexico City has slowly shed its image as intensely violent and is now considered relatively safe, a substantial achievement given its history and size. Some now characterize Mexico City as a relatively secure "island in the middle of a climate of violence that pervades large part of the country," not just because of declining crime rates but also owing to the relative absence of cartel visibility (Olmos 2011).

Such developments are surprising when one looks carefully at the nature, extent, and spatial patterns of *narcomenudeo* in Mexico City, where "micro" drug trade had grown 450 percent in the last nine years. That this rate matches the national average suggests a persistence of drug activities in the capital. Mexico City is considered the fifth most important urban market in the country for *narcomenudeo*, hosting more than 40,000 drug selling points and involving the networked collaboration of more than 200,000 people under the organization of around 40 gangs (Milenio 2010). Most of the drug transactions in Mexico City take place in the districts of Iztapalapa and Cuauhtémoc, in the heart of the city, as well as the neighboring Gustavo A. Madero. Cuauhtémoc concentrates the highest density of *narcotienditas* and reports the largest number of crimes related to drugs in the city (Medellín 2007). Within Cuauhtémoc, there is one neighborhood called Tepito that is the most significant distribution center for *narcomenudeo* in the city.[2]

Evidence suggests that the state's spatially targeted strategies for monitoring and/or protecting urban space help explain the city's successes in territorially pushing back against drug-related violence. For one, recent studies show that large-scale drug trading en route to the USA now avoids territories within Mexico City, with most activities that originally passed through Iztapalapa and

Tepito now finding their way into the municipality of Ecatepec in the neighboring State of Mexico (Olmos 2011). For another, local authorities in Mexico City now use a new spatially focused security strategy aimed at street-level drug trading, in which urban-planning authorities as well as police are working together to monitor and transform micro-land uses in those city neighborhoods where drug-trafficking persists.

The local government's capacities in these regards have been partly enabled by recent legislation allowing city authorities to target particular neighborhoods like Tepito for these new policing operations. In prior years, local governments were not allowed to directly intervene in the investigation, pursuit, or prosecution of drug trafficking because it was considered a "national" crime, falling under the administrative domain of the federal executive. Yet in a challenge to this division of powers and under pressure from local mayors, municipalities, and opposition party leaders, when Calderon launched the "war on drugs" in 2006, he faced pressures from local municipalities to complement this strategy with a reform of the health law that would differentiate large-scale drug-trading from street-level drug trafficking. With this new law, local authorities were afforded an opportunity to craft their own security strategies for fighting drug-related criminal activities, because the change in legislation allows for a conceptualization of *narcomenudeo* as a local activity that unfolds in city spaces. This made it possible for local authorities to police particular areas of the city through novel more territorially targeted strategies that differed from those undertaken by federal police in their national crime-fighting efforts.

Yet even with this legislation, most other cities in Mexico did not take advantage of it to introduce more localized strategies, thus further raising questions about how and why Mexico City did. We can find answers through examination of the controversy over La Fortaleza, a 5,800-square-meter housing estate in the center of one of Mexico City's oldest hubs of crime, the neighborhood of Tepito. The property, known as "The Fortress," was among the largest centers of counterfeit goods and piracy, and the site for commercialization of more than 10 percent of the *narcomenudeo* in Mexico City (Mora 2007). The residents of the property and its surrounding neighborhood had long fought against state efforts to intervene in their community, despite the presence of illicit trading. But in 2007, Mexico City's mayor expropriated the property, using a legal tool justified by the spirit of the new health legislation as the basis for securitizing the city, with aim being to remove *narcomenudeo*. An examination of Tepito and how citizens and the state both struggled to regulate and control urban space both before and after the expropriation will help illuminate the features of the state's rescaling of security strategies on violence and the legitimacy of governing arrangements in Mexico City, then and now.

Tepito: state security strategies before 2006

Although the new health legislation promised to give Mexico City authorities a new mandate for asserting control over urban space in the name of curtailing retail drug trading, the advent of this legislation was by no means the first time authorities sought to intervene at a neighborhood scale to securitize Mexico City. Throughout most of the twentieth century, the Mexico City government tried to use a combination of policing and programmatic changes in urban land-use with the aim of redeveloping central city areas – to mitigate the social, spatial, and economic conditions associated with informality and disorder (Davis 1994) and later crime (Davis 2007). This was especially so with respect to Tepito, long identified as a problematic urban area (Eckstein 1977). Tepito's reputation as a marketplace for the underprivileged, and home to the city's illicit economy traces to the pre-colonial times, when it formed part of the Aztec Tlatelolco market. As early as 1901, Tepito's history as a site of illicit trade created a special form of social cohesion and neighborhood solidarity. The social and cultural identity of *Tepiteños* was built around suspicion of local authorities, a strong historical relationship to the streets and other neighborhood attributes in need of defense from the state, and the neighborhood's market identity (Castro Nieto 1990).

Until the city's main boulevard (Avenida Reforma) cut through Tepito in the first years of the twentieth century, the neighborhood's urban terrain had never been spatially altered by outside forces. Even after that, infrastructure projects that altered the built environment of the neighborhood were few. In the 1970s, the construction of two four-lane thoroughfares (Eje 1 and Eje 2) provoked the first major displacement of Tepito's residents, signaling a major confrontation between *Tepiteños* as an organized entity and what they saw as an overpowering state trying to destroy their neighborhood. Residents were relatively successful in rejecting most of the rest of the urban restructuring elements in the "Plan Tepito."

Their social and political strength in these regards was built on economic foundations. In the 1970s national restrictions on consumer imports created opportunities for local residents to strengthen illegal trade networks by selling contraband foreign merchandise the informal and illicit markets in Tepito. The astonishing growth of illegally imported merchandise, known in Mexico as *fayuca*,[3] had two effects. First, it changed policing in the area, because the huge sums of illicit money passing through the neighborhood created relations of complicity between corrupt police and local traders, enabling the illicit economy to thrive while also limiting the state's capacity to use police effectively for securitizing the neighborhood. Second, these dynamics strengthened the autonomy of Tepito as a socially cohesive neighborhood, thus buttressing residents' efforts to keep local authorities and their interventions at arm's length. Soon Tepito became the hub of the *fayuca* market, serving not merely as a neighborhood-wide informal retailer, but also as a city-wide and national distributor of contraband consumer durables.

The strength of the informal economy provided a barrier to the government's will and capacity to physically enter into the urban territory of Tepito and its centuries old multi-family housing units known as *vecindades*. The street market for *fayuca* and myriad other forms of informal vending expanded and overtook the whole neighborhood. What has been since called the *barrio bravo* (or brave community) became known for its collective form of defense and protection. Here the deteriorating urban infrastructure and strong social networks enacted a flexible yet impermeable membrane that protected illegal activities, rendering the territory semi-independent from city regulators (Castro Nieto 1990).

Things began to change in 1985 when an earthquake wrought major destruction in Tepito, producing widespread damage to the housing stock and bringing many commercial activities to a halt as the neighborhood sought to recover. This situation created the opportunity for government representatives and other state actors to enter Tepito's "forbidden territory," using the post-disaster recovery as an opportunity to reorganize the neighborhood. Now, the logic for entry was not policing so much as urban redevelopment, a framing that gave the government a non-security rationale for its intervention. A redevelopment plan for housing was created, largely financed by the World Bank. With it came external experts, and the "normalization" of the poorest and most heavily destroyed neighborhoods in Tepito and other downtown areas was prioritized (Connolly 1987).

Local authorities in charge of reconstruction initially sought to accelerate the decentralization of those neighborhoods by sending all social housing to the periphery, and redeveloping central city plots for more upscale uses.[4] In response, Tepito residents protested at the site of federal and local government offices located near Tepito (Gamboa de Buen and Revah 1990). However, the earthquake also brought private-property owners who pressured local and national authorities to regularize land, displace tenants, and redevelop the area – a strategy of renovation that threatened to destroy the existent social fabric and cultural life of Tepito residents (Duhau 1987). Protest from both sides stopped when the state enacted an Expropriation Decree laying the groundwork for a new housing program offering land title and property rights to inhabitants with long-standing residence in Tepito prior to the earthquake. The expropriation decree was the first of its kind in the city. By invoking six different laws, it created a powerful spatial tool that would be invoked again almost 20 years later during the expropriation of La Fortaleza. But this was not the only connection to the past.

Tepito was the neighborhood most dramatically altered by the new reconstruction program for the city, with more than double the housing units initially proposed being built, thus producing higher urban densities (Connolly 1987). Furthermore, two of the developments were the massive housing units later called La Casa Blanca and La Fortaleza.[5] These were generic three-story housing blocks of conventional architecture that "fractured" the traditional urban landscape (Connolly 1987). Many of the subsequent increases in insecurity, criminality, and social problems in Tepito can be traced to the altered built environment (Tomas 1994). Tellingly, the building site selected to celebrate the iconic modern architecture of the rebuilt downtown area, displayed on the cover of a publication describing the post-earthquake modernizing project of reconstruction, was 40 Tenochtitlan Street: the building now known as La Fortaleza.

Expropriation for other means: securitizing Tepito, post-2006

The transformation of Tepito into a landscape of intense criminality owed to more than transformations in the built environment after the earthquake. Changes in local employment and commercial activities fueled by the liberalization of the Mexican economy also damaged the neighborhood's social fabric, leading to greater state pressures for intervention.

The approval of the North American Foreign Trade Agreement (NAFTA) in 1994 following post-earthquake housing reconstruction accelerated liberalization of the national economy, making its mark on violence in the city (Davis 2006; Davis and Alvarado 1999). These changes directly affected Tepito because with tariffs on imported goods minimized or removed, the *fayuca* market virtually disappeared, pushing many informal vendors into other black markets. More clandestine and dangerous forms of piracy and the smuggling of counterfeit goods soon grew, with *narcomenudeo* creeping into back-offices and warehouses as a key source of trade. As residents became fearful of dangerous criminal activities and work opportunities declined (with high crime rates, fewer wanted to shop in Tepito), the stable resident population dropped from 120,000 in the mid-eighties to nearly 50,000 today. With these changes, and the loss of residents willing to monitor and protect the community on their own, Tepito became one of the few territories in the city under the total control of violent actors (Pansters and Castillo Berthier 2007).

Faced with a deteriorating community situation and violence in Tepito spilling over into the upscale redevelopment of other downtown areas, local authorities became desperate to secure the area. In 2006, a public debate surfaced over who should have the power to fight crime and impose security measures in the city. A key protagonist in this discussion was newly elected Mexico City Mayor Marcelo Ebrard (2006–12). He supported a restructuring of police and a new special force whose mandate would be limited to the city's historic center, as well as technology-like surveillance cameras to replace corrupt police (see also Botello, this volume). Ebrard advocated approaching retail drug trafficking as a territorial issue, a position influenced by recommendations against violence presented by Giuliani Partners in 2003, when Ebrard was the city's principal police chief (Davis 2007).

After election in 2006, Ebrard's team wanted to hit the ground running, but first needed reliable diagnostics. Because *narcomenudeo* was considered stable and site-specific, Ebrard argued mapping these conditions was crucial. Trustworthy information was needed about where drugs were being sold, leading Ebrard to create a Citizens Observatory, built around cooperative action with residents to obtain information. The Citizen Observatory was the first of two "spatial strategies" the local government developed to securitize the city. It relied on strong relationships with civil society for success. To organize surveillance and data collection, the city was divided into 918 quadrants, with each quadrant headed by a Chief who would communicate with citizens to locate drug retailers, thieves, and other criminal actors. Citizens became proactive in reclaiming their neighborhoods, with reported program participation of 1,300,000 households and more than 30 percent of emergency calls related to drug retailing activities (Asamblea Legislativa 2011). As early as 2007, the security information from this program was translated into an Atlas of Crime that identified drug sale and distribution points in the city totaling 5,174 sites.[6]

Yet information alone was not enough to eliminate the networks of drug-trafficking. This is why Ebrard devised a complementary territorial strategy, inspired by the 2006 health reform which was still facing opposition in congress from those who wanted the war against drugs to remain in the hands of federal authorities working on a national scale under a larger territorial mandate. In pushing for more local power to introduce security measures that scaled down to the neighborhood, Ebrard did not merely turn to the local police, many of whom were highly corrupt and implicated in drug trafficking or contraband in Tepito and elsewhere. Instead, he argued that the best way to eliminate *narcomenudeo* was to isolate and attack so-called territorial hot spots and thus weaken the market logic of the drug trafficking network.

In June of 2007, while still waiting formal congressional approval of the health reform, Mayor Ebrard used the expropriation decree first adopted in the 1985 reconstruction program as the basis for decisive action.[7] The first property to be seized and repurposed was symbolic, and this is where La Fortaleza re-enters the picture. By 2007 it was among the most significant hubs of *narcomenudeo*, a single property responsible for almost 10 percent of street-level retail drug trade in Mexico City and serving as a distribution and strategic site, not merely a retail spot.

When the raid to expropriate the property in 2007 took place, police stated that at least 60 apartments had been used for illegal video production and retail drug trafficking. Such activities had been made possible by the fact that La Fortaleza was an inward-looking complex of fourteen three-story buildings surrounding one large patio, with four apartments per floor for a total of 155 apartments. That it had only four points of pedestrian entry reinforced its reputation as a walled "fortress." Although much documentation of what happened during the raid was concealed by the Secretaria de Seguridad Pública, some was later released to justify the "assertive" nature of the strike by describing the infrastructural ecosystem that had been created within what seemed like an impenetrable structure. Police chronicles showed apartments with double bulletproof doors, multiple high-security locks and electronic alarm systems, secondary entries through the ceiling, *ad hoc* security rooms on the roofs, and false walls that revealed hidden rooms and tunnels hidden behind furniture and mirrors (Proceso 2007). The raid also revealed a major clandestine tunnel, the first of an alleged network of 26 in Tepito, further proving that La Fortaleza and its surrounding neighborhood was indeed an urban trafficking network hub.

During the raid the complex was mostly empty, and information about how much property was seized or numbers of inhabitants displaced was never publicly announced. Even so, some residents were offered a monthly stipend of $200 while they were relocated, and others were given the possibility of indemnification

($25,000 per household) if they had no criminal record and could prove property rights.[8] Both initiatives were intended to establish the state's authority to monitor which populations lived where, while also offering itself as legitimate guarantor of residents' social welfare. The expropriation was also followed by a public presentation of the administration's new plans to redevelop La Fortaleza and all subsequent seized properties as community development centers.

There was little immediate, negative citizen reaction. But soon questions began to emerge from the media and political partisans, who questioned Ebrard's intentions, given Tepito's symbolism and its proximity to tourist zones under development. Some suggested the targeted expropriation was merely a real-estate development project masquerading as a security strategy. An equally controversial set of questions were posed about the authenticity and efficacy of the operation.

Whatever the motivation, the message about the state's new spatial strategies of crime-fighting was clear. Other inhabitants of emblematic yet problematic housing estates from the 1985 redevelopment era, like Casa Blanca, quickly went into prevention mode. They spoke to the media and hung large messages on their facades inviting the police to enter to inspect their contents, just to prove Casa Blanca was "a legitimate and clean community" and not meriting expropriation or destruction (Terra 2007). Owing to citizen outcry, from at least 55 properties planned for expropriation as of 2007, only six were set in motion for recovery; and almost five years later, only La Fortaleza has been razed, in part because the other properties slated for expropriation have been caught up in the judicial system.

Limits to the effective rescaling of state security strategies

After all the controversy, and four years and 10 million (US) dollars later, a new recreational facility and community center of 7,650 square meters opened to the public on the grounds of the former Fortaleza. This was the largest investment ever in Tepito. More than 225 minors will receive special care, as well as psychological and juridical counseling for families, rehabilitation services and recreational activities. In these regards, La Fortaleza was the first, most symbolic, and arguably most successful of the Ebrard's administration's efforts to expropriate land around the city for crime-fighting purposes. It showed how a land-use policy instrument, conceived as a spatially targeted security strategy focused on a key urban site, could be used to disrupt a regional network of drug distribution.

But the costs turned out to be much larger than the city administration had anticipated, leading to a rethinking of approach. What started as a 12-month project turned into four years of uncertainty, with problems encountered in the post-expropriation period practically insuring that this would be the only successful component of a more scaled-out plan to fight *narcomenudeo* and *narcomenudeo*-related violence in Mexico City. Legally speaking, expropriation came to be understood as an expensive and drawn out procedure easily blocked by citizen activists who sought to defend their homes and street turf. It was also a strategy readily slowed down in the halls of justice; even when successful, expropriation required compensation for the affected, which also created incentives for negotiating both before and during the court process.

Most important, perhaps, expropriation was understood as a highly politicized act that brought claims of undue state power in ways that echoed pre-2006 attempts at intervention. The contestation and protest, judicial slow-down, and charges of authoritarian excess this strategy presupposed created a media frenzy and widespread criticism that made it difficult to successfully implement on the larger spatial scale intended by the local authorities. For these reasons, it was not replicated in other locations,[9] and its impact at the La Fortaleza site was limited in terms of its larger overall effect on the neighborhood. Some of this owed to the fact that residents were so well-connected to each other that this single targeted strike only served to mobilize surrounding neighbors in solidarity against further action. This suggests that despite the clear strategic importance of the site within the local drug-trafficking network, and despite the security and crime-fighting logic of targeting this particular building, expropriation failed to fundamentally transform the neighborhood and the types of activities that predominated there, instead mobilizing citizens in reaction against the state's use of this particular strategy.

Faced with limited prospects for using expropriation to sequester other properties, the Ebrard administration began looking for new forms of spatial intervention. There was little enthusiasm for the new policing capacities guaranteed by the 2006 health law, which Ebrard and others had pushed for and which had finally been approved, because other problems with this legislation began to materialize. Part of the concern was budgetary, which explains why this long-struggled-over law has been implemented in only a few states. Giving judicial authority to local administrators to intervene in *narcomenudeo* may be one thing; but finding local resources to pay for these expanded policing activities is another, particularly in locations where the local police may have long-standing relations of corruption that limit their crime-fighting capacity even in the best of circumstances. Although in Mexico City there are more resources than in many other cities in the country, the option of relying on local police for new forms of fighting local drug-trafficking was not ideal, given the history of police corruption, and this was a constraint. It was an especially critical one given the fact that the new health legislation left room for considerable police discretion about what constituted *narcomenudeo*, thus offering new opportunities for arbitrary arrest. This, in turn, could invite negative citizen reaction and the likelihood of protest if the definitional basis for new security measures were to remain in the hands of the police themselves.

These issues were of great concern to Ebrard in the context of longstanding Mexico City police corruption, where trust in police was already low. In an effort to avoid another round of citizen antagonism to his efforts to securitize space, Ebrard thus turned to another legal tool to control property: the so-called law of "dominion extinction," loosely translated as seizure of assets (Asamblea Legislativa 2008; Constitución Política 2009). This spatially targeted strategy could be tailored toward seizing and repurposing assets used in *narcomenudeo* while avoiding the problems associated with direct expropriation of an entire property itself. The use of a similar law for drug-related crime-fighting was first championed in violence-ridden Colombia in 1996 (Gonzalez 2012), and later adopted in Venezuela, Peru, Guatemala, and Chile. Mexico City followed suit in 2008, soon after recognizing problems with the La Fortaleza expropriation.

This new tool gave the local government a legal basis to "depose a person or family from their property when they are considered guilty of a crime" without going through a formal process of expropriation that could end up displacing or disadvantaging numerous residents and their site-based livelihoods.[10] Yet unlike changes introduced by the new health law, when seizing assets the government was not required to prove criminal intent or responsibility of individuals, but only to demonstrate a crime had occurred (i.e. a drug was sold). It provided the city government the right to seize any property used for *narcomenudeo* – from production labs to warehouses and shops – without necessarily justifying or defending this categorization in a court of law either *a priori* or *ex post facto*.

Unlike expropriation, this tool also offered a less politically charged and more bureaucratically streamlined basis intervening in the name of crime-fighting. It neither required compensation for a property nor for the state to prove a given individual committed a crime, only that they were involved at a given location. This also meant the local government could spend less money and time justifying the original seizure, even as it limited citizens' bases for protesting against the government actions. This is not to say that it is a perfect strategy. Questions have been raised by human rights organizations about the legitimate basis for identifying citizens as being involved in criminal activities without actually proving their guilt in court. Yet the law has already been implemented with limited levels of success in a variety of domains, thus giving it some possibility of future success. Of the 113 cases initiated by the city government between March 2009 and February 2012, only three targeted organized crime; and the strategy was seen as so promising that the Federal Congress passed a similar law in 2009 allowing seizure of assets and property related to four types of crime: car theft, human trafficking, kidnapping, and organized crime.

Mexico City is the only city in the country to have adopted this law against *narcomenudeo*-related crimes, perhaps because of prior successes and commitments to using spatially targeted strategies as a mechanism for securitizing its most dangerous neighborhoods. Toward such ends, in 2011 Mayor Ebrard institutionalized this new security strategy by establishing a new security unit to help target properties and identify activities throughout the city that could potentially be the site of "dominion extinction" actions. Among the many gains resulting from this and prior spatial strategies is the city's newfound status as a relatively safe haven, dropped from the list of the most dangerous places in Mexico.

Conclusion

This chapter suggests spatial strategies deployed by authorities in Mexico City in recent years have produced a range of results regarding crime-fighting, security, and citizen response. In the most vulnerable and violent neighborhoods like

Tepito, where criminal activities are deeply integrated into urban life, policing interventions in prior years were limited by social conditions and community resistance, along with police corruption that limited the viability of traditional security strategies. In contrast, newer strategies that emphasized targeted spatial interventions and tied them to legal mandates for expropriating or seizing urban property seem to have had more traction. This owes partly to the fact that crime problems – and the need to turn to heavy-handed legal measures that include expropriation of property – derived from prior housing interventions that changed the character of neighborhood land use.

The chapter also underscored the limits to spatial strategies. When heavy-handed means are used to "enter" into community-run urban spaces, as with the expropriation of La Fortaleza, they generate citizen dissatisfaction and thus are not easily replicated elsewhere in the city. This suggests that room for local state maneuver when using spatial strategies of security – rather than traditional policing models – is also highly circumscribed. While greater criminality may inspire more concerted efforts for strategic spatial interventions and a degree of citizen tolerance, larger community opposition can set limits on state spatial actions and their crime-fighting efficacy. As such, there is often only a tiny window of opportunity for developing viable security strategies in well-organized communities facing violence, spatially targeted or otherwise. With this narrow room for maneuver, strategies that target well-defined sites and properties and that also shun full expropriation have been the most successful, from both the community and security point of view. Such strategies give the state a territorial foothold to remove certain criminal elements without disrupting the entire social fabric of a neighborhood.

What may be most valuable about targeted spatial strategies, however, are not merely their benefits in terms of urban and community improvement, but also their capacity to reduce reliance on police as the main source of urban security. When compared with cities like Rio de Janeiro where crime-fighting in the name of security has been heavily militarized and reliant on police occupation, Mexico City's use of targeted spatial strategies to securitize a location by restoring and reviving key neighborhood sites for the larger community good is relatively laudable. This is the aim that underlies, for example, the expropriation of La Fortaleza and subsequent efforts to turn this contested site into a community development center, as well as the seizure of assets approach. Such strategies departed from the coercion-heavy imposition of police whose aim has been to militarily control entire neighborhoods, as seen in Rio de Janeiro.

While supporters of the Rio program may also argue that their aim is community improvement, use of a militarized strategy of forced displacement of criminal elements and subsequent police occupation to re-establish state control over urban space suggests Rio's is a coercive policing approach, in which violence, abuses of state power, and human-rights violations are more likely (Veloso 2010). Granted, there have been claims of human rights violations in the spatially targeted programs of Mexico, too. When entire neighborhoods remain vulnerable to networks of illicit activities, as in both Mexico and Rio, site-specific, targeted strategies can also be contested. Even so, the case of Mexico City suggests there are benefits to pursuing the slow but steady spatial expansion of securitizing urban territory, property by property, because the nature and form of coercion used is much less discretional and more circumscribed. These strategies hold more potential to enhance overall community buy-in. By combining security and community development aims, and insuring that responsibility for security remains a shared objective, targeted spatial strategies can unite citizens and the state around common goals of urban renovation rather than contributing to resident estrangement.

Notes

1 Statement by Monte Alejandro Rubido García, *Subsecretario de Prevención, Vinculación y Derechos Humanos de la Secretaría de Seguridad Pública*, as reported by *Proceso* (2010).
2 Drugs are not produced in DF. Cocaine comes from Colombia and arrives through the airport or by boat, from the coast of Michoacan. Marijuana comes from diverse sources from all around the Sierra Madre and is housed in warehouses in Centro, most of them within Tepito (Fernandez and Salazar 2008: 68-69).
3 "*Fayuca:* The word meant contraband, illegally imported merchandise: stereos, televisions, calculators, cameras, silk shirts, tennis shoes, blue jeans, blenders, and blouses" (Quinones 2001: 239).
4 Decades of rent control had limited incentives for owners to upgrade rental properties.
5 A total of 13 such buildings were constructed throughout the poorest city neighborhoods. See Renovación Habitacional Popular (1987).
6 According to published information by SSP by 2009 the total number of sites reached 40,000. See http://www.ssp.df.gob.mx/.
7 On March 21, 2007 Ebrard expropriated Tenochtitlán 40 y Jesús Carranza 33, both in Tepito.
8 Only between 40 and 50 percent of residents had property rights.
9 La Ford, in Iztapalapa, was also expropriated a few months later, but as a strategic operation attributed to car-theft networks rather than *narcomenudeo*.
10 For text of the law see Constitución Política (2009: Art. 22).

References

Arias, D. (2006) *Drugs and Democracy in Rio de Janeiro: Trafficking, Social Networks, and Public Security.* Chapel Hill, NC: University of North Carolina Press.
Asamblea Legislativa (2008) *Iniciativa de Ley de Extinción de Dominio para el Distrito Federal*, Mexico City: Asamblea Legislativa del Distrito Federal, 17 September.
Asamblea Legislativa (2011) *Promete Mondragón Atlas de Incidencia Delictiva*, Mexico City: Asamblea Legislativa del Distrito Federal, 29 September.
Brenner, N. (2004) *New State Spaces*, Oxford: Oxford University Press.
Castro Nieto, G.G. (1990) "Intermediarismo político y sector informal: el comercio ambulante en Tepito." *Nueva Antropología*, 9(37): 59–69.
Connolly, P. (1987) "La política habitacional después de los sismos." *Estudios Demográficos y Urbanos,* 2(1): 101–120.
Consejo Ciudadano (2010) *Estudio comparativo de la incidencia de homicidio doloso en ciudades y jurisdicciones sub-nacionales de los paises del mundo*, Mexico City: Consejo Ciudadano para la Seguridad Pública y Justicia Penal.

Constitución Política (2009) *Ley Federal de Extinción de Dominio*, Mexico City: Constitución Política de los Estados Unidos Mexicanos.

Davis, D.E. (1994) *Urban Leviathan: Mexico City in the Twentieth Century*, Philadelphia, PA: Temple University Press.

Davis, D.E. (2006) "Undermining the Rule of Law: Democratization and the Dark Side of Police Reform in Mexico." *Latin American Politics and Society*, 48(1): 55–86.

Davis, D.E. (2007) "El Factor Giuliani: delincuencia, la 'cero tolerancia' en el trabajo policiaco y la transformación de la esfera pública en el centro de la ciudad de México." *Estudios Sociológicos*, 25(75): 639–83.

Davis, D.E. (2009) "Non-State Armed Actors, New Imagined Communities, and Shifting Patterns of Sovereignty and Insecurity in the Modern World." *Contemporary Security Policy*, 30(2): 221–45.

Davis, D.E. (2010) "Irregular Armed Forces, Shifting Patterns of Commitment, and Fragmented Sovereignty in the Developing World." *Theory and Society*, 39(3): 397–413.

Davis, D.E. and Alvarado, A. (1999) "Liberalization, Public Insecurity, and Deteriorating Rule of Law in Mexico City." *Working Papers in Local Governance and Democracy*, 99(1): 95–107.

Duhau, E. (1987) "La formación de una política social: el caso del Programa de Renovación Habitacional de la ciudad de México." *Estudios Demográficos y Urbanos*, 2(1): 79.

Eckstein, S. (1977) *The Poverty of Revolution*, Princeton, NJ: Princeton University Press.

Fernandez, J. and Salazar, A.M. (2008) *The Enemy at Home: Drugs and Drug Dealing in Mexico*, Mexico City: Aguilar.

Gamboa de Buen, J. and Revah, J. (1990) "Reconstrucción y política urbana en la ciudad de México." *Foro Internacional*, 30(4): 677–94.

Gonzalez R., J. de J. (2012) "Extinción de dominio (escenarios internacionales, contexto en México y propuestas legislativas)." Centro de Estudios Sociales y de Opinión Pública Work document no. 128 (May): 23.

Graham, S. (2010) *Cities Under Siege: The New Military Urbanism*, London: Verso.

Massolo, A. (1994) "Las políticas del barrio." *Revista Mexicana de Sociología*, 56: 165–83.

Medellín, J.A. (2007) "Concentran 3 delegaciones 48% del narcomenudeo. *El Universal* (March 13), online. Available at: http://www.eluniversal.com.mx/ciudad/83057.html.

Milenio (2010) "La guerra del narcomenudeo en el DF." *Milenio Semanal* (November 6).

Milenio (2012) "Regresan los narcobloqueos a Monterrey." *Milenio* (February 24), online. Available at: http://www.milenio.com/cdb/doc/noticias2011/e4c4329f7e0945ecf9acff4a c6ac6a59.

Molzahn, C., Ríos, V., and Shirk, D.A. (2012) "Drug Violence in Mexico: Data and Analysis Through 2011." Trans-Border Institute special report, San Diego, CA: UCSD.

Mora, F. (2007) "Anuncia GDF expropiación en Tepito" EsMas (February 14), online. Available at: http://www.esmas.com/noticierostelevisa/mexico/604237.html.

Moser, C.O.N. (2004) "Urban Violence and Insecurity: An Introductory Roadmap." *Environment & Urbanization*, 16(2): 3–16.

Muggah, R. and Savage, K. (2012) "Urban Violence and Humanitarian Action: Engaging the Fragile City." *The Journal of Humanitarian Assistance*, online. Available at: http://sites.tufts.edu/jha/archives/1524 [Accessed: 19 January 2012].

Olmos, J.G. (2011) "The Bubble." *Proceso* (February 25), online. Available at: http://www.proceso.com.mx/?p=263782.

Pansters, W. and Castillo Berthier, H. (2007) "Violencia e inseguridad en la ciudad de México: entre la fragmentación y la politización." *Foro Internacional*, 47(3): 577–615.

Proceso (2007) "Se descubre túnel en predio expropriado en Tepito." *Proceso* (February 24), online. Available at: http://www.proceso.com.mx/?p=205803.

Proceso (2010) "Narcomenudeo genera 13 MMDP en México: SSPF." *Proceso* (March 2), online. Available at: http://www.proceso.com.mx/?p=108133.

Quinones, S. (2001) *True Tales from Another Mexico*, Albuquerque, NM: University of New Mexico Press.

Ratcliffe, J. (2010) "Crime Mapping: Spatial and Temporal Challenges." in A.R. Piquero and D. Weisburd (eds) *Handbook of Quantitative Criminology*, New York: Springer Science Business Media.

Renovación Habitacional Popular (1987) "Programa de Renovación Habitacional Popular en el DF." Progress report, Mexico City: Renovación Habitacional Popular.

Rotker, S. (ed.) (2002) *Citizens of Fear: Urban Violence in Latin America.* New Brunswick, NJ: Rutgers University Press.

Terra (2007) "Exigen vecinos de Tepito detener expropriaciones" *Terra* (10 April). Available online at: http://www.terra.com.mx/noticias/articulo/227932/Exigen+vecinos +de+Tepito+detener+expropiaciones.htm.

Tomas, F. (1994) "La ciudad y las estrategias socioespaciales." *Revista Mexicana de Sociología*, 56(4): 209–25.

United Nations (2008) *The Threat of Narco-trafficking in the Americas*, New York: United Nations Office on Drugs and Crime.

Veloso, L. (2010) "Governing Heterogeneity in the Context of Compulsory Closeness: the 'Pacification' of Favelas in Rio de Janeiro." *Research in Urban Sociology*, 10: 253–57.

8 Legal tails

Policing American cities through animals

Irus Braverman

Today, through our ideologically loaded narratives of their lives, animals "hail" us to account for the regimes in which they and we must live. We "hail" them into our constructs of nature and culture, with major consequences of life and death, health and illness, longevity and extinction.

Haraway (2003: 17)

Introduction

Armed with a baton, Chief Officer Michael Armatys cautiously walks to the back of the house and then toward the barking dog. "Hi doggie, good boy," he says reassuringly. The dog, for his part, is unconvinced. He seems ready to leap free of the flimsy rope that ties him to the tree. I keep a safe distance, just in case the rope doesn't hold. While doing so, I notice the body of a dead bird on the ground, a rugged mailbox barely screwed to the house overfilled with mail, tons of peeling white paint, and a few neighbors that have come out to watch the show. One of the neighbors shouts to us, "They come only at night, and the dog is out in the sun all day." Officer Armatys looks around one last time and then heads back toward the side door, where I am standing. "Will you seize the dog?" I ask. "Well, it's officer discretion," he says. "If the dog was hot and panting back there then it would be a no brainer: we would take the dog." "Although he had some water in a little container, the shelter is inadequate," he continues to explain as he tags a notice on the doorknob. "ESPCA: NOTICE TO COMPLY," reads the top of the notice in bold letters. A yellow highlighter marks that this is a violation of Article 26, Section 353-B of New York State's Agriculture and Market Law.

We are in East Buffalo, a decaying urban neighborhood rife with abandoned houses. Officer Armatys – short, bulky, and dressed in a blue-and-white uniform adorned with badges and protected by a bulletproof vest – knows his way around the City's neighborhoods, pointing out the houses he has visited in the past. He has been doing this since 1973, he tells me proudly. Over the years, he has dealt with thousands of animal abuse cases, made hundreds of arrests, and rescued thousands of animals. "As New York State peace officers," he explains, "we have the power to make an arrest and the power to execute search warrants." Still, "we try to work closely with the police department, and the fire department, and child protection," Armatys tells me. "It's all related, if they are going to beat an animal they are definitely going to beat a spouse. You see that a lot." Bald eagles, red-tail hawks, alligators, and even elephants – Officer Armatys has indeed seen it all. Yet at the end of the day, it is not these animals that concern him the most. "I don't worry about the four-legged animals," he explains. "It's the two-legged animals I am concerned about."

Likewise, this chapter's concern is not so much with four-legged animals as with the stories they relay about how two-legged animals are policed in US cities. Specifically, it is concerned with the role of animals in governing humans in urban space. In this sense, the story of policing animals in the city reveals aspects of the policing of humans. Although legal norms often contain assumptions about human agency, they just as often have assumptions about the *lack* of agency on the part of the animals they purport to protect. As a result, the project of policing animals does not target animals directly. Rather, it is performed through the regulation of humans. Moreover, although seemingly enacted to control animals, animal laws and ordinances are very much a way to monitor and control the conduct of humans. In the city, human–animal relations are expressed, regulated, and surveilled more closely than anywhere else. Such regulations and systems of surveillance define not only the limits of human conduct, but also the limits of the city itself. The "hailing" Donna Haraway refers to in this chapter's epigraph is the call that forms the subject – in this case, an animal subject whose non-humanity is already assumed, that is hailed through its regulation in urban space.

I interviewed Officer Armatys twice, the first time at his office in Erie County's Society for the Protection of Animals (ESPCA). Established in 1867, this local branch of the SPCA is the second oldest nonprofit organization in the country. A few months later, I joined him for a ride-along in the city for what he called a "routine workday." Additionally, I interviewed ESPCA executive director Barbara Carr, ESPCA's Chief Investigator Lindsey Styborski, the organization's Wildlife Administrator Joel Thomas, Director of Animal Control for the City of Buffalo in the Department of Public Works Kelly McCartney, and Buffalo's City Clerk Jerry Chwalinski. In addition to these interviews, this chapter considers the laws and ordinances of both New York State and the City of Buffalo. I draw on these sources to convey a story about how Buffalo polices its nonhuman and human population, what I refer to as "legal tails." The complexities of human–animal interactions are illustrated here through anecdotes that expose the material interactions between humans and animals in the city.

In previous work, I have written about the management of various types of animals in the city. My book *Zooland: The Institution of Captivity* (Braverman 2012c) identifies certain technologies through which animals are known, reproduced, regulated, and – more generally – governed by contemporary North American zoos, which have evolved in cities. In other work (Braverman 2012a, 2012b), I explore how laws categorize animals in ways that attempt to capture their mobility and impose order upon them, and how these laws are resisted and mobilized to reflect the fluidity of these constructs. In this chapter, my focus is on the establishment and enforcement of dog laws in the city and what such dog laws teach us about the regulation of humans in urban space. Although, as they pertain specifically to the laws of New York State and the City of Buffalo, the insights obtained here are relevant to many cities in the United States and around the world.

Companion animals in contemporary United States

The animal studies literature refers to the large mass of nonhuman animals in cities as a "shadow population" or a "subaltern animal town" (Wolch *et al.* 1995: 736). Although these references are markedly true of wild, pest, laboratory, and farm animals in the city (Braverman 2012a), they seem outdated and perhaps even irrelevant with regard to companion (or pet) animals. Walking on the streets of any American city, one cannot but notice the ubiquity of pets. I dare suggest, moreover, that the thriving state of pets in the city, alongside the absence of all other nonhuman animals from this space, is what quintessentially defines the modern city vis-à-vis the country or rural society (in the United States, at least). Expelling farm animals to the country and replacing work animals with machines have been central to the making of the postindustrial city. Although pets are by no means confined to city spaces, they have nonetheless flourished in urban settings and, in this sense, have become a distinctly urban phenomenon. Integral to the average modern urban household in the United States, these animals also provide a justification for forms of policing that take place in the intimate and constitutionally protected setting of the home. Through their pets, human owners become subject to various forms of regulation, including an insistence on licensing and proper care.

Dogs in particular are increasingly a fundamental part of the American family. In August 2011, approximately 78.2 million people owned dogs in the United States (Humane Society of the US 2012).[1] The total expenditure for pets in the United States in 2012 is estimated at $52.87 billion, more than the gross domestic product of many countries (*CNS News,* Manning 2012). Pet health insurance has also become common, as well as malpractice insurance for veterinarians, partly fueled by the success of legal arguments that companion species cannot be valued as ordinary property (Haraway 2008: 52), a point I consider below. Moreover, a recent survey commissioned by *Milo's Kitchen*™ and publicized in "Business Wire" reveals that 81 percent of Americans consider their dogs equal members of the family, while 77 percent admit to talking about their pups as if they are human family members (Business Wire 2011). The survey also shows that 54 percent of Americans consider themselves to be "pet parents" instead of "pet owners" and that, in fact, 58 percent of American dog owners are comfortable calling themselves nicknames such as "Mommy" and "Daddy" when referencing their dogs and 35 percent even refer to their dog as "son" or "daughter." The following sections consider the regulation of dogs and other companion animals and, through these animals, in the policing of humans in American cities.

Companion animals and the law

Whereas a large and growing literature is dedicated to studying direct forms of policing of human populations in the city, little has been written about the regulation of humans through policing animals in this space and about the relationship between these two forms of policing. I have previously argued that laws order the messy materialities of animal–human life into neat classificatory schemes (Braverman 2012a). Animals provide an immense challenge to law's imperial classification project (Douglas 1966). In no place is this more apparent than the city. It is in the city that law attempts to civilize nature, which by definition cannot be civilized. The first and foremost project in the regulation of animals is their classification into distinct legal categories defined by their relationship with humans.

The vast majority of the animal kingdom falls into some or all of the following legal orders: wild, domestic, agriculture, pests, and laboratory animals. Each category represents a particular set of human–animal relationships that translates into specific temporalities and materialities. The city is partly defined by the particular animal–human relationships that are permitted within its territories. Most strikingly, agricultural animals are out, pets are in. This, then, is the city's civilizing mission: to house, control, or even manufacture such animals that in turn may provide a safe mirror to man's otherness and proof of his humanity, while simultaneously proving man's domination over animals and nature.

Animal categories are not always consistent; they change through time and space (Braverman 2012a: 9). City by city and state by state, laws differ about whether and how animals may be kept in urban environments. Animal laws define entire animal kingdoms according to the level of legal protection that they are afforded from human-inflicted harm. Specifically, every animal is classified as either "protected" or "unprotected," prescribing the legal actions humans may or may not direct at the animal and its environment. Although protected wild animals can be neither confined to "wilderness" areas nor excluded from cities, they are nonetheless prohibited from entering into the private urban home. By contrast, pets are welcome inhabitants in the urban household and receive legal protections as city dwellers. Animal Geography scholars Jody Emel and Jennifer Wolch explain that invisible lines

> historically divided the animal world into those worth protecting because they were seen as either part of nature (wildlife) or the human community (pets), and those not worth protecting because they were neither (farm animals) and constituted sources of profit and value.
>
> (Wolch and Emel 1998: 14)

Whereas the city is the quintessential home for animal pets, the country is the only place for farm animals.

In Buffalo, New York, the Animal Control Agency is responsible for enforcing laws that protect humans from pets in the city and the ESPCA enforces animal protection laws, namely laws that protect animals from humans. Such latter protections include Title 18, Chapter 3 of the federal US Code, which governs crimes against animals, birds, fish, and plants. In New York State, Sections 350 through 377 in Article 26 of the New York Agriculture and Markets Law protect certain animals in the city through the following non-exhaustive list of prohibitions: animal fighting; overdriving (overworking), torturing and injuring animals; failure to provide proper sustenance; failure to provide appropriate shelter for dogs left outdoors; prohibitions regarding confinement of companion animals in vehicles in extreme temperatures; prohibitions against the abandonment of animals and against throwing substances injurious to animals in public places; and prohibitions against clipping or cutting the ears of dogs, dog stealing or removing, and seizing or transporting dogs for research purposes (NY Agric. & Mkts Law sections 350-77). Although dogs are defined as human property, legal prohibitions make clear that dog owners cannot do with them as they please, even in the confines of their own home.

Historically, domestic animals were farm and working animals and were recognized as having "intrinsic value" under common law (Frasch *et al.* 2011). In many instances, courts refused to expand the term to include pets, which were assumed to lack intrinsic value (*Commonwealth v. Massini*).[2] Today, the Code of Federal Regulations (CFR) defines "pet" as: "[A]ny animal that has commonly been kept as a pet in family households in the United States, such as dogs, cats, guinea pigs, rabbits, and hamsters. The term 'pet' excludes exotic animals and wild animals" (9 CFR section 1.1). New York State regulations are clearer but still circular in defining a pet as "any domestic animal that has been adapted or tamed to live in intimate association with people but is not limited to, dogs, cats, rodents, fish, birds, snakes, turtles, lizards, frogs and rabbits" (NY Gen. Bus. Law section 750-a). The definition of pets through their companionship with humans allows extension of these legal norms to more and more animal species that enter the city under the rubric of "pet" animals, thus prescribing their protection from humans and legitimizing the policing of owners' homes and backyards.

Alongside dogs and cats, birds, reptiles, amphibians, and other animals have been defined as companion animals, thereby paving the way for their legal entry into the city. For example, in *People* v. *Garcia* (2006), a New York court held that a goldfish was a companion animal under an anti-cruelty statute. In that case, the boy who owned the goldfish regularly attended to it and even named it after himself.[3] The court determined the legal status of this animal based on the particular human–animal relationship that had developed. Courts have also considered various characteristics of the animal, such as the duration of its captivity and its training and behavior, to find that a monkey was a domesticated pet, in one instance (*City of Rolling Meadows* v. *Kyle*), but that a pet monkey was a wild animal under a rabies control statute because monkeys are not a "common domestic species," in another instance (*Keeble* v. *Cisneros*).

Whereas criminal law has made strides in addressing animal cruelty, as reflected in the detailed norms described later in this chapter, pet owners face an uphill battle in the civil arena. When a human is injured or killed due to the intentional or negligent act of another, that individual usually has the right to sue the responsible party for damages and acquire legal compensation for an injury. Yet despite the importance that urban society in the United States attaches to pets, these same remedies are often unavailable for injury to these animals. In the United States, as in many other common law countries, pets are considered the personal property of the owner and have no independent standing in courts (Wisch 2003). As a result, when a pet is injured or killed, it is the owner who must file a lawsuit to recover damages. For the most part, the traditional computation of damages for the loss of a pet is the pet's *market value* – the monetary sum someone else would pay for the identical pet of the same age, breed, and condition. Because most companion animals are not pedigreed or are of mixed breed, they have little or no market value. Thus, their owners are often left with no compensation.

However, US courts are increasingly grappling with the possibility of awarding damages for loss of the pet's companionship and for the emotional distress suffered by the owner (Wisch 2003). Whereas the majority of states still reject such damages for various reasons, a few states have broken away from traditional private property notions, providing recovery for these nonhuman household members. Alaska, Florida, Hawaii, Idaho, Kentucky, New York, New Jersey, and the District of Columbia have all expressed a willingness to accept claims requesting damages beyond market value (Wisch 2003). Causes of action for emotional distress, loss of companionship and, on a more limited basis, damage to the "intrinsic value" of the pet are becoming increasingly common, thereby strengthening the unique status of the pet in the city.

In *Corso* v. *Crawford Dog & Cat Hospital*, a New York court considered the intrinsic value of pets under the law. There, an elderly woman brought a claim for damages after the animal hospital mishandled the euthanization and funeral arrangements for her pet poodle. Upon opening the casket for a last goodbye, she found the body of a dead cat, rather than her beloved dog. The court specifically distinguished a pet from other sentimental inanimate objects. "A pet is not just a thing but occupies a special place somewhere between a person and a piece of personal property," the judge reasoned. "To say it is a piece of personal property and no more is a repudiation of our humaneness. This I cannot accept" (*Corso* v. *Crawford Dog & Cat Hospital*: 183). Certain legal scholars have even suggested that it should not only be incumbent upon the owner to recover for damages to their pets but that the animal itself should have standing, through a legal guardian, to bring a claim (Favre 2000). Such standing would allow the animal to receive damages for their injury, which will likely be awarded to a trust or other fund from which their care will be paid (Chute 2012).

Alongside the increasing remedies granted to pet owners, they are also subject to increased scrutiny in the form of detailed regulations that prescribe certain standards for care. This care includes matters such as proper shelter, restraints, licensing and identification, and medical treatments. In Buffalo, New York, such regulations pertain almost exclusively to dogs. The City Ordinance requires dogs over four months of age to be licensed, restricts the maximum allowable number of dogs to three for the entire premise, and obliges dog owners to physically prevent their dogs from leaving their premises, unless securely held on a leash. Finally, the City Ordinance establishes that it shall be the duty of every dog owner or person having possession, custody, or control of a dog to remove any feces left by said dog on any property within the City of Buffalo and deposit the feces in a sealed container lawfully used for the disposal of refuse.

(Buffalo, NY, Code Chapter 78–19, Article IV)

On the books, humans may bring certain animals into the city, but only under strict conditions so that these animals do not frighten fellow human dwellers and that their feces do not contaminate its streets.

Dog laws are not unique to New York State or to the City of Buffalo. Many other states also mandate rabies vaccinations with accompanying fees and certifications and require precise dog shelter design (Butler 2011). According to an Oklahoma statute, for example, dog breeders must provide at least the following for a dog's enclosure:

The mathematical square of the sum of the length of the dog in inches (measured from the tip of its nose to the base of its tail) plus 6 inches; divided the product by 144, times 2. Mathematically, the space the commercial pet breeder must provide for the first dog equals $2 \times [(\text{length of dog in inches} + 6) \times (\text{length of dog in inches} + 6)/144]$.

(Oklahoma Admin. Code, section 532:15-3-3)

Dog disposal is also heavily regulated by federal norms that define the proper ways to transport and sell dogs (7 USCA section 2131). Again, human–dog relations are intensely regulated and policed to ensure the dogs' proper presence in cities under the strict guardianship (care) of their specific human owners.

Walking the beat: enforcing dog laws in Buffalo, New York

At least three agencies enforce the federal, state, and municipal legal norms that apply to companion animals in the City of Buffalo, New York: Buffalo's City Clerk, the City's Animal Control in its Department of Public Works, and the local SPCA branch. Article 7, Section 109 of New York's Agriculture and Markets Law provides that, "The owner of any dog reaching the age of four months shall immediately make application for a dog license." The section also provides that the application for an annual license must be submitted to the city clerk and that:

The application shall state the sex, actual or approximate age, breed, color, and municipal identification number of the dog, and other identification marks, if any, and the name, address, telephone number, county and town, city or village of residence of the owner . . . . The application shall be accompanied by the license fee . . . and a certificate of rabies vaccination.

(NY Agric. & Mkts Law section 109)

Section 111 adds that each licensed dog

> shall be assigned, at the time the dog is first licensed, a municipal identifica-
> tion number. Such identification number shall be carried by the dog on an
> identification tag which shall be affixed to a collar on the dog at all times,
> provided that a municipality may exempt dogs participating in a dog show
> during such participation.
>
> (NY Agric. & Mkts Law section 111)

Buffalo's City Clerk Jerry Chwalinski explains that his role in regulating
animals is limited to licensing, noting that "the only reason we license dogs
is to mandate people to get a rabies certificate." Chwalinski complains that
although the annual license fee is only $13.50 – "less than a visit to the zoo
or a vet" – many people fail to apply. To deal with such recalcitrant behavior,
every summer the City sends interns to comb its streets and detect unlicensed
dogs. "They walk around equipped with the addresses of licensed people,
looking for those unlicensed people who are playing with dogs in their backyards," Chwalinski tells me. He explains the rationale behind the City's preoccupation with dog licenses: "We want to make sure that the people are
indeed the owners – it's the law." "We manage to catch hundreds of unlicensed dogs every year," he concludes proudly.[4] Thus, the only way for animals to lawfully dwell in the modern city is under the designation of
companion species. The city, for its part, enforces this relationship to the
letter: through the application of licensing and identification requirements,
the city ensures that each and every dog has an owner.

But such efforts of controlling both nonhuman and human populations are
often frustrated. "Unfortunately, I would have to say that 90 percent – if not
higher – of the dogs that we take in are unidentified dogs," says Director of
Animal Control Kelly McCartney in an interview. As a result, the City has no
means for finding their human owners. "Dogs sit here without their owners ever
reclaiming them," McCartney says. She explains that the Animal Control shelter
receives approximately 3,500 dogs per year:

> We bring in strays, seizures, raids, whatever the case may be, and these dogs
> are held for a minimum of 72 hours, after which they become the property
> of the City. If they pass an assessment by a behavioralist, they go up for
> adoption.
>
> (McCartney, Director of Animal Control, interview)

After a dog sits in the shelter for over four weeks without being adopted, it is
transferred to the SPCA or to one of the different dog rescue groups and coalitions
that operate in the City.[5] Dogs are allowed back into Buffalo only when claimed
by a human who assumes the responsibility for their care.

Along the same lines, stray dogs are deemed inherently dangerous and are not
tolerated by the City of Buffalo. McCartney tells me that six officers are in charge of

enforcing "the ordinances of the City of Buffalo to basically protect the people from dangerous dogs roaming at large, unlicensed dogs, nuisances, quality of life issues, that sort of thing." She further explains how a dog may be deemed "dangerous" and the ensuing procedures:

> If somebody were to be bitten by a dog and were to seek medical treatment, or the dog control officers were on the scene or were at least called to the scene, then of course we tell those people that they have an option to file a "dangerous dog" report. So the dog control officers are in court with the dangerous dogs, where a Special Term Judge would then determine the disposition of that dog.
>
> (McCartney, Director of Animal Control, interview)

"It's very, very seldom that a judge would deem an animal for euthanasia," McCartney emphasizes, making it abundantly clear that the City does, in fact, have such powers.

Another means of dog control – namely, of ensuring that each and every urban dog has a specific human caretaker – is the City Mayor's Complaint Line. McCartney explains:

> [A]nybody in the city limits can call, and if they have a complaint about . . . an animal or unlicensed dogs, they put those in and those are printed out on a daily basis and dispatched to the Dog Control Officers depending on districts. The Dog Control Officer visits every single address and checks out the situation and either tickets, gives warning – or, in some instances, depending on the condition of the animals, will remove them. So that's another means of dog control. The phones are constantly ringing and there's also the police radio.
>
> (McCartney, Director of Animal Control, interview)

The City's Dog Control Officers enforce the classification of animals in the City: only pet animals are allowed into the City; as such, they must be coupled with a human caretaker and dwell in a human home; and upon their departure from this home, they are no longer considered to be legal urban dwellers and must temporarily be managed by the City, until it finds them a new human home.

Alongside the exclusion of dogs without owners from Buffalo's streets, specific New York laws enforce certain conduct pertaining to the dogs' management within the home. Article 26, Section 371 of the New York State Agriculture and Markets Law authorizes peace officers to summon or arrest any person that perpetuates an act of cruelty upon an animal protected under the law (NY Agric. & Mkts Law section 371). In Massachusetts and New York, agents of humane societies and associations are appointed as special officers and are authorized to enforce statutes outlawing animal cruelty (Arluke 2004). Erie County's SPCA (ESPCA) is the largest local organization in New York State. Three of its officers are authorized to act as peace officers for the enforcement of animal cruelty laws in the City of Buffalo and its surroundings.

Chief Officer Armatys of the ESPCA is one of the three peace officers. He believes that many animal abuse cases are intertwined with criminal conduct toward humans, implying the broader importance of policing human–animal relations in the city. Officer Styborski states more explicitly: "We see the correlations between animal and human abuse. First comes bedwetting, then animal abuse, and, finally, burglary and murder." Certain human–animal relations are thus thought to serve as early indicators for future criminal conduct toward humans. Because criminal conduct toward animals is often linked with criminal activity that is unrelated to animals, such as illegal betting and drug use, it often necessitates cooperation among various policing agencies. Officer Armatys uses organized dogfights as an example for this type of cooperation. "The organized stuff is really hard to get a handle on because, naturally, you are not going to be invited in. They move all the time, and it's big money for betting," he explains. "There is narcotics, firearms, or some kind of weapons at these fights. That's why, if we are busting somebody, it is always handy to have some kind of police action with you" (Armatys Interview 1). This statement demonstrates how animal police and human police work together to enforce laws protecting both humans and nonhumans. The following example highlights that similar to many other crimes, the causes of animal abuse are complex and that family histories and social and economic contexts play an important role in their trajectories.

> [O]ne time I had a complaint in the City of Buffalo's Eastside about a dog who was short chained to the fence in the hot sun and all that. So I roll up and I see this dog, and the owner comes out of the house and he was kind of irate. I said, "Look, we had a call about this dog here. He is in the hot sun, short chained, he can't move." I said, "He has no water." He was a good-looking pit-bull. I said: "You have to move the dog to a secure area …. Put him in the house or the backyard or the shade where there is water." So he did that. I asked, "Let me see some identification." So he gives his driver's license and I'm writing down his name and I look at his last name and I say, "Don't I know you?" He says, "No, you don't know me." And I said, "Did I arrest you for something some time back?" And he said "No." And I said, "Didn't I arrest you for dog fighting?" He looks at me with a big smile and says, "No, you arrested my dad."
>
> (Armatys Interview 1)

But dog and cockfights are still at the extreme and rare end of human–animal crimes in the City. More often, Armatys' job is to educate the public about how to properly care for their animals. In these everyday instances, the enforcement of humane laws toward animals often bumps up against human prejudices toward other humans. For example, neighbors will use animals as a way to imply racial statements. Armatys tells me that he once received a complaint about Sudanese residents on Buffalo's West Side. In his words:

The way the call went out it said, "Children abusing a cat is occurring right now." So I happened to be in the area and swung by. [T]he guy that made the complaint was white and the kids were black. These kids were sitting there with a string and all they were doing was playing with the kitten. So I talked to the adults and I went to question them and the kitten was fine, there was no problem. The kids were being cared for, too. So I looked at the guy and I said "Really." He just went back into his house.

(Armatys Interview 1)

Animals, humans, race, class, and crime – all play a role in animal law enforcement in the city. The city's density, both in terms of physical space and in terms of population size and location, provides fertile ground for policing human–animal and human–human relations, which then manifest in specific urban laws and regulations.

The regulations that define the place of pet animals also perform an important role in determining the boundary between country and city. Recently, the ESPCA has been investigating an unusual case of animal hoarding by what one ESPCA officer labeled "a rich girl who just thinks she is entitled to do anything." "She had seventy-three horses, fifty-three cats, and four dogs," tells me one of the ESPCA officers. "And the [animals] were living in squalor. There wasn't an inch that wasn't covered in waste, and everything there had feces . . ., and no food, no water." After a veterinarian examination, one horse had to be euthanized. The woman – Beth Lynne Hoskins – was charged with 125 counts of misdemeanor animal cruelty. On May 21, 2012, a nonjury criminal trial on animal abuse got under way in New York's Aurora Town Court. Unsurprisingly, the opening statements received much press. "This is a case of animal abuse by neglect," the Assistant District Attorney said, later ticking off all the horses' names. The Defense Attorney denied this categorization: "It is a breeding farm. Horses are bred and fed. They are like cows, livestock. They are not like dogs or cats" (*Buffalo News* 2012). Such legal arguments reveal the importance of animal classification for defining permissible and impermissible human conduct. While the ESPCA's individual naming of the horses purports to treat horses and dogs on equal grounds and implies the extension of the legal protections afforded to dogs onto horses, the adverse party's claim is that pet laws should not apply to farms or, in other words, that the country is not the city.

Conclusion

> Citizenship across species ties many knots, none of them innocent.
>
> Haraway (2008: 118)

Legal stories about companion animals – especially dogs – illuminate aspects of policing in the American city that are often invisible otherwise. In this sense, dog laws have more than cuddly and furry tales to tell. Such tales expose the underlying classificatory schemes that distinguish pet dogs from farm horses. Alongside their illumination of overlooked human–animal relations, these stories also reveal hidden aspects of law's "humane" enforcement. We learn that while some animals – such as wild geese – are allowed to temporarily pass through the city, not all animals are welcome as permanent residents of this space. Animal laws instruct us which animals are allowed into the city and under what conditions. Beyond regulating the everyday of urban life as it pertains to animals, humans, and the interrelations thereof, such laws and their enforcement help define the very essence of the city. Through its distinct matrix of animal–human relationships, the city is distinguished from its significant other, "the country," where a different set of animal–human relations takes place.

I have shown how certain laws protect humans from specific dogs by identifying them as "dangerous animals" and how other laws grant powers to city clerks to identify and license all dogs in the city, ensuring that every dog has a registered human owner. These clerks have the power to roam city streets, looking for human offenders who have taken the liberty of caring for unlicensed dogs. A hotline system enables telephone calls about stray dogs and other nuisances to flow into the City's switchboard, triggering the dispersal of Dog Control Officers. These officers collect such problematic dogs into their shelters for screening and then release them back out again into the city, this time to more adequate homes. Meanwhile, cases of animal abuse and cruelty are dealt with by a small workforce of nongovernmental officials, who work closely with the City's police and the public to enforce these norms. Such legal tales reveal not only the detailed policing of the interrelations between humans and animals that occurs in the city but also the importance of such policing for the very definition of this space. At the end of the day, whether one has created a proper shelter for his or her dog is a question of legal geography, enforced on both humans and nonhumans in and through the city.

Notes

1 According to a 2012 survey, 62 percent of US households owned a pet (APPA), in comparison with 50 percent in Canada and Britain, and 15 percent in China (Ontario Vet. Med. Assoc. 2012).
2 See, e.g., *Commonwealth* v. *Massini,* where the court refused to expand an animal cruelty statute beyond the precise wording of the statute: "equine animal, bovine animal, sheep, goat and pig."
3 In this case, the defendant stomped to death the pet goldfish of a nine-year-old boy. The Court found that child's pet goldfish was a "companion animal" under the statute, thereby convicting the defendant of aggravated cruelty to animals in violation of the Agriculture and Markets Law section 353a(1).
4 Incidentally, although we have never owned a dog, in summer 2011 we received a series of official notices indicating that the City had evidence we had an unlicensed dog. After the third notice my partner accused the City of harassment and the notices ceased to appear.
5 The Humane Society of the US estimates that animal shelters care for six-to-eight million dogs and cats annually in the United States, of whom approximately three-to-four million are euthanized. Local humane societies, Societies for the Prevention of Cruelty to Animals (SPCAs), and other animal protection organizations urge people to neuter their pets and adopt animals from shelters instead of purchasing them from breeders or pet stores (Humane Society 2012b).

References

American Pet Products Association, Inc. (2012) APPA National Pet Owners Survey. Online. Available at: http://www.americanpetproducts.org/press_industrytrends.asp [accessed 2 May 2012].

Arluke, A. (2004) *Brute Force: Policing Animal Cruelty,* West Lafayette, IN: Purdue University Press.

Braverman, I. (forthcoming) (2012a) "Animal Mobilegalities: The Regulation of Animal Movement in the American City." *Humanimalia: A Journal of Human-Animal Interface Studies.*

Braverman, I. (forthcoming) (2012b) "Animal Frontiers: A Tale of Three Zoos in Israel/ Palestine." *Cultural Critique.*

Braverman, I. (2012c) *Zooland: The Institution of Captivity,* Stanford, CA: Stanford University Press.

Buffalo News (2012) "Contrasting Views as Hoskins Trial Opens." Online. Available at: http://www.buffalonews.com/city/police-courts/courts/article867302.ece [accessed May 21, 2012].

Business Wire (2011) "New Study Reveals That the American Family Has Gone to the Dogs: More Than 8 in 10 Pet Parents Say Their Dogs Are an Equal Member of the Family." Online. Available at: http://www.businesswire.com/news/home/20110502006312/en/ Study-Reveals-American-Family-Dogs [accessed 2 May 2011].

Butler, W. (2011) "Welcoming Animals Back to the City: Navigating Public Health Tensions of Urban Livestock to Achieve Healthy and Resilient Communities." Working Paper Series, Florida State University.

Chute, L.A. (2012) "Helping Animals Stand on Their Own Four Feet: The Inadequacy of Current Legal Rights and Standing for Animals in New York State." (Unpublished paper.)

Douglas, M. (1966) *Purity and Danger: An Analysis of Concepts of Pollution and Taboo,* New York: Praeger.

Favre, D. (2000) "Equitable Self-Ownership for Animals." *Duke Law Journal,* 50: 473: 501–2.

Frasch, P., Hessler, K., Kutil, S., and Waisman, S. (2011) *Animal Law in a Nutshell*, St. Paul, MN: West Publishing.

Haraway, D. (2003) *The Companion Species Manifesto: Dogs, People, and Significant Otherness,* Chicago: Prickly Paradigm Press.

Haraway, D. (2008) *When Species Meet,* Minneapolis: University of Minnesota Press.

The Humane Society of the US (2012a) U.S. Pet Ownership Statistics. Online. Available at: http://www.humanesociety.org/issues/pet_overpopulation/facts/pet_owner ship_statistics. html [accessed 22 May 2012].

The Humane Society of the US (2012b) "Shelters." Available at: http://www.humanesociety. org/animal_community/resources/qa/common_questions_on_shelters.html#How_many_ animals_enter_animal_shelters_e. [accessed 22 May 2012].

Manning, S. (2012) "Americans Spent Nearly $51 Billion on their Pets in 2011." Cnsnews. com. Online. Available at: http://cnsnews.com/news/article/americans-spent-nearly-51-billion-their-pets-2011 [accessed 2 March 2012].

Ontario Veterinary Medical Association (2012) "Pets: An Integral Part of the Family." Online. Available at: http://www.ovma.org/pet_owners/ownership_benefits/part_of_ family.html [accessed 29 May 2012].

Wisch, Rebecca F. (2003) "Quick Summary of Pet/Companion Animal Damages." Animal Legal and Historical Center, Michigan State University. Online. Available at: http://

www.animallaw.info/topics/tabbed%20topic%20page/spuspetdamages.htm   [accessed 23 May 2012].

Wolch, J., and Emel, J. (1998) *Animal Geographies: Place, Politics, and Identity in the Nature-Culture Borderlands,* London: Verso.

Wolch, J., West, K., and Gaines, T. (1995) "Transspecies Urban Theory." *Environment and Planning D: Society and Space,* 13(6): 735–60.

Cases cited

City of Rolling Meadows v. *Kyle,* 494 N.E.2d 766 (Ill. App. Ct. 1986).
Commonwealth v. *Massini,* 188 A.2d 816 (Pa. Super. Ct. 1963).
Corso v. *Crawford Dog & Cat Hospital,* 415 N.Y.S. 2d 182 (Civ. Ct. 1979).
People v. *Garcia,* 812 N.Y.S.2d 66 (N.Y. App. Div. 2006).
Keeble v. *Cisneros,* 664 F.Supp. 1076 (Tex. 1987).

Statutes cited

9 CFR (2012) section 1.1.
7 USCA (2011) section 2131.
Buffalo, NY, Code Chapter 78-19, Article IV (2005). Online. Available at http://www.city-buffalo.com/files/1_2_1/CityClerk/Ordinances/Article 3.pdf [accessed 29 May 2012].
NY Agric. & Mkts Law (2011) section 109 ch. 69, art.7.
NY Agric. & Mkts Law (2011) section 111 ch. 69, art. 7.
NY Agric. & Mkts Law (2011) sections 350–377 ch. 69, art. 26.
NY Agric. & Mkts Law (2011) section 371 ch. 69, art. 26.
NY Gen. Bus. Law (2011) section 750-a.
Okla. Admin. Code (2011) section 532:15-3-3.

Interviews cited

Armatys, M. (10 Oct. 2011) Chief Officer Erie County SPCA, Buffalo, NY.
Armatys, M. (17 May 2012) Chief Officer Erie County SPCA, Buffalo, NY (Ride-along).
Carr, B. (5 Oct. 2011) Director, Erie County SPCA, Buffalo, NY.
Chwalinski, J. (23 May 2012) Buffalo City Clerk (Telephone).
McCartney, K. (14 Oct. 2011) Director of Buffalo Animal Control, Department of Public Works, City of Buffalo, NY (Telephone).
Styborski, L. (13 Oct. 2011) Chief Investigator, Erie County SPCA, Buffalo, NY.

Part III

Policing city spaces and regulating conduct

9 Reconfiguring urban Britain

Policing, spatial justice and postmodern (in)security

John Flint

Introduction

In July 2012, a major controversy erupted over security arrangements for the London Olympic Games when the private security firm G4S was unable to meet its contractual obligations (Syal 2012). G4S had a total of £284m of contracts for outsourced support functions with English and Welsh police forces, including a 10-year £230m contract with Lincolnshire Police (Lister 2012). These contracts represented a structural shift in the organization and delivery of British policing in the wider context of reductions in policing budgets, and the introduction of elected Police Commissioners to provide external 'democratic' oversight (Crawford 2012; Lister 2012). One legacy of the Olympic Games was to be major new housing developments financed and managed by the private sector (for critiques, see Fainstein 2011; Minton 2012). London was already the site of controversial plans by Borough Councils to relocate some public housing tenants to northern cities in response to welfare reforms, including Housing Benefit changes, during a continuing national housing affordability crisis (Flint 2012; Ramesh *et al.* 2012). These controversies epitomize contemporary debates about urban security, the relationships between public and private policing and the right of particular populations to reside in urban space. These debates are magnified by the policing and governance of hyper-visible (Rhodes 2010) global urban events, such as the Olympic Games. But they are equally relevant to urban regeneration programmes and reconfiguring the spatial and social realities of public housing, including its policing.

This chapter locates the contemporary policing of British cities within a wider 'governmentality of unease' (Bigo 2002; Gilbert 2009) responsive to new forms of postmodern insecurities, particularly related to housing. Drawing on housing and urban studies, urban geography, sociology and criminology, the chapter argues that beyond the focus on symbolic arenas such as stage-set events, privatized city-centre developments and gated communities, much of the reconfiguration of urban Britain, and the USA, is occurring through public (and formerly public) housing and its policing. Following an account of these developments, the chapter describes how conceptual frameworks of spatial justice and the right to the city offer important lenses through which to understand the policing of cities. It also argues for a stronger historical detached perspective (Elias 1987) that links contemporary trends to remarkably similar precedents of urban governance and planning. The chapter concludes that contemporary insecurities are linked to a decline in the civic notion of 'shared fate in place' (King 2010: 135) and the reconfiguration of urban governance characterized by a declining public vision for cities.

Postmodern (in)security

The contemporary policing of British cities may be located within sociological arguments that we have entered an age of economic, physical and political insecurity (Judt 2010), characterized by anxieties about the scale and pace of change and declining social solidarities. Our ontological security (Giddens 1990) is reduced as the constancy and permanency of our social and physical environments dissolves in new forms of 'liquid life' (Bauman 2005) and exposure to risk (Beck 1992), inducing what Young (2007) terms the 'vertigo of late modernity.' The overarching narrative is a loss of control and authority, including by police and security services and governments, to forces beyond their reach (Bauman 1998; Judt 2010). Such narratives of decline and crisis are ubiquitous to the urban condition and may not accurately reflect comparative levels of urban security in previous historical periods (see Flint and Powell 2012). But, this conceptualization of an urban crisis and a responsive 'governmentality of unease' (Bigo 2002) has certainly influenced the planning and policing of British and US cities.

Much scholarly attention has been devoted to catastrophic events that render the insecurity and fragility of the urban condition, and its order and governance, prominent and visible. These include the terrorist attacks of 9/11, the London bombings of 7 July 2005 and subsequent failed attacks in the English capital and in Glasgow. They also extend to environmental disasters and systemic urban regime failure, such as the response in New Orleans to Hurricane Katrina (Rhodes 2010) and episodic urban disorder, including in French Banlieues in 2005 and, more recently, the riots across cities in England in the summer of 2011 in which policing practices were significantly implicated (Flint and Powell 2013; Riots Communities and Victims Panel 2012; Slater 2011). Police forces in Britain also have increasingly prioritized responding to urban disturbances related to marches and protests of the English Defence League, an extremist social movement motivated, in part, by insecurities of urban change (Copsey 2010; Jackson 2011). These episodes represent eruptions within a wider urban imaginary and governmentality driven by continuing fears of immigration, urban fundamentalism and anti-social behaviour (Alsayyad and Massoumi 2011; Gilbert 2009; Flint 2009; Home Office 2012).

A defining feature of such governmentalities of unease is the quest to provide spatial solutions to these generalized insecurities (Mann 2012). This is enacted through new forms of architecture, policing and militarism (Graham 2008, 2009; Minton 2012, see also Silberberg and Walby and Lippert, both this volume). Sorkin (2008) terms this 'the garrison state' that aims to control and regulate urban space, whilst simultaneously being rooted in the notion that space is increasingly 'indefensible' and that states are actually governing national insecurity. Attempts to police and secure an 'urban renaissance' in Britain (Atkinson and Helms 2007) – a concept premised on recovery from previous urban crisis – epitomize the key techniques deployed in public and privatized spaces. These include the 'march of the bollards' (Boddy 2008: 286) through a defensive and exclusionary architecture, use of Secure by Design principles, 'open-street' camera surveillance systems, private security patrols, legal mechanisms such as Anti-social Behaviour Orders and Dispersal Orders that ban individuals and/or populations from designated urban areas. Exclusionary architecture and policing practices are extensively deployed in gated communities (Webster *et al.* 2002) and large-scale privately owned, managed and policed developments in major British cities, including Liverpool One and the Stratford City and Westfield complexes in London (Atkinson and Helms 2007; Crawford 2012; Minton 2012).

These exclusionary practices remind us that urban space is hierarchical, segregated and zoned (Mann 2012; Minton 2012). Policing the city requires some control over its visual landscape and is enacted through socio-spatial practices of power (Mann 2012; Minton 2012; Rhodes 2010; Zukin 1991). It is argued that contemporary policing and security techniques are premised upon urban imaginative geographies (Graham 2008) that have increasingly become geographies of paranoia (Sorkin 2008), exemplified by the growth of gated communities (Low 2003; Webster *et al.* 2002) and the Zimmerman case in the USA involving a vigilante shooting a young black man (Barry *et al.* 2012). What Mann (2012) terms the 'psychotopographical landscape of cities' reveals entrenched urban socio-spatial divides, although governmental spatial logics of concealing these divides, and containing the 'problematic' populations underpinning them, are also present (Rhodes 2010). For Minton (2012: xii-xiii) this represents 'the architecture of extreme capitalism' in which 'the privatization of poor housing' is a key feature.

Reimaging, reconfiguring and policing urban residential space

Urban public housing in Britain and the USA has been a crucial stage upon which contemporary anxieties and insecurities are enacted (Mann 2012). Rhodes (2010) argues that the urban poor are excluded from the imaginary of remodelled cities such as New Orleans, and Belina and Helms (2003) describe how zero-tolerance policing strategies in Western European cities are framed within a wider rejection of the industrial past within urban reimagining projects. State and municipal provision of public housing for the working classes were core elements of the welfare state and have been conceptualized, from the nineteenth century, as instruments of urban progress. However, public housing and its populations on both sides of the Atlantic are also regularly used to symbolize urban crisis and to represent a contagious threat to the existing order (Wise 2008; Mann 2012). Public housing in the

US has been subject to increased policing through measures such as the 1994 Violent Crime Control Law Enforcement Act and zero tolerance initiatives (Beckett and Godoy 2010; Flint 2013; Mann 2012).

The architectural and demographic realities of cities in the USA also have been remade in the 'most significant effort to reimage American cities in the last 50 years' (Goetz 2012). Through the federal HOPE VI programme (now Choice Neighborhoods Initiative) and localized variations of this model, entire public housing stocks in cities such as Atlanta, Baltimore, Chicago, Las Vegas and Memphis have been subject to what the Chicago Housing Authority explicitly terms 'A Plan for Transformation' (Goetz 2012; Mann 2012) and in cities such as New Orleans, investment in public housing has been significantly reduced (Rhodes 2010). In England, the Housing Market Renewal programme sought to reconfigure large areas of social and private rental housing in the north of the country, and similar national initiatives have been deployed in many advanced liberal democracies (see Flint 2012). These projects of government have been based on neo-liberal rationalities that public housing is economically, socially and politically 'obsolete' (Goetz 2012). For example, the Cabrini Green apartments in Chicago were labelled in official reports as 'tombstones on quarantined turf' and 'warehouses of terminal poverty' (Mann 2012; see Mooney 2009 on British public housing estates). These governmental initiatives have also been premised on the primacy of securing private sector leverage and increasing the proportion of privately owned and rental stock (Flint 2012; Goetz 2012). In Britain, this represented a continuation of policies such as the Right to Buy and housing stock transfer which aimed to transfer public housing to respectively private individual home-owners and private-debt funded (but still quasi-public) social landlords. In addition to the direct provision of public housing, in both Britain and the USA (through Section 8 vouchers), the state subsidizes large numbers of low-income households to reside in the private rental sector. These developments have had significant consequences for how cities, including their residential areas, are policed.

The zero tolerance policing model pioneered in New York was based on environmental determinism and an actuarial focus upon 'reclaiming public spaces of the city' (Flint 2013). Although the extent to which zero-tolerance policy transfer occurred between the USA and Britain is debated (Jones and Newburn 2002), public housing (or social) landlords in England and Wales were committed to 'visibly upholding standards of behaviour in public spaces' (Flint and Pawson 2009: 426). This resulted in extensive use of Secure by Design and target-hardening mechanisms (new locks and windows, alarm systems and the gating of alleyways), landscaping public areas to create 'defensible space' and the extensive use of open-street camera surveillance systems, though more widely in Britain than in other nations, including the USA (Flint 2013; Flint and Pawson 2009). A key policing mechanism is the expanded deployment and visibility of security patrols and the increasingly diverse delivery of these security services by public, private and resident actors (Crawford *et al.* 2005). For example, the New York Police Housing Bureau provides customized policing of the 338 public housing developments in

New York City (see Flint 2013). In Britain, social landlords purchased additional specialized security patrols from the private sector or directly from the police (Flint and Kearns 2005). Replicating similar processes between the police and private security providers (such as G4S and Lincolnshire Police), the insignia and symbolism of security became increasingly blurred. For example, an 'ASBO patrol car' provided by an Arms Length Housing Management Organization in the city of Manchester included landlord as well as police emblems and responded only to anti-social behaviour incidents rather than other routine or emergency calls (see Flint and Pawson 2009). The use of resident security patrols, such as the tenant patrol and lobby and block watch initiatives in New York public housing in which residents monitor and control access to residential areas (Flint 2013), is replicated in Britain by the continuing promotion of volunteer street patrols within a policy paradigm of local community activism, including 'community trigger' powers that enable residents to compel police forces to address anti-social behaviour concerns (Home Office 2011). In both Britain and the USA, the emphasis within public housing policing often has been on 'quality of life' issues and 'anti-social behaviour', especially problems of noise and young people's conduct (Flint 2013).

A key policing technique within public housing, as much as within privatized city-centre Business Improvement Districts or Development Corporations (Hoyt, 2004; Minton 2012) or gated communities (Low 2003), is the exclusion of individuals and groups from public urban spaces. In the USA, public housing is characterized by strict allocation policies that screen out 'undesirables', severe 'one strike rules' that lead to eviction for criminal offences and the use of exclusion and trespass notice schemes, such as the Not Wanted List of New York City Housing Authority, which bans individuals from public housing sites (see Flint 2013). In British cities, other mechanisms have been deployed. Public and social landlords, as well as the police, have become centrally implicated in the use of Anti-social Behaviour Orders and Dispersal Orders, which may ban individuals and groups from properties and public areas. Despite the UK coalition government criticizing the effectiveness of these measures, these powers will remain through new Criminal Behaviour Orders and Crime Prevention Injunctions (Flint and Pawson 2009; Home Office 2012). British landlords' powers and grounds of eviction have been continually strengthened since the 1990s and are currently being expanded further (Flint and Pawson 2009; Home Office 2012; Scottish Government 2012), with greater use of probationary tenancies, linking evictions to more categories of criminal offences and enabling further discretion to exclude those with a history of anti-social behaviour. However, it is important to recognize that the policing of conduct in British public housing has also, particularly since the mid-2000s, been characterized by intensive forms of early and family intervention. These directly link sanctions such as eviction and Housing Benefit penalties to the provision of holistic family approaches, delivered by public, private and voluntary sector organizations. These interventions aim to address underlying causes of vulnerability and problematic behaviour. Public and social landlords, therefore, have seen enhanced legal powers mirrored by increasing obligations and duties to provide support to the most vulnerable tenants (see Flint 2013; Flint and Pawson 2009). This is a model not currently used in the USA, where there are few programmes aimed at 'socializing tenants' to sustain their tenancies.

These techniques of policing need to be situated within the wider reconfiguration of British cities and public housing and, in particular, changing conceptualizations of the security of urban spaces for particular populations. What is common to these urban restructuring programmes in Britain and the USA is the extensive processes of displacement and the growth of private sector provision of housing and, increasingly, related welfare services (although the models are different, for example, the conversion of public housing to condominium developments in the USA has not been replicated in Britain). At the individual household level, there has been an erosion of the 'elective fixity' of working-class populations (Paton 2012) – that is their ability to continue to reside in particular urban neighbourhoods. This increase in spatial insecurity is the consequence of complex and inter-linked processes of housing affordability crises, gentrification, the use of Compulsory Purchase Orders and demolition to displace and disperse the urban poor within regeneration programmes and tightening conditions of tenure and reframed allocation policies in public and social housing (see Flint 2013; Minton 2012). This is epitomized by Housing Benefit reforms which cap the amount a household may receive and introduce new conditions and restrictions on eligibility, with the result that some Borough Councils in London are seeking to house some tenants in public housing stock in northern local authority areas up to 200 miles away (Ramesh *et al.* 2012). In addition, local authorities are increasingly able to discharge their homeless obligations through the private rental sector, which is already accommodating many of the poorest households. This has generated considerable problems for the police, however, as it has in US cities, in attempting to responsibilize private landlords to control and support these populations (Flint 2013).

Thus, public or social housing in Britain is becoming closer to the US model where it is conceptualized (although does not in reality function) as a tenure of temporary crisis, rather than as long-term residences (Flint 2013). New policies are likely to drop the requirement for a proportion of social housing to be delivered on new housing developments as the private rental sector continues to be strongly promoted (Jowitt 2012). This is combined with significant reductions in a visible policing presence, as police officers, Community Support Officers and neighbourhood wardens are reduced by public sector austerity cuts. It is less certain whether the private rental sector will be encouraged to play a key role (including partnerships with the police) in delivering supportive interventions to the 120,000 'troubled families' identified by the government to require it (HM Government 2012).

This wider landscape of urban housing insecurity provides the context for policing the city. Unlike some previous housing crises, middle-class households are experiencing unprecedented forms of insecurity, for example individuals being unable to access home ownership often until their mid-thirties (in addition to employment-related insecurities). The consequences of this national housing crisis for political resistance, unrest and policing are unclear. For example, one feature of the aftermath of the English urban riots of 2011 was the emergence of the residents' clean-up campaign (De Castella 2011) and attempts by social landlords to evict tenants found guilty of riot offences were challenged by the judiciary. The politics of housing and welfare will be central to how urban citizenship is defined and contested. While the UK government calls for 'a new contract with the British people' in relation to welfare reform (HM Government 2012: 36), it now explicitly acknowledges that it cannot fundamentally resolve the housing and employment crisis (Cameron 2012). Therefore a key dimension of the (imagined) social contract through which government and policing authority always has been based – providing security and predictability to the population (Hobbes 1651) – is being realigned.

Spatial justice and the city

Urban restructuring programmes and policing techniques are socio-spatial practices of power and conflict (Mann 2012; Rhodes 2010; Zukin 1991) which require appropriate theoretical frameworks through which they may be understood and assessed. The work of Soja (1983, 2010) and Harvey (1973) on spatial or territorial social justice recognizes that processes and outcomes are dependent on, and reproduce, urban spaces. As Ferrari (2012) argues, multi-scalar geographies are required to construct these socio-spatial definitions of justice, necessitating a 'polymorphic' understanding of the different formulations of space, including territories, places, scales and networks through which policing and security mechanisms are enacted. Ferrari (2012) further states that competing logics of normative assessment are related to the particular socio-spatial scales at which they are deployed. If, for example, we view exclusionary practices of policing at the scale of particular public housing developments, we may conclude that such practices are justified by the benefits accruing to the wider public housing population, despite detrimental consequences for some individuals. However, if we reframe our lens at the scale of the individual households or the city, we may posit that exclusion displaces rather than addresses problems of crime and anti-social behaviour, and indeed necessitates a continuing and often escalating policing of these problems.

Pinnegar (2012) argues that 'for the city' paradigms are therefore crucial to enable 'more than local geographies' to be deployed which may facilitate concepts of wider publics and an 'urban commons' through which traditional distinctions in interests may be reconsidered within a 'shared fate of place' (King 2010). This leads to concepts of the 'just city,' understood as being underpinned by democracy, diversity or equality (Fainstein 2011) or as the goal of class-based struggles against accumulation by dispossession arising from urbanization's key role in surplus creation in capitalist economic systems (Harvey 1973; Marcuse *et al.* 2009). The concept of the just city is related to theories of 'the right to the city' (Lefebvre 1968; Harvey 2008; Attoh 2011; see also Mitchell and von Mahs, both this volume), which is fundamentally the right to both legitimately participate in (access) and appropriate (occupy) urban space. These rights of access and occupation, particularly for working-class populations, are threatened across a spectrum of policy and policing interventions: from the demolition strategies of urban renewal programmes (Duke 2009; Goetz 2012); through the displacement of households arising from the retrenchment of housing benefit welfare systems (Flint 2012); to the exclusionary practices of restrictive allocation policies, eviction and trespass laws in public housing (Flint 2013) and expanding grounds of conditionality denying urban citizenship rights to immigrant populations (Gilbert 2009).

Pinnegar (2012) argues that the city must be understood, governed and policed as it is inhabited, rather than as a site of property (see also Minton 2012). As Mann (2012) states, public housing developments may be viewed as integral sites within urban systems or as isolated and disconnected 'exceptional' locales which are 'in' but not 'of' the city (Alsayyad and Roy 2006). One of the legacies of British (and French) nineteenth-century urban planning and, to an extent, policing is that (albeit driven by fears of contagion and the inability to segregate disease and disorder and insulate more affluent populations), they were based on both a public vision for the city as a whole and facilitated state intervention that partially superseded the traditional primacy of individual property rights (Smith 1980; Wise 2008). These paradigms of reclaiming space for the public realm and citizenry were usually based on opening up working-class housing areas and their populations to government intervention and ensuring the authority of the state and its agencies (Smith 1980), paradigms that have their contemporary manifestations in zero-tolerance policing in US cities and responses to the recent urban riots in England and France. But, equally, this paradigm of reclamation of the public realm could be applied to the increasingly privatized urban form, including city centres and low-income housing, where the effects of informal and under-regulated renting are already evident (Minton 2012). Two conclusions to be drawn are, first, that the policing of cities requires to be embedded in the wider and proactive governance of residential neighbourhoods, including the provision of adequate housing and supporting the most vulnerable populations rather than deploying tactics of displacement. Second, policing the city needs to be framed within an understanding of the polis, with the implications for multi-scalar interventions and concepts of the public and civic this inherently entails.

Historical perspectives

This emphasis on policing as practices of socio-spatial power and their consequences for conceptualizing of spatial and urban justice needs to be combined with historical investigations revealing how previous urban imaginaries and governmentalities have shaped the topography of cities. The legacies of urban form, including the tenacities of physical segregation and distinctions within populations (Berman 1988), frame contemporary practices. This necessitates detached longer historical term perspectives (Elias 1987; Flint and Powell 2012) that reveal that cities always have been sites of exclusions and segmentations linked to specific urban forms and organization, including policing (Alsayyad and Roy 2006). Recent work has, for example, explored the precedents of the postmodern urban condition in medieval cities (Alsayyad and Roy 2006; King 2010; Woods 2010) while Rhodes (2010) has developed the concept of the 'besieged city.' In this understanding, the medieval city offers a trans-historical analytical category for imagining the present and fundamental components of urban landscapes (Alsayyad and Roy 2006). This enables us to avoid a 'retreat into the present' (Elias 1987; Flint and Powell 2012) and to explore universal social patterns inherent to urbanism in different periods (Woods 2010), such as exclusionary territorial logics (King 2010) that continue to frame contemporary policing and governance techniques.

Using the symbolic sites of gated communities and camps, Alsayyad and Roy (2006) describe how the contemporary landscape of urban citizenship is increasingly fragmented and divided in new urban geographies of competing and territorially exercised 'fiefdoms' or 'miniature sovereignties' (Woods 2010). They argue that these forms of citizenship were also located in medieval urban enclaves and 'honeycombs of jurisdiction' (mirroring the complexity of modern policing and security regimes), including seccessionary spaces of internal regulations and codes that may be seen as ancestors of gated communities and the 'privatized fiefdoms' of flagship urban developments in British cities (Minton 2012). Woods (2010) shows how private coercion is not primarily a modern social development linked to capitalism, but rather that protection and military power were, in medieval cities, primarily a private good and a means of generating wealth through violating city-states' claims to a monopoly on violence.

Contemporary trends in public–private policing clearly have historical parallels, as do attempts by the state to reclaim public spaces in the name of the citizenry (Alsayyad and Roy 2006). However, Alsayyad and Roy's work reconceptualizes our understanding of the city (including the neo-liberal exclusionary city) and requires us to move beyond processes of segregation, walling or quarantine, towards a 'post-city urbanism' in which states of exception (including the exceptional sites of public housing) are the dominant paradigm (see Flint 2009). By this, Alsayyad and Roy (2006) mean that different urban spaces and populations are subject to flexible forms of sovereign power and citizenship and that these spaces of exception should not be understood as beyond or peripheral to the city, but rather constitute the very modalities that produce the city. King (2010) offers a different emphasis, suggesting that whilst urban citizenship was always tightly controlled and policed, commerce and daily routines in medieval shared urban spaces, and above all a shared fate in place, enabled the emergence of limited forms of toleration and cooperation and modest relations of recognition. Governance through free chartered cities became partly grounded on interests and rights, rather than nobility and virtue.

Woods (2010) extends his analysis to bourgeoisie control over public space in the Victorian city, and there are strong parallels between slum clearance programmes of the nineteenth century and the contemporary reconfiguration of public housing and its policing. For example, Minton (2012) refers to the contemporary housing market renewal program in England as 'the twenty first century slum clearances'. Similarly, Smith (1980: 99) reveals how Victorian urban planning was influenced by 'entrenched images of the city and society and class prejudices and stereotypes' (see also Wise 2008). In language resonating with the contemporary description of Chicago's public housing cited above, the 'moral degradation of the poor' was linked to their 'unclean and miserable homes.' Thus, Smith (1980) and Wise (2008) identify key elements of schemes in Edinburgh and London from 1850 onwards as including: public investment being restricted and maximizing economic returns; redevelopment being led by market trends; the absence of voice for displaced residents in clearance areas, ambiguity about obligations to re-house displaced; a focus on technical – rather than political – rationalities; and, perhaps above all, the notion that 'public enterprise should do nothing that private enterprise was willing and able to do' (Smith 1980: 132). These elements replicate almost verbatim the critiques of contemporary urban renewal programmes in Britain and the USA (Minton 2012; Goetz 2012). In addition, as Wise (2008) describes, Victorian slums and their regulation and policing were linked, in complex webs of relations, with slum landlordism and profiteering (often implicating those in positions of official authority over controlling the conduct of, and welfare provision to, the poor). The growing role of the private rental sector in Britain, and the problems of policing its landlords and tenants and meeting the needs of the most vulnerable, would certainly appear to represent one form of 'back to the future.' Identifying the spatial dimensions and contexts of contemporary policing practices requires an understanding of the historical legacies of urban form and governance and their interrelationships. Elements of medieval and Victorian urbanism 'still lurk at the heart of the modern city' (Alsyaad and Roy 2006: 16). Spatial and historical approaches facilitate the policing of cities to be examined within wider conceptualizations of challenges to urban security, including the growing insecurity of access to affordable urban housing.

Conclusions

This chapter has located the contemporary policing of British cities within a wider context of insecurities and a reconfiguration of urban spaces through large-scale regeneration programmes. These processes are characterized by socio-spatial practices of power based on the reimagining of cities that has resulted in the displacement and increasing housing insecurity of working-class populations. In Britain and the USA, public housing is both a symbol of contemporary urban crisis and the site of new forms of policing. These are often exclusionary, based primarily on the regulation of public space enacted through environmental mechanisms, enhanced visible authority and legal measures. However, in Britain, both the police and social landlords also have been involved in forms of housing-based intensive interventions that have sought to open up the domestic realm of 'troubled families' to address underlying vulnerabilities, generating new obligations for agencies to provide support.

The chapter also highlights the importance of spatial and historical perspectives in framing our understanding of the contemporary policing of cities and identifying previous precedents. This also evidences the value of an interdisciplinary approach that draws upon social and ethical theory, using the work of criminologists, geographers, historians, sociologists and scholars working in the traditions of housing, socio-legal and urban studies. Such an approach facilitates a more nuanced understanding of urban policing and also provides concepts such as the just city and right to the city that provide a normative framework through which the processes and outcomes of urban policy may be robustly assessed. Transformations of cities raise significant questions about how the security of urban populations, particularly the poorest and most vulnerable, may be maintained; including their secure right to occupy urban space. This is a necessary complement to concepts of security based on the policing of urban crime and disorder.

References

Alsayyad, N. and Massoumi, M. (eds) (2011) *The Fundamentalist City? Religiosity and the Remaking of Urban Space*, Abingdon: Routledge.

Alsayyad, N. and Roy, A. (2006) "Medieval Modernity: On Citizenship and Urbanism in a Global Era." *Space and Policy*, 10(1): 1–20.

Atkinson, R. and Helms, G. (2007) *Securing an Urban Renaissance: Crime, Community and British Urban Policy,* Bristol: Policy Press.

Attoh, K.A. (2011) "What *Kind* of Right is the Right to the City?" *Progress in Human Geography,* 35(5): 669–85.

Barry, D., Kovaleski, S.F, Robertson, C. and Alvarez, L. (2012) "Race, Tragedy and Outrage Collide After a Shot in Florida." *New York Times*, 1 April.

Bauman, Z. (1998) *Globalization: The Human Consequences*, New York: Columbia University Press.

Bauman, Z. (2005) *Liquid Life,* Cambridge: Polity.

Beck, U. (1992) *Risk Society: Towards a New Modernity*. London: Sage.

Beckett, K. and Godoy, A. (2010) "A Tale of Two Cities: A Comparative Analysis of Quality of Life Initiatives in New York and Bogota." *Urban Studies*, 47(2): 277–301.

Belina, B. and Helms, G. (2003) "Zero Tolerance for the Industrial Past and Other Threats: Policing and Urban Entreprenuerialism in Britain and Germany." *Urban Studies*, 40(9): 1845–67.

Berman, P. (1988) "Mysteries and Majesties of New York." *Village Voice*, 15 March.

Bigo, D. (2002) "Security and Immigration: Toward a Critique of the Governmentality of Unease." *Alternatives*, 27(1): 63–92.

Boddy, T. (2008) "Architecture Emblematic: Hardened Sites and Softened Symbols." In M. Sorkin (ed.) *Indefensible Space: The Architecture of the National Insecurity State*, New York City: Routledge.

Cameron, D. (2012) Welfare speech, Bluewater, Kent, 25 June 2012. Available at: www.number10.gov.uk/news/welfare-speech [accessed 19 November 2012].

Copsey, N. (2010) *The English Defence League: Challenging Our Country and Our Values of Social Inclusion, Fairness and Equality*, London: Faith Matters.

Crawford, A. (2012) "Thinking About Public/Private Relations in Policing." Paper presented at the Public Policing and Private Security Seminar, University of Leeds, 14–15 June 2012.

Crawford, A., Lister, S.C., Blackburn, S.J. and Burnett, J. (2005) *Plural Policing: The Mixed Economy of Visible Patrols in England and Wales*, Bristol: Policy Press.

De Castella, T. (2011) "England Riots: Are Brooms the Symbol of Resistance?" BBC News (Online), 20 August. Available at: www.bbc.co.uk/news/magazine-14475741 [accessed 19 November 2012].

Duke, J. (2009) "Mixed Income Housing Policy and Public Housing Residents' 'Right to the City'." *Critical Social Policy*, 29(1): 100–20.

Elias, N. (1987) *Involvement and Detachment*, Oxford: Blackwell.

Fainstein, S. (2011) *The Just City*, New York: Cornell University Press.

Ferrari, E. (2012) "Competing Ideas of Social Justice and Space: Locating Critiques of Housing Renewal in Theory and Practice." *International Journal of Housing Policy*, 12(3): 263–80.

Flint, J. (2009) "Cultures, Ghettos and Camps: Sites of Exception and Antagonism in the City." *Housing Studies,* 24(4): 417–31.

Flint, J. (2012) "Housing Policy, the Right to the City and the Construction of Knowledge." *International Journal of Housing Policy*, 12(3): 253–61.

Flint, J. (2013) "Policing Public Housing: New York and UK Cities." *Safer Communities*, 12(1): 13–23.

Flint, J. and Kearns, A. (2005) *Evaluation of Reidvale Housing Association Community Policing Initiative,* Glasgow: Reidvale Housing Association.

Flint, J. and Pawson, H. (2009) "Social Landlords and the Regulation of Conduct in Urban Spaces in the United Kingdom." *Criminology and Criminal Justice,* 9(4): 415–35.

Flint, J. and Powell, R. (2012) "The English City Riots of 2011, 'Broken Britain' and the Retreat into the Present." *Sociological Research Online,* 17(3): 20, Available at: www.socresonline.org.uk/17/3/20.html [accessed 19 November 2012].

Giddens, A. (1990) *The Consequences of Modernity*, London: Polity Press.

Gilbert, L. (2009) "Immigration as Local Politics: Re-Bordering Immigration and Multiculturalism through Deterrence and Incapacitation." *International Journal of Urban and Regional Research*, 33(1): 26–42.

Goetz, E.G. (2012) "Obsolescence and the Transformation of Public Housing Communities in the U.S." *International Journal of Housing Policy*, 12(3): 331–45.

Graham, S. (2008) "Cities and the 'War on Terror' In Indefensible Space: The Architecture of the National Insecurity State." in M. Sorkin (ed.) *Indefensible Space: The Architecture of the National Insecurity State*, New York: Routledge.

Graham, S. (2009) "Cities as Battlespace: The New Military Urbanism." *City*, 13(4): 383–402.

Harvey, D. (1973) *Social Justice and the City*. Athens, GA: University of Georgia Press.

Harvey, D. (2008) "The Right to the City." *New Left Review*, 53: 23–40.

HM (Her Majesty's) Government (2012) *Social Justice: Transforming Lives*. London: HM Government.

Hobbes, T. (1651) *Leviathan, or the Matter, Forme and Power of a Common-wealth Eccelesiaticall and Civil*. Harmondsworth: Penguin.

Home Office (2011) *More Effective Responses to Anti-social Behaviour*. London: Home Office.

Home Office (2012) *Putting Victims First: More Effective Responses to Anti-social Behaviour.* London: Home Office.

Hoyt, L. (2004) "Collecting Private Funds for Safer Public Spaces: an Empirical Examination of the Business Improvement District Concept." *Environment and Planning B: Planning and Design,* 31(3): 367–80.

Jackson, P. (2011) *The EDL: Britain's 'New Far Right' Social Movement,* Northampton: RNM Publications.

Jones, T. and Newburn, T. (2002) "Policy Convergence and Crime Control in the USA and the UK: Streams of Influence and Levels of Impact." *Criminal Justice,* 2(2): 173–203.

Jowitt, J. (2012) "Ministers Likely to Drop Requirement for Social Housing." *The Guardian,* 21 July: 6.

Judt, T. (2010) *Ill Fares the Land: A Treatise On Our Present Discontents.* London: Penguin.

King, L. (2010) "Liberal Citizenship: Medieval Cities as Model and Metaphor." *Space and Polity,* 14(2): 123–42.

Lefebvre, H. (1968) *Writings on Cities,* Oxford: Blackwell.

Lister, S. (2012) "Reflections on the growth of police out-sourcing arrangements in England and Wales." Paper presented at the Public Policing and Private Security Seminar, University of Leeds, 14–15 June 2012.

Low, S. (2003) *Behind the Gates: Life and the Pursuit of Happiness in Fortress America,* London: Routledge.

Mann, N. (2012) "Do Not Believe the Hype: The Death and Resurrection of Public Housing in the American Visual Imagination." In C. Richardson and H. Shott-Mytre (eds), *Habitus of the Hood,* Bristol: Intellect, pp. 273–98.

Marcuse, P., Connolly, J., Nowy, J., Olivio, I., Potter, C. and Steil, J. (eds.) (2009) *Searching for the Just City: Debates in Urban Theory and Practice,* Abingdon: Routledge.

Minton, A. (2012) *Ground Control: Fear and Happiness in the Twenty-First Century City,* London: Penguin.

Mooney, G. (2009) "The 'Broken Society' Election: Class Hatred and the Politics of Poverty and Place in Glasgow East." *Social Policy and Society,* 8(4): 437–50.

Paton, K. (2012) "Exploring Housing and Class in Hard Times: Working-class Place Attachment and 'Elective Fixivity'." *Housing, Theory and Society.* iFirst Article, DOI: 10.1080/14036096.2012.683296, 1–17 http://www.tandfonline.com/doi/pdf/10.1080/14036096.2012.683296

Pinnegar, S. (2012) "For the City? The Difficult Spaces of Market Restructuring Policy." *International Journal of Housing Policy,* 12(3): 281–97.

Ramesh, R., Mulholland, H. and Walker, P. (2012) "London Looks to Export Council Tenants." *The Guardian,* 24 April. Available at: http: www.guardian.co.uk/uk/2012/apr/24/london-exporting-council-tenants [accessed 19 November 2012].

Rhodes, J. (2010) "Managing the Parameters of Visibility: The Revelations of Katrina." *Urban Studies,* 47(10): 2051–68.

Riots Communities and Victims Panel. (2012) "After the riots." London: Riots Communities and Victims Panel. Available at: www.guardian.co.uk/uk/2012/apr/24/london-exporting-council-tenants [accessed 19 November 2012].

Scottish Government (2012) *Affordable Rented Housing: Creating Flexibility for Landlords and Better Outcomes for Communities.* Edinburgh: Scottish Government.

Slater, T. (2011) "From 'Criminality' to Marginality: Rioting Against a Broken State." *Human Geography,* 4(3): 106–15.

Smith, P. J. (1980) "Planning as Environmental Improvement: Slum Clearance in Victorian Edinburgh." In A. Sutcliffe (ed.) *Planning and the Environment in the Modern World:* Vol. 1, *The Rise of Modern Urban Planning 1800–1914*, London: Mansell.

Soja, E.J. (1983) "The socio-spatial dialectic." *Annals of the Association of American Geographers*, 70(2): 207–25.

Soja, E.J. (2010) *Seeking Spatial Justice*. Minneapolis, MN: University of Minnesota Press.

Sorkin, M. (ed.) (2008) *Indefensible Space: The Architecture of the National Insecurity State*. New York: Routledge.

Syal, R. (2012) "G4S Contracts at Risk as Private Firms Leave Trail of Chaos in Public Sector." *The Guardian,* 21 July: 18.

Webster, C., Glasze, G. and Frantz, K. (2002) "The Global Spread of Gated Communities." *Environment and Planning B*, 29(3): 315–20.

Wise, S. (2008) *The Blackest Streets: The Life and Death of a Victorian Slum*, London: Bodley Head.

Woods, J. (2010) "Medieval Security in the Modern State." *Space and Polity*, 14(3): 251–69.

Young, J. (2007) *The Vertigo of Late Modernity*, London: Sage.

Zukin, S. (1991) *Landscapes of Power: From Detroit to Disneyworld*, Berkeley, CA: University of California Press.

10 Governing security in public spaces

Improvement districts in South Africa

Julie Berg

Introduction

Security governance has long been undertaken by a number of authorities beyond the state – both in global and local contexts (Wood and Shearing 2007).[1] Many societies have witnessed the rise of multiple sovereignties or new sites of authority, in which a multiplicity of non-state auspices and providers of security operate in networked arrangements (Loader and Sparks 2002). In light of these developments, this chapter explores a system of polycentric security governance – Improvement Districts (IDs) in South Africa – to shed light on the functioning of these systems with respect to the main security auspices and a mapping of their mentalities (ways of thinking), technologies (tools or methods of governing), resources and power. The chapter also investigates how the challenges of public urban space management have facilitated the development of this polycentric system, which in turn has shaped the regulation of public urban space.

The argument here is that polycentricity is a governance adaptation that developed to manage complex urban issues, which in turn has broadened the regulation of space and the scope of policing the city. Regulating urban space may entail both regular law enforcement and the control of individual transgressions but also broader urban space management techniques – exclusionary techniques to manage undesirable populations, reframing and reshaping public and private spaces, architectural design, and use of surveillance hardware – all designed to pre-empt or reduce potential risks of disorder and undesirable behaviour (Beckett and Herbert 2008). In this way, the spatiality of the city – its design, the nature of its private, public and hybrid spaces, and the infrastructural opportunities to change people through spaces – influences the types of security governance configurations that develop (Hentschel and Berg 2010).

'Polycentric governance' is difficult to define. Writing in reference to political systems, Ostrom *et al.* (1961: 831) describe polycentric governance as having 'many centers of decision-making which are formally independent of each other'. These decision-making centres account for each other 'through processes of cooperation, competition, conflict, and conflict resolution' (Ostrom 1991: 225). Polycentric governance systems thus involve a multiplicity of autonomous, independent authorities that have differing capacities, forms of power and resources;

may operate at different scales; are of varied sizes; and have varying degrees of specialization (Ostrom 2001). These governing auspices may be state or non-state, private or public and may include local government, special districts, private associations and NGOs (Ostrom 2001). Polycentric systems of governance may thus operate within an overarching set of rules but where no single overarching auspice monopolizes authority – power is dispersed throughout the system (Ostrom 2001). This is different from a neo-liberal objective where there is a single governance auspice steering a plurality of providers (Osborne and Gaebler 1992). Instead, what is found is a plurality of auspices of governance, coalescing around common issues and geographical spaces.

But what happens when *security* governance is polycentric, when there are not only multiple *providers*, but multiple *auspices* of security focusing on the same issues or operating in the same spaces? Considerable research has been conducted on the interactions between nodes of policing in such circumstances (see, for instance, Abrahamsen and Williams 2011; Dupont 2006). There also has been a long-standing criminological interest in urban spaces (sometimes with a normative dimension), for instance, the theory of broken windows (Wilson and Kelling 1982), situational crime prevention (Clarke 1992) and the analysis of mass private property (Shearing and Stenning 1992). However, there is still a predominant focus by criminologists on individual offenders (policing and punishment thereof), and less on the role of urban space in the development of new security governance configurations and reducing crime and disorder (Eck and Eck 2012).

Improvement Districts (IDs) are a polycentric governance formation but they are also a spatial governance innovation, which compels one to engage with more space/place-based understandings of policing and regulation. To investigate this phenomenon, I conducted empirical research in six urban IDs in and around Cape Town in 2002, 2006, 2007 and 2010, as well as in Johannesburg in 2007.[2] The research was conducted from a criminological perspective using nodal governance theory as a conceptual tool to understand how polycentric security governance systems work – through exploring the 'mentalities, institutions, technologies and practices' of 'nodes' (Wood and Shearing 2007: 27).[3] The purpose of the research was to explore how polycentric governance has emerged as an urban management innovation and the impacts on the policing of space. South Africa is an appropriate case study, since its cities have, over the past two decades, undergone significant changes in how they are policed. The emergence of IDs has been a noteworthy development resulting in the creation of polycentric systems of security governance in South African urban centres. The multiplicity of auspices within these arrangements and the challenges of urban unsafety in South Africa have meant that these IDs have promoted certain styles of policing and spatial ordering hinged on the economic and social needs of specific areas.

What follows is a discussion of the origins and normative framework of IDs and then elaboration of the mentalities, technologies, resources and power of the various authorities that operate within them. From this, I infer the relationship between polycentricity and public urban space formation and regulation.

IDs: a polycentric formation?

IDs are known by several names – Business Improvement Districts, Business Improvement Areas, City Improvements Districts or Special Rating Areas. They originated in Canada in the 1960s and have been adopted and adapted in various countries since, including South Africa (Caruso and Weber 2006). They develop in light of contextual specificities but they may also share some features (Wolf 2006; Ward 2010). This includes the fact that they are usually non-profit, public–private corporations which have been created by (local) government as a supplement or top-up to local government services (meaning they may have to report back to local government on activities and spending); there is usually a petition process involved in their formation; and they operate in localized, demarcated urban spaces (Caruso and Weber 2006; Wolf 2006). These features are present in South Africa. The levies received by IDs may also be supplemented by public or donor money received for urban development projects (Morçöl and Zimmermann 2006b). The public urban spaces they occupy are relatively small, usually only a few city blocks. They may operate in commercial/industrial areas or in a mix of commercial/residential areas (Wolf 2006). The types of top-up services they provide may be anything from consumer marketing to parking control and public security (Morçöl and Zimmermann 2006a; Wolf 2006).

There are many reasons for IDs' existence, but a main one is perceived economic, and subsequent political benefits, especially since the state stands to benefit through drawing-in the private sector to assist in urban revitalization (Clough and Vanderbeck 2006). The creation of IDs is also usually part of larger urban renewal projects underpinned by neo-liberal thinking and a desire to engage with inefficiencies of 'unwieldy' government departments – this is certainly the case in the USA where IDs were created to offset inner-city urban degeneration (Clough and Vanderbeck 2006). IDs in South Africa were originally implemented in the mid-1990s by the state as part of a broader neo-liberal, urban renewal strategy (a strategy started in the 1980s) to ensure more effective delivery of services offered by the state (cleansing, security and so forth). There are thus expectations that they *currently* operate as neo-liberal systems. However, in practice they operate more like 'general-purpose governments'; they are thus not simply providers under state auspices, but instead a complex meeting place of state and non-state knowledge, capacity, resources and power (Morçöl and Zimmermann 2006a: 77; Caruso and Weber 2006; Lippert 2012). This evolution from a neo-liberal to polycentric system has taken place to some extent in South Africa, where in some contexts, the nature of political changeovers, changing demands and challenges of urban spaces, the state's role and the nature of security and insecurity has led IDs to become hybrid systems, with multiple sites of authority.

Thus IDs provide an interesting case since they are not only a polycentric arrangement, but are also a site at which state, market and community governance co-exist in legitimate and complex ways. The formation of IDs in South Africa was a government initiative, with the Department of Provincial and Local

Government driving their establishment. In light of past development deficits and inequities of the Apartheid era, the challenge for local government was to find sustainable, cost-effective and innovative ways to address these imbalances. One means identified to achieve this was public-private initiatives. Thus the Local Government Municipal Property Rates Act or MPRA (2004) was enacted to permit local government to establish IDs and to levy and collect additional rates in those areas.[4] Each municipality in South Africa is entitled to establish its own ID by-law. Rather than outline the by-laws of all South African municipalities, the City of Cape Town will serve as a case study. Cape Town's first ID was created in 2000, followed by several others, many of which are mixed-use (commercial/industrial and/or residential components). Cape Town established its first ID by-law in 1999 and replaced it with a new by-law in 2009 (City of Cape Town 1999, 2009a). According to the 2009 by-law policy the main purpose of IDs is to top-up municipal services for the purposes of 'improving or upgrading the area' (City of Cape Town 2009b).[5] An interesting clause in the policy is the requirement that IDs 'will not be used to reinforce existing inequities.'[6] This speaks to the features of the city itself: Comprising approximately 3.2 million inhabitants, it is diverse in culture and language. According to 2006 and 2007 figures, about 11 per cent of the population was unemployed and 22.5 per cent lived in an informal dwelling (Small 2008, 2009). The City is also the tourist capital of South Africa. Parts of Cape Town are characterized by affluence and privilege, while others are characterized by hardship and poverty, marking distinct inequities in wealth and opportunity. It is within this context that IDs developed.

Regulating space in a polycentric world

Within Cape Town's IDs, several authorities are charged with regulating public space. The main authorities are the Cape Town Partnership; ID managing bodies (including the private security companies contracted by them); the South African Police Service (SAPS); and the City of Cape Town (including Law Enforcement personnel, Traffic Services and the Metropolitan Police Service).

The Cape Town Partnership

The Cape Town Partnership was formed in 1999 and serves as a managing body for the central Cape Town ID and other IDs. This body also provides advice to areas wanting to establish an ID. Overseen by a Board of Directors drawn from both the public and private sectors, it is a not-for-profit organization funded on a 50/50 basis by the City of Cape Town and the private sector. The Partnership is mandated to focus on broader urban regeneration issues within the City, and seemingly beyond it, and it views its activities as being focused on developmental issues that 'go way beyond clean and safe' (although cleanliness and safety are prominent foci too) as well as urban management (Cape Town Partnership 2007). What is interesting about the Partnership is its desire to connect private and public, and affluent and poverty-stricken urban spaces: '... you cannot have an island of prosperity in a sea of poverty, you've got to connect town and township' (Cape Town Partnership 2007).

At the time of my research, the Partnership was focused on making the City centre more accessible through walking tours, outreach programmes (through facilitating visits to the central city from the townships), creating affordable housing and improving public transport:

> ... whoever needs to get here [Cape Town] must be able to get here, cheaply, easily, efficiently and safely through public transport and that's obviously a much bigger, wider set of issues than just here in town. It's a restructuring of the whole public transport system ...
>
> (Cape Town Partnership 2007)

These issues go beyond the abilities and resources of the Partnership, meaning that it has to find other ways to implement its ways of thinking about urban management. The main method of governance used by the Partnership is mobilizing and enrolling what it calls the 'big players' (from both the public and private sectors) to address these bigger issues. Thus the role of the Partnership is 'to constantly try and put the right people together' (Cape Town Partnership 2007).

The aim is to resolve issues within and beyond the City by finding the right nodes able to contribute in a meaningful way. For instance, if the public sector is struggling with an issue, the Partnership may contact relevant persons from the private sector to assist with funding or expertise. The Partnership, itself, may have little knowledge or expertise on the issue at hand, but is able to identify others who do have this knowledge. This entails 'building up trust, credibility [and] contacts' (Cape Town Partnership 2007). As Rhodes (2006: 18) argues, trust is the most important feature of a polycentric system and 'the central co-ordinating mechanism.' Yet trust is also fragile and can be completely undermined by contracts and competition (Rhodes 2006). Thus the Partnership has to constantly enrol others to fulfil its aims. This is an interesting form of power. It is not legal (it cannot force others to confront these issues) or economic, but it works through a capacity to enrol others. This befits a Latourian understanding: to exercise power means to have others perform the action. Thus the exercise of power is shaped by the projects of those enrolled – one's power is affirmed and demonstrated through enrolling others to fulfil one's aims (Latour 1986).

Thus the Partnership attempts to extend beyond its borders through enrolling state and non-state actors to resolve issues bigger than its capacities and resources can accomplish and through making City spaces more public, accessible and inclusive.

ID management bodies and private security[7]

In contrast to the broad mandate of the Partnership, the IDs are parochial by design. They are 'paid' by the ratepayers within demarcated spaces and thus are not obligated or mandated to function beyond them. IDs operate at a local level, focusing primarily on safety within their spaces. A focal concern for many, if not all IDs, is improving physical security. It has been identified as the 'biggest issue' with the bulk of ID budgets spent on contract private security companies (Cape Town ID chairperson 2006). This is in light of the high crime challenge facing South Africa. The types of safety issues vary depending on the type of ID and its needs. For instance, in one industrial ID the main security issues related to informal trading, illegal squatting and the non-payment of rent. In contrast, another ID was created largely because of a spate of murders and/or attacks on students and staff in the public spaces surrounding a local university – the primary challenge thus was to protect individuals from physical assault. In IDs with a large residential component, the main challenges may include home burglaries and theft of and from motor vehicles.

The diversity of issues to be dealt with may impact on how IDs conceive and act on security. They all have particular ideas about urban management of space and the links to safety. However, IDs' main focus is monitoring of and crime prevention within public spaces. They focus on crime prevention through patrolling (foot, bicycle, motorcycle, and/or vehicle patrols) and visibility; information-gathering; problem-solving; and being as proactive as possible. However, they also play a role of order maintenance through monitoring physical signs of disorder – such as illegal parking, illegal dumping, faulty street lights, blocked drains, dirty streets, unsightly spaces, derelict buildings and so forth. In one ID, both security and cleaning were sub-contracted to the same security company and the cleaners, fitted with radios, served a security function as well by reporting crime. The rationale was that 'there is a direct correlation between cleanliness and crime' (Executive Manager of an ID 2006). This is consistent with the findings of Huey *et al.* (2005) and Sleiman and Lippert (2010) in their research on Ambassadors in the USA and Canada, with one ID in Johannesburg for instance, using the term 'public safety Ambassadors' to describe its personnel (Kagiso Urban Management 2007). These Ambassadors engage in a hospitality service while also monitoring signs of physical and social disorder, perpetuating an underlying logic of 'clean and safe' (which stems from Wilson and Kelling's broken-windows hypothesis) (Sleiman and Lippert 2010). In South African IDs, variations of the clean-and-safe and broken-windows logics can be found through the activities of private security – the degree of which depends largely on the rationale of the ID and the types of crime and security issues experienced by that ID.

Similarly, some IDs have established their own social development units to deal with vagrancy where conventional policing does not work or is only effective in the short term. This is in light of the fact that IDs do not have the authority to remove street children off the streets. IDs thus have to work closely with NGOs and/or deploy their own social workers in the City, who *do* have this authority and who can liaise with various shelters to find accommodation for street children. One of the IDs has also created working programmes whereby homeless adults are given skills training and reintegrated into the city, through the provision of jobs (ID Security Manager 2007).

Similar to the Partnership, their mentalities may go beyond their own (legal) powers, capacities and resources. They do not have the same legal powers in public spaces as state authorities – the nature of the space has in a large part determined the types of activities they adopt, but also influences the nature of relationships with others. IDs have to co-ordinate activities of others to be able to fulfil their mandate effectively. For instance, they may have to work closely with government social workers or NGOs to manage vagrancy, as mentioned; with SAPS to manage crime; with Metropolitan police to manage by-law violations; with the City to address public street maintenance issues and so forth. This is consistent with the research of Lippert and Sleiman (2012) who similarly found that IDs used their knowledge collection as a means to enrol other institutions to more effectively fulfil their mandates. IDs manage disorder and regulate through shaping spaces (beautification and cleaning for instance) and deal with unwanted individuals or groups in various ways. One way is through enrolling them in rehabilitation programmes or welfare institutions, as mentioned. Another way is through excluding them by getting them to 'move along' to other parts of the City or out of the City altogether (in one ID for example, a group of vagrants had congregated immediately outside of an ID boundary) (see also Huey *et al.* 2005). An additional way is through extracting them from ID space by having state authorities arrest them for by-law or criminal offences.

As with the Partnership, IDs have power to enrol others, but they also have symbolic power to assert authority over public spaces through their acquired legitimacy (Dupont 2004). Private security in the IDs is 'very recognizable' (Cape Town ID Chairperson 2006). They are known by property owners and play a reassurance role by accumulating much information (Lippert 2012). The IDs are not physically gated, but they show physical signs of a protected space and this gives the ID a different feel. IDs also have social capital 'that allow[s] the constitution, maintenance and expansion of social networks' (Dupont 2004: 86). This is essential for creating and maintaining support networks given their lack of legal authority in many respects.

The South African Police Service (SAPS)

The SAPS are considered the main authority regarding crime control, roadblocks, criminal investigations and general deterrence. This is mainly due to their legal power to legitimately use coercive force and effect arrests, particularly in public spaces. SAPS, as a national institution, is large (with over 190,000 employees), centralized (with national, provincial and local levels) and bureaucratic (South African Police Service 2011). All of this may impact on local level co-operation with other nodes. For instance, some IDs reportedly took years to develop a working relationship with SAPS (ID Security Manager 2007). As stated in the White Paper on Safety and Security: 'The objectives of the South African Police Service are to prevent, combat and investigate crime, maintain public order, protect and secure the inhabitants of the Republic and their property, and uphold and enforce the law' (Department of Safety and Security 1998: 30). However, in practice,

SAPS is the least flexible institution. This may be due to two reasons. First, given its constitutional mandate and the way it has been interpreted, SAPS is more focused on (serious) crime issues first and foremost before 'grime' issues, especially due to the potential draining of limited resources (SAPS Captain and Communications Officer 2007). Second, the large amount of legal, coercive power it possesses on public spaces (compared with other nodes), may reduce the need for it to be more innovative through exploring other ways of asserting power. In other words, SAPS is predominantly focused on law enforcement, crime control and crime prevention. Therefore there is a very narrow approach to spatial regulation as the focus is on individual transgressions and punishment thereof – and its legal power is geared towards fulfilling that focus. However, there is still a strong need by many of the other authorities within the IDs to develop good relations with SAPS, thus SAPS often enrols others and co-ordinates their activities. The IDs (especially their contracted private security companies) have more resources and staff at their disposal as well as certain types of local level information that are sometimes valuable to SAPS. Likewise, SAPS is valuable to other nodes due to its arrest powers but also the types of broader, crime-related information it collects and collates. SAPS initiated and/or participated in a number of security-related meetings with other security role-players. For instance, in some IDs, there were weekly meetings among SAPS, Metropolitan Police and private security to address crime issues. There were also monthly meetings held to address operational issues with respect to comparing crime statistics, sharing information about and/or planning joint operations.

In many respects, other security role-players will support the activities of SAPS. For instance, consider the role that private security may take:

> Well what we do most of the time is compile information for them [SAPS] and we hand it to them and then they obviously do there whatever they need to do. Sometimes when they also have issues like when there is a spate of robberies happening on this corner here, they obviously can't stand with police officers there 24-hours a day, they will inform us to say 'look we are having a concern in this area can you actually look at deploying?' And then we will actually put more visibility in that area to prevent that crime from occurring.
>
> (ID Security Manager 2007)

In other words, due to broader security needs and priority crimes SAPS will often deploy other security role-players to fulfil its mandate:

> [Other security role-players] police certain issues that we [SAPS] can also police but then again they take [the] task away from us so we can specialize on the serious crimes .... Remember police officers have the power to look at all crimes. We can do traffic, we can issue traffic fines; we can arrest people for drinking and urinating in public. But our focus is more serious crimes.
>
> (SAPS Captain and Communications Officer 2007)

The IDs and other nodes may thus buy-in to SAPS mentalities and technologies (temporarily or permanently) by identifying a breach of the law, gathering evidence (or keeping the suspect in place), possibly filling out the relevant documentation on behalf of SAPS (depending on the expertise of the security company involved) and then reporting the incident to SAPS or Metropolitan Police. In sum, SAPS, through its legal mandate and strong cultural capital is able to enrol and co-ordinate other nodes in fulfilling its mandate to prevent and control crime (Dupont 2004). However, this is a narrow mandate relatively speaking, since the IDs focus on much broader issues of spatial regulation and in some areas social ordering may be a greater priority. Thus, SAPS will dominate crime-related governance due to their 'unique expertise' but not necessarily other forms of spatial governance (Dupont 2004: 86).

City of Cape Town

The City of Cape Town is a primary authority within the IDs. It has a duty and the resources to regulate space. For instance, it is mandated to provide services such as cleaning, street maintenance, traffic control, law enforcement, crime prevention, and so forth, and is in charge of broader projects of urban regeneration across the Metropole.[8] Thus the City is legally mandated to provide most services directly impacting on spatial regulation and also charged with the by-laws to give effect to this. The City has thus mandated (directly and indirectly) various other authorities to enforce specific types of spatial ordering through its range of by-laws created to this effect (see City of Cape Town 2007).[9]

But the City is also a 'meta-regulator' of the IDs through ensuring that the ID managing bodies comply with City provisions (Loader and Walker 2006). In fact a ward councillor is elected to attend ID meetings and the ID managing body is obligated to annually report to the City. The City is also responsible for levying the additional rates on property owners in the ID and collecting these rates on IDs' behalf (City of Cape Town 2009a).[10]

As mentioned, the IDs are mandated to top up services that the City is meant to provide, and many IDs have a service-level agreement with the City to ensure this happens. Therefore the co-ordinating relationship is a two-way street, as the IDs may demand service delivery from the City should it renege on its service-level agreement.

Three departments, managed by the City, fulfil the security governance aspect of the City's mandate: the Metropolitan Police Service, Traffic Services and Law Enforcement. There are 1,500 Metropolitan, Traffic and Law Enforcement personnel to cater to the needs of the almost three-and-a-half million residents in the Cape Town Metropole (City of Cape Town 2012). It is thus not surprising that many IDs reported having a more *ad hoc* relationship with these departments compared with the more sustained relationship with SAPS. However, these nodes are authorities in their own right in terms of their specializations. For instance, by-law enforcement is a problem identified by most IDs, and is in fact the focal concern for the types of social ordering within the IDs. Since SAPS specializes in priority crimes, many IDs are dependent on these City security departments for their legal authority and peace officer status to enforce by-laws. These nodes may thus act as co-ordinators of security governance operations depending on the context:

> ... remember we [Metropolitan police] are experts in our own field and SAPS are also experts in their own field. So when it is traffic-related problems they will lean towards us. When it is a by-law related problem they will lean towards us. When it is a hard-core crime-related problem we will lean more towards them ...
>
> (Metropolitan Police Commander 2006)

Whether or not by-laws are effectively enforced has a large effect on the types of spatial regulation that occur. IDs can have a huge impact on how spaces are regulated (in terms of dealing with aggressive panhandling, illegal parking and other traffic infringements, illegal dumping, informal trading and so forth) if they are able to mobilise the state to effectively enforce the by-laws.

Urban space and polycentricity

There is no single, static co-ordinator of (public) urban space regulation within the IDs. How spatial regulation is conceived (as simply controlling crime within these spaces or shaping the spaces themselves) determines which authority takes the lead and co-ordinates the system or parts of it. There are shifting centres of co-ordination in which urban space itself plays an important role. Urban space is therefore not only a physical site in which security governance strategies take place but is itself an important player in governance arrangements.

As a player within governance arrangements, urban spaces have a large role to play in determining the types of relationships between various authorities and the types of power formations created. The demands of urban space regulation, particularly within cities, which at times perpetuate unique challenges of crime and disorder, encourage or may necessitate innovations and 'inventions' (Robinson 2006). This has been found in other studies, such as research on mass private property, where the characteristics of those spaces and their unique needs and challenges perpetuate certain styles of governance (Shearing and Stenning 1992). Different authorities have different powers, opportunities or abilities to manage space. The nature of City (public) space, and the challenges of managing it, has thus perpetuated the evolution of the ID security governance system in the City from a neo-liberal system to a polycentric system. City spaces have contributed towards the redefinition and/or creation of new relationships between (state and non-state) governance authorities. This has resulted in a shift away from the normative aspiration of the state being the centre of governance to recognition that governance has increasingly become more pluralized.

As mentioned, though, urban space is also a physical site in which governance takes place. Thought of in this way, space can be manipulated to shape behaviour (Merry 2001). The normative and empirical shift away from state-centrism means authorities in the polycentric system can demonstrate their power through their ability to regulate space in various ways (Allen 2006). However, the issue then becomes whose authority dominates and the implications thereof. It is clear that ID spaces are not normatively state-dominated spaces as non-state authorities may dominate. For instance, SAPS is conceived of having the most power (legally), but it is not mandated specifically to regulate spaces, but rather to regulate or punish people/individuals. The IDs are mandated specifically to regulate spaces and through their enrolment strategies can have profound impacts on what types of technologies of spatial regulation are more or less active in a given space. In theory, all may benefit from entering that space, but in practice certain groups may be targeted and excluded by virtue of suspicion or over-enforcement of certain by-laws (Miraftab 2007). In other words, IDs/polycentric systems may be accused of being undemocratic. The very nature of IDs means that particular areas are protected from crime and disorder more than others. IDs are also reliant on extra rates from property-owners, meaning they can be very expensive to run. They thus cannot be set up in informal settlements (due to non-rateable property) and may not be sustainable in less affluent areas.

The implications of unequal space-based governance in South Africa are profound, given this country's recent past. Security always has been unequally provided in South Africa and even two decades after the transition from Apartheid rule to democracy, inequalities in security provision persist (Marks and Wood 2007). The key challenge for the state is to address past inequalities and provide services in previously disadvantaged areas, at times by shifting focus and resources from more affluent areas.

The question of whether polycentric systems of governance aggravate or perpetuate inequalities in security provision is however an empirical question. On the one hand, IDs are parochial in nature. On the other hand, IDs, through the relationships of trust and mutual support developed with the state, may extend their activities and support to the state beyond their immediate boundaries. Consider too the activities of the Cape Town Partnership in broadening the accessibility of the City to all groups. New spatial configurations need not be negative and exclusionary but can be inclusive, through the creation of 'special places' and the use of more subtle forms of regulating space (Allen 2006; Hentschel and Berg 2010).

Also, there is a normative argument that polycentric governance should be something to aspire to because it may be more democratic than monocentric systems (where there is one central authority). It is argued for instance by Ostrom (1973) that polycentric systems are more able to assure individual freedoms than large, centralized, bureaucratic systems (as individuals have more opportunities to have their voices heard). This may be the case for IDs; however, for Ostrom (1973), freedom is conceived as freedom of the individual rather than as the freedom of the majority to not be subverted by minority rule (for instance, during the Apartheid era).

President Zuma recently stated in a speech that the (white) minority in South Africa still lays claim to the economy of the country (Myburgh 2012). Therefore, the challenge is now to effectively cater to the rights and needs of the majority through addressing persistent economic and spatial divisions and inequalities. This will require at least a rethink of broader, spatial and economic governance policies and practices within the context of political dynamics, crime and fear of crime, as well as the legacies of racial segregation practices (Herbert and Brown 2006).

Conclusion

Given the development of polycentric governance systems and the decentring of the state as main governance auspice, there is an ongoing normative debate within criminological circles as to the way forward with respect to these systems. The demands of public space management and the nature of space itself may result in shifts in authority and power as well as innovative practices. However, the effects of a multiplicity of authorities on the regulation of space may also raise challenges with respect to aligning polycentric systems to notions of democracy and spatial cohesion rather than in perpetuating exclusivity and spatial fragmentation (Robins 2002).

The conventional normative solution to undemocratic polycentric or plural practices always has been that the state be charged with aligning governance to democratic values and a common good. This is because the state has always been viewed as the means to ensure this. The challenge then becomes how to do this in polycentric systems where the state does not necessarily anchor these systems to democratic values and/or where the state itself has perpetuated democratic inequalities and withdrawn from public space (Loader and Walker 2006; Wood and Shearing 2007). The challenge is to ensure that polycentric regimes aspire to good governance principles as well as to ensure that weak nodes are empowered when strong nodes predominate (Braithwaite 2006).

There are two possible, alternative responses to the claim that polycentric systems are undemocratic. The first takes into account the end of Westphalia and consists of finding a new formula of governance or normative goal besides that of a state-centric ideal. The second response is to adopt the solution of the Ostroms, the nodal governance school and others: that this is an empirical question to be explored on a case-by-case basis (Ostrom *et al.* 1961; Wood and Shearing 2007). Taking into account the seemingly natural evolution of polycentric, spatial formations and the specificities of context this is perhaps the better option. However, whatever option is chosen, the challenge remains to further develop the conceptual tools needed to address the empirical realities of shifts in urban governance.

Notes

1 For the purposes of this chapter, governance means 'organized efforts to manage the course of events in a social system' (Burris *et al.* 2008: 2).
2 The chapter is based on the approximately 50 interviews that were conducted, as well as direct and participant observation within ID areas. I am grateful to Ricky Röntsch for her assistance with the interviews and to the Open Society Foundation for South Africa for their generous funding.
3 A node is a 'site of governance' which has four features: a way of thinking or mentality; methods or technologies for governing; resources to support its activities; and an institutional structure (Wood and Dupont 2005).
4 *Local Government Municipal Property Rates Act,* 6 of 2004, sections 22(1)(a)–(b).
5 Section 5.1.
6 Section 5.2.
7 The private security industry is an authority or auspice in its own right. However, in many respects the ID as client works very closely with contracted security companies and they largely share mentalities and technologies – influencing each others' ways of thinking and doing things.
8 According to the South African Constitution (1996) local government is mandated to provide democratic and accountable government to communities; provide services in a sustainable way; promote social and economic development; promote 'a safe and healthy environment'; and encourage community participation. To fulfil its purpose, local government (municipalities) 'may make and administer by-laws' (Constitution of the Republic of South Africa, 1996, section 152(1) and 156(1)).
9 By-laws include prohibitions on: behaviour associated with begging; behaviour considered to be inappropriate in public spaces (abusive language, fighting, urinating or defecating, bathing, spitting, sleeping, starting fires, being drunk, gambling, etc.); control over parking infringements; control of the activities of public vendors and other types of spatial ordering.
10 Special Rating Area By-law 2009, section 12(4).

References

Abrahamsen, R. and Williams, M. (2011) *Security Beyond the State: Private Security in International Politics,* New York: Cambridge University Press.

Allen, J. (2006) "Ambient Power: Berlin's Potsdamer Platz and the Seductive Logic of Public Spaces." *Urban Studies,* 43(2): 441–55.

Beckett, K. and Herbert, S. (2008) "Dealing with Disorder: Social Control in the Post-industrial City." *Theoretical Criminology,* 12(1): 5–30.

Braithwaite, J. (2006) "Responsive Regulation and Developing Economies." *World Development,* 34(5): 884–98.

Burris, S., Kempa, M. and Shearing, C. (2008) "Changes in Governance: A Cross-disciplinary Review of Current Scholarship." *Akron Law Review,* 41(1): 1–66.

Cape Town ID Chairperson (2006) Interview with R. Röntsch, 23 October, Cape Town.

Cape Town Partnership (2007) Interview with J. Berg, 22 March, Cape Town.

Caruso, G. and Weber, R. (2006) "Getting the Max for Tax: An Examination of BID Performance Measures." *International Journal of Public Administration,* 29(1–3): 187–219.

City of Cape Town (1999) "By-law for the Establishment of City Improvement Districts." *Provincial Gazette,* 5337 (26 March).

City of Cape Town (2007) "By-law Relating to Streets, Public Places and the Prevention of Nuisances." *Provincial Gazette* 6469 (28 September). Online. Available at: http://www.capetown.gov.za [accessed 29 June 2012].

City of Cape Town (2009a) "Special Rating Area By-law." *Provincial Gazette*, 6651 (27 May).

City of Cape Town (2009b) Special Rating Areas Policy 2010/2011.

City of Cape Town (2012) "What the City Peace Officers Do." *City News*, 37: 5.

Clarke, R. (1992) "Introduction." In R. Clarke (ed.) *Situational Crime Prevention: Successful Case Studies*, New York: Harrow and Heston.

Clough, N. and Vanderbeck, R. (2006) "Managing Politics and Consumption in Business Improvement Districts: The Geographies of Political Activism on Burlington, Vermont's Church Street Marketplace." *Urban Studies*, 43(12): 2261–84.

Department of Safety and Security (1998) White Paper on Safety and Security: In Service of Safety 1999-2004, Pretoria: Department of Safety and Security.

Dupont, B. (2004) "Security in the Age of Networks." *Policing and Society*, 14(1): 76–91.

Dupont, B. (2006) "Delivering Security through Networks: Surveying the Relational Landscape of Security Managers in an Urban Setting." *Crime, Law & Social Change*, 45(3): 165–84.

Eck, J. and Eck, E. (2012) "Crime Place and Pollution: Expanding Crime Reduction Options through a Regulatory Approach." *Criminology & Public Policy*, 11(2): 281–316.

Executive Manager of an ID (2006) Interview with R. Röntsch, 6 October, Cape Town.

Hentschel, C. and Berg, J. (2010) "Policing South African Cities: Plural and Spatial Perspectives." In M. Cools, S. De Kimpe, A. Dormaels, M. Easton, E. Enhus, P. Ponsaers, G. Vande Walle and A. Verhage (eds) *Police, Policing, Policy and the City in Europe*, The Hague: Eleven International Publishing.

Herbert, S. and Brown, E. (2006) "Conceptions of Space and Crime in the Punitive Neoliberal City." *Antipode*, 38(4): 755–77.

Huey, L., Ericson, R., and Haggerty, K. (2005) "Policing Fantasy City." In D. Cooley (ed.) *Re-imagining Policing in Canada*, Toronto: University of Toronto Press.

ID Security Manager (2007) Interview with J. Berg, 19 March, Cape Town.

Kagiso Urban Management (2007) Interview with J. Berg, 6 December, Johannesburg.

Latour, B. (1986) "The Powers of Association." In J. Law (ed.) *Power, Action and Belief: A New Sociology of Knowledge?*, London: Routledge.

Lippert, R. (2012) "'Clean and Safe' Passage: Business Improvement Districts, Urban Security Modes, and Knowledge Brokers." *European Urban and Regional Studies*, 19(2): 167–80.

Lippert, R. and Sleiman, M. (2012) "Ambassadors, Business Improvement District Governance and Knowledge of the Urban." *Urban Studies*, 49(1): 61–76.

Loader, I. and Sparks, R. (2002) "Contemporary Landscapes of Crime, Order, and Control: Governance, Risk, and Globalization." In M. Maguire, R. Morgan, and R. Reiner (eds) *The Oxford Handbook of Criminology* (3rd edn), Oxford: Oxford University Press.

Loader, I. and Walker, N. (2006) "Necessary Virtues: The Legitimate Place of the State in the Production of Security." In J. Wood and B. Dupont (eds) *Democracy, Society and the Governance of Security*, Cambridge: Cambridge University Press.

Marks, M. and Wood, J. (2007) "The South African Policing 'Nexus': Charting the Policing Landscape in Durban." *South African Review of Sociology*, 38(2): 134–60.

Merry, S. (2001) "Spatial Governmentality and the New Urban Social Order: Controlling Gender Violence Through Law." *American Anthropologist*, 103(1): 16–29.

Metropolitan Police Commander (2006) Interview with R. Röntsch, 8 November, Cape Town.

Miraftab, F. (2007) "Governing Post Apartheid Spatiality: Implementing City Improvement Districts in Cape Town." *Antipode*, 39(4): 602–26.

Morçöl, G. and Zimmermann, U. (2006a) "Metropolitan Governance and Business Improvement Districts." *International Journal of Public Administration*, 29(1–3): 5–29.

Morçöl, G. and Zimmermann, U. (2006b) "Community Improvement Districts in Metropolitan Atlanta." *International Journal of Public Administration*, 29(1–3): 77–105.

Myburgh, J. (2012) "South Africa's Zuma wants to Wrest Economy from White Minority." *Jakarta Globe* (June). Online. Available at: http://www.thejakartaglobe.com/afp/safricas-zuma-wants-to-wrest-economy-from-white-minority/526982 [accessed 29 June 2012].

Osborne, D. and Gaebler, T. (1992) *Reinventing Government: How the Entrepreneurial Spirit is Transforming the Public Sector,* New York: Plume.

Ostrom, E. (2001) "Vulnerability and Polycentric Governance Systems." *Newsletter of the International Human Dimensions Programme on Global Environmental Change,* 3: 1–4.

Ostrom, V. (1973) "Can Federalism Make a Difference?" *Publius,* 3(2): 197–237.

Ostrom, V. (1991) *The Meaning of American Federalism: Constituting a Self-governing Society,* San Francisco: Institute for Contemporary Studies.

Ostrom, V., Tiebout, C., and Warren, R. (1961) "The Organization of Government in Metropolitan Areas: A Theoretical Inquiry." *The American Political Science Review,* 55(4): 831–42.

Rhodes, R. (2006) "The Sour Laws of Network Governance." In J. Fleming and J. Wood (eds) *Fighting Crime Together: The Challenges of Policing and Security Networks,* Sydney: University of New South Wales Press.

Robins, S. (2002) "At the Limits of Spatial Governmentality: A Message from the Tip of Africa." *Third World Quarterly,* 23(4): 665–89.

Robinson, J. (2006) "Inventions and Interventions: Transforming Cities – An Introduction." *Urban Studies,* 43(2): 251–58.

SAPS Captain and Communications Officer (2007) Interview with J. Berg, 11 April, Cape Town.

Shearing, C. and Stenning, P. (1992) "From the Panopticon to Disney World: The Development of Discipline." In R. Clarke (ed.) *Situational Crime Prevention: Successful Case Studies,* New York: Harrow and Heston.

Sleiman, M. and Lippert, R. (2010) "Downtown Ambassadors, Police Relations and 'Clean and Safe' Security." *Policing and Society,* 20(3): 316–35.

Small, K. (2008) 2006 General Household Survey Analysis for Cape Town Summary, City of Cape Town: Strategic Development Information and GIS Department, Strategic Information Branch. Online. Available at: http://www.capetown.gov.za/en/stats/CityReports/Documents/Households/GHS%202006%20Report%20Summary.pdf [accessed 13 August 2012].

Small, K. (2009) Labour Force Trends in Cape Town September 2005 to September `2007, City of Cape Town: Strategic Development Information and GIS Department Strategic Information Branch. Online. Available at: http://www.capetown.gov.za/en/stats/CityReports/Documents/LFS_Trends_Report__Sep_2005_to_Sep_2007.pdf [accessed 13 August 2012].

South African Police Service (2011) Annual Report of the South African Police Service 2010/2011, Pretoria: Government Printers.

Ward, K. (2010) "Entrepreneurial Urbanism and Business Improvement Districts in the State of Wisconsin: A Cosmopolitan Critique." *Annals of the Association of American Geographers,* 100(5): 1177–96.

Wilson, J. and Kelling, G. (1982) "Broken Windows." *Atlantic Monthly,* 249(3): 29–37.

Wolf, J. (2006) "Urban Governance and Business Improvement Districts: The Washington, DC BIDs." *International Journal of Public Administration,* 29(1–3): 53–75.

Wood, J. and Dupont, B. (2005) *Democracy, Society and the Governance of Security,* Cambridge: Cambridge University Press.

Wood, J. and Shearing, C. (2007) *Imagining Security,* Cullompton: Willan.

11 Get lost!

The impact of punitive policy on homeless people's life chances in Berlin

Jürgen von Mahs

Introduction

"Get lost," in German "*verschwinde*," "*hau' ab*," or "*verpiss Dich*," is something homeless people in Berlin, Germany, hear often. However, not all homeless persons are the target of such condescending words or of more severe consequences that threatening vocabulary can accompany. Rather, upon analyzing the experiences of 28 homeless service users in Berlin I found that there are substantial differences in the encounters with and consequences of punitive policy in public, semi-public, and private places on homeless people's immediate and long-term chances to overcome homelessness.

This chapter is based on an ethnographic investigation I conducted in Berlin in 1998 and 1999 – at the height of the most recent homelessness crisis. I provide a more nuanced analysis of the impact of public policy, including punitive and social policy, on homeless people's immediate life circumstances and long-term attempts to overcome homelessness. I demonstrate that homeless people's experiences with public policy depend on their life course trajectories, that is, how they lived their lives prior to becoming homeless. Specifically, I show that the extent of "normality" in these people's lives is determined by how and how often punitive policy was encountered. I deliberately use contentious language because respondents themselves used such terms to describe their lives and their relationship *vis-à-vis* the societal mainstream.[1] Specifically, homeless people who had more unsettled lives or "irregular" life courses are more noticeable, more likely to congregate in city centers, and more likely to engage in shadow work (e.g., panhandling, scavenging). As such they tend to become easier targets of police and private security patrols, sometimes with severe financial and legal consequences. Homeless people with greater previous integration and social ties in the city and thus comparatively speaking more "regular life courses," in contrast, experience punitive measures and legal exclusion less frequently and with lesser consequence simply because they often stayed inside the neighborhood in which they previously resided. For them, and arguably all others, other types of spatially manifested barriers imposed by substandard shelter provision in impoverished neighborhoods (what I term "service exclusion") and lack of success in (re)accessing labor and housing markets (or "economic exclusion") played a more important role in their ongoing social and spatial exclusion than occasional harassment by police or private security. Economic exclusion therefore also explains why homelessness and legal exclusion declined since 2000 and under more favorable market conditions, but that it still exists, as former respondents and key informants report. My ethnographic study therefore supports the Right to the City debates' key assertions about the extent, unlawfulness, and detrimental effects of punitive policy, yet it also suggests it is important to consider the impact of other types of policies on homeless people's daily lives and chances to overcome homelessness. Below I describe where, why, and how homeless people experience displacement or persecution in public and private spaces and how this relates to people's life course trajectories and other types of policy and service intervention. I begin by providing some context about the proliferation of punitive policy in the USA and cities across the globe, with a focus on Berlin.

Punitive policy in the USA and Germany

When I started researching the impact of public policy on homeless people in Berlin and Los Angeles during the mid-1990s, I was inspired by several influential articles and books published during that time that focused on the increasing criminalization and deliberate displacement of homeless people. I remember reading Neil Smith's *The New Urban Frontier* (1996), Talmadge Wright's *Out of Place* (1997), and Don Mitchell's "The Annihilation of Space by Law" (1997). These studies provided me with a clear-eyed assessment of the deliberate exclusion of homeless people in US cities for primarily economic reasons. This still-growing body of literature is now often called the "Right to the City" debates that encompass several academic disciplines.[2] Such academic literature, along with a slew of reports by advocacy groups and think tanks,[3] unanimously reported a proliferation of punitive policy in virtually every North American city, whereby local governments and law enforcement had developed a broad range of explicitly anti-homeless ordinances to regulate homeless people and their behaviors in public spaces. Such ordinances, alongside existing regulations pertaining to public order and safety (i.e., prohibitions against public urination and alcohol consumption), have been used with a vengeance against, first, homeless people directly and, over time, against feeding and outreach programs designed to help them (Mitchell and Heynen 2009). Virtually every study on the criminalization of homelessness, regardless of city or country, indicated that the deliberate targeting, displacement, and criminalization of homeless individuals is unlawful and unconstitutional (for the USA, see Mitchell 1998a, b; for Germany, see Hecker 2002). Moreover, most commentators also emphasized that the underlying rationale behind this "sanitization" and "securitization" of commercially important urban quarters is nothing short of "revanchism," to use Smith's (1996) well-known term. In other words, the real aim of anti-homeless measures is to reclaim the city and its most important economic and residential areas for commercial and monetary purposes. Dating back to Wilson and Kelling's (1982) now infamous thesis on how to fight urban decay, homeless people and other social fringe groups are perceived as "broken windows" that must be removed to enhance the urban experience of shoppers, tourists, upscale residents, and other more affluent visitors of the city. The deliberate exclusion of homeless people through punitive means and displacement, then, is rationalized as a necessary step to reclaim the city and halt and reverse city center deterioration.

Punitive policy in post-unification Berlin

Over the past decade, increasing evidence emerged indicating that proliferation of punitive approaches to homelessness is not only a North American phenomenon – rather, it is an increasing practice in the world's cities, as recent case studies from Korea, Russia, France, Sweden, and Germany have shown (see von Mahs 2011a; see also Doherty *et al.* 2008). The main difference is that in Europe, at least, such exclusionary measures are less the result of explicit anti-homeless ordinances than of selective enforcement of existing public order and safety laws and regulations (Doherty *et al.* 2008). Germany and its capital Berlin, as my and others' research (Eick 1996; Schneider 1998; Robe 1999) has shown, are no exception. If anything, Berlin exemplifies German experiences with punitive policy and the deliberate spatial exclusion of growing numbers of homeless people throughout the 1990s and beyond.

After unification and with an immediate and rather steep increase in rental prices due to speculation, the numbers of homeless people in Berlin, previously found only in the West but now also appearing in the East, began rising dramatically. They reached a peak of 11,000 officially registered homeless people and another 3,000 to 4,000 estimated on the streets by late 1997 when I started fieldwork (Senatsverwaltung 1997). Yet, as these numbers rose, so did the local government's desire to become a competitive and growing capital city, to attract capital, investment, and upscale residents to the city and to generate revenue for ambitious urban restructuring plans, including the relocation of much of Germany's large federal administration and parliament from Bonn to Berlin (Mayer 1997).

In this light, it is perhaps unsurprising that Berlin's Interior Senate, responsible for public order and safety, including Berlin's police service, was quick to embrace a more rigorous approach to reclaiming those "social fire pits" (*soziale Brennpunkte*) in the commercial center that had become notorious. Soon after unification, Berlin's police developed "operative groups" that targeted perceived disorder, most notably the Operative Group West, whose jurisdiction included the notorious Bahnhof Zoo and the adjacent Breitscheidplatz around the Kaiser Wilhelm Gedächtniskirche, areas that since the 1970s had attracted a range of "social fringe groups" (*soziale Randgruppen*), including punks, drug users and dealers, sex workers, transient foreign nationals, and scores of apparently homeless people (Eick 1996). The local business community strongly welcomed the new police presence and this proactive approach to "cleaning up the neighborhood." To bolster these efforts, Berlin's Internal Senator Jörg Schönbohm, a retired German Army general, invited then-NYPD chief William Bratton to share his experience with "zero-tolerance" approaches celebrated for ridding Manhattan's theater district of "broken windows" and credited as one foundation of the revitalization of many deprived Manhattan neighborhoods. Like official voices from NYC, Berlin's public officials quickly came to embrace the anti-homeless rhetoric and forceful crackdown on perceived deviant behaviors in prime urban spaces. The subsequent economic revitalization, it is claimed, justifies the disciplining and displacement of deviant individuals for the benefit of locals and guests alike (Eick 1997; Belina 2007; Busch-Geertsema 2008).

This political step toward a punitive approach was accompanied by another major transformation in Berlin, the ongoing privatization of public spaces and the expansion and hiring of private firms to provide security and determine access to such spaces (Eick 2008; Busch-Geertsema 2008). In Germany, private and semi-private spaces are governed by private property law. Any property owner or landlord has the ability to establish "house rules" regarding conduct and activities on the premises, including explicit prohibition of loitering and solicitation. Landlords also have the right to employ private security to ensure house rules are enforced. The result, as in US cities, is that private security firms, often owned by large corporations, expanded greatly during this period (Eick 1996). Nowhere is this trend more obvious than in Berlin's privatized but publicly used transit system, where much of the reported crackdown on social fringe groups has occurred (Eick 1997; Schneider 1998). There, up to five different public and private security organizations provide security and control access, including Berlin's police and federal border security in railroad stations shared by the privatized German Railroad (Deutsche Bahn AG, DB) and the Berlin Transit Authority (Berliner Verkehrsgemeinschaft, BVG).

With this expanded presence of private security, one might conclude that homeless people with no place to reside would be disproportionately affected, although this is not known with certainty. This expanded presence raises the question: How extensive are such punitive approaches and who is targeted? According to Eick (1998), the deliberate displacement activities by police and private security in central Berlin are enormous; he cites some 228,000 reported incidents of displacement in 1997 alone. The problem is that such numbers, often internal, do not differentiate displaced people by housing status or other characteristics that may help determine how many are homeless. We also know little about the extent of repeat violations and thus the possible double-counting. Therefore, it is unclear who among the homeless experiences punitive policy and deliberate displacement; the reasons for these actions (and whether they are justified); and, more importantly perhaps, the consequences of punitive policy for homeless people's life chances.

Limitations of contemporary research

My contention about contemporary academic preoccupation with the criminalization of homelessness is not with the basic message about the illegality and economically determined nature of punitive policy; rather, I question the empirical basis of such claims. Virtually every study on the topic contains case studies and personal testimony from a range of actors involved, but hardly any have systematically researched the extent and consequences of punitive policy and how it potentially affects people's long-term chances to overcome homelessness. Such omission is problematic for three primary reasons. First, the homeless population in any industrialized country – and Germany is no exception – is diverse and its most visible segments constitute only the proverbial tip of the iceberg. Most homeless people (less so in the USA) reside in often publicly financed homeless shelters and transitional housing facilities. It is therefore important to find out who among the homeless experiences punitive policy. Second, it is generally assumed that an encounter with police or private security automatically has negative consequences. Yet, an empirical basis for this assumption is lacking, notwithstanding common-sense conjecture that displacement might be associated with loss of income (e.g., being displaced while panhandling) or more serious consequences such as the impact of a criminal record on one's chances of finding employment or housing. Third, as DeVerteuil, May, and I argued elsewhere (2009), there are policy changes other than criminalization and punitive policy that may, after all, have a more profound effect on homeless people's life chances, most notably a diminishing level of social protection, welfare state restructuring, and concurrent privatization of homeless service provision.

Methods and data to assess homeless people's experiences in Berlin

To provide answers, I focused my fieldwork in Berlin on the encounters and experiences with punitive policy among 28 single homeless shelter residents and service users. I contrasted such encounters with their simultaneous experiences with social policy within Berlin's relatively extensive system of shelter and service providers as well as with other public agencies involved in providing services. To do so, I selected three case studies (a transitional shelter, a day center, and a street-newspaper agency) in which I established contact with patrons and conducted semi-structured in-depth interviews along with numerous follow-ups (on average five per respondent), and thus was able to document the experiences of 28 respondents, including four women, during one year. In addition, I explored the context of such homelessness through archival research, key-informant interviews, public opinion surveys, and cartography, thus adding the top-down approach to provide an analysis of homelessness in Berlin from multiple perspectives, which I was able to compare with existing findings and a more developed empirical basis in Los Angeles (von Mahs 2005). This interdisciplinary approach allowed me to create a longitudinal assessment of public policy effects and provide a differentiated analysis of outcomes, including effects of punitive approaches. I developed a grounded, five-fold typology of homeless people based on similarities in people's life courses, which I then used to differentiate the impact of policy on homeless people. I established possible outcomes too, ranging from finding both housing and work, to finding housing but remaining on public income support, to remaining unsuccessful, living in shelters and on welfare. The life course types then constitute two principal groups differentiated by the extent of regularity, previous societal and residential integration, and stability in a person's life: people with more "regular" and "irregular" life courses (for discussion, see von Mahs 2013: Ch. 2).

The 12 respondents with more "regular" life courses had all lived in Berlin for many years and are further differentiated by age in that older homeless people (over 35 years) with regular life courses tended to be fully integrated both socially and residentially, leading rather inconspicuous lives until unemployment set in motion a gradual social decline, often accompanied by increased alcohol problems, that eventually ended in an inability to pay rent and subsequent homelessness. The four younger homeless people with regular life courses typically had a stable upbringing, completed high school, and became homeless in a more abrupt fashion, usually after conflicts with their parents with whom they had been living.

By contrast, the 16 respondents with more "irregular" life courses are characterized by lesser social and economic integration, greater economic and residential instability, and more debilitating personal problems. Among this group were eight people of different ages with comparatively "transient" life courses who led unsettled lives characterized by frequent moves and few local affiliations. Another four younger respondents, including a 19-year-old female heroin addict, had what could be considered "deviant" life courses characterized by foster care, drug use, criminal activity, multi-year incarceration, and social disaffiliation. Like the transient group, they never developed any roots and lived residentially unsettled lives. Finally, four people, including two women, constituted homeless people with "disabilities" who had either lifelong or accident-induced physical or mental health problems and were consequently unable to work. They did not receive assistance and became homeless as a result.

Below I use this life course typology to provide a more nuanced understanding of who, among homeless people, is particularly prone to experiencing punitive policy; what, if any, the consequences of such repressive action are; and how punitive policy relates to other types of public and social policy intervention. Although an ethnographic exploration of the experiences of only 28 respondents cannot produce representative, quantifiable results, the findings nevertheless provide a more nuanced understanding of the nature, extent, and consequences of policy effects on homeless people and their ability to overcome homelessness.

Homeless people's experiences with punitive policy in Berlin

Considering the evidence about the increasingly repressive approach of Berlin's public and private security during the late 1990s, it seemed prudent to ask the 28 respondents about their experiences with punitive policy. A surprising three-quarters of respondents were acquainted with one form of punitive policy or another. At least eight respondents reported regular experiences, and six incurred substantial financial penalties that added to their often debilitating mountain of personal debt. The previously outlined life course typology was helpful in differentiating who, among the homeless, experiences punitive policy, for what reason, and the ultimate consequences. Given that different legal and procedural contexts apply in urban spaces, I first provide an account of the extent of encounters with punitive policy in public (i.e. parks, sidewalks), semi-public (i.e. railroad stations, trains, stadiums) and private spaces (i.e. malls, department stores, restaurants, etc.), all of which are governed by different legal standards and controlled by different security forces, including public (i.e. police, border patrol, operative groups) and private entities (i.e. private security guards, electronic surveillance).

Extent of punitive policy encounters

When I interviewed homeless people, I asked every respondent if, when, where, and for what reasons they had encounters with police or private security and thus punitive measures. In this context, it is important to note that, subjectively speaking, only four of the 28 respondents resembled the stereotypical image of a homeless street person in appearance or demeanor and were immediately noticeable as "out of place."

In ostensibly public places, such as parks, plazas, streets and sidewalks Berlin police are responsible for upholding public order and safety ordinances and have considerable discretion about issuing a warning, temporary order to leave (*Platzverweis*), permanent ban (*Platzverbot*), temporary arrest and deportation (*Verbringungsgewahrsam*) or, in the most severe instances, a formal arrest for more serious charges. In my study, half the respondents (14) reported instances of being asked to leave by the police, eight of them repeatedly, whereupon five people, typically upon disagreeing or arguing with a police officer, received a permanent ban. Three of them, as well as two people who had no prior warning, told of being temporarily arrested, shoved into a police van, and driven and released on the city's outskirts and into the jurisdiction of suburban Brandenburg police. Marita, a 19-year-old female sex worker and heroin user, and four other respondents, including Hans, who had a comparatively inconspicuous life course, experienced this exclusion as daunting and potentially life threatening. Although this practice was discontinued after a hearing in Berlin's parliament in 1996, it shows how brutal police practice can be, as the discussion of the consequences of punitive policy below also shows (Abgeordnetenhaus 1996).

Displacement from private spaces where "house rules" apply was reported by more respondents; 17 respondents experienced such practices, almost exclusively on the premises or trains of Berlin's privatized Berliner Verkehrsgemeinschaft (BVG). In such a semi-public space, the house rules dictate that loitering and simply occupying the promises of a railroad or subway station for prolonged time is reason enough for presumably homeless people to be asked to leave. House rules also prohibit any type of commercial activity, which includes selling street newspapers, an activity five respondents pursued at some point. All of them, deliberately defying current circumstances to make their point, had multiple encounters with "the blues," as BVG's private security is commonly called (see Eick, this volume).[4]

However, rather than direct displacement, it was a subtle form of persecution associated with fare dodging that was most frequently reported and ironically had the most severe consequences. BVG uses a trust system in which passengers are expected to pay advance fare. Since deliberate fare dodging amounts to a substantial loss in revenue, BVG hired a private security company to conduct random checks for fare dodgers, with the incentive that the company would receive a share of the recovered revenue. In 1998, a conviction resulted in a DM 60 ($40) fine, payable within one week and subject to substantial interest thereafter. I witnessed how efficient the controls were, once counting seven random checks in one day by plain-clothed, badge-carrying security personnel. Sachse's response was typical:

> Man, this happens all the time, you know? Can't afford the ticket so I am already always on the lookout. I get out sometimes but sometimes they come from both sides. Trapped! Another ticket. How many you ask? Oh, eight or nine. [Pauses.] With interest? Hmm, over DM 1,000 ($700) by now, I believe.
> (Sachse, 35, shelter resident, older regular life course, 17 February 1998)

Although the BVG and its private security agents could not deliberately target homeless individuals on the premises of the public transit system – after all, most are indistinguishable from the general public – the consequences are, arguably, worse for these and other poor people who cannot pay the resulting fines. Ingo Thederan, spokesperson for BVG's subway security, countered:

> You have to understand that a railroad station is not a service agency. And we do provide discounted fares for poor Berliners. It is not our fault that some people choose to spend the money on alcohol instead. The social ticket is affordable.
> (Ingo Thederan, spokesperson for BVG, 12 September 1998)

This justification tries to release BVG from wrongdoing, pointing to both alleged individual behavior and the fact that subsidized passes are available. One problem was that most respondents were unaware of the existence of such passes because they were never told by their welfare case workers. This suggests one of many reasons why people face displacement. Neglect by other public entities denied homeless people the option to circumvent fare-dodging charges.

Reasons for displacement

The question arises as to why such apparently inconspicuous homeless people experienced displacement so frequently. The most frequently mentioned reason (17 people) was simply hanging out, which resulted in accusations of loitering and not using the corresponding space for its intended purposes. Of these, 11 conceded such inquiries came while they were consuming alcoholic beverages, which, while not illegal in Germany, may be used by police or security to invoke rules around disruptive conduct, noise, or endangering bystanders. Eight respondents admitted the original charge against them may have been justified given their advanced stage of intoxication and because they argued with officials. Of those, six said that security agents behaved appropriately and in fairly polite yet firm fashion, thereby deescalating the situation. The other 11 respondents had less favorable experiences, reporting condescending attitudes and intimidation, especially from younger, presumably ambitious officers intent on proving themselves.

Aside from loitering and public intoxication, a third frequently cited reason for displacement was to dissuade people from engaging in shadow work, most notably panhandling. Half the 16 people who reported relying on panhandling to generate income said they were singled out and asked to leave by police or private security while trying to make money this way. In these instances, all but one respondent complied immediately, left, and resumed panhandling elsewhere at a sufficient distance from police or security.

Finally, four respondents sold street-newspapers, typically on the premises of subway or railroad stations and in subway trains. The reason they did this is that vendors buying the papers then sold them for twice as much, and kept the profits and tips. These vendors needed high turnover because most people are disinclined to purchase a paper or have already done so. However, BVG disallows the sale of street-newspapers in public transit without explicit permission because it is deemed a commercial activity. Ingo Thederan of BVG expressed his sympathy for vendors' initiative, but explained rather plainly why a ban had to remain:

> We know that most vendors are polite and do not bother anyone but it is impossible for us to sort out the aggressive vendors. And since allowing their activities would set a precedent for all kinds of commercial activities, an all-encompassing ban of any sales activities has to remain in effect.
>
> (Ingo Thederan, spokesperson for BVG, 12 September 1998)

As a result, all four vendors had been repeatedly caught and risked arrest on trespassing charges. Stefan Schneider, then director and operator of the *Strassenfeger* street newspaper, related that eight regular vendors, because of inability to pay fines and sometimes in conjunction with other charges, were in jail at the time. Others, like Sioux and Matze, found a *modus vivendi* with security guards who did not even bother writing citations anymore; the guards' reaction, as Sioux put it, was "Oh no, you again. You know the drill. Get out at the next station. Ciao! See you tomorrow!" In the case of the ongoing confrontation between vendors and BVG, vendors showed tremendous resilience and sometimes deliberate defiance in the face of this perceived injustice. And although vendors knew their displacement and legal persecution is unconstitutional (Hecker 2002), they saw few chances for change other than via collective action. Martin explained:

I know that my constitutional rights are being stepped upon. I learned in school that the human dignity is untouchable. But, look, who is the judge going to believe? Me, the bum, or them, the police officers? You make the call. That's why we have to [starts singing the famous Bob Marley tune] "Get up, stand up, stand up for your rights" [others chiming in].

(Martin, 33, transient life course,
Berlin Breitscheidplatz, 9 February 1998)

To this day, no compromise between the street-newspaper agencies and the BVG has been found and the standoff continues as Sioux, one of the vendors I stayed in touch with over the years, as well as key informants continue to tell me.

Consequences of punitive policy by life course type

The experiences of street-newspaper vendors certainly showcase the vigor with which people are willfully spatially excluded and prevented from generating income. Through their resistance, they experience punitive policy much more frequently and, as with incarceration, with daunting long-term consequences. This, however, did not apply to all homeless respondents, as differences in the life course mattered profoundly. The vast majority – over two-thirds – of all instances of displacement, bans, and deportations were directed against homeless people with comparatively irregular life courses, while fewer – half of all people – with regular life courses experienced displacement. There are multiple reasons for this: First, homeless people with more regular life courses still often had important social ties in their previous residential community (which Berliners fondly refer to as their *Kieze*) and thus had more chances to blend in or meet with non-homeless people. Furthermore, respondents' *Kieze* were typically located in small urban centers outside the city center where most instances of displacement occurred. These respondents also had better alternatives to generate income (through day labor or social networks) and engage in leisure than people with more irregular life courses, especially transient folks, who tended to be less familiar with Berlin's social and economic infrastructure and to possess fewer ties to social networks in the city.

Homeless people with more irregular life courses, in contrast, were more likely to spend their days, in the absence of alternatives, in commercial center city locations congregating with other homeless people around the Bahnhof Zoo or the Alexanderplatz, resulting in loitering charges. They were also much more likely to employ informal survival strategies in public and to do so more frequently. Two-thirds of the 16 people who occasionally or regularly panhandled as well as almost all of those who scavenged, sold sex, or sold illegal drugs were people with irregular life courses who by the nature of these activities had no choice but to do so in commercially active public spaces with greater pedestrian volume. After all, not everybody makes donations, buys illegal drugs, or hires a sex worker. Yet by doing all this in public and commercial areas in a city center, these respondents inevitably attracted the scrutiny of police or private security more easily and frequently than homeless people who had opportunity to stay out of sight. As such, they were also less apt to avert more severe consequences such as deportations. In all, four of the five respondents who experienced such harsh forms of displacement were people with more irregular life courses having been deported from the city center to the urban fringe.

In the end, perhaps an even more consequential form of persecution than being singled out and displaced involved the sometimes substantial financial consequences of fare dodging. Over one-third of the people who had been repeatedly caught had accumulated more than $500 in fines, which only added to their substantial debt. Although some of them achieved a temporary suspension of debt repayment obligations (one provision of welfare law), they would eventually face repayment once off welfare. This alone kept at least three people with personal or alimony debt in excess of $100,000 from trying to move off welfare. This, in turn, demonstrates that the deliberate spatial exclusion of people through legal means is often facilitated by welfare state deficiencies, and thus is only one of many types of social and spatial exclusion homeless people face.

Punitive policy in context: one of three types of spatial exclusion

The aforementioned experiences of single adult homeless service users in Berlin provide much-needed clarifications about the extent and impact of punitive policy, suggesting that both need to be more carefully differentiated based on people's distinct life course experiences. In other words, punitive policy that underlies the legal exclusion of homeless people is not experienced in the same fashion by all homeless people and is often less consequential than other policy deficiencies inherent in service and economic exclusion, again depending on life course trajectory (von Mahs 2005, 2013).

The foregoing discussion has shown that legal exclusion is experienced most severely by homeless people with more irregular life courses. Unfamiliar with alternatives and unable to find formal employment, they often have no choice but to stay in the commercial center city to generate income and live. They are consequently more noticeably out of place and thus singled out, facing punitive policy more frequently; in the case of people with deviant life courses and among street-newspaper vendors, almost regularly. It is telling that most experiences and typically the most severe consequences affect these two groups. People with a more regular life course, by and large, experienced punitive policy less frequently and with less severe consequences. The most severe consequences for them were the more subtle forms of punitive action, notably in the context of persecuting fare dodging. Considering that most respondents with regular life courses were familiar with the city, often staying in their home districts, they were largely indistinguishable from the general public. As a result, their encounters with police and private security were comparatively rare, and when an order to leave was issued, it was usually complied with. Rather than suffering particularly from legal exclusion, homeless people with regular life courses, especially older ones, were most adversely affected by service exclusion, characterized by warehousing homeless people in usually dilapidated shelters which themselves are in the most deprived urban quarters surrounding the commercial center. This had devastating personal consequences.[5]

Yet perhaps the most consequential form of exclusion of homeless people's experience – regardless of life course type – is what I call "economic exclusion": their inability to (re)access housing and labor markets. One year after my initial interviews, only four respondents had found jobs, and slightly more than half – 16 respondents, primarily with regular life courses – had found housing yet remained on welfare. Such economic exclusion is largely facilitated by insufficient assistance and referrals through local labor and welfare offices. It is telling that only four out of 22 active job seekers in this sample found employment at a time when local unemployment rates reached and in some neighborhoods exceeded 20 per cent (Statistisches Landesamt 2000).

The importance of economic exclusion is further exemplified by the fact that the numbers of homeless people in Berlin declined by over one-third since 1997 in large part because pressures on the housing market due to speculation subsided and rental prices stabilized after peaking in the late 1990s (Senatsverwaltung 2004). Moreover, employment rates – due to Germany's stellar economic performance – increased, which might have meant more job opportunities for homeless people with previous job experiences. In addition, there is evidence for improvements in assistance and shelter provision showing that Germany's comprehensive welfare system performs substantially better than that of the USA.[6] The local system further benefited from declining numbers by being able to refer homeless people to higher quality shelters more able to provide case-appropriate assistance.

All these factors contributed to a noticeable decline in street homelessness and thus the necessity of individuals relying on shadow work and congregating in city centers. It also resulted in lower instances of displacement by police or private security. This, however, does not mean that the displacement and persecution of homeless people has stopped as key informants and homeless respondents I kept in contact with over the years continue to report.

Conclusion

The Berlin study suggests that legal exclusion is interrelated with other forms of exclusion with very clear spatial ramifications. Specifically, homeless people's removal from the vital center city (legal exclusion) is accompanied and reinforced by the simultaneous containment and warehousing in low quality shelters (service exclusion) in the city's most deprived communities outside the city center. Such settings, then, offer few economic possibilities to find housing and jobs (economic exclusion) thus resulting in what I have termed "socio-spatial exclusion" (von Mahs 2005, 2013). The "Right to the City" debates consequently need to extend the range of inquiries to other types of policy intervention beyond public order and safety and investigate how other social and economic policies affect both the short- and long-term life chances of people in their quest to overcome homelessness. Doing so requires a more interdisciplinary approach that draws from a range of academic disciplines, and provides insight into the economic, social, and political context of homelessness and homeless policy to understand the exclusions it causes. Specifically, the intersecting geographies of legal, service, and market exclusion require urban geographers to think beyond criminalization. It further implies inclusion of political economy and a nuanced understanding of markets at multiple scales. Examining the intersections also requires using a range of research methods to explore both the context and the personal circumstances of homelessness and thus pay attention to homeless people's life courses and personal circumstances, limitations, and strengths. This ethnographic research has barely opened the door as we still have to learn a lot about how different types of policy intersect to either facilitate or hinder exit from homelessness and thus find ways to help homeless people to overcome this predicament for good.

Notes

1   For further discussion of how this life course typology, including its contested terminology was developed, see von Mahs (2013: Ch. 2). In this chapter, I provide an analysis of people's life courses in order to develop a grounded typology. I am aware that terminology such as "regular," "irregular," "mainstream," or "disability" is contested, subjective and potentially stigmatizing but chose such terms because the respondents themselves used such terms to describe their experiences.
2   Notable authors include Peter Marcuse (1988); Mike Davis (1990); Neil Smith (1996); Nick Blomley (2001); Don Mitchell (1997, 2003); Michael Duneier (1999); and Randal Amster (2008).
3   The National Coalition for the Homeless, the National Alliance to End Homelessness, and the National Law Center on Homelessness and Poverty regularly report civil rights violations, unlawful practices, and deliberate removal of homeless people in virtually every US metropolitan area. Most of the reports contain testimony from affiliated advocates on the ground and often exemplary case studies.
4   The blue uniforms set private security apart from Berlin's police which customarily wear green jackets and khaki trousers (see Eick, this volume).
5   All four agglomerations can be found within the bottom 10 of 336 traffic cells in Berlin regarding social index, poverty, and unemployment. Such service agglomerations contain between 10 and 15 homeless service facilities within a 1 km radius. Compared with US cities, they can be considered second order agglomerations, which are less dense than US Skid Row areas. In Los Angeles Skid Row, we find 36 homeless service and shelter providers (Wolch and Dear 1993).
6   Although Germany has restructured its social welfare and unemployment assistance systems (the so called 2005 Hartz IV Reforms) since my study, the basic pillars of the German welfare system remained unchanged and, if anything, have noticeably improved (see von Mahs 2011b).

References

Abgeordnetenhaus von Berlin (1996) Besprechung gemäß § 21 Abs. 5 GO Abghs über Vertreibung von Obdachlosen aus den Bahnhöfen und rechtswidriges Verbringen von Personen an den Stadtrand von Berlin durch die Polizei [Hearing of Berlin's State Parliament pertaining to paragraph 22, section 5 of public order law regarding the displacement of homeless people from railroad stations and the unlawful deportation of people to the urban fringe through the police], Wortprotokoll des Auschuß für Soziales, 7. Sitzung am 3.06.96, Soz 13/7. Berlin: Kulturbuch Verlag.

Amster, R. (2008) *Lost in Space: the Criminalization, Globalization, and Urban Ecology of Homelessness*, New York: LFB Scholarly Publishing.

Belina, B. (2007) "From Disciplining to Dislocation: Area Bans in Recent Urban Policing in Germany." *European Urban and Regional Studies*, 14(4): 321–36.

Busch-Geertsema, V. (2008) "Urban Governance, Homelessness and Exclusion: Homelessness and Access to Space in Germany." In J. Doherty and B. Edgar (eds) *In My Caravan, I Feel Like Superman: Essays in Honour of Henk Meert, 1963–2006*. Brussels: FEANTSA.

Davis, M. (1990) *City of Quartz*, London: Verso.

DeVerteuil, G., May, J. and von Mahs, J. (2009) "Complexity, not Collapse: Recasting Geographies of Homelessness in a Punitive Age." *Progress in Human Geography*, 33(5): 646–66.

Doherty, J., Busch-Geertsema, V., Karpuskiene, V., Korhonen, J., O'Sullivan, E., Sahlin, I., Tosi, A., Petrillo, A. and Wygnańska, A. (2008) "Homelessness and Exclusion: Regulating Public Space in European Cities." *Surveillance & Society*, 5(3): 290–314.

Duneier, M. (1999) *Sidewalk*, New York: Farrar, Straus and Giroux.

Eick, V. (1996) *Mein ist die Stadt...: Das Berliner Sicherheitssystem und die Zugangsbedingungen der Stadt für Ihre Bewohner* [The city is mine...: Berlin's security system and access to the city for its residents], master's thesis, Otto-Suhr-Institut FU Berlin.

Eick, V. (1998) "Neue Sicherheitsstrukturen im Neuen Berlin: 'Warehousing' öffentlichen Raumes und staatlicher Gewalt" [New safety structures in the New Berlin: The 'Warehousing' of public space and state power.] *PROKLA*, 28(1): 95–118.

Eick, V. (2008) "Verlängertes Gewaltmonopol? Der kommerzielle Teil der 'neuen Sicherheitsarchitektur'." ["Extended monopoly of power? The commercial aspect of the 'new security architecture'."] *Bürgerrechte & Polizei/CILIP*, 91(3): 61–8.

Hecker, W. (2002) "Der öffentliche Raum in der Bundesrepublik Deutschland – Bettel- und Alkoholkonsumverbote, Aufenthaltsverbote, Privatisierung: zum Stand der Entwicklung." ["Public space in Germany – anti-panhandling laws and alcohol bans through privatization: current status."] In M. Berthold (ed.) *Wohnungslosenhilfe: Verbindlich verbunden ! Kooperationen – Verbundsysteme – Bündnisse* (Issue 51 of *Materialien zur Wohnungslosenhilfe*), Bielefeld, Germany: Verlag Soziale Hilfe.

Marcuse, P. (1988) "Neutralizing Homelessness." *Socialist Review*, 18(1): 69–86.

Mayer, M. (1997) Berlin–Los Angeles: Berlin auf dem Weg zur, Global City?" [Berlin–Los Angeles: Berlin on the Way Toward a "Global City"?], *PROKLA*, 27(4): 519–44.

Mitchell, D. (1997) "The Annihilation of Space by Law: the Roots and Implications of Anti-homeless Laws in the United States." *Antipode*, 29(3): 303–35.

Mitchell, D. (1998a) "Anti-homeless Laws and Public Space I: Begging and the First Amendment." *Urban Geography*, 19(1): 6–11.

Mitchell, D. (1998b) "Anti-homeless Laws and Public Space II: Further Constitutional Issues." *Urban Geography*, 19(2): 98–104.

Mitchell, D. and Heynen, D. (2009) "The Geography of Survival and the Right to the City: Speculations on Surveillance, Legal Innovation, and the Criminalization of Intervention." *Urban Geography*, 30(6): 611–32.

Robe, C. (1999) "Und Raus bist Du!: Wie soziale Probleme in der Berliner Innenstadt ausgegrenzt werden" [And You Are Out!: How Social Problems Are Excluded in Berlin's Inner City]. In M. Knecht (ed.) *Die Andere Seite der Stadt: Armut und*

Ausgrenzung in Berlin [*The Other Side of the City: Poverty and Exclusion in Berlin*], pp. 30-42. Cologne, Weimar, and Vienna: Böhlau Verlag.

Schneider, S. (1998) Wohnungslosigkeit und Subjektentwicklung: Biographien, Lebenslagen und Perspektiven Wohnungsloser in Berlin [Homelessness and the Social Construction of Subjects: Biographies, Life Circumstances and Perspectives of Homeless People in Berlin], PhD diss., Free University, Berlin. http://userpage.fu-berlin.de/zosch/diss/index. html.

Senatsverwaltung für Gesundheit und Soziales (1997) *Empfänger und Leistungen im Bereich Soziales: II. Quartal 1997* [Recipients and Services in the Area of Social Policy: 2nd Quarter of 1997]. Berlin: Referat Gesundheits- und Sozialstatistik, Gesundheitsberichterstattung, Epidemiologie, Gesundheitsinformationssysteme.

Senatsverwaltung für Gesundheit und Soziales (2004) *Empfänger und Leistungen im Bereich Soziales: I. Quartal 2004* [Recipients and Services in the Area of Social Policy: 1st Quarter of 2004], Berlin: Referat Gesundheits- und Sozialstatistik, Gesundheitsberichterstattung, Epidemiologie, Gesundheitsinformationssysteme.

Smith, N. (1996) *The New Urban Frontier: Gentrification and the Revanchist City,* London: Routledge.

Statistisches Landesamt Berlin (2000) "Ten Years of Unity in Berlin – a Narrative and Statistical Analysis of the Unification." *Statistische Monatsschrift,* 1–6: 1–164.

von Mahs, J. (2005) "The Socio-spatial Exclusion of Homeless People in Berlin and Los Angeles." *American Behavioral Scientist,* 48(4): 926–60.

von Mahs, J. (2011a) "Introduction – an Americanization of Homelessness in Post-industrial Societies." *Urban Geography,* 32(7): 923–32.

von Mahs, J. (2011b) "Homelessness in Berlin: between Americanization and Path Dependence." *Urban Geography,* 32(7): 1023–43.

von Mahs, J. (2013) *Down and Out in Berlin and Los Angeles: The Sociospatial Exclusion of Homeless People,* Philadelphia: Temple University Press.

Wilson, J. and Kelling, G. (1982) "Broken Windows: The Police and Neighborhood Safety." *Atlantic Monthly,* 249(3): 29–38.

Wolch, J. and Dear, M. (1993) *Malign Neglect: Homelessness in an American City,* San Francisco: Jossey-Bass Publishers.

Wright, T. (1997) *Out of Place: Homeless Mobilizations, Subcities, and Contested Landscapes,* Albany: State University of New York Press.

12 Contentious policing in Paris

The street as a space for emotional public solidarity

Virginie Milliot and Stéphane Tonnelat

Introduction

Since 2008, informal flea markets have been spreading throughout poor areas of Paris. Many people, including immigrants, have resorted to selling and buying recuperated goods in order to make a living during tough economic times. As in other cities around the world (Low 2000; Bromley 2000; Cross 1998), the police have been cracking down on street peddlers, although with mixed results. Such repression, at the behest of inhabitants and local elected officials concerned with security and cleanliness, often puts police officers at odds with the informal order of the street, causing vendors, clients, and passers-by to react to arrests and brutality. Policing thus becomes the catalyzing agent for the formation of publics mobilized for a cause.

The analysis in this chapter stems from a research project on the experience of public spaces in large cities. Hoping to test the hypothesis made by Isaac Joseph that multi-ethnic neighborhoods are the crucibles for the formation of urban mentality, we conducted an ethnographic inquiry in the Barbès neighborhood of Paris between 2007 and 2009. We focused on the modes of management of co-presence, on the daily adjustments that urbanites make to deal with the breaches of civility and accessibility that happen in the neighborhood streets (Milliot 2013a). This chapter thus contributes to the literature on public space, but with a specific focus on the role of the police in instant social mobilizations. The scene that we describe below takes place adjacent a subway entrance, in a transitory area between a major thoroughfare, a market and a neighborhood. This area is neither clearly regulated by the rules of anonymity and mobility of pure spaces of flow, nor by the commercial and moral transactions proper to the market, nor by the characteristic traits of neighborhood life (Hunter 1985; Tonnelat 2010). The reaction of the crowd to the police intervention is in fact revealing of a specific social order, which we attempt to analyze. We first describe the scene. We situate it in the Paris context before analyzing the confrontation of public orders and the emergence from the street of a shared conception of justice. We will then discuss the collective emotive reactions of the crowd to the action of the police that we observed.

The city, the crowd, and emotions

In urban studies, thoughts on emotions have been tied to theories of the crowd. From the late nineteenth century on, two different conceptions have been opposed. On the one hand, Gustave Le Bon (1895) described the crowd as emotionally versatile, receptive to all sorts of influence and subject to unpredictable behaviors. These properties make the crowd behave as if governed by one fickle mind. Crowds therefore are mostly irrational. They can become dangerous and must be carefully controlled and monitored. Opposed to this conception of the crowd, Gabriel Tarde (1901) and Robert Park (1972 [1903]) were more interested in the crowd as a first step towards a more organized social form and ultimately towards social change. For them, passers-by are only scrambled until the moment when a common faith or goal moves them together. Tarde (1901: 21) noted: "As soon as a new spectacle focuses their gazes and their minds, as an unforeseen danger or sudden indignation turns their hearts in the same direction, they begin to aggregate obediently, and this first degree of aggregation is the crowd." The crowd thus emerges when attentions converge through a process of emotional contagion in direct interactions. For Tarde, the crowd can give rise to a more elaborate form of association, which is the "public." In this case, people are scattered but their minds interact at a distance and produce simultaneity of convictions in time, if not in space. Whereas the crowd is close to an animal aggregate, the public is a more "evolved form of sociability and association" (Joseph 2001: 213). For Park, the only difference between the crowd and the public lies in the modes of organization of attention and of joint activities. The former characterizes a gathering in a physical location, whereas the latter comprises a collection of individuals in different locations. But both are "agents of social change opposed to norms producing forms such as groups and sects" (Joseph 2001: 215). Park thus does not understand emotions as psychological reactions, but as a social dimension of experience. In this regard, crowds and publics are reactive forms of social organization that can generate social change by forging new norms and values independently of already existing groups and institutions.

In our work on public space, it is this question of the emergence of social ties independent of specific statutory spaces that we are looking to explore via the sociology of emotions. In this regard, the recent development of the theory of social movements and more specifically, the work of James M. Jasper, is important to our thinking. Almost a century after Park and Tarde, Jasper's theory of emotions and social movements (Jasper 1998) builds on this early tradition. Notably, he argues individuals who have been exposed to "moral shocks" that have pushed them to become engaged for a specific cause are often at the origin of social movements. Although Jasper does not discuss the urban dimensions of such an emotional experience, it is reminiscent of Tarde's theory of simultaneous convictions brought about by common emotions.

It is this precise moment that interests us. This ephemeral eruption in public space can only be grasped through experience. This is why we begin this chapter with an extensive description of an incident between the police and street vendors, in the form of a testimony written shortly after the event. This testimony contains the empirical support for the theoretical interpretation we propose in this chapter. According to Dulong (1998), a witness must be morally responsible for their reaction to an event, their feelings and their judgment. It is therefore as much upon the facts reported here as upon the moral consistency of our testimony that we base our analysis (also see Katz (2002) about causal inferences in ethnographic descriptions).

A disputed arrest in la Goutte d'Or

March 25, 2009, early afternoon; the crowd is dense in front of the Barbès subway exit under the elevated tracks. Shoppers navigate the public space, encumbered with bags. Next to the regular market, a few street vendors display ill-assorted objects on improvised cardboard mats laid on the concrete. These twenty-first-century scavengers are becoming a more common feature of the Parisian landscape. On their improvised stands, retirees, refugees and casual workers transform the leftovers of the society of consumption into resources. This economy of survival renders visible a misery that one thought belonged to the past.

Suddenly, people gather around three uniformed policemen. They have just arrested a vendor. A woman, distraught, is clinging to his arm. She wants to go with him. The police refuse categorically. In her arms, a terrified four-year-old child cries for his father. Witnesses are gripped by the scene, and some speak up: "He is not hurting anybody" ; "He isn't dangerous to nobody." A policewoman justifies the arrest by explaining that the man is illegally selling canned food donated by a charity. A voice answers, "to be poor and to try to survive, is it a crime?" The policemen violently separate the man from his wife. The child is screaming with terror. The excessive force used by the police is not tolerable to the people gathered: "It's a shame to do this to a kid!" "The shame is to use a kid as a shield," replies the policewoman. When the policemen drag the man to their car, parked a dozen yards away on the Boulevard de la Chapelle, the crowd follows suit with a wide clamor of protest. Nobody opposes the police and all stay at a respectable distance. But one policeman, visibly overwhelmed by the situation, sprays the crowd with tear gas without warning. The vendor is manhandled. The policemen grab him by the neck; make him kneel down on the road, hands cuffed behind his back. Stéphane Tonnelat steps forward to film the scene and remind the police that they are under the citizens' watch. The same officer walks to him, grabs his camera and smashes it. Then he comes to me, Virginie Milliot, and tries to seize my cell phone. Unable to take it, he throws me forcefully to the ground. A couple of women help me get up. "What a shame. They think they can do anything!" The event provokes angry comments. "Ten meters away, there are people who sell drugs and they never arrest them. They go after the poorest," says a woman. "This is what they use public money for! They should arrest true criminals instead. There are thieves everywhere in the market. You just have to look. They let them be." A man confides to us, "I also sell at the market. I know him. He is a nice man. He's never caused any trouble." Another woman repeats several times: "You can't let them do this. We cannot help, but you can. You have to log a complaint." Another woman asks if we were able to take pictures. "This is good. You need proof. I don't dare. I am afraid. Several other women also tell us about their fear of the police. Meanwhile, the officers have called for reinforcement. Several vans full of policemen arrive within a few minutes. Several subway security guards in riot gear join them. The display of force is out of proportion. They take the man into the police car and drive away, leaving his wife on the sidewalk, crying tirelessly: "fascists, fascists." Her son, shocked, sobs in her arms, calling for his father. Several women quickly gather around the mother and her child. "It's a shame. They have nothing better to do than arrest innocent people?" "You have to take them to a community organization. They must be prevented from expelling her husband," worries a young woman of Maghrebi descent. A woman from the neighborhood points us to a local organization. "I cannot take her, you go ahead."

We end up at the Goutte d'Or community center. The tension gradually lessens. The child, exhausted, calms down and falls asleep in his mother's arms. We discuss the event, the possibility of testifying and pressing charges. A young woman who accompanied us apologizes: "I cannot do it. I am afraid." She will not explain why, but her fear, similar to the other women we talked to on the street, denotes an extreme feeling of vulnerability in the neighborhood. We learn that Maria is Russian, her husband, Alec, is Armenian. They fled Russia because of police violence. They asked for asylum and have legal status. They live in social housing but they don't have enough money to live (they each receive 316.20 euros per month as asylum seekers) and they do not have the right to work. Maria does not understand what happened. She expresses the need to explain. "We cannot live on what they give us. If I could work, we wouldn't have any problems. In my country, I was a pediatrician …. My son cannot eat only canned food. He needs vegetables, fruits … we try to make ends meet, we do nothing wrong." The episode brought back bad memories. "This is France, isn't it? This is not a dictatorship." The head of the organization then took up the case with great care and professionalism. She told us that she was used to these types of "incidents." Several complaints from the neighborhood were made last year to The National Commission for Police Professional Ethics. She then gave us a lawyer's contact information and tried to contact the *arrondissement* deputy mayor for security. She also attempted to get information from the police station about the place of detention. The next day, we learned that he had been detained without charge for 24 hours at the local station. His body was covered with bruises. He was finally released after signing a police statement that he was not given a copy of and that he did not understand, for lack of a translator.

La Goutte d'Or, a Paris neighborhood rife with tension

North East Paris where this police action took place has long been one of the most multicultural neighborhoods in the city. In this old working-class *faubourg* (the part of the city that was outside former walls), immigrants from Eastern Europe, Northern Africa, and Western Africa have been succeeding one another since the beginning of the twentieth century (Toubon and Messamah 1990). More than a third of its residents are born abroad (compared with 20 percent in Paris as a whole). Immigrants have always found commercial activities that have allowed them to take advantage of this central location (Lallemant 2010). People visit daily by road and public transportation from many places in the metropolitan area to shop for imported products and receive news from their home country. Street-level businesses are a fixture. The occupation of public space by male and immigrant populations has been repeatedly constructed by media as a "public problem" (Gusfield 1984). Anti-communitarian rhetoric has been used for thirty years to justify successive operations of urban renovation.[1] The Goutte d'Or neighborhood has been marked as a target zone for urban policy since 1984 (it has been also labeled a "sensitive urban area" (*zone urbaine sensible*) since 1996[2]) and went through several phases of urban renewal. Despite these state interventions, the neighborhood retains a strong image in the Parisian imagination. It is heavily marked by the public street life that develops around commercial activities and sociabilities unique to the worlds of immigrants.

While the types of items sold on the street change all the time, ranging from small radios to phone cards to cigarettes, informal street peddling at the Barbès metro station is a continuous activity. At another local metro station, Chateau Rouge, one can find grilled chestnuts, African vegetables, and clothing. Subutex (a prescription drug) and cannabis are sold on the smaller streets. Camerati's (2006: 88) observations in the neighborhood showed the instant shifts provoked by the police presence: street vendors move and behave as simple passers-by.[3] He describes police presence as an element of the "ecology of space": "Local police work by looking for a balance, an honorable compromise, between, on the one hand, the public order and, on the other hand, activities tied to the local context, even if they are illegal." The police thus perform an adjustment to a liminal space, where the categories of formality and informality, legality and illegality, are confused.

Since 2008, street peddling has been deemed to be causing trouble by encumbering the public spaces of the neighborhood. At the Goutte d'Or community board meeting of November 27, 2008, precinct captain Pecquet declared:

> We have reached the limits of police action. We need other types of responses, judicial and legislative. When someone is arrested for street peddling, the person only gets a summons, and after 24 hours, sometimes 48 hours, he is back out on the street.[4]

For the police, the problem seems to be the lack of any deterrent effect of this penalty and of fines given to insolvent people. At a public meeting on street security at the City Hall of the eighteenth *arrondissement*, the police captain also complained about the obstacles faced by officers to intervene in the neighborhood's public spaces. The work of the 700 agents in this area was made difficult by the territory's problems, such as drug dealing and street peddling combined with a changing relationship with the local population. "We are working more and more on the edge in difficult conditions," he explained.[5]

During 2007-09, we observed that police actions often caused public comments. In most cases, they were discussed satirically, symbolically reversing power relations. They could also elicit more general discussions among witnesses about justice and injustice, legitimacy and illegitimacy, legality and illegality (Milliot 2013b). But the scene described earlier was different. It was not experienced from a detached point of view, but from an emotional and reactive one.

What is the nature of these emotions and what drives them? In his later theory of emotions and social movements, Jasper (2011) makes a distinction between "reflex emotions," such as surprise, fear and anger, and "moral emotions," such as shame, pride and indignation, which carry a judgment on the situation at hand. Leaders of social movements and organizers of ritualistic events strive to transform reflex emotions into moral ones, which can be shared and used as durable motivators for engagement. For this, they use diverse props and techniques, such as a stage, a speakerphone, singing, marching, etc. called "sensitizing apparatuses" (Traïni cited by Jasper 2011: 14.8).

In the example that we analyze, emotions quickly spin into an indignation that is not merely supported by political, religious or community values, since the people involved come from numerous cultures. Whereas we have observed on other occasions public reactions based on a sentiment of belonging to a given community, or to the more general category of immigrant, in this case, the crowd is too diverse for this to constitute a valid explanation. Also the market is too pervaded by the street to work as a cosmopolitan canopy, as described by Anderson (2011). Everything happened as if the police action was spontaneously received as an infraction to a tacit public order.

The confrontation of two public orders

In the event described above, two conceptions of public order have clashed. On the one hand, the public order enforced by the police is based on a discretionary interpretation of common law. As guardians entitled to the "monopolistic use of force towards all" (Montjardet 1996), the police must apply the many rules written in law. This incident illustrates the priorities made by the officers about which rules to apply. In this case, repression of street peddling seems to be primary. We call this the public institutional order.

On the other hand, the public order of the street, which we call the public interaction order (Goffman 1963), is regulated by a small set of tacit normative principles such as cooperative mobility, civil inattention, restrained helpfulness and civility towards diversity (Lofland 1998). These principles do not function as strict rules, but they are all the more potent when the location is patronized by an anonymous flow of people, for example, next to a subway station. As one goes more deeply into the neighborhood, the principles of public order weaken as they mingle with other norms and values anchored in specific local cultures

(Tonnelat 2010). But even in the most crowded areas, variations and offenses, as well as reparations and disputes, are many. Thus, public life in this urban neighborhood constantly puts these principles to test, redefining their reach. For example, informal economic activities produce specific types of visual attention as well as forms of public address. The larger sociability emerging from the different worlds of immigration, mostly based on recognizable signs of ethnic cultures, is more open to improvised relations than in more homogenous urban areas. Conflicts also erupt between users defending a right of way and others claiming a space for activities (e.g., informal vending, daily prayer for Muslims, and social gathering of immigrants of the same origin). The street is thus an ongoing stage, where episodes of reciprocity, friction, negotiation, controversy and repair test the street as a public good. The principles of this public order, although at an infra-social level, are powerful regulators of interactions in public space. One of its main ethical foundations is what Isaac Joseph called the "presumption of equality" which is "a presupposed given of public space and social encounters. The question is not whether this equality is established: a presupposition is a regulatory device and a principle for the interaction order" (Joseph 2007: 15). This presumption of equality and its attached reciprocity guide the interactions between unknown urbanites. One consequence is the common rule "first come, first served," which does not distinguish between the type of person (for example by gender), but only ranks them according to the order inherent to the flow of circulation. It organizes the lines in front of the stands, and even the distribution of selling spots. Only certain people, pregnant women, children, the elderly, and the disabled, enjoy a partially dispensatory status in public space, linked to a perception of vulnerability attached to motherhood, age, and/or disability. While, at the Barbès metro station, cigarette street vendors lead a perpetual struggle against the newspaper vendor in his licensed kiosk, the latter striving to control the sidewalk against the overflow of informal trade, these peddlers commonly help women with strollers and older persons climbing up the stairs to the subway mezzanine.

Logically, the public institutional order and the public interaction order should not come into conflict. Whereas the first order regulates infractions of the law, the second order organizes public behaviors so as to maintain existing activities while avoiding offenses to individual selves and to the gathering (Goffman 1963; Rawls 1987). A form of normative continuity should connect them, notably by calling on the police only when the order of interaction proves unable to manage conflicting situations. Ideally, there would be a form of subsidiary principle between the two public orders. However, the incident described at the chapter's outset shows a situation where the public institutional order, represented by officers of the law, conflicts with the public order of interaction.

An emerging and shared concept of justice

What begs inquiry here is this critical moment, the sense that a reversal of the hierarchy of institutional and interactional public orders occurred. Instead of counting on the police to make up for the shortcomings of the public interaction order with their own authority, the crowd attempted to use the norms of the public order of interaction to limit the powers of the police. Could the police abandon their claim of control over the crowd? What could the consequences be in a neighborhood already rife with tensions? Everybody felt the stakes of that "tipping point" (Collins 2001: 41). The public was energized and emboldened to resist the work of the police while the officers immediately called for reinforcement. The speed, the number, and the range of police who quickly arrived reveal the extent of the means deployed to reduce the risk of losing power, and reaffirm the preeminence of the institutional order over any attempt of public self-organization.

To manage a public space, there are two basic systems, declares Jean Loup Gourdon (2001): the material and mechanical physical setting and the ordering, regulatory and appeasing presence of police force. In this case, we can only observe the counterproductive effect of police action, which, instead of appeasing, generated a contested social order. What is at stake? Pierre Favre remarks:

> In their daily concrete work, the police draw a general and hierarchic order of what is authorized and forbidden, of what is urgent and what can wait, of what is potentially dangerous and what is harmless, of what is just and what is unjust, of what is acceptable and unacceptable, of what is normal and pathological.
>
> (Favre 2009: 1035)

But this intervention was experienced as an offense to public order, primary because it contravened the presumption of equality by arbitrarily picking one "criminal" among the street vendors. The comment of a nearby vendor: "I sell on the market, I know him, he is a nice man, he never caused any trouble," expresses the inconsistency of the arrest for the people gathered around the event. In addition, as another comment illustrates, "It is a shame, to do this to a kid," the officers' choice contradicted even the exception to the rule by targeting a couple with a young child. It negated the dispensatory benevolence that the parents and the child were benefiting from in the public order of interaction. The arrest thus voided the tacit principles of the interaction order and tended to disqualify it as a means of regulation. As a consequence, the hierarchy of social order imposed by police action fed a shared sentiment of injustice and indignation and provoked a normative reaction. The comments exchanged during the event thus opposed another conception of justice to the legal norm justifying the action of the police, which questioned anew the dominance of the institutional order. Because the people targeted as delinquent by police intervention were poor and vulnerable in the eyes of the gathering,[6] the action caused the crowd to transform into a public from which emerged a benevolent watch aimed at repairing the offense to the social order of interaction. Emotions took the spectators in and pushed them to redefine the situation by exchanging comments about the fragility and harmlessness of the couple and about the arbitrariness of police actions. The spontaneous communication attempted to repair public order by reaffirming the value of the presumption of equality. The words and the actions of people caught in the scene thus tried to reconstitute around the woman and her son a specific public order with its own conception of justice. This solidarity impulse was by consequence not only a response to the exposed vulnerability of individuals to the law applied by the police, but also to the weakening of the public order of interaction, on which rest the commercial informal agreements that allow everybody to survive. The impulse arising out of the feeling of injustice thus produced a public characterized by "simultaneity of convictions" (Tarde 1901: 9). The indignation experienced by the witnesses can be compared to the idea of a "moral shock" proposed by James M. Jasper (1998). Examining the role of emotions in collective mobilizations, he uses this concept to analyze social experiences caused by a disconcerting event, a sudden change in the environment that elicits acute emotional reactions, which imme- diately call for involvement and reaction. Based on a discrepancy between the situation in which individuals are caught and the values which they carry, these tests bring people to reevaluate their expectations, or to the contrary, to work towards fixing the situation to fit their expectations. The values under stress can be anchored in diverse cultures, religions, political and professional opinions. But what is interesting in the case described here is that the spontaneous reac- tion of the crowd brought forth a shared conception of justice that was directly tied to the public order of interaction,

What is also striking in the event is the perception of an inequality in power and status between the individuals involved. The crowd was principally com- posed of people belonging to ethnic minority groups, mostly from northern Africa and sub-Saharan Africa. Whether these people hold French citizenship, legal immigration status, or have no legal title, does not seem to matter here as all appear defenseless against the institutional order enforced by the officers. As suggested earlier, several people told us of their fear of the police and their unwillingness to testify. Several people also incited us to press charges. We, and a dozen others,[7] were the only "white" witnesses of the event. Whereas the relationship between minority and majority is somehow reversed in this neigh- borhood's public spaces, it came back distinctly in this event. The people gathered did not feel entitled to act beyond the space of the street. They somehow man- dated us to attempt to repair the injustice in arenas in which they did not have legitimate access. A woman resident put us in contact with a local community organization (we do not live in the neighborhood), who helped us take the event from the street into the political and judicial spheres. We were put in contact with a local elected deputy mayor who in turn called the local police commis- sioner, and with a lawyer who used our testimonies to argue the case of the arrested vendor. In this way, the public perspective of the order of interaction was translated into the language of the institutional order. Only at the price of this mediation and translation, by "white" people who testified, by social work- ers who reframed their words into legal language, and by a local elected official who brought the complaint to the ears of the precinct captain, was a form of communication established between the holders of public force and the public of the event, between the values of the order of interaction and the values of the institutional public order.

The role of the street in mobilizing a public against the police

What do these street corner interactions "reveal for those who study public good and the impulse of public morality" (Joseph 2002: 90)? The analysis of this scene gives us a first-hand measure of the effects that two concurrent trends have on the work of the police in French urban public space. On the one hand, informal and survival street trade is growing in the working class neighborhoods of Paris (Milliot 2013a). Street peddling is one of the "public problems" repeatedly discussed at neighborhood meetings. The reaction of local elected officials to this phenomenon described as "out of the ordinary" and "very worrisome as regard to security and illegal occupation of space as well as the poverty of the population given to these activities" (Paris Municipal Council, May 10-11, 2010) is a quasi-unanimous call for repression. In the eastern *arrondissements*, issues of circulation and cleanliness bring local councils to demand police reinforcement from the prefecture of Paris.[8] In response to these calls, the police prefect reminded them that more than 10,000 tickets had been written for unauthorized street selling in 2009 and declared that police work would not be a sufficient problem response. Indeed, police repression has occurred at all overflowing informal markets, and has only pushed the vendors and their related "problems" to other places. During the summer of 2012, the Goutte d'Or neighborhood, which is particularly affected by the development of street vending, was targeted by the secretary of domestic affairs (*ministre de l'intérieur*) as a "Security Priority Area." The police are now more mobilized to enforce rules of cleanliness and circulation against occupations of the sidewalks by informal markets.

On the other hand, the police have been under pressure by the government to improve statistics (of custodies, arrests, crime solving, etc.), which modifies police work on the ground by reducing their ability to interpret the diversity of situations they encounter (Mucchielli 2008; Mouhannna 2009). Faced with activities at the legal margins, police officers are less and less able to act as "good professionals" (Bearman 2005). In other words, they are less and less able to adjust the legal frame of their mission to local contexts and situations. As Fabien Jobard (2002) showed, this tendency, when applied to immigrant and working-class neighborhoods and populations easily produces police blunders and shootings. In fact, many "incidents" of police violence have happened in the last few years in la Goutte d'Or.

Inhabitants and local elected officials logged several complaints with the National Deontology Police Commission against police wrongdoings in the neighborhood. The most famous is the 2007 case of a young woman of sub-Saharan origin, obviously pregnant, who was beaten in public and then taken into custody without access to a lawyer, because she was selling fruit without a license. Here too, the mechanism of public indignation showed the growing opposition between the public order of the street and the institutional public order, the moral order of small street trade and the legal order. NGO Amnesty International used this incident in its 2009 report on French Police entitled, "Police Officers Above the Law." To respond to government demands and repress informal street trade, police officers are pushed to overlook even the republican principles that legitimate their action.

One might think that the choices made by officers on the ground, following the process of hierarchic inversion, which lets lower ranking officers take the initiative (Monjardet 1996), could be controlled or at least contained by higher ranking officers and police administrators. But the contrary is happening. Their actions are legitimated, if not condoned. Almost none of the complaints logged with the Inspection Service of National Police (IGPN) have resulted in sanctions. Almost all have been dismissed. Blunders are thus in a way legalized after the fact by the State (Mohammed and Mucchielli 2006), which rubberstamps the rupture between the police and the city. Finally, the law itself has been recently changed to provide more power to police agents. The vote of LOPPSI 2 (*loi d'orientation et de programmation pour la performance de la sécurité intérieure*) at the National Assembly, on February 18, 2010, and its ratification by the Constitutional Council a year later, transforms unlicensed street selling from an offense to a misdemeanor. The penalty changed accordingly from a ticket to a six-month prison sentence and a 7500 euro fine. With this law, the translation of the public perspective into the language of institutions may well become inaudible to the State and its administrations. One can wonder about the justification, in a period of economic crisis and growing poverty, of such an apparatus of repression of informal street vending that criminalizes the poorest and systematically pits its police and its institutional order against inhabitants and the public order of interaction. Research in US cities points to similar use of repressive strategies (Low and Smith 2006; McArdle and Erzen 2001). The impulse behind them may be diverse, but one point illustrated here could probably apply generally: the general diffidence towards regulatory principles of the public interaction order.

Finally, this incident provides insights into an emerging and shared conception of justice. The catalyst here is the emotion provoked by a situation perceived as intolerable. The indignation that brought together passers-by, inhabitants and visitors, during the event, crossed social categories – "white" middle class which we represented and an immigrant population of diverse ethnic and class origins represented by women and men who pushed us to testify and press charges in the name of all. This is not a form of universal cosmopolitanism but rather a pluralist ethics, built *in situ* during the interactions in urban public space. This argument reaches back to the relationship between emotions and the city. According to Collins (2001), to get engrossed in specific emotional dynamics, people must be ready. They need to have a compatible "conscience constituency" (Collins 2001: 31), which gives them an orientation similar to that of the social movement. Here, in addition to already existing tensions between the local immigrant population and the police and to a sentiment of belonging to a community of conditions, the principles of the interaction order of public space have provided a common axiological grammar (Lemieux 2009). As the principles of the public interaction order are applied, reworked and adopted by all, they can serve as a setting for common reactions to events that disturb the ongoing urban order. This event thus shows that there can be strong moral and political dimensions attached to the simple ability of denizens to share the space of the street and that these values can indeed, as Tarde had theorized, link together the crowd and the public as two successive forms of social organizations aimed at social change.

But these values are rarely visible. They are not only seldom expressed, because it is difficult to get indignant on the street, but they are also ephemeral, as emerging expressions remain in the realm of speech. For values to be shared in the immediate circle, events need to be strong enough to provoke instant mobilization. To spread beyond the gathering, they need to give way to a narration that can carry emotions through time. Here we have observed the almost instant passage of a shared emotion to a collective action, and how this dynamic feeds off the problematic disjunction of two public orders in urban public space, in the rift widening between the values upon which publics form and act and the principles that motivate State Police action. If public space is the pulse of urban societies, this incident provides us a measure of the fault lines that divide them and that could push them toward greater democracy.

Notes

1 Conservative representative and chief of staff for the ministry of domestic affairs, Jean-Pierre Bloch, initiated in 1978 a policy of securitization of the neighborhood (closure of brothels, arrests of street vendors). He declared to the press: "Harlem will not exist in Paris," "I will break la Goutte d'Or" and "the police must take control of la Chapelle-Goutte d'Or" (*Le Monde*, July 26, 1978).
2 It was designated this way because of unhealthy housing conditions and high indexes of poverty (28 percent of household income is below poverty level, 33 percent of the population are single parent families, 15 percent is eligible for Medicaid). See report by l'Observatoire des quartiers prioritaires, 2010, APUR, Ville de Paris.
3 See Tonnelat's (2007) work on Times Square, New York, for a similar reaction to the police by peddlers.
4 Minutes available at: www.mairie18.paris.fr/mairie18/document?id=14680.
5 Field notes from the public meeting "Vos libertés, votre sécurité. Parlons-en ensemble" at the City Hall of the eighteenth *arrondissement*, April 29, 2009 (21 h).
6 For two years, an organization called CLAP or Collectif contre les abus policiers (Collective against police abuse) has published a chronicle of police repression of street vending in the neighborhood.
7 This event happened as we were taking a tour of the neighborhood with a group of ethnology students and colleagues. A good proportion of that group was "white" and more educated than most neighborhood residents.
8 The *préfecture* is under the authority of the National Secretary for Domestic Affairs. The city of Paris does not have a municipal police force.

References

Amnesty International (2009) *France, des policiers au-dessus des lois*, London: Amnesty International Publications. Available at: http://www.amnesty.fr/Documents/Rapport-France-Des-policiers-au-dessus-des-lois [accessed 20 November 2012].

Anderson, E. (2011) *The Cosmopolitan Canopy: Race and Civility in Everyday Life*, New York: W.W. Norton & Co.

Bearman, P. (2005) *Doormen*, Chicago: University Of Chicago Press.

Bromley, R. (2000) "Street Vending and Public Policy: A Global Review," *International Journal of Sociology and Social Policy* 20(1/2): 1–28.

Camerati, N. (2006) "La 'performance' de la police dans l'espace public," *Sociétés* 94(4): 77–90.

Collins, R. (2001) "Social Movements and the Focus of Emotional Attention," in J. Goodwin, J. M Jasper, and F. Polletta (eds) *Passionate Politics: Emotions and Social Movements*. Chicago: University of Chicago Press.

Cross, J. C. (1998) *Informal Politics: Street Vendors and the State in Mexico City*, Stanford, CA: Stanford University Press.

Dulong, R. (1998) *Le témoin oculaire: les conditions sociales de l'attestation personnelle*. Paris: EHESS.

Favre, P. (2009) "Quand la police fabrique l'ordre social. Un en deçà des politiques publiques de la police ?," *Revue française de Science politique*, 59(6):1231–48.

Goffman, E. (1963) *Behavior in Public Places; Notes on the Social Organization of Gatherings*. New York: Free Press of Glencoe.

Gourdon, J.L. (2001) *La rue. Essai sur l'économie de la forme urbaine*, La Tour-d'Aigues: Éditions de l' Aube.

Gusfield, J. R. (1984) *The Culture of Public Problems: Drinking-Driving and the Symbolic Order*, Chicago: University of Chicago Press.

Hunter, A. (1985) "Private, Parochial and Public Social Orders: The Problem of Crime and Incivility in Urban Communities." In G. Suttles and M. Zald (eds) *The Challenge of Social Control: Citizenship and Institution Building in Modern Society – Essays in Honor of Morris Janowitz*, NJ: Aldex Publishing.

Jasper, J. M. (1998) "The Emotions of Protest: Affective and Reactive Emotions in and Around Social Movements." *Sociological Forum*, 13(3): 397–424.

Jasper, J. M. (2011) "Emotions and Social Movements: Twenty Years of Theory and Research." *Annual Review of Sociology*, 37(1): 285–303.

Jobard, F. (2002) *Bavures Policières. La force publique et ses usages*. Paris: La Découverte.

Joseph, I. (2001) "Tarde avec Park." *Multitudes*, 4(7): 212–20.

Joseph, I. (2002) "Pluralisme et contiguities." In *L'héritage du pragmatisme. Conflits d'urbanité et épreuves de civisme*, Cefaï Daniel et Joseph Isaac (dir), La Tour-d'Aigues: Éditions de l'Aube.

Joseph, I. (2007) Parcours: Simmel, l'écologie urbaine et Goffman. In D. Cefai and C. Saturno (eds) *Itinéraire d'un pragmatiste*, Paris: Economica.

Katz, J. (2002) "From How to Why: On Luminous Description and Causal Inference in Ethnography (part 2)." *Ethnography* 3(1): 63–90.

Lallement E. (2010) *La ville marchande: enquête à Barbès*, Paris: Editions Téraèdre.

Le Bon, G. (1895) *Psychologie des Foules*, Paris: Felix Alcan.

Lemieux, C. (2009) *Le devoir et la grâce*, Paris: Economica.

Lofland, L.H. (1998) *The Public Realm: Exploring the City's Quintessential Social Territory*, Hawthorne, NY: Aldine de Gruyter.

Low, S. (2000) *On the Plaza: The Politics of Public Space and Culture*, Austin: University of Texas Press.

Low, S. and Smith, N. (2006) *The Politics of Public Space*, New York: Routledge.

McArdle, A. and Erzen, T. (2001) *Zero Tolerance: Quality of Life and the New Police Brutality in New York City*, NYU Press.

Milliot, V. (2013a) "Indignations et mobilisations autour des marchés de la pauvreté à Paris." Forthcoming in *les Annales de la recherche urbaine*, 107.

Milliot, V. (2013b) "Pluralist Ambiance and Urban Socialisation: Ethnography of Public Space in the Goutte d'Or Neighbourhood of Paris." *Ambiances. International Journal of Sensory Environment, Architecture and Urban Space / Revue Internationale sur l'Environnement Sensible, l'Architecture et l'Espace Urbain*, 1.

Mohammed, M. and Mucchielli, L. (2006) "La police dans les Quartiers Populaires : un vrai problème!" *Mouvements* 2: 58-66.

Montjardet, D. (1996) *Ce que fait la police. Sociologie de la Force Publique*, Paris: La Découverte.

Mouhannna, C. (2009) "Politique du chiffre et police des étrangers." *Plein droit*, (3): 3–6.

Mucchielli, L. (2008) "Le nouveau management de la sécurité à l'épreuve : délinquance et activité policière sous le ministère Sarkozy (2002-2007)." *Champ pénal/Penal field. Nouvelle revue internationale de criminologie*, Vol. V. Online. Available at: http://champpenal.revues.org/3663 [accessed 20 November 2012].

Park, R.E. (1972) *The Crowd and the Public, and Other Essays*, Chicago: University of Chicago Press.

Rawls, A.W. (1987) "The Interaction Order Sui Generis: Goffman's Contribution to Social Theory." *Sociological Theory*, 5(2):136-49.

Tarde, G. (1901) *L'opinion et la foule*, Paris: Felix Alcan.

Tonnelat, S. (2007) "Keeping Space Public: Times Square (New York) and the Senegalese Peddlers." *Cybergeo*, article 367. Online. Available at: http://www.cybergeo.eu/index4792.html [accessed 20 November 2012].

Tonnelat, S. (2010) "Walking to the Subway: The Ambiguity of Public Social Norms at Work in and Around Subway Stations in New York City." Paper presented at the American Anthropological Association meeting, New Orleans, November 17.

Toubon, J.-C., Messamah, K. (1990) *Centralité immigrée. Le quartier de la Goutte d'Or, Paris*, Paris: L'Harmattan.

Part IV

Securitization of twenty-first century cities

13 Municipal corporate security and risk mitigation companies in Canadian cities

A new military urbanism?

Kevin Walby and Randy K. Lippert

Introduction

Despite Western cities' long history as settings for democratic politics and freedom of public movement in open streets, markets, and squares, in the twenty-first century, cities are increasingly viewed as major sites and sources of risk. The risks include terrorism and street crime. But cities are also deemed to be sources of risk insofar as they are thought to create conditions that harm citizens, for which city governments can be held liable. As both site and source of risk, many organizations have sought to securitize and police cities. Their efforts take multiple forms, from building secured residential high-rise developments, to deploying sophisticated camera surveillance systems in commercial districts, to stepping-up municipal police and private security patrols in residential neighborhoods, to posting signs listing hazards to persons and property in city-owned parking lots and recreation facilities, and more. Indeed, there is neither a shortage of agencies rethinking the city as a site or source of risk nor of securitizing and policing strategies that see and remake the city this way. As we noted in this book's Introduction, this is one reason[1] why we say cities throughout the world are becoming *policing cities*. This pluralization of policing in cities is fascinating given that municipal public police services in the West now openly acknowledge what has been known since their modern Peelian beginnings in nineteenth-century London; public police cannot be everywhere at once and must share the substantial load of security provision (see Shearing and Marks 2011). Indeed, Sir Robert Peel implied the public should help shoulder this load in espousing his famous idealized view of London's police as the public, and the public as the police. But this chapter focuses on a decidedly more clandestine collection of agents than the public police and with whom this seemingly escalating burden is to be shared. Their distinctive securitizing and policing strategies that are mundanely practiced with little fanfare seem antithetical to traditional ideals of democracy and freedom of movement in cities. They may even befit a creeping militarization of the urban.

Graham (2010) has recently offered the idea of the new military urbanism as a way of conceptualizing how risk and security traverse twenty-first century cities. The new military urbanism refers to a major "shift that renders cities' communal and private spaces, as well as their infrastructure – along with their civilian populations – a source of targets and threats" (Graham 2010: xiii). This is not tantamount to merely paying greater attention to risk and security in cities, processes about which criminologists and other scholars have already written at length. It is instead a strategy of borrowing the language and technologies of war and insidiously injecting them into the flows of everyday urban life along with promises of eliminating risk and providing security. Urban geographers like Graham (2010) have paid close attention to how the material form of cities is mutating due to these emphases on risk and security. It is our contention that sociologists of policing and security, as well as criminologists interested in urban policing, can learn from geographers' understanding of risk and security, especially this idea of military urbanism. We think this idea is more fruitful than seeing the developing character of urban security provision and policing as marking the rise of a new kind of state or Leviathan (see Hallsworth and Lea 2011). However, questions remain as to whether this idea of military urbanism can be universally applied or might itself benefit from refinement. To this end, in the conclusion we suggest it could be supplemented with consideration of legality drawn from the sociology of law literature (see Ewick and Silbey 1998).

Our research focuses on two agencies implicated in these risk and security processes in Canadian cities: municipal corporate security (MCS) and risk mitigation companies. MCS offices operate in the public sector; risk mitigation agencies in the private sector. Both agencies monitor and investigate employees of governments and private corporations, and the latter are also engaged in security consulting for corporations in cities. Below we focus on MCS offices and risk mitigation companies to assess the purchase of military urbanism and its six-fold framework. In so doing, we contribute to a cross-disciplinary discussion about security and risk in sociology, criminology, and geography.

This chapter is organized in four parts. First, we comment on our research program, including interviews with MCS personnel and risk mitigation professionals and document analysis. Second, we unpack the concept of military urbanism and its six elements with emphasis on the shape of these processes in Canadian cities. We then use case studies of MCS and risk mitigation to think through the idea of military urbanism and its worth for conceptualizing urban security and risk in the twenty-first century. Finally, we discuss how our analysis of MCS and risk mitigation adds to an understanding of possible futures of risk and security; we comment on the blurring of the public–private distinction among organizations focusing security and risk and of public–private city spaces and to possible future avenues of research using this idea of military urbanism.

Note on method

Before commenting on our theoretical framework and empirical material, we review our research study design. We conducted interviews with MCS personnel in multiple Canadian cities as well as their municipal government risk manager counterparts. Our purpose was to understand how MCS agencies have become established in municipal governments across Canada, how they form policy, and how they procure technology for application in municipal buildings and on municipal lands. Our interviews also focused on the work of MCS staff, including their monitoring of municipal employees, regulation of conduct on municipal lands, securitization of buildings, surveillance camera use, and assessment of risk and threat in buildings and during temporary events on municipal land. In addition, we interviewed risk mitigation company representatives and professionals from two risk mitigation companies. Private corporations with concerns about critical infrastructure contract with risk mitigation companies for various services and threat assessments, however, municipal governments increasingly contract the services of risk mitigation firms too. In addition to interviews, we analyzed publicly accessible documents pertaining to MCS and risk mitigation companies in Canada, and documents acquired from freedom of information requests with MCS offices. While risk mitigation in the private sphere diverges from MCS in the public sphere, below we focus on their continuities and whether military urbanism helps to make them intelligible.

MCS units and risk mitigation companies are similar in several respects. First, both assess threat and risk using tools from the American Society of Industrial Security, or ASIS, and other security associations that establish security and risk standards. Second, their work involves security and risk assessment in cities as sites of major industrial development and population growth. Although risk mitigation companies have a different corporate culture, and avoid some bureaucratic delays that MCS offices encounter due to their location in the public sector, MCS and risk mitigation professionals think about risk and security in similar ways and equally contribute to regulation in Canadian cities. Third, given these agencies' similar work, resources, and approach to security, MCS and risk mitigation agencies might comprise what O'Reilly (2010) calls a state–corporate symbiosis where public and private organizations are folded into one another. Indeed, in the conclusion we reflect further on the apparent dissolution of public and private distinctions in risk and security work.

The new military urbanism

The new military urbanism is an intriguing and multi-faceted concept with six elements (Graham 2010). The first element is a new urban scale of security doctrine; security has traditionally been thought of as an issue pertaining to nation states and international relations. Recently the link between security doctrine and cities has been explicitly articulated. The urban scale of security doctrine focuses on how cities become sites and sources of risk requiring continuous securitization. The second element of military urbanism is the technological application of securitization to address those risks. This application of technology takes many forms, including screening entry to municipal buildings, surveillance on municipal lands, surveillance of employees of government and corporations in the city, and increasing reliance on technologies to produce information about potential threats and risk. The third element of military urbanism refers to security industries that are encouraging and capitalizing on this new urban scale. These industries market their technologies and strategies directly to municipal governments, and also to private corporations. Claims about the vulnerability of cities have become incorporated into the marketing strategies of corporations that sell security technologies and strategies. The fourth element of military urbanism refers to the capture of additional spaces by the process of urbanization. The process of urbanization is no longer separable from securitization. As cities continue their relentless spread into rural areas, security follows. All riverbanks, ravines, and green spaces become objects of scrutiny for risk assessment and securitization. The fifth element of military urbanism is the urban threat discourse that reframes all persons, places, and things within the city to be in need of risk assessment and constantly under threat, but also recasts the city as a threat in and of itself. The final element of military urbanism regards cultural performances of security. This entails reporting on issues of terrorism or other urban threats that create a spectacle of security and a demonstrable need for security, which weaves the very idea of risk and security into everyday consciousness of urbanites. These processes are not organized at a single point (Graham 2012); instead they operate through networks, such that it is difficult to make claims about singular causes or sources of military urbanism.

These six elements comprise the concept of military urbanism. Given its coverage of issues having to do with everything from architecture and physical design of municipal spaces, to urbanization, to cultural knowledge of risk, and to the political economy of the security industry, military urbanism is of potential interest to geographers, sociologists, and criminologists. The idea has been used to think through advanced forms of regulating graffiti (Iveson 2010: 131), the new kinds of surveillance and intelligence gathering used in graffiti-prevention efforts, and the growth of attendant security markets. Iveson argues the new military urbanism precludes "the possibility that anything visibly out of the 'ordinary' might be innocent." The analytical potential of the military urbanism concept to understand particular contexts is exciting, but also challenging given that any given case study may not involve all six elements. Graham (2012) argues that most examples he used to conceive of the idea of new military urbanism pertain to US agencies such as the US Department of Defense. But he goes on to suggest that "much work needs to be done to satisfactorily understand how contemporary trends towards the securitization of cities are refracted through different national security and military cultures and the various urban political and legal traditions" (Graham 2012: 150). It remains to be seen whether particular cases in other countries and outside the traditional military domain can help extend and substantiate the idea of military urbanism.

Most cities Graham discusses in *Cities under Siege* in relation to military urbanism are characterized by high levels of violence, or at least high relative to others. For this reason, in this chapter we are keen to discern whether the notion of military urbanism may have application in Canadian cities that are typically not characterized thus. While there is geographical variation, with generally higher rates of violence in Western Canadian cities than in the East, overall Canadian cities experience levels of violence (at least as measured by official crime rates) more akin to cities of Europe than to their US and Mexican urban North American counterparts. This is also true of major terrorist acts in public urban spaces, which, unlike in New York City, Madrid, London, and Mexico City, have not been experienced in Canadian cities. We think that considering the analytical purchase of military urbanism in Canada, therefore, where preoccupation with risk and security seems less justifiable, may be more revealing than in other regions' cities. It remains to be seen whether and to what extent MCS and risk mitigation practices and work arrangements cohere with the idea of military urbanism.

Municipal corporate security

As mentioned above, we conducted research on MCS agencies and risk mitigation firms. First, we will discuss MCS agencies, with a focus on how their practices intersect with the notion of military urbanism. Since the early 2000s, MCS agencies have become embedded in municipal governments across Canada. MCS engages in several kinds of work within municipalities and assesses risk in physical security and architecture and building design using threat assessments. MCS monitors municipal employee conduct, including criminal activity. MCS surveils and polices municipal lands insofar as they remove homeless persons and other persons defined as risks or nuisances who enter the sight or cross the path of MCS personnel. As well, MCS trains municipal employees to think about risk and security in their everyday working lives. MCS contracts private security services too for tasks not requiring expertise or specialized training, although this varies by city. MCS procures its technologies and strategies from organizations at the international scale of security such as ASIS. The use of these strategies requires procurement of technologies such as ID card scanners, camera surveillance systems, door and alarm monitoring systems, asset protection cataloguing systems, and so on.

We argue that MCS demonstrates the tendencies of new military urbanism in several ways. First, MCS reflects the emergence of an urban scale of security doctrine, insofar as the kinds of boundary maintenance and border regulation that were once deemed the terrain of national security agencies have been transferred to cities. MCS personnel erect these boundaries, and also test to determine if they are porous:

> [W]e'll do Security Penetration Tests Incorporation. So we're out there making sure that people are following policy and procedure, you know, locking up laptops and making sure cash handling procedures are being adhered to, and stuff like that . . . . It's interesting too, the auditor's office loves it, and they think it's a fabulous idea . . . . Actually my guys are having a great time doing it. They'll dress themselves up and try to penetrate the perimeters.
>
> (MCS 1)

The city is seen anew through a security doctrine partially borrowed from grander scales of security. In this sense, MCS embodies the first element of military urbanism. More and more boundaries are erected by MCS, leading to spheres of security (Klauser 2010) on and within municipal properties. MCS work involves targeting everyday urban life as risky.

As well, MCS implements new security technologies on municipal lands and in municipal buildings to track inhabitants of those spaces and to exclude others. There are numerous examples of these practices, ranging from the use of camera surveillance, to ID card scanners, to door monitoring systems. In one Western city:

> We administer the access card program, so my analyst actually does a lot of the scheduling ... and my admin assistant has a clerk doing all of the card programming and stuff, for names and access. ... We have a process, a 3–1–1–call center and within that is called 'Inside Information.' Everyone goes there to get the photo taken, to get the access put on the card, and through POSSE our security database it flows to us. And then we put the appropriate level of access on the card. The card is already given to the employee at 'Inside Information'... the type of card that we're using: HID card, has a chip in it. So as for counterfeiting ... it is possible, but the security measures that we have in them would make it quite difficult . ... You'll notice City Place, Maple Hall and City Hall, are all must-wear facilities. So employees must have their cards visible; it's kind of an unwritten rule at the rest of the facilities, and they know that they can be challenged at any given time and they must display their card. ... But these three facilities, given that city administration and councilors are in there ... are all must-wear facilities.
>
> (MCS 1)

Through such use of surveillance technologies, MCS embodies the second element of military urbanism – the application of new security technologies. New styles of tracking and keeping track (Graham 2009) are perpetually applied to the city to mitigate risk.

The third element of military urbanism is the political economy of security industries that market to municipalities and treat these government bodies as clients. MCS embodies the third element of military urbanism insofar as security industries market security strategy and technology and supply MCS and other municipal agencies with this security knowledge. The security industry and its new focus on cities intersects directly with MCS. ASIS is again the key organization here:

> I find them truly being the one that's bringing everyone together, sharing best practices, providing those networking opportunities, sharing solutions, working in other areas, . . . that one-stop shop to be able to prevent things from occurring. I just came from Orlando last week, where the big ASIS seminar was . . . giving you an opportunity to see all the latest and greatest technologies in one building, at one time and talk to thousands of people from all around the world. I was talking to a guy from Buenos Aires, and it was very interesting to hear: different part of the world, same security issues.
>
> (MCS 1)

As with other agencies traditionally working outside the ambit of security studies, such as port authorities (see Eski 2011), MCS is joining international security markets as a consumer. Unlike most of these consumers, though, MCS is a government agency. This new surveillant economy amounts to a marketization of municipal government (Graham 2009; Dorn and Levi 2007), insofar as MCS knowledge points back to ASIS and other private security industry Meccas. However, it is vital to point out that this marketization (see Rose 1999) also changes how municipal government works from within, in that MCS begins to see municipal government departments or divisions not only as service users but as paying clients too:

> The way security started at the City ... was that it was still some smaller groups and there were many divisions that either did their own security or didn't have any security and we started to get involved in those divisions. ... So the way we did it, we tackled different divisions based on risk ... saying you know let's look at your risks. Let's see if there are some benefits of combining security in here . .... One of the first [municipal government] divisions that we did was social services ... we deem them a client because they pay us for the security and ... we provide 18 fulltime staff to them . .... They used to be contract guard firms now its in-house security staff at those locations and its worked out wonderful [*sic.*] but that model kind of sold other divisions when they saw ... these tremendous benefits . .... The way our budget works is that well more than half my budget is charge-backs from other divisions.[2]
>
> (MCS 2)

The fourth element of military urbanism – urbanization and subsequent securitization – is evident in MCS practices too. As the municipality procures new lands and buildings, these are measured using threat assessment tools. Every building must be thought through using security logic:

> You see the crime stats for some of these cities; I'm going to suggest that it's not just out on the streets, it's going to filter into their community services sites and pools and transit centers and that's another point to know.
>
> (MCS 1)

The number of sites keeps expanding, and the application of security logic follows:

> [W]e have 60 new facilities coming online, in the next 10 years. Some very major facilities as well – a major rec[reation] center is one of our largest rec centers with something like 90 CCTV cameras in it right now.
>
> (MCS 1)

MCS units are responsible for numerous expanding spheres of security: "In my section there's roughly 1200 buildings and roughly 900 parks that the City ... owns or operates spread over 2700 square kilometers ... there's a lot of ground to cover" (MCS 3). These spaces are to be securitized using various technologies, and they must be visualized through a risk and security lens. This is true as much for immense municipal lands such as parks as for tighter inner spaces of municipal properties. In one major city,

> the software we're looking at to basically be the core of our security program involves GIS mapping. It ties into not only Google Earth to give you that whole sort of big street view thing. And you can insert ... floor plans and designs and links from the floor plan, so if you have a camera on the floor plan and you double click it, it will open up the image associated with that. Or you double click an alarm point on the floor plan and it gives you the instructions or what that device is . ... That sort of an interface that's intuitive as opposed to text based is where we need to go because it's much faster for them to interact with. ... it's something you can buy off the shelf and then you customize it with your floor plans. So we bought that software, we're implementing it now, we're building our database and that information to make that work ... the great thing about that is ... the operation center is communicating to the alarm response guard they can give them very detailed information about 'you should see this' or 'you should be able to turn left there.
>
> (MCS 3)

Here the architecture of municipal properties is securitized in a material way, becoming an intelligence tool in itself. Komninos (2011: 176) refers to these kinds of technological developments as "instrumentation intelligence" insofar as they generate real-time data for assessing risk across the city. While a human agent (a guard) is still thought to be necessary to respond within these arrangements, these guards are merely tools of the primary intelligence system.

The fifth element of military urbanism is the emergence of a pervasive urban threat discourse that reframes all persons, places, and things within the city as sites and sources of risk. This is central to the security imaginary that animates MCS work. Any door left ajar, any item left unattended is a potential source of risk or a liability, and could cause harm to an employee or someone else on municipal property, and so must be eliminated. As one city risk manager remarked:

> There's the public liability claims and as a municipality ... we're a huge target. Someone hurts themselves on, outside anywhere, we're going to get blamed for it ... if it's a park, a road, a sidewalk, whatever it is, you know, something shines too bright or something isn't bright enough, or a sign wasn't visible, or whatever, we'll get blamed for it ... so we are a huge liability target.
>
> (MCS 4)

MCS in a major Western city recently audited and upgraded its camera surveillance systems at the downtown public library. One planning document notes that "the technology in use is becoming a risk in itself as it becomes outdated, unsupported and more prone to failure." Here, even MCS surveillance becomes a risk. In a major Eastern city,

> we would go in and said what the nature of the business is, what are the risks involved, what are the threats, what are the assets, what are you trying to protect here, you know, the vulnerabilities and come up with some sort of plan to mitigate those risks and so that's what we do here and part of those recommendations is . . . [to] install CCTV. Now we have knowledge here as to what the new technology is. We are starting to set some standards within the region as to how to move forward and what kind of cameras would be appropriate.
>
> (MCS 5)

Everything is described and assessed as a potential threat or risk. Similarly, the corporate security policy of Canada's largest city, Toronto, reads:

> The City of Toronto also has a duty to protect City of Toronto employees and members of the public from foreseeable dangers. Knowing the current and foreseeable threats may provide the City of Toronto with a duty to act and implement applicable counter-measures.
>
> (City of Toronto 2009: 10)

That this particular statement is found in a section of the corporate security policy called "legislative reasons for security" is significant and is a point we return to in the conclusion of this chapter.

The final element of military urbanism, cultural performances of risk and security, is not evident in MCS work insofar as MCS is not well known to the general public. MCS offices and practices are without a public face or ritual, unlike, for instance, municipal public police services media relations persons and their drug-bust media spectacles featuring officers posing with oversized marijuana plants or attending elaborate public funeral processions for officers who died on the job in full dress uniforms and white gloves. It is hard to locate information about MCS offices or their personnel as they work behind the scenes in municipalities. That they are without cultural performances of security is interesting given their recent rise in municipalities in recent years. Thus, in some ways the idea of military urbanism can be usefully applied to the MCS example, but there are also limitations.

Risk mitigation companies

Our second case study is of risk mitigation firms, particularly those based in Canada. Risk mitigation firms do work similar to MCS offices, except the former are private. As O'Reilly (2010) has shown, there has been a massive expansion of risk mitigation companies worldwide as part of the growth in transnational security consultancy. Various clients, including municipalities, contract these firms' services. Risk mitigation companies do a wide-range of work involving consultation with clients such as energy sector companies working with critical infrastructure (see Sheptycki 2002), surveillance of employees, pre-employment screening and background checks for human resource departments, workplace monitoring, managing labor disputes, and supporting litigation. As an example of how public and private security teams work side by side in the twenty-first century (see White 2012), municipalities in Canada with or without MCS units have contracted risk mitigation companies for their expertise. In some cases, they do risk mitigation on municipalities' behalf.

The question becomes whether the idea of military urbanism can be applied to the work of risk mitigation companies. We argue that risk mitigation demonstrates the tendencies of new military urbanism in several ways. Consistent with the first element of military urbanism, risk mitigation companies think of risk at the urban scale. In fact, they are interested in multiple scales including the rural, corridors cutting through the rural and the urban, and so on. Therefore, because of the nature of the clients risk mitigation companies work with, their scale of risk must shift and is necessarily broader than the urban. Like other security agencies that do not fall under the ambit of any particular state (see Aydinli and Yon 2011), the scale of security for risk mitigation companies can be zoomed in or out. In this way, the work of risk mitigation companies implies new fluid scales of security doctrine, but one which nonetheless includes the urban. In terms of technology (the second element of military urbanism), risk mitigation companies are not as involved in hands-on revision of buildings and spaces and application of surveillance and monitoring technologies as MCS personnel. However, these firms have expertise in applying relevant technologies and also deploy various techniques to monitor and account for risk. Here we extend the idea of technology to the techniques and procedures used to assess risk:

> Cap Index Risk Reports . . . they're a risk report service where they've collected all the data from the insurance industry and demographics of the police services . . . if we're working on a project for a client and they've got a specific address, we'll run this Cap Index Report as just one of the tools that we'll put into the equation as it relates to risk mitigation.
>
> (Risk Mitigation 1)

Some municipal governments contract all legal claims adjustment work and some legal services. The firms are asked not only to investigate and settle claims but also provide information to the risk management unit since they are the "eyes and ears on the street." Risk mitigation is also provided through insurance brokerage services which in one city "are covered by a company called A, and through A we have access to loss prevention and loss control consulting services if required" (Risk Management 1). Risk mitigation companies have a goal consistent with the new military urbanism: to identify and eliminate threats before they manifest themselves (also see Graham 2012).

The third element of military urbanism is the development of security industries that target cities. This is what Graham (2012) calls the new political economy of security. Risk mitigation specialists attend the security expositions and purchase strategies from ASIS and apply these in scenarios they assess for risk. To an extent, the risk mitigation industry can be conceptualized as a player in a broader security industry that targets cities. As one risk mitigation professional explains:

> There definitely is more of a market, and that comes from a lot of different reasons. It's increased exposure to loss and that loss could come from litigation, it could come from loss of business, so if a company doesn't have good risk mitigation program it doesn't mean they're potentially going to lose that client they have, and that client is going to go to another vendor.
>
> (Risk Mitigation 1)

Nonetheless, as noted, risk mitigation companies are not explicitly city-based, because client demand determines both the scale of risk for the company as well as the subsequent marketing and promotions work that risk mitigation companies must do to attract clientele.

The fourth element of military urbanism is the creation of new spaces of risk and security through urbanization. This implies the suburbs, which are also targeted. For example, the common practice of building residential suburbs without sidewalks due to perceived limited pedestrian traffic is now deemed to expose municipal governments to liability risk. This is because pedestrians may be harmed by vehicles when forced to walk on these streets (e.g., Rennie 2009). It is such trends that municipal governments contract risk mitigation companies to help deter.

The work of risk mitigation companies is pertinent, insofar as they assist in the securitization of energy sector sites, energy corridors, and other rural spaces, bringing technologies and strategies germane to the city to adjacent rural areas to provide security to clients, or help clients create their own solutions to identified risk. They consult with corporate clients who manage pipelines from oilfields to cities to ports, for instance. In these scenarios, risk mitigation companies advise corporate security on how to ensure the infrastructure and commodities of the corporation are secure, and on how to keep employees safe (see Sheptycki 2002: 330).

The fifth element of military urbanism refers to the urban threat discourse that animates these practices. Risk mitigation firms focus on the urban as both a site and a source of risk. All issues are recast in the language of threat and risk:

> the generic term is a 'Threat Risk Assessment,' TRA, so what are the threats to our client? . . . broadly it's under geographic risks, so some things about being in that country: plague, floods . . . But we'll look at the geographic issues, the political issues, crime, health and safety issues. Those are the three broad domains that a lot of things fall under. . . . if we go back to a

municipality here in Canada, the threats that we're going to look at for them are: crime, and all things crime related, whether external or internal, so fraud. You know, what are your purchasing and accounting processes, vendor management processes to insure that there's no internal fraud or external fraud? Vandalism, theft, violence in the workplace is a big issue . . . . What we call 'loss prevention' or 'shrinkage' issues around theft, misappropriation. We'll look at health and safety issues. We'll look at if they're using an external guard force, what standards are imposed.

(Risk Mitigation 2)

All persons, places, and things become recast as a site and source of risk. Here, even security becomes a risk to be monitored, assessed, and mitigated.

Cultural performances of risk and security, the final element of military urbanism, by risk mitigation companies are non-existent. Like MCS offices, risk mitigation firms are not on the front stage of risk and security work. They are entities with tentacles that reaching everywhere in the spaces of the city but they are without a public face. They work behind the scenes without media scrutiny or the attention of politicians.

The main idea animating this concept new military urbanism is that all city spaces, be they private or public, are becoming recoded as targets and threats. The new military urbanism does not simply imply the application of military technology and strategy to cities in zones of conflict, occupation, and war. The new military urbanism goes beyond this to re-envision relatively safe and tranquil spaces free of violence as sites of potential security breaches. This applies as much to downtown cores and suburban spaces as it does to world financial centers and war-torn or occupied cities. The insides and outsides of municipal properties are divided up into more or less risky zones. And the new military urbanism involves both technology and strategy as ways and means of transforming city spaces, involving *en masse* target hardening and redesigning of city spaces to render them risk-proof and controllable.

Discussion and conclusion

Our examination of MCS demonstrates that the idea of military urbanism can be used to illuminate the multiplicity of practices of risk and security agencies in cities. In turn, attention to the practices of these risk and security agencies helps flesh out the theoretical model that military urbanism implies. MCS and risk mitigation agencies do not perform risk management and security provision in a spectacular way. Rather, these agencies tend to operate behind the scenes. At the same time, they are involved in many aspects of military urbanism, including reproducing an urban scale of security doctrine, applying security technologies, contributing to the growth of security industries targeting cities, deploying an urban threat discourse that re-conceives urban persons, places, and things as risky, and more broadly helping to tighten the tether between urbanization and securitization.

Another key point, alluded to above, that we encountered in relation to most every feature of the practices of MCS and risk mitigation firms, whether emergency management legislation, workplace harassment legislation, legal claims against city governments, or criminal law, is the centrality of legality, that is, the notion that these agencies and, by extension, military urbanism works through law in very complex ways. Legislative changes affect not only the tools available to MCS and risk mitigation to manage risk and security space, it also shapes how and whether they engage in a particular practice. The example of the "legislative reasons for security" in Toronto above is the tip of an iceberg of legality. A refinement of military urbanism would entail adding an element of legality.

Perhaps the most innovative aspect of Graham's (2012) idea of military urbanism is how it draws together knowledge from geography and sociology to explain changes in twenty-first century cities. We have shown that MCS agencies and risk mitigation firms are integral parts of the policing and securitization of cities. We have been careful not to suggest this new military urbanism involves complete privatization (see also Lippert and Walby 2012). In conclusion, we reflect further on public and private dichotomies regarding urban risk and security. The consequences of these processes for the future of risk and security are interesting, and there are two issues we address here.

The first is the dissolving of the public and private distinction as it regards the agencies involved in risk and security work. MCS is a public body and a government agency, but it derives its strategy and technology from the private security sphere; it contracts private security guards (see Thumala *et al.* 2011) to work on municipal lands and in municipal buildings, and it is integrated with the private security industry. The crossover between the private sphere and the public sphere with this sort of agency leads to a blurring of the public and private. Municipalities' engagement with risk mitigation companies further blur that line; they are a private company with knowledge from the private security industry, but they are increasingly working in consort with public bodies, and conducting this work in and around municipal property. We ultimately see the operation of a network consistent with the rise of military urbanism. Municipal risk management offices contract with private risk mitigation firms and municipal corporate security offices contract with private security firms while both offices also form direct and indirect links with ASIS and other international associations, as well as exchanging information with one another about risk. O'Reilly (2010) notes that the scale of agencies in these processes blurs, not only the distinction between public and private, but also between municipal and international. The future of security in the twenty-first century may be witness to a dissolve between the public and the private, a near complete marketization of government agencies (also see Dorn and Levi 2007), which raises interesting questions about accountability and the future of municipal government given its integration with private bodies (also see Berg 2008).

The second is the increased blurring of the public and private distinction regarding the control of city spaces. As more municipal lands become securitized using security technologies that restrict entrance to and movement in public spaces, they are effectively privatized (Button 2003). Although they remain nominally public and municipal, the spaces that MCS agencies and risk mitigation companies work on lose their openness and publicness, and become subject to further surveillance and forms of security that make it harder to access those sites. Another interesting development is the application of security categorizations to municipal space itself, with some spaces being accessible to everyone, while others accessible only to pre-screened municipal employees. More and more city spaces are becoming neither public nor private as they are graded according to a risk protocol adopted from private industry and applied to all spaces. Perhaps memories of the use value of public spaces will fade as military urbanism enlarges spheres of security in our cities. The result of this new military urbanism, for Graham (2009: 400), is a potential lock-down on democratic politics, insofar as public urban space becomes harder and harder to come by.

The idea of military urbanism is critical for thinking through issues such as security strategy and technology, the political economy of how strategy and technology is marketed and procured, the creation of more urban spaces and secure spaces therein, and how threat and risk are measured and monitored. Our finding that the practices of MCS and risk mitigation agencies are devoid of spectacular aspects and are enmeshed in forms of legality, however, points to significant avenues for future research and imply a need for conceptual refinement. Regardless of whether they ultimately are representative of military urbanism, however, the profound material changes these agencies are plainly enacting and their contributions to the increasing securitization of Canadian cities that is inconsistent with democratic politics and freedom are cause for great concern.

Notes

1 Another reason, as we note in the Introduction, is that we think "policing" already encompasses regulation, security provision, and policing in cities, and that the mostly disciplinary distinctions backing these terms are less than analytically useful and may well stunt rather than foster fruitful conceptual exchanges among geographers, criminologists, sociologists, political scientists, and others seeking to understand how urban life is governed.
2 The cost of risk is also charged back to municipal divisions as a consequence of damage payouts from litigation (Risk Management 1).

References

Aydinli, E. and Yon, H. (2011) "Transgovernmentalism Meets Security: Police Liaison Officers, Terrorism and Statist Transnationalism." *Governance: An International Journal of Policy, Administration, and Institutions,* 24(1): 55–84.

Berg, J. (2008) "Holding South Africa's Private Security Industry Accountable: Mechanisms of Control and Challenges to Effective Oversight." *Acta Criminologica,* 21(1): 87–96.

Button, M. (2003) "Private Security and the Policing of Quasi-Public Space." *International Journal of the Sociology of Law,* 31(3): 227–37.

City of Toronto (2009) *City of Toronto City-Wide Corporate Security Policy.* Available at: http://www.toronto.ca/legdocs/mmis/2009/gm/bgrd/backgroundfile-20217.pdf [accessed 20 November 2012].

Dorn, N. and Levi, M. (2007) "European Private Security, Corporate Investigation, and Military Services: Collective Security, Market Regulation and Structuring the Public Sphere." *Policing and Society*, 17(3): 213–38.

Eski, Y. (2011) "'Port of Call': Towards a Criminology of Port Security." *Criminology and Criminal Justice,* 11(5): 415–31.

Ewick, P. and Silbey, S. (1998) *The Common Place of Law*, Chicago: University of Chicago Press.Graham, S. (2009) "Cities as Battlespace: The New Military Urbanism." *City*, 13(4): 383–402.

Graham, S. (2010) *Cities Under Siege: The New Military Urbanism*. New York: Verso.

Graham, S. (2012) "When Life Itself Is War: On the Urbanization of Military and Security Doctrine." *International Journal of Urban and Regional Research*, 36(1): 136–55.

Hallsworth, S. and Lea, J. (2011), "Reconstructing Leviathan: Emerging contours of the security state." *Theoretical Criminology,* 15(2): 141–57.

Iveson, K. (2010) "The Wars on Graffiti and the New Military Urbanism." *City*, 14(1–2): 115–34.

Klauser, F. (2010) "Splintering Spheres of Security: Peter Sloterdijk and the Contemporary Fortress City." *Environment and Planning D: Society and Space*, 28(2): 326–40.

Komninos, N. (2011) "Intelligent Cities: Variable Geometries of Spatial Intelligence." *Intelligent Buildings*, 3(3): 172–88.

Lippert, R. and Walby, K. (2012) "Municipal Corporate Security and the Intensification of Urban Surveillance." *Surveillance and Society*, 9(3): 310–20.

O'Reilly, C. (2010) "The Transnational Security Consultancy Industry: A Case of State-Corporate Symbiosis." *Theoretical Criminology*, 14(2): 183–210.

Rennie, G. (2009) "Claims Drain Municipal Coffers." *Windsor Star,* 5 December. Available at: http://www2.canada.com/windsorstar/news/story.html?id=a8eb7c96-c1f3-40ba-a10a-4cc0540db08e&p=2. [accessed 20 November 2012]

Rose, N. (1999) *Powers of Freedom,* Cambridge: Cambridge University Press.

Shearing, C. and Marks, M. (2011) "Being a New Police in the Liquid 21st Century." *Policing,* 5(3): 210–18.

Sheptycki, J. (2002) "Accountability Across the Policing Field: Toward a General Cartography of Accountability for Post-Modern Policing." *Policing and Society*, 12(4): 323–38.

Thumala, A., Goold, B., and Loader, I. (2011) "A Tainted Trade? Moral Ambivalence and Legitimation Work in the Private Security Industry." *British Journal of Sociology,* 62(2): 283–303.

White, A. (2012) "The New Political Economy of Private Security." *Theoretical Criminology*, 16(1): 85–101.

14 Securitization strategies

Gated communities and market-rate co-operatives in New York

Setha Low

Introduction

This chapter examines neoliberal securitization strategies embedded in corporate legal structures and institutions as a way of problematizing the concept of privatization (also see Mitchell 2003; Low and Smith 2006; Miller 2007). A focus on private governance in two types of collective housing schemes found in New York City and the adjoining suburbs, gated condominium communities and co-operative apartment complexes (i.e. co-ops) uncovers the spatial, legal, and financial barriers constructed to provide "security" and "safety" and that organize and regulate people according to economic, social, political, and cultural ideals. Drawing from ethnographies of gated communities and co-ops in New York City and Nassau County, New York, these two forms of collective home ownership will be used to illustrate the impact of private governance structures on the politics, emotions and social relations of residents. They suggest that other forms of privatization also employ securitization as a means of mobilizing support for what would otherwise be seen as race and class segregation through exclusionary practices.

In the United States, where private home ownership has been touted as the primary means for citizens to achieve financial security and social status (cf. Saegert *et al.* 2009), the governance structures that regulate collective home ownership are being privatized and increasingly organized as corporations with ever more restrictive institutional practices. In a study of gated communities completed in 2005, I found that the greatest impact on social relations within the residential development was how private governance was structured, and not simply the physical walls and gates that stimulated my initial concern. In fact, the governance structure of the homeowners' association board and other elements of common interest development (CID) housing, better known as condominiums, changed the nature of home ownership and the so-called "American Dream" (also see McKenzie 2009; Harris 2011; Lippert 2012). They use an extreme form of social segregation to monitor and control "community" to create a "secure environment," raising questions as to whose economic, social, political and cultural ideals are enforced by both the physical and metaphorical walls and gates (also see Low 2003).

To further understand the impact of private governance on home ownership and housing schemes, a second study of another form of private governance, co-operative apartment complexes, was undertaken to determine if some of the same outcomes – desire for safety and security, fear of others, moral minimalism, lack of representation and civic engagement, and exclusionary and racist behavior on the part of residents – would also be observed. This chapter draws upon these two ethnographic studies to examine privatization of housing schemes through the framework of corporate private governance, concluding that securitization may be an additional way to conceptualize the observed social impact of private governance practices, and to understand the privatization of public urban space in other contexts.

Although my use of the term securitization emerged from the discourse of interviewees during my fieldwork, it is similar to Røyrvik's (2010) concept of securitization that draws from both economic-financial securitization and political-military securitization as expressed in the home environment (Low 2009). He identifies two major trends: the "securitization of the social" and the "sociality of securitization" that create distrust and distancing, cultures of fear, militarism, and deep patterns of global inequality (Røyrvik 2010). McDonald (2008) develops the concept further by unpacking its discursive construction and the under-specified elements in the context of speech acts. In this research, however, while interviewees employ security discursively, I am using the term to describe interlocking and overlapping spatial, legal, institutional, governmental, and financial strategies of producing "security" in CID housing environments.

Ethnography of gated communities in New York

The gated-community research began with gaining entry into two upper-middle- and middle- income gated subdivisions in 1994 and 1995, both in Nassau County on Long Island. Communities of middle income and of middle to lower-middle income in the New York City area were added in 2000 and 2005, to answer questions about class and cultural differences that arose later in the project. Three gated communities – one with single-family housing (approximately 3,500 square feet), one with attached townhouses (approximately 1,200-1,500 square feet), and one apartment complex (800-1,200 square feet) – were studied in the two regions (Low 2003). Utilizing family contacts and real-estate agents to gain entry to these communities, the research group employed a snowball sampling technique using each interview respondent to lead to the next. It was a slow process to recruit interviewees. A total of 25 households were interviewed for this New York based part of the study.

The two-hour open-ended interview was organized around a semi-structured residential history conducted in the home with the wife or single woman, husband or single man, or husband and wife together. The majority of the interviewees were heterosexual European Americans and native-born couples. However, four interviews were conducted in households in which one spouse was from Latin America, West Africa, Asia, or the Middle East. Interviewees were 18–75 years of age. The absence of minority residents is indicative of the middle- and upper-middle-class composition of their gated communities. The men interviewed were mostly professionals such as doctors, lawyers, and teachers and those working in industry as businessmen, managers, and foremen. Others were retired from these pursuits. The majority of the women were stay-at-home mothers. Those women that worked were employed part-time. Of the three single, widowed or divorced women, two worked full-time and one was retired from full-time employment.

Participant observation was ongoing in the shopping, transportation, and recreational areas near each development. The analysis of participant observation field notes focused on identifying empirical evidence of changes in the local environment. Further, it produced data on naturally occurring conversations and everyday observations that provide a test of ecological validity for the interviews. Field notes and interviews were coded by emerging themes throughout the research process. A thematic content analysis of the interviews and documents collected from the media, marketing, and sales materials provided the documentation of the range of discourse available.

Ethnography of market-rate co-op apartment buildings in New York City

The study began in July 2006, and data collection completed September 2007 after interviewing 24 co-op residents in 23 buildings in New York City to compare with the 25 gated-community residents interviewed in the New York area. A total of 22 of the interviews were conducted with single participants, while the twenty-third was with a couple. Through personal contacts and interested colleagues, the research team located residents willing to be interviewed. In some cases, a key informant referred others who might be willing to speak to us. As opposed to the gated-community study, it was less complicated to identify possible participants, but more difficult in that the interviewers could not contact multiple residents in any one building or apartment complex. Instead, every effort was made to sample small to large buildings in three of the five boroughs (i.e. counties) of New York City: Manhattan, Brooklyn, and Queens, and to include a variety of age, marital status, sexual orientation, ethnic and/or racial, and gender characteristics to capture a broad range of resident experiences, opinions, and attitudes.

The sample included only participants who owned and resided in market-rate co-ops in New York City. An attempt was made to solicit participants with varied backgrounds where possible, yet the sample remained fairly homogenous. Participants ranged in age from 27 to 71 years of age; seven interviewees identified themselves as men. Eighteen participants identified themselves as white or Caucasian, and six identified themselves as African-American, Latino, Filipino, and Asian. Six identified themselves as homosexual, fourteen as heterosexual, and four individuals did not identify their sexual orientation. All participants had completed college. Most participants noted that they had or were nearing completion of an advanced degree. Occupations included lawyers, professors, artists, graphic designers, computer programmers, corporate vice presidents, and research directors. Interviewees lived in apartment buildings throughout the city, from trendy SoHo to the family-oriented Upper West Side, and from Forest Hills in Queens to Park Slope in Brooklyn. Most participants resided in studios and one- or two-bedroom apartments ranging from 400 to 1,700 square feet, averaging around 900 square feet. Seven buildings had fewer than 30 apartments, fourteen had 90-140 apartments, and three buildings had over 150 units. Participants had occupied their present co-op for six months to 20 years, with a median of six years of occupancy. Most buildings became co-ops in the early 1980s, and a few were converted in the mid-1990s. Few participants had been in their buildings long enough to have experienced the conversion process. Almost all participants experienced a complicated application and interview process, and 10 had served on their co-op board.

The open-ended interview was organized around a semi-structured series of questions that included the same residential history used in the previous gated-community study with additional questions about doormen, the co-op board, the building conversion, and the application process. Interviews were conducted in the home with the individual or the couple together, and ranged from 40 minutes to one hour and 45 minutes. Audio recordings of the interviews were conducted for accuracy and transcribed before the coding process commenced. Field notes were also taken on site by the interviewer to account for visual cues that could later be used to help contextualize the analysis of interviewee responses. The same themes that emerged in the gated- community study were used and new themes that emerged were added to complete the comparative data analysis.

Gated communities and co-ops

In the gated-community study, I found that gates increased fear and anxiety about "other" people entering. But some of my findings – such as sparse neighbor interaction, restriction of civil rights, and minimal participation and sense of representation – could not be explained adequately by spatial enclosure. Instead, they appeared to be due to the articulation of the walled space with the legal institution (CID or condominium) that organized the collective ownership of the facilities and the governance structure of the homeowners association that regulates and monitors it. This interlocking of spatial, legal, and governance systems in gated communities is what creates a "securitized" environment. Gated communities respond to residents' desire for safety and security, as well as status and privacy, by using spatial enclosure and collective private property arrangements that promote a socially exclusionary and disengaged residential neighborhood.

Since there are other kinds of collective private housing schemes, such as market-rate co-operative apartment buildings in New York City, known as "co-ops," I completed another study, discussed above, to see what impact they have on residents to compare to my gating research. Although co-ops are explicitly committed to democratic practices and non-discrimination, in practice they are less than democratic and stimulate exclusionary practices, similar to gated communities. Exactly how this social exclusion varies by size of the building, neighborhood, and social composition of the residents, remains to be seen. However, thus far I have noticed gated communities and co-ops have features in common such as the creation of a securitized environment that is partly due to urban neoliberal policies, especially in New York (Low *et al.* 2012). Specifically, the similarities appear to be the result of the comparable legal and governance structures, not just the spatial configuration, and in the case of co-ops, an additional financial screening component.

Both forms of collective private housing schemes evolved from a racist history of deed restrictions, restrictive covenants, and selective mortgage lending in the United States. In 1948, the US Supreme Court ruled that enforced racial covenants violated the equal protection clause of the United States constitution, and hoped that the case of *Shelley* v. *Kraemer* (334 no. 1 1948) would end racial segregation since these covenants would no longer be enforceable (Rose 2009). Of course, strategic mortgage lending, red lining, and real-estate collusion continued in force (Hayden 2003), but other more invisible forms of social control also began to be used to spatially monitor and limit who belongs within a community. First developed in 1928, CIDs created collective private property regimes with homeowner associations, and existing residential co-operatives with boards, used by the wealthy and artists since the early 1900s, increasingly became a means for organizing and limiting residential membership (Hayden 2003).

The major difference between co-operative housing and gated communities is the structure of ownership. Co-op residents purchase shares in a corporation, and do not own their units. Gated-community residents retain fee-simple ownership of their unit and common ownership of facilities. This means that gated-community residents can sell or rent their units without the approval of the homeowners' association board, while a co-op board must approve buyers or renters and has the power to grant or withhold approval based on an extensive financial review. Although they are not allowed to discriminate by race, ethnicity, age, gender, and sexual orientation, they can refuse those they feel are a financial risk.

In terms of representation, board participation, and social interaction with their board and neighbors, residents living under these two private governance regimes reported similar experiences. However, we found a divergence in how safe and secure residents feel and we think this difference is revealing (Low 2009; Low *et al.* 2012). While gated-community families say they feel safe and secure, they often express considerable ambivalence about the matter. Residents talked about a constant anxiety about workers and "others" as illustrated in Karen's comment:

> That's what's been most important to my husband, to get the children out here where they can feel safe, and we feel safe if they could go out in the streets and not worry that someone is going to grab them . . . we feel so secure and maybe that's wrong too. You know, we've got workers out here, and we still think 'oh, they're safe out here.'
>
> (Co-op Resident 1)

Another resident added, "It's like they can slip in and slip out. Where there's no record of these guys at all. They're here today and gone tomorrow" (Co-op Resident 2). Here, as with other residents, the relative anonymity and inconsistent presence of "workers" are perceived as a breach of security.

Co-op residents, however, are less concerned and attribute this to the combination of the financial screening process and gate-like actors, such as doormen, or a secured key entry. As Yvonne put it: "I've seen them stop people at the door whom they don't recognize and so you feel kind of safe, you know, you're going to be in the building with people that are supposed to be here" (Co-op Resident 3).

But it is as much the co-op application process and the financial vetting of potential residents that is deemed to create this sense of security. Vanessa explained:

> There is a certain feeling like knowing that everyone else had to go through the same agony to get by the co-op board . . . that my next door neighbor isn't this ex-murderer or that they are not paying their rent by selling drugs [laughs].
>
> (Co-op Resident 4)

Similarly, Patricia said, "I really trusted the homogeneity of that building, that I was not going to find someone so very different from me" (Co-op Resident 5).

Even though some residents begrudged the financial vetting by the co-op board and outwardly questioned it, in the final analysis, residents like Kerry, a young woman, suggested it is probably "a good thing":

> First I'm thinking . . . 'oh, that's a drag. Who are they to say?' . . . But how do you know how to vet people? . . . if you're vouched for by an employer or two and you have the money to pay for it, you should be in no matter who [you are] . . . unless you're clearly . . . like a freaky, you know, person. Although I don't know who's supposed to be the judge of that . . . I think that's . . . a good thing, probably.
>
> (Co-op Resident 6)

While an applicant's financial standing is often the reason for access to purchase a property, socioeconomic class and norms are interlocked with financial status in the vetting process. Thus, when residents talk about whether residents "belong" in their building or should be "vouched for" it is ostensibly about the residents' financial ability to pay the mortgage and carrying costs. Yet, this financial discourse references deeper concerns about class and norms of social behavior that residents want protected for their own sense of security.

Some residents, though, perceive the co-op application process as having racist implications and we found instances in which people of color felt they were treated differently. Yul, a self-identified Filipino, talks about what he perceived as racist questions during his application interview, "things they won't ask in a job interview that you could sue for . . . [including] 'Do you cook any ethnic food that smells offensive?'" (Co-op Resident 7). Similarly, Yvette, a Korean-American explains her concern: "I think co-op boards can get away with discrimination without . . . doing it outwardly because they don't have to tell you what they like and what they don't like" (Co-op Resident 8).

Another aspect of this "securitization" process found in both gated communities and co-ops is a unit's purchase price, ability to obtain a mortgage and pay the monthly fees, and the resulting "laissez-faire racism" (Bobo *et al.* 1996). Gary, a White male, laughed knowingly when he explained how this kind of inadvertent racism occurred:

> Cause first of all, there's an income screen. By the time you enter a building like that, people have at least, can afford to rent and they can mortgage a million dollar condo. Like the apartment, I bought this for six-hundred-and-fifty thousand dollars. The one that's identical to this just got sold for a million two. And the person that bought it was not acceptable to the board. Then it got re-sold for approximately a million. So, by the time you're at that level, uh, you're color blind.
>
> (Co-op Resident 9)

These everyday events are experienced as tolerable, told as anecdotal, and are reflected in the discourse of "people like us" that extends beyond race and class to police most aspects of identity and regulate social homogeneity. Thus the desire to live with "similar" people and with people who behave in a similar way is perceived as normative and natural, but the mechanisms to achieve it are structurally complex and hidden even to the residents. Gated communities provide this desired homogeneity through extensive covenants and regulations, and the containment and surveillance of communal spaces with walls and limited access. For this reason, gated communities are viewed by critics as intensifying spatial segregation. Co-ops, in contrast, provide homogeneity through the application and selection process and the ability to determine who can buy or rent a unit, thus creating a social environment that is perceived as "safe" and where residents "feel at home" not through draconian spatial restrictions. Yet this desire for social and economic homogeneity also produces environments in which minority residents feel singled out, and where racist and exclusionary behavior can be more easily exhibited.

The development of neoliberal policies in the United States, that include the growth of privatization and market-driven housing schemes, saturates the state, political culture, and social relations with a "market rationality that effectively strips commitments to political democracy from governance concerns" (Brown 2006: 695). In doing so, undemocratic processes and legal arrangements such as co-operatives and gated communities, that previously might have been interrogated, continue to reinforce social and racial segregation within this neoliberal landscape.

What this research adds to ongoing discussions of privatization and neoliberalism is that spatial enclosure, often identified as a foundational neoliberal strategy (e.g., Brown 2006), does not fully account for the resulting social exclusion and spatial inequality without also considering governance and legal institutional practices. The financialization of daily life (Martin 2002), that measures personal worth and trust in term of income, investments and savings, and private governance structures play an equally important role. It is the interweaving of space, governance, and financial and legal institutions that is so politically and socially powerful, especially when evoked by residents' fear and anxiety and wanting to live with "people like us." The broader concept of "securitization" brings together these interlocking structures with the desire for safety and security, as a significant dimension of the increasing spatial fragmentation and social segregation that is occurring in cities and suburbs today.

Conclusion

Most discussions of privatization correctly focus on the "variegated" geographies (Brenner *et al.* 2010), modalities, and pathways that neoliberalism has taken to inscribe "free market"-based economic and political systems on cities and suburbs in the United States. Many have pointed out that there are cracks and contradictions in these accounts and possibilities for resistance to this seemingly totalizing political-economic regime. The example of New York City Occupy Wall Street, which used a private–public space to set up an encampment in the center of private capital, suggests that this regime is certainly not all-powerful. Within this landscape of inquiry, therefore, I have become increasingly interested in how people reinforce neoliberal strategies and turn state-based concerns with security into an everyday obsession rather than resist its constraints. Private housing schemes facilitate a new level of strangle-hold on social life through the deployment of the emotions of fear and insecurity, especially when tied to legal arrangements such as CIDs and co-ops, and spatial enclosure, such as gated communities or doorman buildings, where the constraints seem almost impossible to pry apart. Co-ops and gated communities employ complex assemblages of spatial, legal, governance, and financial restraints to safeguard "security," the "good" desired by both families and the state, and which is so elusive in this neoliberal environment. For this reason, I suggest we pay more attention to the process of securitization I define as the interlocking of these strategies at the same time as we query other forms of "privatization." Through the use of in-depth ethnographic interviewing over a number of years and an intimate knowledge of residents residential histories and housing concerns, it is possible to uncover how social inequality is produced through private governance of these housing schemes and how a regiment of securitization that is recruited to justify this form of social segregation. I do so in the hopes of better understanding the emotional and social realities of citizens who participate in and reinforce such a politically conservative and revanchist attitude to the poor, the different, the other, and the city.

References

Bobo, L., Kluegel, J.R., and Smith, R.A. (1996) "Laissez Faire Racism: The Crystallization of 'Kinder, Gentler' Anti-Black Ideology." In S. Tuch and J. Martin (eds) *Racial Attitudes in the 1990s: Continuity and Change*, Westport, CT: Praeger.

Brenner, N., Peck, J. and Theodore, N. (2010) "Variegated Neoliberalism." *Global Networks*, 10(2): 182–222.

Brown, W. (2006) "American Nightmare: Neoliberalism, Neoconservatism, and De-Democratization." *Political Theory*, 34(6): 690–714.

Harris, D. (2011) "Condominium and the City: the Rise of Private Property in Vancouver." *Law and Social Inquiry*, 36(3): 694–726.

Hayden, D. (2003) *Building Suburbia: Green Fields and Urban Growth, 1820–2000*. New York: Pantheon Books.

Lippert, R. (2012) "Governing Condominiums and Renters with Legal Knowledge Flows and External Institutions." *Law and Policy*, 34(3): 263–90.

Low, S.M. (2003) *Behind the Gates: Life, Security, and the Pursuit of Happiness in Fortress America*, New York: Routledge.

Low, S.M. (2009) "Maintaining Whiteness: The Fear of Others and Niceness." *Transforming Anthropology*, 17(2): 79–92.

Low, S. and Smith, N. (2006) *Politics of Public Space*, New York: Routledge.

Low, S., Donovan, G. and Gieseking, J. (2012) "Shoestring Democracy: Gated Condominiums and Market-Rate Cooperatives in New York." *Journal of Urban Affairs*, 34(3): 279–96.Martin, R. (2002) *Financialization of Everyday Life*, Philadelphia: University of Pennsylvania.

McDonald, M. (2008) "Securitization and the Construction of Security." *European Journal of International Relations*, 14(4): 563–87.

McKenzie, E. (2009) *Beyond Privatopia: Rethinking Residential Private Government*, Washington, DC: Urban Institute Press.

Miller, K.F. (2007) *Designs on the Public: The Private Lives of New York's Public Spaces*, Minneapolis: University of Minnesota.

Mitchell, D. (2003) *The Right to the City*, New York: Guilford Press.

Rose, C. (2009) "Liberty, Property, Environmentalism." *Social Philosophy and Policy*, 26(2): 1–25.

Røyrvik, E. (2010) "The Sociality of Securitization: Symbolic Weapons of Mass Deception." *iNtergraph: Journal of Dialogic Anthropology*, 2(2): 1–16.

Saegert, S., Fields, D., and Libman, K. (2009) "Deflating the Dream: Radical Risk and the Neoliberalization of Homeownership." *Journal of Urban Affairs*, 31(3): 297–317.

15 Urban securitization in Mexico City

A new public order?

Nelson Arteaga Botello

Introduction

Since the middle of the 1990s, processes of policing, securitization, and regulation of urban spaces have been developing in Mexico City with the objective of addressing the increased violence and crime that the city has lived through (Arteaga 2006). As stated by Zurita and Ramírez (1999), crime increased in a significant way in the 1990s, from 1,700 offenses for every 100,000 inhabitants in 1993, to 2,895 for every 100,000 in 1995. Violent offenses increased 500 percent from 1990 to 1996. In fact, the number of reported violent offenses consistently increased from 1980 to 1996 from 1,000 offenses for every 100,000 inhabitants to almost 3,000 (Ruiz 1999). Robbery, homicide, assassinations, kidnappings, settling of accounts among drug traffickers, isolated acts of urban guerrilla warfare, urban riots, as well as lynching in communities undergoing urbanization painted a violent and criminal picture of the capital during the 1990s.

It is in this context that two forms of policing, securitization, and regulation developed in Mexico City, which I focus on in this chapter. The first was characterized by certain sectors of the population being under siege and limiting the circulation of the inhabitants of the city, whereby the police and the army establish checkpoints and control points. The second one involves a strategy of securitization that seeks to establish a logic of monitoring, classification, and control of the population's movements. It has been put in place through three programs: dividing the city into quadrants, establishing a video surveillance program which covers the main residential, financial, and commercial centers, and reforming the state police force. The objective of this chapter is, first, to show how both strategies lead to order maintenance in urban spaces from the transformation in different ways of public and private spaces, as well as the infrastructure of cities, including their citizens, into sources of targets and threats in two distinct ways from urban militarism (Graham 2012). Second, it seeks to sketch out the implications that they have in the reorganization of the city, as well as the way in which the inhabitants gain access and use it.

In addition to these two strategies of policing, securitization, and regulation of urban spaces in Mexico City, these changes also have been accompanied by reforms to the organization of the state police, and to the legal and judicial framework, which revolve around a specific thread. In the first case, the reforms are structured with the goal of facilitating the detention and assurance of presumed criminals and suspects without judicial order, such as guaranteeing the establishment of the policies known as "zero tolerance," giving support to the strategy of limiting population flow and besieging certain residential zones. Meanwhile, in more recent policies, video surveillance mobilizes political, legal, and judicial reforms. Both are analyzed here, and following Norris (2012) I argue that both supply a symbolic response to the problem of crime that suggests something is being done to guarantee the security of the population. This calls into doubt the idea that, as Graham says (2009a) there exists a constant danger and risk of violence and criminality in everyday urban spaces.

The chapter examines, first, the strategies of urban policing developed to address the increase in criminal acts in Mexico City in the 1990s. Next, I analyze the turn toward surveillance of urban space, particularly the installation of video cameras. This can be understood as an answer to the problem of insecurity and is linked also to policies of urban renewal of the city implemented in the first decade of the twenty-first century. Finally, I examine the connection among the dynamics of surveillance (such as control), the expansion of a particular urban management (e.g. real-estate renovation development) and the practices of the citizenry (facing the logic of segregation and exclusion as a product of the new forms of social sorting) in discussing Mexico City. In closing, I briefly consider these urban processes in reference to other similar dynamics, but trying to accentuate the particular conditions of violence in Mexico.

Urban spaces under siege

During the decade of the 1990s, the feeling of insecurity in Mexico's capital was converted into one factor that delegitimized the city's government. Since 1928, the president of the republic had the right to designate and remove at his discretion the mayor of the city. The delegitimization not only affected the government of the capital, but also directly affected the president of the republic. A strategy of securitization was implemented by the federal government to slow down the violence. But this had the effect of limiting the flow of the population, containing in some cases its mobility and in others, besieging it. Such a strategy is supported through the articulation of three spheres of action: the implementation of police controls in predetermined points in the city, the hardening of criminal laws, and the militarization of the police force.

The first sphere of action was the program called Immediate Maximum Alert Reaction (IMAR) in the middle of 1995. This program was thought of as a police action directed at preventing criminal violations, kidnapping and homicide, as well as "high risk anti-social conduct" (Ramírez 1996), particularly that linked to the consumption and trafficking of drugs. The IMAR program examined the implementation of blockades and points of vehicle and pedestrian control, generating with it police and military filters allowing the detection of presumed delinquents, discouraging crime, and seizing weapons. Security was for the IMAR program a matter of control of the population's movement. Its advocates claimed its success by announcing it lead to an increase in the number of presumed delinquents brought before the corresponding authorities (Aleman 1996a). Despite that the country's Constitution does not authorize the detention of any person without judicial order, and despite the denouncements of human rights defense organizations for violation to individual rights, the then chief of the city's police department, David Garay, announced that the operations would continue to develop because giving back the security to the citizens of the capital of the country was the central objective of the city's government, that it

> supersedes any other program of the capital city's government, neither the program covering unemployment, neither economic, educational, cultural promotion, of public works or social development, cannot go forward if the problem of crime and violence is not attended to beforehand.
>
> (Aleman 1996b: 44)

The second sphere involved a series of reforms of an administrative framework in criminal law, increasing the sanctions and penalties, lowering the age of criminal responsibility from 18 to 16 years old, and denying bail to those charged with minor robbery. The government suggested, also, the initiation of the death penalty for certain major offenses, a proposal that did not materialize thanks to resistance of several human rights civil defense organizations. The government proffered these reforms, arguing that the only way to stop crime was with an example of punishment, that "delinquency cannot be combated with flowers and cotton: it should be fought exactly with the principal idea that every action corresponds to a reaction; with the same force, but in the opposite direction" (Aleman 1996a: 3). This discourse was reinforced with the idea, expressed by the president of the republic, Ernesto Zedillo Ponce de León, of confronting both corruption in the interior and generally in the judicial system, and equipping and training of the capital city police to do so. It was considered necessary to spread between the police a culture of "zero tolerance" for any legal infraction, since avoiding minor mistakes, according to president Zedillo, was "the road to the justification of grave criminal acts" (Vargas and Gil 1998: 3).

The third sphere of action was directed toward the militarization of police and security, a process that was consolidated with the exit of David Garay as the Secretary of Public Security in the middle of 1995 (he was accused of abuse of police power in the repression of a protest of the basic education school teachers). His successor, by presidential designation, was General Enrique Salgado Cordero, who became in charge of transfering a military discipline and criteria of institutional functioning of the army to the police force of the city. The objective was to reduce the levels of police corruption and elevate the efficiency of the prosecution of criminal acts. Approximately 20 generals and 10 colonels were incorporated into the new police department to search, following its new responsibility, "to imbue the principals under those which have been formed [the military]: loyalty, discipline, institutionalism and vocation to service" (Llanos 1996: 35). Its vision included that Mexican society acquire new values and rules since individualism and indifference facing community *problems* had contributed also to the increase of crime and violence.

Under military control, the Mexico City police force established security forces in tourist spaces, large concentrated places, and residential zones. The operations focused on neighborhoods considered to generate delinquency and typified by marginalization and exclusion. A large number of these new security forces were concentrated in the city center and functioned by detaining people who, in judgment of uniformed officers, were suspect. Any vehicle that carried more than three people was detained, officers insisting that they identify themselves, explain their occupation and the reason they were traveling in that vehicle. Pedestrians were also detained when, under judgment of the uniformed officers, exhibited behavior that they considered "suspicious" (Najar 1997). In some neighborhoods, strictly military operations were implemented that lasted three months, in which the army established street patrols and activities of a social character, mainly medical attention for the population, following a model of intervention used in rural communities with a guerrilla presence during the seventies. In this way a militarization of society and the organization of the city has been established, what Graham (2009b) has called as a new military urbanism, in which the techniques, ideas, doctrines, rules and exercises of the military's own power is used to management risk and danger, crime and criminal violence or terrorist acts in the urban space. This type of intervention, along with the security cordons, disappeared in 1997, when an operation to dismantle the commerce of stolen auto parts in the Buenos Aires neighborhood, ended with an uprising of the neighbors, killing of a police officer and a citizen, as well as the disappearance of three young men during the clash – who later appeared dead in a sand mine after being tortured and executed by police who participated in the operation.

This context served as a backdrop for the questioning of the security policies of the city government and the federal government. The main criticism of the city's inhabitants is directed toward questioning the colonization of the city and society by clearly military operations. In 1997, the inhabitants of the capital for the first time democratically elected their mayor, Cuauhtémoc Cárdenas Solórzano, who was a candidate of the Democratic Revolution Party (or PRD based on its Spanish abbreviation). However, these new political conditions did not translate into a reform of the police or urban policing policies. The continuance of a bureaucracy linked to the president's party, with more than 70 years in power, slowed the reform of the police organization and the city's judicial system. The chief of police continued to be appointed by the president – although this decision was made in consultation with the mayor. This meant that the city's security policies were marked by a series of negotiations that severely limited the capacity for action of the new government. Yet, as Davis (2007) points out, the attempt to cleanse the police with the goal of reducing corruption of some elements generated important resistance that manifested itself through the despondency of the police in doing their job and sometimes a greater participation of police in criminal acts.

The first years of the first democratic government of the city did not imply a change in forms of securitization. To this it must be added that Cuauhtémoc Cárdenas was questioned for a series of appointments in the area of security. It was argued by various human rights organizations that some named officials were linked to investigation and political repression during the sixties and seventies. Also, the mayor made his speech on "zero tolerance" that had been pushed by the federal government through the president of the republic. In fact, operations continued based on sieges and security cordons, although not with the same intensity, in some cases with the same consequences. Such was the case of police intervention in the Tepito neighborhood – traditionally considered the core of piracy, contraband, and drug trafficking – that ended in the uprising of an important segment of the population of the barrio that burned automobiles, looted businesses, and closed the most vital avenues in the center of Mexico City.

Cárdenas and his idea for transforming the police and reducing crime and violence did not live up to the expectations placed on the first democratic city government (Davis 2007). When Cárdenas left the post of mayor there was even a decline in the weak cooperation between police elements, which increased the population's dissatisfaction in the same proportion as they felt that the city was one of the most insecure in Latin America. Statistics reinforce this idea. According to Smith (2003), during the period of the Cárdenas government, only 7 percent of crimes committed in the city were solved. This is the lowest figure in the recent history of the country's capital. However, in this period of government, between authorities and society, the militarized practices of tracking and targeting everyday urban circulation, key pieces of a new military urbanism were standardized (Graham 2009b) in a certain way because nobody thought that there would be another way to fight crime and violence in the city. A war zone strategy was created and directed toward separating spaces and zones, as well as routes that need protection from those that need to be separated. This occurred through, as Graham (2010) points out, a military targeting strategy which will be taken to another scale with the introduction of smart CCTV. The new military urbanism, based on the introduction of information and communication technologies, appears to be presented to society as a less "intrusive" and authoritarian alternative the simple operation of sieges and security cordons, that can be remembered from the hardest years of political repression in the country. In other words, as Foster (2004) suggests, the necessity of generating a "defensible space" and of generalizing the display of surveillance is legitimized.

The surveillance turn

Regretful about the problems left unaddressed and in some cases exacerbated by the security policies in the city, again in 2001 the citizenship elected a candidate from the PRD as mayor: Andrés Manuel López Obrador. His arrival in the capital government was a more favorable context than that experienced by his successor. One year before Vicente Fox arrived as president of the republic, the head of the National Action Party (PAN as known by its Spanish abbreviation), ended more than 70 years of rule by the Institutional Revolution Party (PRI, based on its Spanish abbreviation). In this sense, as Davis (2006) points out, the bureaucracy of the Mexico City government, as well as the police structures, had lost their federal government. However, the democratic political environment became difficult. Visions of both the capital and federal government were on distinct paths, which caused police reform proposals to halt.

From the perspective of the government of Andrés Manuel López Obrador, crime and violence resulted from unemployment and poverty. From this perspective, the increase in the number of police and the social control measures of the cordon walls was an insufficient response (Gobierno del Distrito Federal 2001). The capital government designed a security strategy made up of three actions. The first involved attending to poverty and marginalization. The second required consolidating the citizenry's participation. The third required increased security through the installation of what was considered to be the most advanced technical methods, statistics, and surveillance that allowed detection and control of dangerous places, different types of crime, and actors, help for victims, as well as recording times when acts were committed (Gobierno del Distrito Federal). This was a new public order in the making.

Speaking about the first action, the Mexico City government encouraged one of the programs for addressing poverty and boosting social development, directing its forces toward marginalized zones, the elderly, single mothers, and scholarships for students of all academic levels. In the matter of social development, it generated policies of community integration through sports, recreation, and culture with the clear objective of intervening in what were considered the most marginalized neighborhoods. Despite criticism that these policies received by the federal government were populist, the program was reproduced by the federal government as well as other entities of the country, parties separate from the PRD. With respect to the second type of actions, 1,352 public security citizen committees were established with their own resources, with the goal of contracting night watchmen, the installation of wiring for lighting in zones considered dangerous, installing neighborhood alarms, as well as cleaning empty lots that could constitute a refuge for violent people and criminals (Llanos 2000). These examples of community decisions are aligned with preventive police leadership with the goal of designing fully community-based security strategies, taking into account the particular characteristics of each neighborhood, barrio, and residential development, as well as the dynamics of the relationship among neighbors (Gobierno del Distrito Federal 2001).

The third type of action was developed through the import and adaption of technological securitization that Rudolf Giuliani, ex-mayor of New York, established in that city. The proposal of the installation of video surveillance cameras was borrowed from the security project that the consultation team of Rudolf Giuliani presented as a request from the Mexico City government. This project had as its central proposal the modernization of security through the installation of new electronic surveillance technologies, all at the city's historic center. As Davis (2007) states, Giuliani's proposal had a tangible effect on the development of facilities in this particular location of the city. It sought to accelerate the revitalization of this historic center which had been involved in a process of deterioration, being occupied by low-income and homeless people and other marginalized segments (Pineda 2003). As a result of Giuliani's recommendations, there was a focus on recuperation of urban space, proposing changes in the use of land and public spaces. For that reason "the largest part of the cameras and state of the art monitoring technology that the report recommended, was finally installed downtown" (Davis 2007: 661). All of this was complemented with the organization of semi-private police in charge of the surveillance strategies, as well as the use of CompSat (Computer Statistics of Comparative Statistics) technology – a system of geographic information and statistical production for directing police operations. The central point was monitoring activities in the streets of the city's downtown via video surveillance technologies, as well as mapping crime. As Davis points out,

> while the recently renovated spaces downtown continue to be fundamentally public in a sociologically inclusive way, it is precisely the diversity of this new spatial environment that pushes forward the application of new police and surveillance technique measures directed toward new forms of restricting the flow of people and activities.
>
> (Davis 2007: 668)

Surveillance was converted into a new logic of organization of the city's center, a logic that has been used to push forward urban renovation of other city spaces, but also for control of population flow in public transport and on the main highways. In other words, the surveillance was turned into a central mechanism for pushing forward the logic of predatory planning that was found linked, as Graham (2012) states clearly, to both governments and the burgeoning array of private military and security operations. The effect is, as has been happening in other cities on a global scale, "a radical ratcheting up of techniques of tracking, surveillance and targeting, centered in both the architectures of circulation and mobility – infrastructure – and the spaces of everyday life (Graham 2010: 21). This has been accentuated in the third government of the PRD, headed by Marcelo Ebrard Casaubon. During his government the city was divided into quadrants with the goal of establishing a clearer strategy for surveillance camera installation. The program was named "Bicentennial Project: Safe City" and its objective was to respond immediately to "emergencies, crisis situations and criminal acts" (Gobierno del Distrito Federal 2010). The intention was to install 12,000 surveillance cameras and convert Mexico City into one of the safest cities in the world (Gobierno del Distrito Federal 2010). Besides the surveillance cameras, emergency buttons with direct communication with different offices of the police were installed at various points in the city.

According to the city authorities, the project was designed by taking into account the surveillance systems in cities such as Jerusalem, London, Liverpool, Paris, Baltimore, Chicago, Medellin, and Bogota, adapting the success of these systems to the local conditions of Mexico. The project was put forward only after the passing of the Public Security Technology Regulatory Use Law, with the goal of guaranteeing the installation of digital monitoring systems and the use of information gathered by them. This law states that the installation of equipment and systems of surveillance technology will be in places where it is necessary to prevent, inhibit, and combat criminal behavior, as well as guarantee order and the tranquility of the population (Gobierno del Distrito Federal 2010).

The criteria that justify surveillance camera installation are varied, such as zones considered dangerous, public areas, neighborhoods and other concentrated places, affluent and transited by people, and which mean they can practically be installed anywhere in the city. However, the justification for installation came with three requirements. According to the security technology law, the Secretary of Public security and the Attorney General of the City must develop the statistics to find out the areas with high rates of crime – such as neighborhoods, blocks, avenues, and streets. The Sub-Secretary of Transit Control must, at the same time, provide information of troublesome intersections and those that present risk in case of natural phenomena (Gobierno del Distrito Federal 2008). The security technology law also specifies that information derived from surveillance must be managed in particular ways. On the one hand, it is suggested that such information must be used to generate public security policies, and neighborhood and barrio intervention strategies, in order to detect criminal groups and behavior that break the confidence of the community. On the other hand, the information should provide support for the investigation and prosecution of criminal acts, as well as sanction of administrative infractions and the particular use for guaranteeing the punishment of adolescents' criminal behavior. The information that these surveillance technologies produce have a clear weight, such as means of proof in ministerial and judicial procedures. Finally, it signals that the direct information that the surveillance cameras transmit is a necessary tool for the immediate intervention of the police and not only a mechanism of storing and administering the data (Gobierno del Distrito Federal 2008). This last consideration resulted in the training of 500 police officers in direct image analysis with the objective of detecting criminal acts in process and immediately transferring these discoveries to the police quadrant where the criminal acts are taking place.

Based on these criteria, a little more than 11,000 surveillance cameras were installed between 2008 and 2011: 192 directed towards transit control; 3,312 located in the 175 stations that form 11 lines of the Metropolitan Transport System (metro, metro bus, trolley, bus, tram) and 7,452 urban video cameras distributed in the 916 quadrants that the city was divided in for public security strategic reasons (Gobierno del Distrito Federal 2011). 4,176 cameras have been placed at points considered to have a high incidence of crime and 248 in governmental institutions and embassies (Gobierno del Distrito Federal 2011). The cameras which were installed have the capacity to turn 360° and are capable of distinguishing license plates and faces. Some also have sensors that detect gunfire, which allows the rotation of the camera toward the sound of the detonations automatically. The cameras located in the metro system have the capacity to recognize facial features. Other cameras have loudspeakers to sound alarms and panic buttons, which have been located in parks and outside public schools (Cuenca 2008). Each camera also has a visible identification sign so that the citizenry can locate the camera and know they are being watched.

The surveillance cameras are concentrated in two particular fields. The first of these is in the city's public transportation system, where a daily average of 4.7 million passengers passes through the metro stations (Gobierno del Distrito Federal 2011). The second are points considered to have high crime and violence indexes, mainly streets and avenues that have a large circulation such as financial and commercial districts, which are mostly located in the city center. In this way, the surveillance cameras can be found trying to watch over points with the largest population flow. The rest of the cameras are located along the main avenues that connect downtown with residential zones. The concentration of cameras is heaviest in the central zone of the city and lessons as one moves toward the city's periphery. However, camera density increases as one moves toward the border between Mexico City and the State of Mexico. In this way, the eastern border of Mexico City stands out with a large concentration of surveillance cameras, a type of digital protection wall facing the municipalities of the State of Mexico, such as Nezahualcóyotl, Ecatepec, and Texcoco, which witness a daily exodus of the population who work in Mexico's capital.

These cameras that track population flow substitute for the police checkpoints in an unconstitutional manner, demand the citizenry give personal information and of mobility without a judicial order. This implies a change in security strategies of the city in at least three aspects. In the first place, the establishment of policy directed towards the surveillance of population flow replaces military and police dikes. This provides a greater capacity for the displacement of the city's population, and is different than the siege approach of the 1990s. Insecurity has changed from confinement of the population to tracking the city's carefully managed population flow. In the second place, social controls are established through technological means, little by little displacing the use of physical force as a mechanism of control and security.

Direct intervention of the police diminishes because of this new approach of following the behavior of groups and persons in the city. Face-to-face physical control gives way to forms of technological controls. This means that finally, the consolidation of particular forms of social sorting result in urban segregation. In this last process, the surveillance cameras are not the only actor. The "Bicentennial project: Safe City" is a mechanism that promotes the installation of cameras in different spaces of the city with the goal of reinforcing real-estate development, the financial districts, and consumption spaces for the middle- and upper-class sectors of the city, thus replicating the strategy of the project headed by Giuliani of revitalizing the historic downtown area of Mexico City.

There does not exist an evaluation that allows one to determine how the installed surveillance cameras have reduced criminal and violent acts in the city. The official data only points out that between 2009 and 2011, 16,389 people have been detained by the commission of different criminal acts (pedestrian, house, vehicle, public, transport robbery, and murder), as well as 18,281 people for misdemeanor offenses (alcohol and drug consumption in public spaces, informal commerce, graffiti, indecent behavior, public scandal, littering) (Gobierno del Distrito Federal 2011). Leaving aside an analysis of the capacity that surveillance cameras have for diminishing crime, the symbolic weight of the surveillance cameras is key here, as they play an important role in: (1) spreading an anti-crime policy across the city; (2) revitalization and real estate renovation of the city; and (3) displacement of the logic of restriction and its replacement by the logic of control and monitoring of the flow of the population considered key in the functioning of the city.

Urban segregation and flow control

In the last two decades Mexico City has lived through two forms of securitization: one which drove "traditional militarization" forms of urban space, and the other which established a new military urbanism. The first one utilizes sieges, checkpoints, cordons, isolation, and dike flows; the second, electronic surveillance devices, statistic calculations of risk, securitization technologies, accompanying urban space revitalization programs by predatory urban planning. The new military urbanism, contrary to the old military urbanism, developed with the financial support of national and multinational corporations. However, it is still the old form of militarization that transformed urban spaces into main targets and a large part of its inhabitants into potential threats to security, all done with resistance and social criticism. The new military urbanism, made it possible on the other hand for the normalization of militarized practices of tracking and targeting everyday urban circulation.

The old military urbanism could not resist public opinion criticism because militarization of urban space was understood as an element more for exercising authoritarian power by the federal government within the city. It was even the object of criticism when the first democratic government decided to keep in operation this strategy, and it is in this way that the sieges, checkpoints, cordons, isolations, and dike flows were strategies that could affect any inhabitant – nobody was exempt from being detained, questioned, and brought down, if this was the case, to the police station. They were military strategies that converted any citizen into a threat, and in a city such as Mexico, with its enormous contrasts and inequalities, represented a mechanism of de facto social equality. This woke up and exasperated criticisms from certain sectors of the population – in particular those of middle and high income – who considered that such strategies pointed them out as potential criminals, that it put them at the same level as those sectors considered traditionally to be "dangerous classes," and that also such measures were a violation of the freedoms of circulation and privacy.

Thus, the introduction of securitization based on video cameras was a way to resolve the effects of utilizing sieges, checkpoints, and police cordons, because they operated from the principal differentiating the flow of the population of homogeneous maintaining of enclaves of urban development. This implies the recognition of the differences in the access and use of the city by different social groups. The governmental strategy defined in this sense comprises three forms of observation of the city: first, surveillance of the avenues and streets that connect them, particularly of private automobiles; second, and maybe most importantly, monitoring of the flow of the population in public transportation, in particular, the metro system, where a majority of the population of the city travels – almost all of low income, living on the margins of the city, who regularly are considered by authorities as potential criminals; third, the production of urban segregation processes and social exclusion linked to policies of renovation and real-estate rescue. In this sense, they are a support that first seeks to maintain order in urban spaces.

The first two strategies are directed toward monitoring of large displacements of the population as well as public systems such as private transport. The third is to safeguard the residential zones of the middle and upper class, as well as financial and commercial centers. In the first case the main objective is the protection of social sectors with medium and high income. The second deals with the control of risks that represent the flow of the population in public transport, mainly those of low income. Thus, only a few social sectors are in the line of constant monitoring that includes those spaces where people live, work, and socialize; in the same way, the streets and avenues – some upper- and middle-class sectors. The surveillance cameras are, in this sense, the cement that solidifies the logic of urban segregation and control of population flow, but also connects both processes. It is the common denominator over what rights of access and citizenry exclusion are built. The cameras play a central role as urban modernization mechanisms, not only because of their effects on the production and reproduction of inequality, but also as a clear symbol in the narrative of securitization that seeks order and maximum control of risks.

In Mexico City, there is also success in normalizing these urban policing strategies, from the displacement of exercising direct force in the control of the population by forms of electronic surveillance that are less violent, but not by themselves less intrusive in how they affect people's privacy and their movement in urban spaces. The surveillance cameras are registered as a particular form of sorting, administration, and control of spaces and population, where the behaviors, attitudes, faces, and aspects are potentially analyzed with the goal of preventing apparent risks to social order.

Graham (2012), following the works of Agre (2001), shows that one of the key elements that direct the new military urbanism is to think and act in terms of "battlespace," a conception of military matters that includes absolutely all, temporal and geographical; there is no front or back, no beginning or end; it is found on all sides and not limited to a "battlefield." The two forms of urban policing in

Mexico City opened the door so that this military thinking began following two movements. The first, establishing the city as a battlespace, where the group of its inhabitants stayed involved in the same way under the establishment of a series of military operations face to face, with the presence of not only police, but military that demonstrated in a direct way the presence and force of the State. Social pressures that resisted this form of urban policing brought the battlespace to another level: digital and electronic surveillance systems. In the second movement of urban policing, the presence of the force of the State was diluted in a cloud of data correlation, in the imprecise identification of persons, that is, not left to be perhaps more intrusive or profound. In this way, the resistance to more direct forms in the use of force in the first urban policing experiences for confronting violence and crime in Mexico City ended by expanding the battlespaces through the everyday sites, spaces, and experiences of city life.

Conclusion

The consolidation of urban policing supported in the establishment of a logic of monitoring, classification, and control of the population's movements through the use of video surveillance is not a phenomenon exclusive to Mexico City. There exist distinct securitization processes that respond to the framework of the new military urbanism, in which the installation of surveillance cameras, and other electronic surveillance devices, is linked to the spaces where commercial and financial transactions converge, whose objective is to generate a new aspect to the city, an attractive face to investment and tourism, and offer the sensation of producing adequate conditions for consumption and coexistence in public spaces (Hempel and Töpfer 2009; Coleman and Sim 2000). As in other cities, the cameras in Mexico City respond in line with neoliberal conceptions of the appropriate use of public spaces (Phillips and Curry 2003; Coleman 2004). What results from these types of processes are urban and social segregation that reproduce and in some cases institutionalize certain logics of social exclusion (Lyon 2007; Hasam 2000; Norris *et al.* 1998).

The peculiarity of Mexico City is that, contrary to the experiences of other Global Northern cities, the view of the cameras is combined in Mexico City with the abysmal inequality, with grossly inefficient or, sometimes, nonexistent public services and massive unemployment in the context of a polarized urban economy. It is these surveillance cameras, inserted under the logic of the new military urbanism, that symbolize the poor, the excluded, the unemployed and underemployed, as well as the violence, which millions of people in the city live with. This constitutes one more link in the chain which impedes the practice of the citizenry and the access to the city of important groups of the population. The result is a paradox which, contrary to other countries where the political parties of the Right promote this type of urban policing (Graham 2012), in Mexico City, it is precisely the Leftist party that aims to standardize, with practically no resistance, the operation of military strategies in the city. In this sense, Mexico City has become a space for the normalization of these urban policing strategies, where there exists a displacement of exercising direct force in the control of the population by forms of electronic surveillance that are less violent, but not by themselves less intrusive in the way in which they affect people's privacy and their movement in urban spaces.

There does not exist and apparently there will not exist – at least in the short term – criticism that aims to slow down the installation of surveillance cameras as is happening in other contexts (Smith 2012). This can be explained by the fact that violence in Mexico does not respond to a simple failure of democracy and its institutions, but that is an integral part of it, as a necessary component of their maintenance, as an instrument for popular challenges to their legitimacy (Goldstein 2003). As in other Latin American societies, in Mexico City,

> violence emerges as much more than a social aberration: violence is a mechanism for keeping in place the very institutions and policies that neoliberal democracies have fashioned over the past several decades, as well as an instrument for coping with the myriad problems that neoliberal democracies have generated.
>
> (Arias and Goldstein 2010: 24)

In this sense, the State, the social elite, and other social groups employ the violence in order to establish regimes of citizenship, justice, right, and democratic social order. Urban policing that today prevails in Mexico City appears to give new support to the construction of the city and the exercise of the citizenry through the construction of a battlespace directed toward the institutionalization of the new military urbanism.

Police and judicial authorities anchored in authoritarian practices and with the capacity to handle and administer information of ample sectors of the population, do not favor conditions for the development of the citizens and individual freedoms. In some cases, the electronic surveillance systems also had a political use, in particular when facing social movements which claim access to urban services, to better life conditions and even, a more democratic administration of the city. It is now possible to exercise control and exercise excessive power over pre-determined social groups, thanks to the information which authorities obtain through different surveillance mechanisms. Surveillance is converted, then, into a form of governing the population, which establishes new forms of social sorting in the organization of urban space in a context of economic degradation, unemployment, marginalization and exclusion. In this way, it seems to create a panorama of a city that is organized according to urban spaces and social groups undergoing hyper- and infra-surveillance.

A large part of contemporary literature on the real impact of the installation of surveillance cameras indicates that the dystopic dream of the panoptic is not a reality (Hier 2010). However, in the case of Mexico, it contributes to feeding the dystopic reality of a citizenry that lives in a weak institutional and social support network. In spite of surveillance cameras not creating a feeling of protection among the citizenry (see also Doyle *et al.* 2012), social inequality is used as a mechanism of legitimization of surveillance. Graham (2010) suggests allows separate spaces and privileged zones of mobility free of risk – where those that need protection are found – from the risky surrounding population and infiltration, the surveillance cameras symbolize. As Norris (2012) feels – and the case of Mexico City is no exception – the effective management of the problem of crime and violence is offered as the way to place the city on the same level as cities in developed countries, and to compete as a node of interconnection for the process of a globalized economy.

References

Agre, P. (2001) "Imagining the Next War: Infrastructural Warfare and the Conditions of Democracy." *Radical Urban Theory,* 14 September. Online. Available at: http://polaris. gseis.ucla.edu/pagre/war.html [accessed 10 May 2012].

Aleman, R. (1996a) "La violencia no debe responderse con violencia." *La Jornada* (29 May): p. 1.

Aleman, R. (1996b) "Garay: Seguridad, prioritaria sobre *todos* los demás programas del DDF." *La Jornada* (23 February): 44.

Arias, E. and Goldstein D. (2010) "Understanding the New Democracies of Latin America." In E. Arias and D. Goldstein (eds) *Violent Democracies in Latin America.* Durham, NC: Duke University Press.

Arteaga, N. (2006) *En busca de la legitimidad: Violencia y populismo punitivo en México,* México: Universidad Autónoma de la Ciudad de México.

Coleman, R. (2004) "Watching the Degenerate: Street Camera Surveillance and Urban Regeneration." *Local Economy,* 19(3): 199–211.

Coleman, R. and Sim, J. (2000) "'You'll Never Walk Alone': CCTV Surveillance, Order and Neo-liberal Rule in Liverpool City Centre." *British Journal of Sociology,* 51(3): 623–39.

Cuenca, A. (2008) "Lanza el GDF licitación para instalar videovigilancia." *El Universal* (28 February): 1.

Davis, D. (2006) "Undermining the Rule of Law: Democratization and the Dark Side of Police Reform in Mexico." *Latin American Politics and Society,* 48(1): 55–86.

Davis, D. (2007) "El factor Giuliani: delincuencia, la 'cero tolerancia' en el trabajo policíaco y la transformación de la esfera pública en el centro de la ciudad de México." *Estudios Sociológicos,* 25(3): 639–81.

Doyle, A., Lippert, R., and Lyon, D. (2012) "Introduction." In A. Doyle, R. Lippert, and D. Lyon (eds) *Eyes Everywhere: The Global Growth of Camera Surveillance,* New York: Routledge.

Foster, H. (2004) "Polemics, Postmodernism, Immersion, Militarized Space." *Journal of Visual Culture,* 3(3): 320–35.

Gobierno del Distrito Federal (2001) *Programa de Desarrollo General del Distrito Federal (2001–2006),* Mexico: Gobierno del Distrito Federal.

Gobierno del Distrito Federal (2008) "Decreto por el que se establece la Ley que regula el uso de la tecnología para la seguridad en el Distrito Federal." In *Gaceta Oficial del Distrito Federal,* 27 Octubre, Mexico: Gobierno del Distrito Federal.

Gobierno del Distrito Federal (2010) *Proyecto Bicentenario,* Mexico: Gobierno del Distrito Federal.

Gobierno del Distrito Federal (2011) *Reporte de Resultados del Centro de Emergencia, Atención y Protección Ciudadana,* December 17, 2009–June 19, 2010.

Goldstein, D. (2003) *Laughter Out of Place: Race, Class, Violence, and Sexuality in a Rio Shantytown,* Berkeley: University of California Press.

Graham, S. (2009a) "The Urban Battlespace." *Theory, Culture & Society,* 26(7–8): 278–88.

Graham, S. (2009b) "Cities as Battlespace: The New Military Urbanism." *City,* 13(4): 384–402.

Graham, S. (2010) *Cities Under Siege: The New Military Urbanism,* New York: Verso.

Graham, S. (2012) "When Life Itself Is War: On the Urbanization of Military and Security Doctrine." *International Journal of Urban and Regional Research,* 36(1): 136–55.

Hasam, S. (2000) "Privatización de la seguridad: guerra económica y social." In K. Horst (ed.) *Globalización de la Violencia,* México: Colibrí/Goethe-Institut Mexiko.

Hempel L. and Töpfer, E. (2009) "The Surveillance Consensus: Reviewing the Politics of CCTV in Three European Countries." *European Journal of Criminology,* 6(2): 157–77.

Hier, S. (2010) *Panoptic Dreams: Streetscape Video Surveillance in Canada,* Vancouver: U.B.C. Press.

Llanos, R. (1996) "Queremos imbuir principios, no suplantar a la policía: Salgado." *La Jornada* (5 October): 35.

Llanos, R. (2000) "Propone López Obrador una cruzada contra la delincuencia." *La Jornada* (26 July): 43.

Lyon, D. (2007) "Surveillance, Security and Social Sorting: Emerging Research Priorities." *International Criminal Justice Review,* 17(3): 161–70.

Najar, A. (1997) "'Tenemos agente que las detectan muy bien': asegura una funcionaria." *La Jornada* (23 August): 19.

Norris, C. (2012) "There's No success like Failure and Failure's no Success at all: Some Critical Reflections on the Global Growth of CCTV Surveillance." In A. Doyle, R. Lippert, and D. Lyon (eds) *Eyes Everywhere: the Global Growth of Camera Surveillance,* New York: Routledge.

Norris, C., Moran, J., and Armstrong, G. (1998) "Algorithmic Surveillance: The Future of Automated Visual Surveillance." In C. Norris, J. Moran, and G. Armstrong (eds) *Surveillance, Closed Circuit Television and Social Control,* Aldershot: Ashgate.

Philips, D. and Curry, M. (2003) "Privacy and the Phenetic Urge: Geo-demographics and the Changing Spatiality of Local Practice." In D. Lyon (ed.) *Surveillance as Social Sorting: Privacy, Risk and Digital Discrimination,* London: Routledge.

Pineda, M. (2003) "El Centro Histórico, más vivo." *Certeza: Economía y Negocios,* 6(54): 17–32.

Ramírez, I. (1996) "La militarización de las fuerzas armadas, grave riesgo social." *Proceso,* 1002 (15 January): 13–14.

Ruiz, R. (1999) *Inseguridad y mal gobierno,* México: Sansores & Aljure.Smith, G. (2003) "Mexico City's Battle to Beat Crime." *Business Week Online,* 20 de agosto, Online. Available at:http://www.businessweek.com/bwdaily/dnflash/aug2003/nf200330820_5793_db017.htm?chan=search [accessed 21 February 2007].

Smith, G. (2012) "What Goes Up, Must Come Down: On the Moribundibity of Camera Networks in the UK." In A. Doyle, R. Lippert, and D. Lyon (eds) *Eyes Everywhere: the Global Growth of Camera Surveillance,* New York: Routledge.

Vargas, R. and Gil J. (1998). "Delincuencia y Corrupción, *La Jornada* (27 August): 1.

Zurita, B. and Ramírez T. (1999) "Trends and Empirical Causes of Violent Crime in Mexico" (discussion paper), Washington DC: The World Bank/Mexican Health Foundation [FUNSALUD]. Online. Available at: http://wbln0018.worldbank.org/LAC/LACInfoClient.nsf/5aaa39a87ab8daf985256cc6006f355b/7eb8495c22df44b68525688 0007ee937?OpenDocument [accessed 14 March 2010].

16 Pretext securitization of Boston's public realm after 9/11

Motives, actors, and a role for planners

Susan Silberberg

Introduction

The events of September 11, 2001 and continued threat of terrorism have led many municipalities as well as the US government to rethink issues of public accessibility, open space design, and perimeter building protection. Critics argue that overzealous government officials and security professionals are linking "terrorism" with "urbanism" in a manner that amplifies perceptions of threat everywhere and anywhere (Marcuse 2006; Sorkin 2004). Further, the (re)design of space to secure the public realm is said to degrade and militarize the urban experience with every additional bollard, barrier, checkpoint, security zone, and public space restriction (Graham 2010; Sorkin 2008) (Figures 16.1 and 16.2).

Figure 16.1 A blocked sidewalk at the John F. Kennedy Federal Building.

Figure 16.2 Jersey barriers block the way to the Barking Crab restaurant on the South Boston waterfront.

One line of research on the socio-political aspects of urban security and planning has explored the erosion of traditional social, physical, and free speech "rights to the city" (Lefebvre 1996) and the role of securitization in exclusion from social, economic, and political urban life (Flusty 1994; Nemeth 2009; Savitch 2008). Scholars assert that security measures and restrictions on public gatherings and free speech under the guise of counterterrorism are part of a political agenda that exploits fear and insecurity (Marcuse 2004, 2006) and promulgates a sense of vulnerability and anxiety (Gray and Wyly 2007). Other research has examined security zones (Coaffee 2003) and securitized public space, with some scholars arguing that these zones qualify as a unique land use because they preclude a diversity of users and "privatize" public space (Hollander and Whitfield 2005; Nemeth 2010; Nemeth and Hollander 2010). Still others examine institutional relationships and political frameworks to explain the processes and actors determining security policy, finding evidence of cross-sector and public–private collaborations that span nations (Coaffee and O'Hare 2011).

My chapter explores the role of public space in city living and the politics and motivations of urban securitization. I draw on a study of the city of Boston, which investigates how planning practices, securitization strategies, and key actors shape the public realm and how the extant literature applies to its financial district and government center. Field research from 2007 through 2012 provides a framework for understanding and discussing collaborations, influences, and motivations that have shaped the post-9/11 (re)design of Boston's public spaces. I assess the pretexts for these changes and discuss the actors responsible and their motivations for securitization. Planners' roles also are examined to advance understandings of how they fit within the urban securitization agenda, and suggestions are offered for how planners may ensure a meaningful presence in the new order of things.

High profile/high scrutiny

A review of the urban securitization literature reveals a progression from early reactions against high-visibility counterterrorism interventions at iconic sites, toward a study of broader strategies employed by municipal and state authorities. However, much of this literature, both pre and post-9/11, has focused on a few high-profile/high-density cities around the globe. London, Belfast, Jerusalem, New York City, Washington, DC, and Los Angeles receive extensive scrutiny in these efforts to understand the urban planning processes and goals of institutional stakeholders and government officials in securing public space (Benton-Short 2007; Coaffee 2003, 2004; Davis 1992; Nemeth 2010). Other cities at the periphery of the security focus, including Boston,[1] face different circumstances and planning environments, even as security measures create significant changes in the public and private realms. According to Coaffee and Wood (2006), not all cities respond equally to threats of terrorism. In the United Kingdom, risk assessment and management are intrinsic parts of local governance; authorities enter into multi-level collaborations to prepare all levels of government for a broad array of emergency situations (Coaffee *et al.* 2009a; see also Berg, this volume). The situation is different in the United States, as illustrated by the RAND Corporation (2010) summary of its study of security and government action that found "A challenge facing law enforcement is how to manage the expansion of these information-sharing networks, ensure the participation of all stakeholders and ensure flexibility in homeland security grant programs to account for variation in local needs and capabilities." This trend toward localized and multi-level collaborations is evident in the security approach shift from a globalized and abstract "war on terror" to one emphasizing local urban resilience that has been described as the combination of physical, planning and management efforts that attempt to reduce vulnerability of people, places, and businesses (Coaffee and O'Hare 2008).

The urban design ramifications of securitization

Measures to enhance urban security affect millions of people across the United States, with a handful of metropolitan areas receiving a significant amount of funding, expertise, and public scrutiny for counterterrorism efforts.[2] Like many US cities since 9/11, Boston has been host to a proliferation of secure urban design interventions: bollards, that ubiquitous symbol of security and stalwartness, are ever-present in the city; some barricade models designed for crowd control are used seemingly as a terrorist truck bomb deterrent; and "temporary" as well as permanent barriers and fences dot the urban landscape.

Why are these post-9/11 changes to public space of interest to urban advocates? While profound changes in response to potential threats continue to impact our public realm, urban dwellers are often not conscious of their occurrence. As one Boston Redevelopment Authority (BRA) planner believes, these concrete barriers are "white noise" – objects now familiar to many and thus fading into the background of urban life (BRA planner 1). For half a decade I have been researching the alteration of public spaces post-9/11, documenting this transformation in Boston through an urban design lens to understand how the quest for security is affecting the city's public realm and planners' desires for an urban space that fosters community and civility.

This balance of security and civility is as old as urbanism itself. *Securitas* (after the Roman goddess of security) was at the right hand of early rulers and city builders and *securitas* has coexisted with *civitas* – the citizens and larger community of urban settlements. Citizens' ability to gather and move freely about the city, and be part of a larger community is supported by openness and accessibility, which are the hallmarks of public spaces in democratic societies (Lefebvre 1996). The treatment of public space in the post-9/11 city focuses on security at the expense of civility. Peter Marcuse has argued that the persistent focus on counterterrorism and urban securitization, particularly when applied indiscriminately or by a diffuse array of actors, is neither effective nor practical and could be harmful to civic life: "The false responses to the threat of terrorism . . . create a form of existential insecurity" (Marcuse 2006: 924). He defined existential insecurity as "the human, psychological sense of pervasive danger, a deep and fundamental threatening anxiety, without a sharp focus on a specific danger" (Marcuse 2006: 924). Ironically, focus on security creates insecurity, which then supports increased urban public space interventions. This amorphous and unfocused sense of danger rooted in part in the attacks of 9/11 and terrorist acts around the globe is a recurring theme in the study of urban securitization.

Good public realm design

Planners are necessarily invested in this coexistence of *securitas* and *civitas*; the post-9/11 focus on counterterrorism measures and proliferation of players affecting the public realm beg one question: If we enhance urban *securitas*, what places and spaces support *civitas* and how is the balance achieved? Standards for urban design practices and public space supportive of *civitas* abound. In Boston, the goal of good spaces and a vibrant public realm is deemed important enough to warrant a Boston Civic Design Commission (BCDC) that provides "a forum for the general public and the professional design community to participate in the shaping of the city's physical form and natural environment" (BCDC, n.d.). On a wider scale, "The Place Diagram" shown in Figure 16.3, developed by the

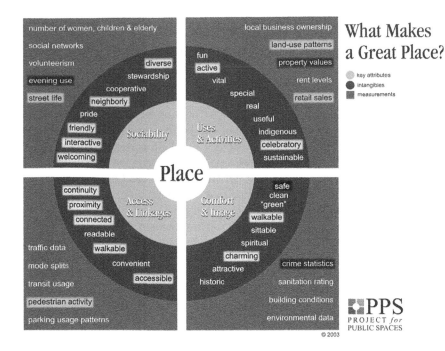

Figure 16.3 The Place Diagram, developed by Project for Public Spaces to illustrate those elements that make a place great. The elements highlighted in dark boxes are supported by security interventions; light boxes indicate elements negatively affected by securitization of the public realm. (Base diagram source: Project for Public Spaces, used with permission. Box highlights by author.)

non-profit Project for Public Spaces (PPS), is useful for identifying what makes a good or bad space. Ongoing research has offered evidence that security design can have a positive effect on "perceived safety," which can translate into stabilized property values, a welcoming and comfortable feeling, and possibly less crime (Newman 1972; Poyner and Webb 1997). However, security interventions that restrict movement, prevent public gatherings and other uses, and restrict public services can detract from public spaces and *civitas*.

Research methodology

The purpose of this case study of Boston pre- and post-9/11 was to gain a better understanding of public realm securitization; test assumptions about the motivations for changes to public space; and characterize planners' roles in the post-9/11 city. The financial district, government center, and surrounding areas are host to a density of activity, buildings, and uses that are similar to areas in other US cities often assessed as terrorist targets.

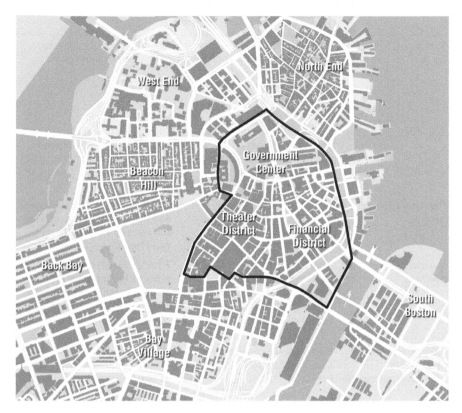

Figure 16.4 Map of the study area, showing Boston's financial district, government
center, Downtown Crossing, and adjacent areas.

An empirical assessment of the study area (Figure 16.4) was conducted to
document changes to the urban landscape after 9/11, including barriers to movement and changes to public services, entertainment, and dining in privately
owned public space. The security elements are shown in Table 16.1.

Data were collected and marked on maps acquired through the City of
Boston's online mapping portal and photographs taken of all sites. These field
conditions were compared to pre-9/11 conditions wherever possible. Interviews
with over 20 government officials, city planners, public space advocates,
building owners and managers, and business leaders were conducted to determine motivations for securitization decisions and (re)design of the public
realm. This taxonomy of securitization motivations serves to illustrate Boston's
planning environment and contributes to an understanding of the challenges
encountered by planners in balancing *civitas* and *securitas* in the twenty-first-
century city.

Table 16.1 Urban design security tools/interventions

Barrier/tool type	Description	Reason for use
Temporary fences/ barriers	Movable concrete barriers (Jersey barriers) and metal fencing that is movable and can be adapted to a particular landscape or temporary situation	Block or control pedestrian and vehicular movement
Bollards	A short vertical post that may or may not be retractable that sits in the pavement, sidewalk or landscape. Used in groupings	Impediment to vehicles. Crash-resistant bollards withstand truck and vehicle impact. Can increase standoff distances from buildings
Permanent fences/ barriers	Concrete barriers (Jersey barriers), reinforced walls, planters and reinforced benches	To block or control pedestrian and vehicular movement. Can increase standoff distances from buildings
Restricted lobby access	Turnstiles, security desks, ID checkpoints and other measures that screen visitors to buildings and limit access to approved visitors/tenants only	Restrict access to non-public areas of buildings and screen visitors to buildings to ensure the safety of occupants, property and the building structure
Loss of commercial space/public services/public space	Elimination of public services and retail business in or near buildings	Limit public access and infiltration to non-public areas of buildings or sites. Protect occupants and property from damage, theft and/or terrorist acts
Restricted open space use	Barriers to group gathering and loitering in open spaces through security screening, policing, and other methods	Limit crowd situations and potentially dangerous chaotic public scenes that could make it easier for crime and terrorist activity to take place. Curtail crowds of dissent and public demonstrations
Stand-off distances	A prescribed distance from which vehicles are prevented from entering without security screening. Can be achieved with concrete barriers, walls, movable bollards, gates or landscape devices that collapse from vehicle weight	Prevent vehicle approach to buildings and property to protect from explosives

Boston as a case study

Boston is a city of over 500,000 residents within a larger metropolitan area of approximately 4.5 million.[3] Despite its DHS Tier I designation, Boston has not experienced terrorist activity[4] like other cities in the top rankings, nor has it received the same level of scrutiny. Boston is a peripheral city – a city not at the epicenter of scrutiny, research or security efforts, but an important city nonetheless because of the presence of world-class universities, high-tech companies, medical institutions, and the financial industry.

Within the study area, the BRA's public realm goals emphasize connectedness and accessibility; in 2007, Robert Kroin, senior urban designer at the BRA, stated that the Authority has had a long-standing policy of encouraging and mapping through-block connections[5] in office buildings in the financial district and Downtown Crossing areas of the city. What is the balance between these goals and the securitization of public space in the financial district and government center?

The physical landscape pre- and post-9/11

While there is no record of the precise number and type of security elements in the city prior to 9/11, the BRA did record one aspect of the public realm that can be compared to changes since the terrorist attacks. Figures 16.5 and 16.6 show changes to porosity and connectedness in the financial district through the loss of through-block connections after 9/11. Figure 16.5 is the BRA map of through-block office lobbies[6] while Figure 16.6 shows which connections have survived the post-9/11 securitization of the district. Conditions after the terrorist attacks, first mapped in 2007, reveal a vastly changed public realm, with over 50 percent loss of through-block connector access points due to security guards, ID checkpoints and turnstiles, or keycard-only admittance through locked doors.

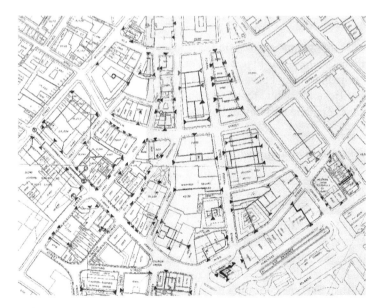

Figure 16.5 Through-block connectors and public access points in Boston financial district and adjacent areas. (Source: Boston Redevelopment Authority, date estimated to be around 1985.)

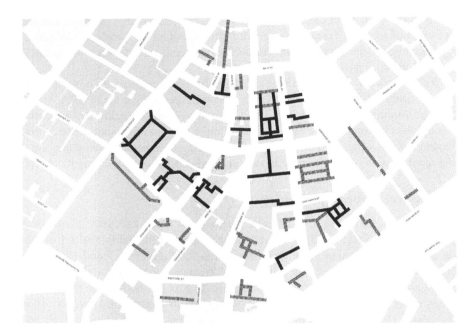

Figure 16.6 Loss of through-block connectors and public access points, in Boston's
financial district and adjacent areas post-9/11. The black pathways are
retained public through-blocks, while the hatched pathways have been lost
since 9/11, 2012.

In addition, field surveys, interviews, and a study of photographs show other
security interventions in the area. Figure 16.7 offers an emerging picture of an
altered and reduced public realm but it illustrates only the visible manifestation of
the securitization of Boston's public realm. Behind the scenes, the actors involved
and their motivations complete the story of how these security elements came to be.

Security (re)design: actors and motivations

The changes to public space illustrated in these maps are not surprising in themselves. Boston's financial district plays host to major corporations, law firms, and
financial service providers; a short distance across the harbor and visible from many
upper-floor offices is Logan Airport, the point of origin for two of the four hijacked
planes on 9/11. According to interviews in 2007, six years after 9/11, Boston planners and city officials were either unaware of the many security interventions, or
they believed them to be temporary in nature or inconsequential to the quality of the
public realm and urban experience. Officials also seemed unaware of the web of
actors and motivations responsible for this securitized urban landscape. Yet, if city
officials were not part of the decision-making process, how did securitization of the

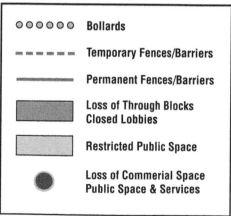

○○○○○○	Bollards
▬ ▬ ▬ ▬ ▬	Temporary Fences/Barriers
▬▬▬▬▬	Permanent Fences/Barriers
	Loss of Through Blocks Closed Lobbies
	Restricted Public Space
●	Loss of Commerial Space Public Space & Services

Figure 16.7 Security interventions in Boston's public realm.

public realm occur? Interviews conducted in conjunction with mapping illuminate a decision-making landscape that often conceals varied actors and motivations under the guise of security (re)design. The story of these motivations begins at government center, where the city's goals for connectedness collide with federal security guidelines and "temporary" barriers still in place more than a decade after 9/11.

Federal security guidelines and assessments

Boston City Hall with its vast plaza, along with the John F. Kennedy Federal Building, forms the centerpiece of government center. The Kennedy Building's perimeter security on Sudbury Street (Figure 16.8) was upgraded after 9/11 to include video surveillance systems, traffic barriers, bollards, and crash walls (Classic Site Solutions, n.d.). Jersey barriers were placed along the façade facing City Hall Plaza (Figure 16.9); this upgraded perimeter building security provides a hardened target that addresses GSA Security standards for standoff distances.[7] These unsightly barriers reinforce the perceived inhospitableness of what has been deemed "The World's Worst Plaza" by PPS (PPS, n.d.) in its ongoing work to foster a vibrant public realm and provide guidelines for good urban space design.

The GSA is a formidable barrier to humanizing and activating the plaza; the events of 9/11 have exacerbated this already sticky problem. As Ann Donner, the Executive Director of the Trust for City Hall Plaza, explained in 2007: "All discussions with GSA end up with 'can't do that because of security.' If you want to do anything, you'd have to go toe to toe with the Federal Government to convince them to do something."

Figure 16.8 Security (re)design of the John F. Kennedy Federal Building in government center.

Figure 16.9 "Temporary" barriers create standoff distance between City Hall Plaza and the Kennedy Federal Building.

Perceived threats

While government regulations and formal threat assessments dictate securitization in federal facilities, in some private buildings, perceived threats drive security decisions. At 60 State Street, a Class A office tower wedged among City Hall, historic Faneuil Hall/Quincy Market and the Downtown Crossing shopping district, post-9/11 interventions were minimal until months after the attacks when visitors from New York City allegedly complained, "Why is it such an open door here? The building looks vulnerable compared to what we see in NYC" (security manager 1). As explained by the operations director of a major tenant in the building, the owner installed security improvements in response to these concerns (operations director 1). At this office tower, the security policies of a building 200 miles away and the perception of threats, including the fact that visitors could see Logan Airport's control tower from upper floors, rather than on-site security guidelines and assessments dictated security (re)design.

Market competition

In competing for tenants and striving for a market edge, building owners face pressure to react to perceived threats with visible security interventions. The actions of competitors and the wishes of tenants are taken seriously in the quest to enhance property value. In this scenario, the tendency is to assuage fears and appear state-of-the-art while not overdoing the "fortress" approach, as shown by the lack of perimeter building protection at 60 State Street. However, competitors' security interventions will drive security decisions and protection will be ramped up to correspond to the "new normal." The building owner "took some time after 9/11 – it gauged actions in other buildings before taking any actions at 60 State Street" (operations director 1).

Shock reaction

Not all securitization moves were as studied or delayed. Some Boston interventions were a shock reaction to 9/11. These "temporary" fixes have not benefited from threat assessments or design consideration; many are still in place more than a decade later. The result is that some interventions do not do as designed; temporary French Barriers around City Hall Plaza are designed solely for crowd control (Figure 16.10), not to withstand vehicular force or act as perimeter building protection from truck bombs. In fact, all these fences do is block pedestrian access to the plaza. At the same time, this "security barrier" is breached to allow MBTA workers and others to park (Figure 16.11). This is only one example of a security intervention installed without consideration of equipment limitations or public realm consequences.

Figure 16.10 These "temporary" barriers at City Hall Plaza have been in place for more than a decade.

Figure 16.11 The break in barriers allows parking on City Hall Plaza.

Legal and fiduciary pressures

Concerns regarding legal liability and investment protection also play a role in securitization. A principal of a major Boston landscape architecture firm noted that lawyers can call the design shots without specific reasons: "If there is ever a lawyer on a building and design client committee, the lawyer brings up security and liability issues *every* time and elements end up being incorporated into the project" (design professional 1). Lending institutions also hold great sway over designs and public accessibility. In 2007, the BRA announced the selection of a developer for what was to be the city's tallest building. The press release described the proposed 1.5-million-square-foot office and retail tower as a very public building containing "one acre of public space" and "a mix of uses," including and "a year-round public market" (BRA 2007) and "a roof garden with glass exterior walls" (Palmer 2008). Mayor Thomas Menino championed these public amenities and spaces in response to public outcry over the project's height and mass. While the project went dormant after a 2008 FAA ruling showing concern about encroachment on Logan Airport's airspace (Palmer 2008), the building's extensive public facilities were a serious concern for the designers, project lawyers, and lenders. Sources with knowledge of the project worried that the public space and amenities desired by the mayor and BRA were unrealistic when matched with the security expectations of the project's legal and financial teams.

The search for profits

Security is a fast-growing sector of the economy: Homeland Security spending increased in the decade after 9/11 from $16 billion to $69.1 billion annually – a 301 percent increase (National Priorities Project 2011). A Boston architect admitted that most security information and specifications used by his firm were obtained from security product manufacturers: "The office was getting blitzed from security companies regarding bollards, planters, and fencing. Only one year after 9/11, all of these security products for landscape were fully in the marketplace" (design professional 2). Most design professionals are not trained in security, and the security industry has much to gain by filling the knowledge void. In overt and subtle ways, these companies pressure designers to provide more, not fewer, security features; manufacturers' websites deliver the message that security design is becoming the standard for *any* commercial or public building. For example, the 2007 Website for SecureUSA claimed, "For this corporate entrance SecureUSA used retractable bollards, fencing, lights, and access control to create a state of the art solution that is becoming a standard in corporate headquarters" (SecureUSA 2007). By 2012, this same company provided a full range of consulting and risk assessment services to complement its product line and offered an online sales pitch by quoting a building owner/client:

> *'I would never have thought I needed a security consultant. I always assumed my security staff or engineering personnel handled all that.' Sound familiar?* In this changing world of increased terrorism, technology and equipment offerings, it is extremely difficult for in-house personnel to keep abreast of the best solutions to meet the demands for protecting at risk assets.
>
> (SecureUSA 2012; original emphasis)

By providing expertise and consulting services that determine the need for the products they sell, the security industry thus becomes a team member – driving decision-making about securitization. Sales pressure from the industry and the reluctance of designers, buildings owners, and planners to say "no" to protection from ever amorphous threats create a potent force no matter where the project or the risk.

Response to threat assessments

Some larger private corporations in the financial district have conducted extensive threat assessments. These corporations have in-house security expertise and work hand-in-hand with consultants to create a comprehensive security strategy. A vice president for operations of a major financial firm (executive 1) confirmed that many financial district corporations actively collaborate with the Boston Police in an environment in which local building owners and tenants work closely with public safety officials to coordinate response efforts and (re)design; this vice president, along with executives from other financial district institutions (executive 2 and 3; operations director 1; security manager 2; chief compliance officer 1) described a "new kind of relationship" between building managers and police department personnel. Regular meetings with the district police office are used to discuss securitization, assess current and projected threats, share security assessments, and coordinate with other agencies such as the MBTA and DHS (police 1).

Design follows the money

While DHS funding has been reduced in recent years, with cities receiving funding mostly for operations, training and equipment for preparedness response (US Conference of Mayors 2011), the private sector provides security interventions by reallocating money from other business operating expenses. Security funding will create security needs and every problem will have a security solution. This means, once again, design will follow the money. As reported by a major financial firm executive, "9/11 has made it easier to get the money needed . . . the security team here gets whatever it wants. We don't argue" (chief compliance officer 1).

High-level security = high-level prestige

The need for a high level of security is akin to the corner office – it engenders an element of prestige. In field research, the phrase "top ten" was frequently invoked in response to questions about threat assessments and funding priorities. Consistently, public officials, private security experts, and design professionals mentioned particular buildings, monuments, and sites as a "top 10 target" to justify increased security (Figure 16.12). It appears a great number of buildings and sites can be on the "top ten" list. No interviewees provided details about a specific list or which government agency had produced the ranking. Some public officials and business executives mentioned the existence of "security envy" – the greater your importance, the more stringent is your organization's security concerns. Rather than a burden, some prioritized security concerns bring prestige, additional funding, and placement higher on the pecking order – an incentive to embrace security expenditures and visible securitization (re)design.

Figure 16.12 A sample of Boston sites and buildings on the mythical national "top ten" list of terrorist targets: (a) the Federal Reserve building, (b) South Station, and (c) the USS Constitution.

Reclamation of privately owned public space

Perhaps a more pernicious motivation for security urban design is the desire to reclaim privately owned "public" space for private use. While Boston does not have the incentive zoning found in New York City to create public plazas, atria, and arcades in privately owned buildings in exchange for increased floor area, it has been a BRA policy to negotiate public space and amenities in private development wherever possible. Once such "public" space was the top-floor observatory in the John Hancock Building, the city's tallest structure – the closest Boston had to a museum of the city. Just two days after 9/11, it was announced by the building's owners that the Hancock Observatory would be permanently closed (Figure 16.13).

The decision was never revisited, even as public access was reinstated in iconic, high-risk structures such as the Empire State Building and Statue of Liberty in New York City. The BRA and City officials pushed for a reopening, but to no avail. "We believe it was part of the original agreement, but we have never been able to find it on paper . ... It was always intended as a public space" (Park 2005), said Susan Elsbree, spokeswoman for the BRA in 2005. Thus, a public space and visitor destination has been reclaimed for office space – probably the most prestigious and expensive in Boston.

There are other lost public amenities and space in Boston. At 245 Summer Street, the restaurant closed to the public due to security screening difficulties. At 100 Federal Street, the lower-level salon, golf shop, and other services can only be reached by making an appointment, which must be shown on the building

Figure 16.13 The top-floor observatory at the Hancock Building has been lost for public use since 9/11.

security computer network to gain passage. Loss of public parking, car rental outlets and ground-floor retail has occurred and is a less-noticed result of security concerns that also serve to chip away at quality-of-life. Of greatest concern are comments by executives of some of the major firms in the financial district that they "would think differently about having ground floor public uses" in the future (executive 1; executive 4; operations director 1).

What does it all mean?

A web of actors and motivations are involved in the securitization of Boston's public realm. While security is certainly a motivation for public realm (re)design, interviews with key actors reveal that physical changes have more to do with private interests than public security agendas. What is also striking is that planners are absent from the discussion. What is the planner's role in curating the public realm when, as Peter Marcuse (2006: 919) accurately stated, "Some responses to

Table 16.2 Security (re)design in Boston: a complex web of motivations and actors

Motivations	Actors
Legitimate	
Federal, state, and local security guidelines and assessments	Federal, state, and local officials, security professionals, design professionals
Threat assessments	Insurance companies, lawyers, lenders, security professionals, building owners, government officials
Target deflection	Building owners, managers and tenants, lawyers, lenders, insurance companies, security professionals, security product manufacturers, government officials
False	
Perceived threats	Government officials, building owners, managers and tenants, design professionals, insurance companies, lawyers, lenders, security product manufacturers, security professionals
Market competition	Building owners, security product manufacturers, design professionals, security professionals
Shock reaction	Government officials, building owners, design professionals
Legal and fiduciary pressures	Lawyers, lenders, building and business managers
Search for profits	Security professionals, security product manufacturers, building owners, design professionals, insurance companies, lenders
Design follows the money	Security professionals, security product manufacturers
High-level security = high-level prestige	Government officials, business owners, tenants
Reclamation of privately owned public space	Building owners, building tenants

the threat of terrorism have been legitimately addressed to its dangers; others have been false, and manipulated for purposes other than increasing safety?" Motivations and responses are closely linked. Here, Table 16.2 is organized according to Marcuse's definitions of "legitimate" and "false"[8] (Marcuse 2006: 103-5) to clarify the extent to which securitization decisions have been informed by "false" motivations having little to do with assessments of risk.

Planning in a changing landscape – pretext securitization of the public realm

A look at elements of the changing urban security design landscape provides a useful understanding of the decision-making processes shaping public space. DHS has provided significant preparedness funding to the Boston region, but most of this money has paid for police response training and exercises, planning strategies, and equipment maintenance and replacement. Far from resulting from a post-9/11 public security agenda, most changes to the public realm in Boston's financial district have been rooted in private decision-making and have used, to a great degree, private funding – all outside the web of public regulation and many under public planners' radar. Marcuse used the term "pretext responses" to describe "false responses to the threat of terrorism . . . used to impose restrictions on conduct that is otherwise an essential component of democracy" (Marcuse 2004: 105). This mix of private–public decision-making outside of an overarching public policy and absent public–private collaboration and formal threat assessment may be termed the "pretext securitization" of the city.

The work of Coaffee and Rogers (2008), Nemeth (2010), and Nemeth and Hollander (2010) claims a strong correlation between secured urban space and collaboration between private and public sectors. While this is true for high-profile/high-density cities such as London, San Francisco, Los Angeles, and New York, Boston's securitized public space in the financial district is the result of private-sector action in a public leadership void. Coaffee and O'Hare (2008) pointed out that decision-making has been transferred in recent years to private-sector actors. However, the situation they describe, in part, as the "'co-option' of non-statutory actors for assistance in state security agendas" (Coaffee *et al.* 2009b: 491) still assumes public realm securitization occurs within a public and transparent framework for a stated public benefit. In Boston, the securitization of urban space is a result of private security agendas and spillover and pretext motivations,[9] not public policy.

Balancing costs and benefits – missing actors

Pretext securitization in Boston creates an environment that lacks mechanisms for balancing public costs and benefits of security interventions and that supports pervasive and persistent securitization of public space. In addition, the communities of interest in the financial district are largely controlled by the strong voices of major corporations and building owners. With private-sector control of securitization of public space, it may be argued that the public costs of these pretext responses are disproportionately high compared with any public or private security benefits. For large projects in Boston, the BCDC normally facilitates a review of public impact and design but security (re)design alone is outside of its purview.[10]

Communities of interest – who's in and who's out?

The existence of private security agendas in Boston and the absence of public officials from decision-making processes points to a territoriality in the financial district that seems nested in private spaces and actors. Private enclaves do not extend, in many cases, beyond the building perimeter/site; the issues at stake are often about privately owned public space. This has created a powerful private-sector community of interest in which actors have engaged in a new level of collaboration and cooperation with each other – creating a type of *de facto* private planning agenda lacking active public oversight by planning officials. Private-sector leaders network with each other, Boston Police, and other local, national, and international public safety officials such as the MBTA and even London Police counterterrorism experts, with little or nothing said about urban design or the BRA permitting process. As one financial company vice president said six years after the 9/11 attacks,

> [S]ince 9/11, we share information and strategies with banks and other companies in Boston . . . . we have built and keep a support network of private companies and public safety officials. In fact, public safety officials want us to take the lead on security.
>
> (executive 3)

Security creep is real

Private-sector co-option of the security agenda in the financial district and lack of oversight and tracking by city planning officials have engendered an environment of pretext securitization outside the context of state strategy and public discourse. While public safety officials moderate regular security meetings with the private sector, there appears to be no effort by these officials to provide a broader base of coordination and cooperation with planning officials and public space advocates. As confirmed by a BRA official responsible for oversight of public realm design, "There is no set policy. Policy is set in different City departments" with no coordinating oversight (planner 2). These conditions have resulted in "security creep." The term is used to describe the shift in the stated use of a security device, such as CCTV, from the publicly stated use (such as monitoring congestion in London's city center) to another less public use (tracking potential criminal and terrorist activity). I also use security creep to describe the gradual acceptance of security interventions as a natural part of the public realm – the acceptance and recognition that these interventions have become "white noise" in Boston. Without a clear set of guidelines and policies, temporary interventions become permanent, new interventions are introduced over time, and little is said or noticed.

Moving forward: an expanded role for planners?

The need to understand this new climate of securitization and the forces at work should not be underestimated. The lack of public discourse about public realm restrictions, even the reallocation of scarce resources within the private sector, should concern planners, since these conditions can relegate *civitas* to the bottom of the priority list – chipping away at "the right to the city." The concern goes beyond a reallocation of private-sector spending away from design and toward security. In past years, almost half the cities responding to the US Conference of Mayors annual surveys of its member cities have indicated they had no opportunity to influence spending of DHS preparedness grants; the concern is that municipalities have no say in how money is spent. A resolution at the organization's 2012 annual meeting urges DHS to embrace "greater local involvement" when considering reforms to the preparedness grant program (US Conference of Mayors 2012). Public monies used ineffectively or inefficiently to fund emergency preparedness planning, equipment, and training[11] also pushes urban design and public space considerations lower on the priority list. Six years after 9/11, Terry Savage, the Superintendent of the Boston National Historical Park and Boston African American National Historic Site, lamented the reallocation of monies to security: "The National Park Service has lost over 10 staff members and I can't replace them. It's sort of eating our young in some ways – pushing all this money into security and taking it out of interpretation, construction, maintenance."

Without public leadership that coordinates both DHS efforts and municipal strategies with private-sector interests in securing public and private space, Boston is run amok with private-sector actions furthering private interests. Private-sector security (re)design combats the fear of terrorism (insecurity) as much as the assessed threat of terrorism. Fear is difficult to quantify and address, particularly under the influence of media and political forces. In this context, how can planners engage in the security discussion while advocating for the public realm in meaningful ways? This question is asked in the context of increasing pressures on the profession. Planners are expected to be proficient in a wide range of areas including land-use planning, transportation planning, economic development, and sustainability. These compete with the more recent focus on combating terrorism in an overall environment of reduced budgets and staff. Given the scarcity of resources and multiple roles for planners, the answers may lie in the reassertion of their skills into the securitization process to take control of public realm (re)design. Planners' strengths include listening to many voices and forging new relationships; acting as managers for complex projects with multiple players and goals; and understanding regulatory processes and review for the built environment (zoning and permitting).

The leadership vacuum in the public realm and absence of planners in Boston's securitization is surprising considering the city's history of visionary leadership in planning and urban design. Perhaps the explanation lies in the fact that security is seen to be a highly specialized field into which planners are reluctant to tread. It can be difficult for anyone to assert authority when "The key ideas underpinning securitization theory are that the perceived need for security against particular threats and risk requires 'security actors' to claim that special and exceptional measures are required" (Coaffee and van Ham 2008: 192). One way for planners to take leadership is to recognize and understand the character of private-sector collaboration. If planners become actors where false motivations exist (Table 16.2), by acknowledging and building on common concerns and interests rather than differences, they can add value to the discussion and assert authority as "knowledge brokers."

Zoning and permitting is another area in which planners can reassert authority. Boston faces a new environment of reduced responsibility by the private sector for the public realm. Where once developers and businesses used the creation of publicly accessible space to garner good will, these goals may be ignored today in the interest of security. How does one argue with security concerns without seeming cavalier? Yet, just as the BCDC reviews large development projects for their impact on the public realm, so too could a special commission (perhaps a BCDC subcommittee) with security *and* urban design expertise. Zoning and design guidelines that do not address security and urban resilience concerns are obsolete. Deliberateness in permitting, particularly with respect to ground floor uses, porosity, and open space accessibility would be a start.

Security will always trump urban design without an informed discussion and insistence on standards and public discourse. A common theme during interviews was the absolute power of "the security card" to upend plans and co-opt design and public realm concerns. The ambiguous nature of the perception of threat and fear highlights the need for planners to speak security language in the same way they speak the language of economic development and sustainability. Government warnings and media coverage both contribute to existential insecurity. Planners who are unable to speak the language of securitization and urban resiliency will have difficulty participating in discussions of the public costs and benefits of security (re)design.

Conclusion

The issue of security raises a new line of inquiry into the securitization of peripheral cities. A better understanding of Boston's securitization at a minimum opens new questions for investigation. Is Boston an anomaly? Is the securitization of the public realm in the city common to peripheral cities in the United States – cities that are under less scrutiny?[12] Are the lessons of institutional theory different for peripheral cities? Is there a new specialized role for planners within these new securitization frameworks?

High-profile/high-scrutiny cities deserve serious study. But millions of people are affected by these processes in peripheral cities too. Knowledge and understanding of the processes by which the urban public realm in peripheral cities is (re)designed to handle both legitimate threat responses and false responses become more important as the war on terror is both more globalized and more local than ever before, with the quest for urban resiliency filtering down to every level of government and private-sector entity.

Acknowledgments

My research on the securitization of Boston's public realm post-9/11 was made possible in part, from a Research in Architecture Grant from the Boston Society of Architects. I also wish to thank my MIT Research Assistants Sai Balakrishnan, Gordon Hansen, Diana Jue, Michael Kay, Deborah Morris, Laura Rothrock, Sara Rothrock, Ben Stone, and Sara Zewde, as well as Amy Glasmeier, Department Head in Urban Studies and Planning at MIT. Maps were created by David Curran. Thank you to Project for Public Spaces for permission to use the "What Makes a Space Great?" diagram. Last, but certainly not least, I must thank Paul Kane and Tavan Pechet – two gentlemen without whose encouragement my years of research would not have been transformed into this chapter.

Notes

1 In the United States, the highest-profile cities are but a fraction of the urban areas that have considered or implemented a (re)design of the urban core to respond to concerns regarding terrorist strikes. Some of these urban areas receive federal terrorist prepared-ness funding and have taken significant measures to secure their urban public realms, people and property from destruction and devastation.

2 In 2011, DHS provided $2.1 billion in preparedness grants, of which $662 million was distributed through the Urban Areas Security Initiative (UASI) to 31 high-threat areas. "In order to focus limited resources to mitigate and respond to evolving threats, the 11 highest risk areas (Tier I) were eligible for more than $540 million, while the remain-ing 20 urban areas, designated Tier II were eligible for more than $121 million" (US Department of Homeland Security 2011). As a Tier I urban area, Boston is one of a small group of cities that has received the bulk of UASI funding.

3 US Census Boston Metropolitan Statistical Area, including the City of Boston.

4 While the city's airport was the point of origin for two of the hijacked planes on 9/11, Boston experienced no direct attacks. In fact, there is record of only a single alleged terrorist plot since 9/11: "an alleged shopping mall bombing plot involving US citizen Tarek Mehanna in 2009" (*Washington Post* 2010).

5 Through-block connections usually refer to narrow rights-of-way between buildings or in commercial districts, to ground-floor lobby space that has access and egress from both sides of the building. In encouraging through-blocks, the BRA has recognized the contribution of a porous, connected streetscape to a vibrant and accessible public realm, particularly considering winter weather conditions in New England where pedestrians may find respite from snow and rain and freezing conditions by taking through-block connections.

6 This map was provided in February 2007 by Robert Kroin, Senior Urban Designer at the BRA and estimated to be approximately 20 years old at the time.

7 The GSA guidelines mandate, "All new federal buildings should have a minimum standoff distance of fifty (50) feet. Some specialized facilities may require a higher standard of security" (GSA 2012). The GSA recognizes this may be impractical or impossible to achieve in historic or dense urban settings.

8 Marcuse described legitimate responses to terrorism as targeted ("directed at grounded risks, regardless of costs") or balanced ("attempting to balance risks against economic and civil rights costs"). False responses include spillover ("expanding the meaning of

'security'"), induced ("building a climate justifying unrelated responses") and pretext ("directly justifying unrelated responses") (Marcuse 2004: 103).

9 I have borrowed this term from Peter Marcuse's description of "pretext responses" (Marcuse 2006). While responses and motivations are different, I have transferred the notion that "pretext" refers to an action that directly justifies an unrelated response. My use of the term "pretext motivation" refers to a motivation that results in securitization that has no basis in real threat but rather is unrelated to a formal assessment of terrorist risk. An example of a pretext motivation is the profit motive whereby security product manufacturers "sell" designers and building owners on security products, devices, and services without rigorous threat assessment and corresponding determination of legitimate security concerns for the sake of making a profit.

10 This public review of design would normally be embedded, in some way, in city zoning or design guidelines.

11 An FY 2003 US Conference of Mayors survey to cities that expected to receive funding through the program revealed that "officials in 46 percent of the cities which are in, or are mutual aid partners with, the urban areas receiving funding through the UASI said they have not been involved in the planning process for the use of these funds." In addition, "Among those which have been involved in the planning process, 23 percent did not believe they had a satisfactory opportunity to influence how the funds will be used" (US Conference of Mayors 2004:18). In FY 2004, the survey reinforced these responses: "44 percent of the UASI cities said they were not involved in the planning process for the use of the funds. Among those which have been involved in the planning process, 18 percent do not believe they have had a satisfactory opportunity to influence how the funds will be used" (US Conference of Mayors 2004: 27).

12 Boston is surely not an anomaly among US cities. There are almost 200 "peripheral" cities – these cities received DHS preparedness grants but were not in the 10 percent of total grantees that had Tier I high-threat/high-density designations (US Conference of Mayors 2004). While each city is a case-by-case basis, it can be surmised that if pretext securitization has occurred in Boston, a Tier I city, other cities, particularly ones not the focus of intense "high-threat" scrutiny, may be experiencing the same phenomenon.

References

Benton-Short, L. (2007) "Bollards, Bunkers, and Barriers: Securing the National Mall in Washington, DC." *Environment and Planning D: Society and Space*, 25(3): 424–46.

Boston Civic Design Commission (BCDC) (n.d.) "The Boston Civic Design Commission." Available at: http://www.bostonredevelopmentauthority.org/bcdc/bcdc.asp [accessed 27 August 2012].

Boston Redevelopment Authority (BRA) (2007) "Menino Announces First Official step in Realization of Winthrop Square Tower." Press release, 25 January, Online. Available at: http://www.bostonredevelopmentauthority.org/press/PressDisplay.asp?pressID=350 [accessed 1 August 2012].

Classic Site Solutions, Inc. (n.d.) "John F. Kennedy Federal Building Security Site Improvements." Online. Available at: http://www.classicsitesolutions.com/p_s02johnfk.html [accessed 26 July 2012].

Coaffee, J. (2003) *Terrorism, Risk and the City: The Making of a Contemporary Urban Landscape,* Aldershot: Ashgate.

Coaffee, J. (2004) "Rings of Steel, Rings of Concrete and Rings of Confidence: Designing out Terrorism in Central London Pre- and Post- September 11th." *International Journal of Urban and Regional Research*, 28(1): 201–11.

Coaffee, J. and O'Hare, P. (2008) "Urban Resilience and National Security: The Role for Planning." *Urban Design and Planning,* 161(4): 173–82.

Coaffee, J. and Rogers, P. (2008) "Rebordering the City for New Security Challenges: From Counter Terrorism to Community Resilience." *Space and Polity*, 12(2): 101–18.

Coaffee, J. and van Ham, P. (2008) "'Security Branding': The Role of Security in Marketing the City, Region or State." (Guest editorial.) *Place Branding and Public Diplomacy,* 4(3): 191–95.

Coaffee, J. and Wood, D.M. (2006) "Security Is Coming Home: Rethinking Scale and Constructing Resilience in the Global Urban Response to Terrorist Risk." *International Relations*, 20: 503–17.

Coaffee, J. and O'Hare, P. (2011) "Co-opting Urban Planners into the "War on Terror': A 'Balanced Way' for Domestic Security." *International Studies Review*, 13(2): 376–85.

Coaffee, J., Wood, D.M., and Rogers, P. (2009a) *The Everyday Resilience of the City: How Cities Respond to Terrorism and Disaster*, Basingstoke: Palgrave Macmillan.

Coaffee, J., O'Hare, P., and Hawkesworth, M. (2009b) "The Visibility of (In)Security: The Aesthetics of Planning Urban Defences Against Terrorism." *Security Dialogue*, 40: 489–511.

Davis, M. (1992) "Fortress Los Angeles: The Militarization of Urban Space." In M. Sorkin (ed.) *Variations on a Theme Park: The New American City and the End of Public Space*, New York: Hill and Wang.

Flusty, S. (1994) *Building Paranoia: The Proliferation of Interdictory Space and the Erosion of Spatial Justice*, Los Angeles: Los Angeles Form for Architecture and Urban Design.

General Services Administration (GSA) (2012) "Site Selection Philosophy: Security" (19 June). Online. Available at: http://gsa.gov/portal/category/21709 [accessed 30 August 2012].

Graham, S. (2010) *Cities Under Siege: The New Military Urbanism,* London: Verso.

Gray, M. and Wyly, E. (2007) "The Terror City Hypothesis." In D. Gregory and A. Pred (eds) *Violent Geographies*, New York: Routledge.

Hollander, J.B. and Whitfield, C. (2005) "The Appearance of Security Zones in US Cities After 9/11." *Property Management*, 23(3): 244–56.

Lefebvre, H. (1996) "The Right to the City." In E. Kofman and E. Lebas (eds) *Writings on Cities*, London: Blackwell.

Marcuse, P. (2004) "The 'Threat of Terrorism' and the Right to the City." *Fordham Urban Law Journal*, 32(4): 101–19.

Marcuse, P. (2006) "Security or Safety in Cities? The Threat of Terrorism After 9/11." *International Journal of Urban and Regional Research*, 30: 919–29.

National Priorities Project (2011) "US Security Spending Since 9/11" (26 May). Online. Available at: http://nationalpriorities.org/en/analysis/2011/us-security-spending-since-911/ [accessed 27 August 2012].

Nemeth, J. (2009) "Defining a Public: The Management of Privately Owned Public Space." *Urban Studies*, 46(11): 2463–90.

Nemeth, J. (2010) "Security in Public Space: an Empirical Assessment of Three US Cities." *Environment and Planning A*, 42(10): 2487–507.

Nemeth, J. and Hollander, J. (2010) "Security Zones and New York City's Shrinking Public Space." *International Journal of Urban and Regional Research*, 34(1): 20–34.

Newman, O. (1972) *Defensible Space: Crime Prevention Through Urban Design*, New York: Macmillan.

Palmer, T.C. (2008) "1,000 Feet Too Tall for Hub Tower, FAA Rules." *Boston Globe* (16 May). Online. Available at: http://www.boston.com/news/local/articles/2008/05/16/1000_feet_too_tall_for_hub_tower_faa_rules/?page=1 [accessed 1 August 2012].

Park, M. (2005), "Searching for an Answer on 60th Floor." *Boston Globe* (15 June) Online. Available at: http://www.boston.com/news/local/massachusetts/articles/2005/06/15/searching_for_an_answer_on_60th_floor/ [accessed 15 July 2012].

Poyner, B. and Webb, B. (1997) "Reducing Theft from Shopping Bags in City Centre Markets." In R. Clarke (ed.), *Situational Crime Prevention: Successful Case Studies* (2nd edn), Guilderland, NY: Harrow and Heston.

PPS (n.d.) "Hall of Shame: City Hall Plaza." Project for Public Spaces. Online. Available at: http://www.pps.org/great_public_spaces//one?public_place_id=148 [accessed 26 August 2012].

RAND Corporation (2010) "Local Law Enforcement's Counterterrorism Initiatives Have Evolved Into All-Hazards Strategies." Press release (28 October), referencing RAND Report "Long-Term Effects of Law Enforcement's Post-9/11 Focus on Counterterrorism and Homeland Security." Online. Available at: http://www.rand.org/news/press/2010/10/28.html [accessed 1 August 2012].

Savitch, H. (2008) *Cities in a Time of Terror: Space, Territory, and Local Resilience,* Armonk, NY: M.E. Sharpe.

SecureUSA (2007) "Corporate Entrance." Online. Available at: http:www.safeusa.net/solutions/corporateentrance [accessed 14 March 2007].

SecureUSA (2012) "Consulting Overview." Online. Available at: http://www.secureusa.net/consulting.htm [accessed 14 October 2012].

Sorkin, M. (2004) "Urban Warfare: A Tour of the Battlefield." In S. Graham (ed.) *Cities, War and Terrorism: Toward an Urban Geopolitics*, Oxford: Blackwell.

Sorkin, M. (2008) "Introduction: The Fear Factor." In M. Sorkin (ed.) *Indefensible Space: The Architecture of the National Insecurity State*, New York: Routledge.

US Conference of Mayors (2004) "Second Mayors' Report to the Nation: Tracking Federal Homeland Security Funds Sent to the 50 State Governments" (January). Online. Available at: http://www.usmayors.org/72ndwintermeeting/homelandreport_012204.pdf [accessed 15 August 2012].

US Conference of Mayors (2011) "Mayors, Police Chiefs Urge House Appropriations Committee to Restore Funding for State/Local Homeland Security Programs" (24 May). Press release. Online. Available at: http://usmayors.org/pressreleases/uploads/20110524-release-homelandsecurity.pdf [accessed 16 August 2012].

US Conference of Mayors (2012) "Homeland Security Grant Programs resolution." 80th Annual Meeting, (13–16 June). Online. Available at: http://usmayors.org/resolutions/80th_Conference/csj11.asp [accessed 1 September 2012].

US Department of Homeland Security (2011) "DHS Announces More Than $2.1 Billion in Preparedness Grants" (23 August). Press release. Online. Available at: http://www.dhs.gov/news/2011/08/23/dhs-announces-more-2 1-billion-preparedness-grants [accessed 12 August 2012].

Washington Post (2010) "Top secret America: Massachusetts." Online. Available at: http://projects.washingtonpost.com/top-secret-america/states/massachusetts/print/ [accessed 8 August 2012].

Index

Lightning Source UK Ltd.
Milton Keynes UK
UKOW06f1505120217

294177UK00017B/490/P

9 780415 838498